Competitive Advantage Through Information Technology

CW00429071

Mary Barton

October 1995.

Competitive Advantage Through Information Technology

JACK D. CALLON

College of Business
San Jose State University
San Jose, California

The McGraw-Hill Companies, Inc.
New York St. Louis San Francisco Auckland Bogotá
Caracas Lisbon London Madrid Mexico City Milan Montreal
New Delhi San Juan Singapore Sydney Tokyo Toronto

McGraw-Hill

A Division of The McGraw-Hill Companies

COMPETITIVE ADVANTAGE THROUGH INFORMATION TECHNOLOGY
International Editions 1996

Exclusive rights by McGraw-Hill Book Co.–Singapore for manufacture and export. This book cannot be re-exported from the country to which it is consigned by McGraw-Hill.

Copyright © 1996 by McGraw-Hill, Inc. All rights reserved. Except as permitted under the Copyright Act of 1976, no part of this publication may be reproduced or distributed in any form or by any means, or stored in a data base or retrieval system, without the prior written permission of the publisher.

1 2 3 4 5 6 7 8 9 0 BJE PMP 9 8 7 6

Sponsoring editor: Frank Ruggirello
Editorial assistant: Kyle Thomes
Production supervisor: Natalie Durbin
Project management: Graphics West, Inc.
Copyeditor: Susan Defosset
Interior design: Graphics West, Inc.
Cove design: John Edeen
Cover photo: Richard Wahlstrom Photography, Inc.
Composition: Graphics West, Inc.

Library of Congress Catalog Card Number 95-81166

Information has been obtained by The McGraw-Hill Companies, Inc. from sources believed to be reliable. However, because of the possibility of human or mechanical error by our sources, The McGraw-Hill Companies, Inc., or others, The McGraw-Hill Companies, Inc. does not guarantee the accuracy, adequacy, or completeness of any information and is not responsible for any errors or omissions or the results obtained from use of such information.

When ordering this title, use ISBN 0-07-114106-5

Printed in Singapore

DEDICATION

This book is dedicated to those who must compete in an increasingly complex, dynamic and global business environment. I wish you the best of success in your competitive endeavors and hope that the contents of this book provide the help that is intended.

DEDICATION

CONTENTS

SECTION II   THE SECOND PERSPECTIVE: THE COMPANY ENVIRONMENT   99

CHAPTER 6   Business Vision   101

CHAPTER 7   Implementing a Vision: Strategy, Tactics and Business Plan   127

CHAPTER 10   The Redefine/Define Concept and Change Management   177

CHAPTER 11   Telecommunications as the Delivery Vehicle   197

CHAPTER 12   Using Information Systems to Compete: A Success Factor Profile   231

SECTION IV MAJOR INFORMATION SYSTEMS MANAGEMENT ISSUES 243

PREFACE

Successful use of information systems within a business enterprise is often an elusive goal. This book will provide an understanding and appreciation for the use of information technology to successfully manage an enterprise. The competitive role of information systems, which contributes to the overall success of the business through an effective integration of business strategies, information technology and people, is a major focus of the book. Students will gain an understanding and appreciation for the increasing importance of information systems to obtain organizational efficiencies, broaden individual effectiveness and/or gain a competitive advantage.

This book was written to be used in classes that provide a business focus to the use of information systems. The primary courses where this book could be used include Information Technology and Corporate Strategy, Management of MIS, graduate level MIS courses, MBA classes dealing with business strategy and technology, and an undergraduate capstone MIS class.

The book does an excellent job of merging the technical and business training of undergraduate MIS majors. The author has used much of the enclosed material for four MBA MIS classes and two undergraduate classes during the past year.

◆◆◆ PREMISE OF THE BOOK

Literally every enterprise, whether private or public, faces unprecedented competitive challenges. The source of these challenges is becoming more global, and the pace of change within the business environment is accelerating.

To respond to these challenges an enterprise needs to develop a necessary and logical vision based on an understanding of the business environment and the strengths and potential of the enterprise. The business vision and its supporting strategies drive the role and use of information systems within the organization.

The compression of time and events has significantly increased information needs for the growing number of people involved in making decisions within an enterprise. Information technology is a major contributor to the growing competitive threats and an enabler of possible responses to these same threats.

For the above reasons the potential role of information systems as a competitive resource has increased.

Innovative use of information technology dictates a systematic approach. It is essential that there be an ongoing working relationship between those who run a business and the people charged with a responsibility for information systems.

This book emphasizes the importance of establishing and maintaining three distinct perspectives. The first is an understanding of the *business environment* —the industry within which a company competes. The second is a realistic assessment of the *company environment* and its ability to achieve and sustain a competitive advantage. The third, the *use of information systems,* can then be positioned as a competitive resource following the assessment of the business and company environments.

✦✦✦ KEY TOPICS

- ✦ Challenges: competitive environment, organizational and information technology issues
- ✦ The effects of IT on competition (the way that an enterprise competes)
- ✦ Extended enterprise as a way to compete
- ✦ Competitive analysis methodology and structure
- ✦ Vision, strategy, tactics and business plan
- ✦ Identifying strategic information systems applications
- ✦ The three potential roles of information systems
- ✦ The concept of Roles, Roles and Relationships
- ✦ Information systems as a business within a business
- ✦ The Redefine/Define concept
- ✦ Telecommunications as the delivery vehicle
- ✦ Information systems architectural alternatives
- ✦ Examples of successful organizations
- ✦ A Success Factor Profile
- ✦ Information systems personnel and organizational issues
- ✦ The value of information systems
- ✦ Information systems financial strategies
- ✦ Business and information systems planning
- ✦ TQM and information systems
- ✦ Conclusions on the entire subject of using information systems to compete

✦✦✦ STUDENT ASSIGNMENTS

The author recommends that a term paper involving a business analysis be assigned, which requires the student to apply the concepts being learned by evaluating a specific company. The analysis term paper is a challenging assignment, but a number of companies can be evaluated based entirely on public domain, printed material. There is significant printed material available on companies like Charles Schwab, USAA, Federal Express, American Airlines and Wal-Mart. The recommended outline of the paper and a more complete list of companies that can be evaluated based on public domain material is included in the instructor manual. The outline for the paper is also consistent with the three perspectives covered in the book. Section I of the paper addresses the industry, Section II deals with the company and Section III is an analysis of the use of information systems using the structured analysis concepts covered in Chapters 8 to 12.

A class could also be taught using case studies. There are a number of Harvard Business School cases that address the concepts and management issues covered in the book. A third option would be to assign selected exercises at the end of the chapters.

◆◆◆ INSTRUCTOR SUPPORT

Accompanying this text is a detailed Instructor's Manual, which includes optional course schedules, supplementary readings, lecture suggestions, transparency masters, exam questions, and suggestions for administering the term paper.

◆◆◆ ORGANIZATION

The book is organized into four sections, preceded by an introductory chapter that introduces the challenges and issues that are addressed in each section. The first three sections correspond to the perspectives needed to understand the impact that the use of information systems has on a business. Section I starts where it must start, with a consideration of the business environment. Section II builds on this by examining important factors that impact the individual company. Then, and only then, does it make sense to look at the role and use of information systems, which is presented in Section III. The final section, Section IV, deals with major information systems management issues.

◆◆◆ BASIC TERMINOLOGY

The subject of information technology is complicated enough, but the lack of common usage of terms further adds to the confusion. The following three basic terms are used throughout the book consistent with the definitions provided:

Information technology (IT) is the "pieces and things" that are used to create information systems. It is the mainframes, the personal computers, the disk files, the modems, etc. It is both the hardware and software that is used to implement computer-based systems.

Information systems (IS) include both computers and telecommunications and are the result of a design and implementation process.

The actual design and implementation of information systems are accomplished primarily by the **information systems organization** working closely with the user organizations to define systems requirements. An alternative to this approach would be a joint development effort between the information systems organization and user departments, with the latter playing a more involved role in the technical aspects of the new system. A third approach would be a separate, independent development effort by a user department. There is a difference between information systems and the organization that has a primary responsibility for this organizational resource. This distinction between information systems and the information systems organization has been carefully noted throughout the book.

♦♦♦ THE INFORMATION TECHNOLOGY SPECTRUM

Ask someone what they think they need to know about information technology to function effectively in the business environment of today. Their response will undoubtedly be an indication of their own personal background and experience. It is important to keep in mind that there are multiple levels of information technology, representing a very broad spectrum. Where a person works and functions within this spectrum will greatly influence the answer to the question regarding a logical focus within a business-oriented class. The multiple levels within this information technology spectrum include:

- ♦ **Research**—basic research on physical science and information technologies.
- ♦ **Product development**—translating basic research into marketable IT products.
- ♦ **Manufacturing**—making the actual products.
- ♦ **Marketing**—identifying markets and selling the products.
- ♦ **Design and implementation**—obtaining information technology products and creating information systems through an analysis and development process.
- ♦ **Use of information technology-based systems**—applying information systems to functions and processes within an organization.

✦ **Management of the use of information technology-based systems**—addressing the specific information needs of the organization.

Where within the above spectrum should the emphasis of a business-oriented class dealing with information systems be placed? Most people, including the author of this book, conclude that the focus needs to be on the use of information systems and the management of this use. That is exactly what has been emphasized in this book.

ACKNOWLEDGMENTS

A book like this may be prepared by a single author, but it is actually written by many people. It is with difficulty that I attempt to acknowledge all of those who have contributed to the writing of this book, as I am sure that I will overlook some whom I should recognize. People who have assisted fall into three categories: (1) authors of other publications, (2) personal contacts as a source of information and'(3) those willing to review specific chapters to validate the contents.

The first category is referenced within the book, but particularly significant are Michael Porter (competitive strategy), Kenichi Ohmae (multinational company role in global competition), Peter Keen (vision process and telecommunications), Peter Drucker (business perspective and Redefine/Define concept), Charles Wiseman (Strategic Option Generator), Marilyn Parker and Robert Benson (IS value and planning structure), David Kearns and David Nadler (Xerox and TQM) and W. Edwards Deming (TQM).

Personal contacts were invaluable as an information source and included Robert McDermott of USAA, T.R. Reid and Dan McNichol of Whirlpool, Rhoda Verner of Lifescan, Cyril Yonsouni of Read-Rite, Tom Waitman of UB Networks, Skip Ross of Hewlett-Packard, Dee Hock and Richard Chew of VISA International, Dawn Lepore of Charles Schwab, Donna Mikov of Boeing Commercial Airplane Group, Al Becker of American Airlines, Au Soo Wei of Singapore Airlines, Sue O'Sullivan of British Airways, Steve Anderson of *USA Today,* Congressman Norman Mineta, Jim Feeman of IBM, Allan Ditchfield and Leslie Heinrich of Progressive Corporation, John Vaughn of Intel, Bob Pospischil of Bissett Nursery and Judd Everhart of Xerox.

Particular thanks go to those who were willing to review specific chapters and provide constructive criticism on how they could be improved. This included Tom Waitman of UB Networks (introduction and telecommunications chapters), Rhoda Verner of Lifescan and previously with Xerox (chapter dealing with TQM and IS), Les Clark of Hoechst, Marion and Roussel (business and IS planning chapter), the airline people cited above who critiqued the sections in the airline chapter about their respective companies, and the numerous university faculty arranged by the publisher who reviewed specific chapters and in some cases the entire book.

I would be remiss if I did not thank my students, both graduate and undergraduate, as they have been the ones upon whom the enclosed material has been tested and honed. They are the ones that prove that the material makes sense and that the structured analysis can be a good learning tool. The paper in the appendix written by Ali Eridiaz as an MBA student is offered as tangible evidence of this contention.

Frank Ruggirello was a positive, steadying influence as my editor, and Peter Keen provided insightful critiques and recommendations as a consulting editor. Jehanne Schweitzer did an excellent job in managing the final production, and Susan Defosset was a pleasure to work with as the final content editor of the book. Her biology training was a good check on whether material was understandable to those not possessing an information systems background.

The following reviewers provided numerous helpful and insightful suggestions for improving the book:

Michele Brown, University of Richmond
Albert Harris, Appalachian State
Richard Hauser, East Carolina University
Kenneth Kozar, University of Colorado
Albert Lederer, University of Kentucky
Prashant Palvia, Fogelman College of Business
Rodney Pearson, Mississippi State
John Quigley, East Tennessee State University
Arthur Rasher, University of Tulsa
Robert Trent, University of Virginia

One does not do a project like this without some personal sacrifices, and I particularly thank my wife Linda for her understanding and acceptance of the hours of my time that were needed to complete it. My sons John, Scott and Mark also assisted with proofreading and critiquing, proving that today's generation does know how to spell and can write very well.

BUSINESS AND INFORMATION SYSTEMS MANAGEMENT CHALLENGES

Running a successful business is like doing a jigsaw puzzle. The problem is that the pieces and the picture are both changing.

Cyril J. Yansouni
Chairman and CEO
Read-Rite Corporation

LEARNING OBJECTIVES

This first chapter highlights the challenges faced by companies competing in a business environment as dynamic as the world has ever known. The focus is on business success factors and the role that information systems can play in support of business strategies to contribute to a company's success. Understanding these is the starting point in appreciating major factors that must be dealt with to run a business successfully in today's global business world.

QUESTIONS

The following questions address the major challenges to manage a business successfully:

1. What are the critical elements that contribute to sustainable business success in today's environment?
2. How does the Business Driver Model help to determine the answer to the above question?
3. Why are three different perspectives necessary to understand the significance of information systems within a specific company?
4. Is leadership still important or has it been replaced by employee empowerment?

5. What is the significance of the simultaneous revolutions within the business environment?
6. Why is a systematic approach needed to gain a competitive advantage through the use of information systems within a company?

✦✦✦ IT IS NOT ANY EASIER TO RUN A SUCCESSFUL BUSINESS

If you talk to any business leader, it is quickly apparent that running a business is more complicated than ever before. The new business environment has also complicated the tasks of those who try to determine why certain businesses are more successful than others. Traditional yardsticks to explain successful companies within specific industries do not provide a complete explanation. Financial measurements and market share are indications of how well a company performed but do not explain how they accomplished these results. Specific emphasis programs like total quality management (TQM) or process reengineering are methodologies that work well for some companies but are too narrow in scope to offer a complete explanation. The days of all companies in the same industry benefiting from common economic or industry factors also seem to be gone. How else can you explain the high level of success of some companies and the dramatic and often sudden demise of others within the same industry?

This simply adds to the difficulty of a search for the factors that truly make a difference within successful companies. One can always look to the business knight in shining armor who rides in loaded with clichés to fix the problems. "If it ain't broke, break it! Don't automate, obliterate! Stamp out long-term planning! Empowerment of employee teams is so good that your objective should be a span of control of one to five hundred!" These comments are good verbiage for conference and banquet speeches but fall short of providing a complete solution to the many challenges faced by most enterprises. They most certainly do not explain what it takes to be a successful business in today's business environment.

✦✦✦ BUSINESS SUCCESS FACTORS

Running a successful business is not one-dimensional. There was a time when businesses cited specific functional strengths as the key to their success. IBM had the best marketing organization, GE had the best financial group and Boeing was blessed with the best engineers. In the past, these specific functional strengths translated into organizational and financial success. This is no longer true.

A successful business has to effectively address all major functions better than its major competitors. For a manufacturing company this includes research and development, product development, manufacturing, marketing and sales, distribution, financing, customer support and repair service. A company does not have to do all of these itself, but each of these functions must be addressed in an effective, high-quality manner.

To understand the contribution that information systems can make, it is necessary to understand the key elements that contribute to the success of a business. Factors that make a major difference among successful companies are addressed below. There is some overlap among these factors, but each is considered important enough to receive specific attention. They will be addressed in more detail in subsequent chapters.

Business Leadership

Leadership in the business world has never been more important than it is today. In today's competitive environment a successful company is the direct result of effective business leadership. Leadership is like an umbrella that fits over many of the other important business success factors. It prompts creativity and innovation when and where necessary within all major aspects of a business. The need for innovation in products, marketing and operations is a must in most organizations, but it doesn't stop there. Innovative ways to acquire the capital to fund growth or new business strategies can also be a major success factor. Creative ways to link information systems to business strategies can also make a major difference.

Leaders come in all shapes and sizes in all parts of the world. It is not so much how they lead but the fact that they do and how well they do it. There are certainly common characteristics of great leaders, but also many differences in personality, characteristics and style. A most important role of business leaders is to deal effectively with the long-term viability of the business. Establishing a direction—a vision for the company—and gaining an understanding and an acceptance of this direction throughout the organization is a major business success factor. Supporting key strategies through the use of information systems is then possible through both business and information technology leadership.

Ability to Fit the Pieces into the Increasingly Bigger Business Picture

The smaller pieces—the multiple operations within a company—must fit into a logical business whole. Every operation, policy and strategy must be evaluated to determine how it fits within the bigger picture in which the business operates. This may mean addressing a global business strategy, a completely new organizational approach, radically different business processes and/or emphasizing the importance of a very comprehensive communications network.

Organizational Responsiveness and Resilience

The time to respond has become a major element of the competitive strategy of many organizations. Emphasis programs like TQM and reengineering attempt to take time out of processes. Why? Because lead times, delays and response to a customer problem have a major time dimension. A quick response is valued by the customers, vendors, work associates and management. This can be based on reducing time to market, time to customer or time to internal decisions.

A company also needs resilience to absorb the increasing amount of change in an effective and continuing manner. It is one thing to deal with changing conditions once or twice. A strong resilience says that an organization can accept the need for and make necessary changes on an ongoing basis.

Solving Customer Problems Through a Combined Organizational Effort

What does it take to solve a major customer problem? It is safe to conclude that the solution to such a problem is not provided by a single individual. For that matter, a major customer problem seldom gets resolved in a satisfactory way by a single function within an organization. Effective solutions in a timely manner are the result of multiple functions like marketing, finance, customer support and product development coming together to successfully address the issue.

A Strong Company Culture

Culture is the way things get done within an organization. More often than not, culture reflects an attitude towards customers. While culture impacts every employee, it is the result of values that senior management have instilled within the organization. These values establish the core of a vision and the foundation upon which a strong culture is built. This has both business and information systems implications.

Ability and Willingness to Innovate, Change and Take Risks

Change and innovation are frequently cited as the reasons for success. Does this mean that the more a company innovates and changes, the more successful it will be? Not necessarily. These factors can also be an explanation for failure. Poorly conceived change can be disruptive, time consuming and counterproductive. The challenge is in determining when traditional success factors are no longer valid. If the basis upon which the business was built no longer offers value to the customer, then it must change. Smaller, more specific changes may make sense, but identifying these can be difficult, and gaining acceptance by employees even more challenging.

Accomplishing These Factors While Maintaining a Balance

Facing so many simultaneous challenges makes it difficult to maintain a necessary balance within an organization. This includes doing what needs to be done on a short-term basis while building for a positive, long-term future. It involves knowing when to exert authoritative management while in other circumstances empowering employees. It includes acknowledging the importance and contribution of long-time employees while encouraging and motivating new, younger people. It is maintaining a balanced perspective of the entire business.

Today's business environment is not for the timid. There is risk potential in literally every major function within an organization. The question is where a company is willing to take risks and how to manage its dimensions.

Communication Across the Entire Organization

Functioning successfully as a truly integrated company requires effective and timely communication across the entire organization. The compression of time and events emphasizes the criticality of keeping people informed.

✦✦✦ THREE NECESSARY PERSPECTIVES

No computer in and of itself has ever created a competitive advantage. Computers are merely a combination of hardware and software and thus have no intrinsic value. Achieving a competitive advantage is also not as simple as buying a computer. The way information systems are used in support of a competitive business strategy determine whether a competitive advantage can be achieved.

To properly position a competitive role for information systems, it is necessary to understand three perspectives (Figure 1-1):

1. The **business environment**—the specific industry in which a company operates. This includes the important characteristics of the industry and how an organization successfully competes within this environment.
2. The **enterprise environment**—the company itself, its major characteristics, track record, and strengths and weaknesses.

Figure 1-1

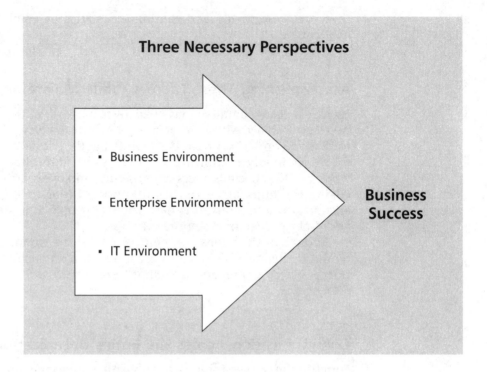

3. The **information technology** (IT) implemented by the organization to gain a competitive advantage. This is the role that information systems has played within the company.

It is crucial to understand the first two perspectives in order to make any sense of why and how information systems are used.

✦✦✦ SIMULTANEOUS REVOLUTIONS IN THE BUSINESS ENVIRONMENT

The difficulty in successfully running a business today is not necessarily based on specific new challenges. Many of the current issues have been around for a long time. The problem is not the difficulty of any one of these challenges, but the requirement to address all of them simultaneously as they continue to change at an accelerating pace. Individually these challenges, shown in Figure 1-2, need at most minimal explanation.

1. An increasing number of new competitors both domestic and foreign.

2. New rules of competition. New competitors often implement new business strategies and try to compete in innovative ways.

Figure 1-2

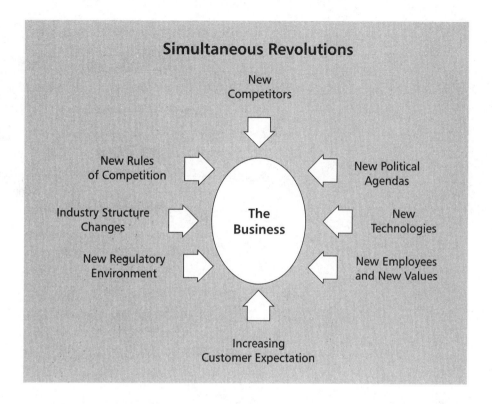

3. Structural changes in many industries and a breakdown in traditional industry boundaries.

4. A new regulatory environment. In some cases this means less regulation and sometimes it means more.

5. Increasing customer expectations. Better company performance leads to higher demands from customers.

6. A change in the number, responsibilities and experience of employees as a result of restructuring and downsizing. New younger employees often have new values and priorities. The reward system within the organization must acknowledge these changes.

7. New enabling technologies including information technology.

8. Political and social change that impacts many of the above factors.

✦✦✦ A BUSINESS DRIVER MODEL

The scope and magnitude of the many simultaneous revolutions prompted the creation of the **Business Driver Model** shown in Figure 1-3. The model can help in understanding the changing revolutions and their relationship with each other.

Figure 1-3

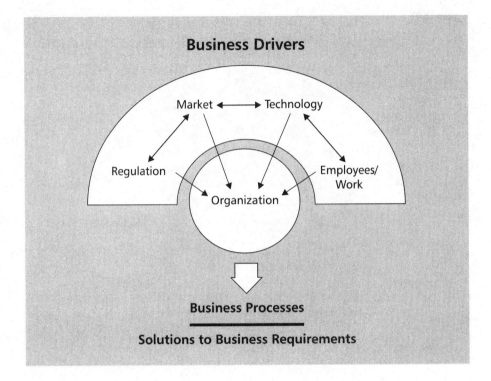

Market

When using the Business Driver Model, some logical advice is "when in doubt, think customer." This starts with an understanding of the market, competitors and competitive rules. It is important to understand and define the market relative to business strategies. It is also important to evaluate the possible impact of market dynamics, globalization, simultaneous fragmentation and segmentation of some industries and company alliances.

Technology

Technology is an enabling resource that is changing rapidly while providing constantly improving price and performance. Organizations do not use information technology without purpose. It is used to address a business requirement.

Regulation

The significance and importance of regulation varies significantly by industry. Regulations can be a major influence on a company's strategies both in terms of what it can do and what it cannot. In the telephone service business, regulation has protected local telephone service monopolies and deterred them from providing long-distance and information services. In the airline business, while there has been some deregulation, a great deal remains.

Employees and Work

Thirty to forty years ago "employees" probably would not have been in the model. This is not to say that they should not have been. Too many factors concerning employees were taken for granted in those times. Today the number of employees to be hired is a strategic decision, and substantial time and energy is spent on this most important competitive resource. Hiring, training, developing, motivating and rewarding employees is at the core of running a successful business.

The model highlights factors that must be considered in addressing business processes to provide solutions to business requirements. Understanding the business environment and defining the business and its key processes are major challenges. For many companies this is far more of an issue than designing and implementing information systems. More and more cost-effective software packages are available that can be used once the business and its processes have been well defined.

✦✦✦ INNOVATIVE USE OF INFORMATION SYSTEMS REQUIRES A SYSTEMATIC APPROACH

The creation of a competitive advantage through the use of information systems involves all of the many challenges of any competitive endeavor. Adding information systems to the equation can actually increase the challenge, because they must be designed, implemented and used effectively. How is this possible? The focus, priorities and leadership of the business need to drive the use of information systems within the organization.

As shown in Figure 1-4, the entire process starts with an understanding of the **vision** for the organization. This is the longer-term direction of the organization, the photograph of the future. Influenced by the length of product life cycles, it is what the organization wants to look like in five, ten, twenty years or longer. Business **strategies** determine how the organization will accomplish the major objectives directed by the vision. **Tactics** are shorter term and more specifically focused on measurable objectives. The **business plan** identifies how resources and funds will be allocated, often in the form of an operating plan or budget.

These major business factors drive the use of information systems. The five elements of the bottom box in the chart are a structured

Figure 1-4

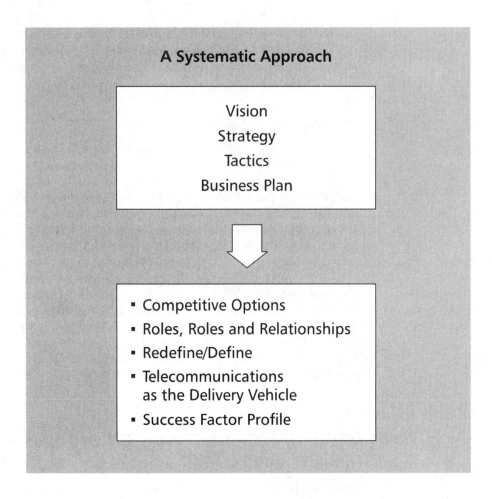

approach that deals with the evaluation, posturing and use of information systems in support of the factors in the top box: vision, strategy, tactics and business plan. These information technology enabling factors
include:

1. A model for the evaluation of **competitive options**.

2. The concept of **roles, roles and relationships**, which addresses
   the competitive role of information systems, the role of senior
   management in posturing information systems as a competitive
   resource and the importance of establishing an ongoing relationship between senior management and the information systems
   organization.

3. The concept of **redefine/define**, which deals with how information systems can change or clarify value to the customer by
   changing the business, products, services, or business processes.

4. The use of **telecommunications as the delivery vehicle**—the link with customers, suppliers and business partners.

5. A **success factor profile** of the primary strengths of companies that have effectively used information systems to compete.

✦✦✦ WHAT IS THE POINT (OBJECTIVE) OF INFORMATION SYSTEMS?

The only logical answer to the above question is to improve the ability of an enterprise, public or private sector, large or small company, to achieve its objectives. In other words, to help it to be successful in the eyes of its stakeholders, i.e., customers, constituents and employees. The demands of the changing environment in which enterprises operate today dictate that providing value to stakeholders, and especially customers, is what really counts.

A positive contribution by information systems can come in three forms:

1. **Efficiency** measured by productivity—doing things better.

2. **Effectiveness** accomplished by broadening the scope of individual tasks, jobs or processes within an organization—doing better things including what an organization could never do before.

3. **Competitive advantage** gained by the enterprise—doing better and new things for the customer.

These three results are often achieved successively over time. As shown in Figure 1-5, information technology tends to migrate through multiple eras or phases within a specific organization. Era I involves the initial company purchase of a computer, which usually becomes the responsibility of a departmental manager. This "owner of information technology" within the organization becomes the regulator of the computer as an organizational resource. In this first era the role of information systems is to gain efficiencies on behalf of the entire organization. Traditionally accounting and finance were the first applications of the new computer. In recent years companies can acquire first-ever computers in multiple application areas based on the availability of software application packages.

Era II welcomed the personal computer, which fundamentally changed organizational computing forever. The IBM announcement of its PC in 1981 legitimatized these desktop devices in corporate America, and the rest is history. While PCs may not be free, they broke the computer monopoly within the company while providing new individual computing capabilities. At the individual level these computers not only provide efficiencies, but also broaden capabilities to address tasks and even entire jobs. Traditional "number crunchers" can be transformed into financial analysts. Bookkeepers can became broader scope accountants since the computer performs the routine tasks.

Figure 1-5

Source: Cash, McFarlan, McKenney and Appleton, *Corporate Information Systems Management,* Richard D. Irwin, 1992, 3/E, p. 11, adapted.

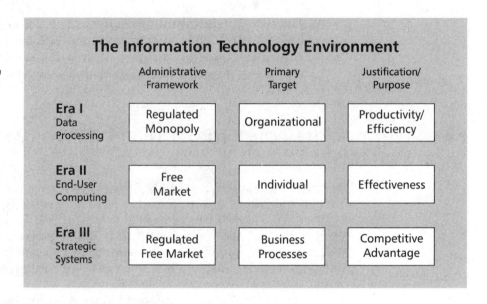

Era III, the strategic systems era, is significantly more challenging than the first two. There is certainly nothing wrong with the first two eras. Most organizations will gladly take all of the possible efficiency and effectiveness benefits that they can get. The Era I and II experiences often provide the basis to pursue strategic systems. Competitively focused applications can be the first computer-based systems within a company, but they are more frequently the result of previous experience with successful information systems. These earlier experiences provide the best of traditional data processing and end-user computing to develop and implement competitive applications. The strategic systems that can involve new or reengineered business processes are an extension of the traditional data processing applications and end-user computing.

♦♦♦ EXAMPLES OF SUCCESSFUL USE OF INFORMATION SYSTEMS TO COMPETE

Some examples of the competitive use of information systems should help to introduce this approach.

Boeing

Strategic Significance: **A New Aircraft Design System for the 777**

Boeing has held the top market share position in the commercial airplane industry for a long time. Because of this it has also been the number one positive contributor to the U.S. balance of trade. But Boeing is facing a major challenge from Airbus Industrie, the European consortium backed by four governments. It is not difficult to find people at Boeing who will say that they are in a fight for survival against Airbus.

This type of challenge often suggests the need for change, and Boeing has responded accordingly. Its 777 aircraft was a response to the market need identified by airline customers. For this reason Boeing fundamentally changed the way it designed the 777. The 777 was the first aircraft ever designed by Boeing that was 100% computer-based. For the first time it did not build a prototype aircraft but relied upon the results of the computer-based design. Why did Boeing make this change? Because it reduced the errors and costly rework associated with manufacturing and redesigning during the build phase.

Boeing has used computers for product design for many years but never as the basis for a complete aircraft. To change the role of the computer in the design process from a tool, as it was in the past, to the platform for the total design was a major change. It is not just a process change but a culture change relative to the role of the computer and the role of design engineers. Engineers are now part of a computer-based design system. Computing played a major communications role in the entire design process. The excitement that surrounded the on-schedule introduction of the 777 and its initial flight would seem to confirm that this was the right decision.

Does Boeing's reduction in the number of employees taint this story? This is a different dimension to the challenges that Boeing faces. While it is struggling to meet the product challenges of a major competitor, its major customers in the airline industry are experiencing the worst financial performance in their history. This has resulted in canceled or delayed orders for aircraft and the unfortunate decision that Boeing must reduce its number of employees. As Peter Drucker has accurately said, corporate size has become a strategic decision.

Wal-Mart Stores

Strategic Significance: A Just-in-Time Retail Inventory Management System

Wal-Mart is a classic American success story. From a single store in Rogers, Arkansas to the largest retailer in the world in twenty-eight years is something to applaud. No wonder it is often lauded as the right way to run an organization. Wal-Mart is a very people-oriented company. This includes customers who are referred to as "the boss" and employees being called "associates." The term "associates" indicates that employees are business associates of senior management and are asked to help run the business better.

There are many reasons why Wal-Mart has achieved its almost unbelievable growth. Its small-town strategy with everyday low prices of nationally advertised brands is the foundation of this success. But it does not stop there. Their store-within-a-store concept where each department is run as if it were a separate business has worked very well. This concept focuses on the importance of making each department successful so that the total store will do well.

Sam Walton's ongoing request to his information systems organization—to get more information to associates running departments in the stores—definitely added to the success of Wal-Mart. A database for each department is maintained on a computer in each store. The database supports an ordering process to restock the shelves in the store. The associate running the department uses the database and a hand-held computer to evaluate ordering history, the margin on the item, an alternate item and its margin in order to make a decision regarding the quantity and the item to order. Contrary to many other retailers, Wal-Mart has pushed this type of decision making down to the hourly associate running the department. Many retailers do this on a centralized computer-based system.

On high-volume products Wal-Mart has been a leader in the use of Electronic Data Interchange (EDI). For instance, Proctor and Gamble (P&G) is linked electronically to the Wal-Mart inventory system and its product analyst monitors the Wal-Mart database. When an agreed upon inventory level reaches a reorder point, the P&G product analyst initiates a purchase order electronically and orders the merchandise to be shipped to Wal-Mart.

Bissett Nursery Corporation

Strategic Significance: A Visual Landscape Design Marketing Program

Innovative business strategies backed by the use of computer-based systems are not limited to large companies. Small companies must also fight for success and even survival. Bissett Nursery in Long Island, New York uses the landscape design talents of Jim Vazzana and a PC image-processing application to provide a major marketing tool to their landscape contractor customers. Computer-generated pictures show new home owners what their home would look like completely landscaped. Vazzana takes a photograph of the prospect's home, scans it into the computer and graphically landscapes it from his custom-built database of more than 4,000 images. The final rendering shows plants, trees, sidewalks, ponds or anything else that would provide a salable landscape plan to a potential customer.

This program was initiated in 1991 when landscape contractors were encountering a decline in residential sales. It proved to be a three-way winning approach. The home owners love seeing their homes in their new landscaped environments. Ninety-five percent of the prospects that are presented with a rendering sign a contract to have the landscaping done. The contractors pay $200 to $400 for a rendering but benefit from the increased business from contracts gained through this approach. A growing number of contractors have become true believers of the benefits of images versus traditional drawings. Since the Bissett images help them to get landscaping contracts, they buy more products from Bissett.

Bissett Nursery is a privately held, family-run wholesale nursery supply company in operation since 1964. It has grown to be the largest re-wholesaler in the tri-state area of New York, Connecticut and New Jersey from its two locations in Holtsville and Dix Hills. It sells 6,000 products to 7,500 customers—landscape contractors, architects, schools, cities and states. Jimmy Bissett, President, and Bob Pospischil, Chief Financial Officer, both feel that the information systems have had a very positive impact on the business. This includes both the landscape-imaging system and their main computer system, which deals with the more traditional applications of order entry, customer billing and inventory control. Both of these systems helped them to not only weather some very tough recession years but to actually drive growth in the products they handle and the customers they serve. Equally important has been a growth in both revenue and profits realized from their improved competitive position.

For service companies like Federal Express, Charles Schwab, USAA, L.L. Bean and Progressive, major use of computers is not really an option but a requirement in their respective industries. Each of these companies provides services and their businesses have high information content. A look at these five organizations confirms this point.

Federal Express

Strategic Significance: A Time-Sensitive Package-Tracking and Delivery System

The claim of Federal Express is well known: "Absolutely, positively overnight delivery and we'll tell a customer at any point in the delivery process where the package is, whether it has been delivered and who signed for it." Delivery is the service, but information is the key added-value to this process. Why else would UPS have spent $1.4 billion to duplicate this capability to compete with Federal Express in overnight delivery?

Charles Schwab

Strategic Significance: A Computer-based Discount Brokerage Business

Once a low-cost discount broker, Schwab has shifted its business strategy to providing the best possible customer service. The ability to confirm a trade while the customer is on the telephone was at one point a major advantage for Schwab. Since other brokers now have this capability, Schwab continues to offer new computer-based services. StreetSmart supports a client who wants to execute his own trades through a dial-up capability. Telebroker executes 30% of Schwab trades through the use of a touch-tone telephone. A unique system to process mutual fund trades is its latest example of computer-based client support.

Early in its efforts to become the success that it is in its industry, Schwab management made a decision that it would not offer products that were not computer-based. This has never been more evident than at the present time.

USAA[1]

Strategic Significance: **Best Possible Customer Service through Information Systems that are Customer Convenient, Operator Efficient and Cost Effective**

Unless you are a member of USAA as a former military officer or one of their dependents, you probably do not know this company based in San Antonio, Texas. If you are a member you realize that it is possibly the best property and casualty insurance company in the country. Evolving to a financial services organization, it is unique in that it has no field insurance agents. This savings in sales commissions is passed on to its members (customers). Meanwhile, according to members it offers the best service in the industry. How is this possible? By keeping its products and services properly focused on the demands of the market and being the leader in information technology use. Its latest accomplishment is an image-processing system that electronically captures member correspondence so they can dispose of the original document. From that point the document is handled electronically. It is processed, filed and retrieved if needed by a customer service agent and ultimately archived electronically. Most customers use 800 numbers to contact the company, and the USAA customer service representative sits in front of the computer terminal with access to the electronic images.

L.L. Bean

Strategic Significance: **A Redefined Order Entry and Distribution Process**

This well-known mail order company is not what some people perceive it to be. Viewed as a conservative, laid-back, woodsy company in Freeport, Maine, it is actually a modern, extremely well-managed business with extensive computer use. It is a misnomer to refer to it as a mail order company, because 85% of its orders during the Christmas buying season come via 800-number telephone calls. The service representative is seated in front of a computer terminal that triggers the entire distribution process, including the warehouse picking list, in the most efficient order

---

[1] The complete name is United Services Automobile Association. The abbreviation is normally used because its products and services deal with more than automobiles.

for the items to be collected. Another important computer application is its customer mailing list, which targets customers with any one of twenty-one catalogues.

Progressive Corporation

Strategic Significance: **New Customer Acquisition and Service Systems**

Progressive, the seventh largest U.S. auto insurer, based in Cleveland, Ohio, has redefined its strategy driven by a strong belief that lower prices, more information, more options and immediate, local, hassle-free service is what is needed to delight customers. Information systems play a significant role in each of the three customer experiences with Progressive: buying a policy from them, ownership of the policy, and claims service and support. Buying a policy in some markets is aided by a system that provides quick response to price quotes for Progressive as well as other major competitors. It is also supported by an on-line systems connection with nearly 8,000 of the 30,000 independent insurance agents throughout the U.S. Ownership is supported by a customer master file and a premium billing system. A quick response to claims is assisted by having access to a database containing everything a representative needs to know about the customer. This also includes a representative who arrives at the scene of an accident armed with a laptop computer and prepared to write the customer a check to cover the damage.

✦✦✦ A QUICK INFORMATION SYSTEMS ASSESSMENT

A quick assessment of the business environment to determine the current role of information systems and the potential for growth in the future entails asking the following questions:

✦ How is business? It is difficult for an organization to invest in information systems, including those intended to gain a competitive advantage, if it is not realizing profits that can be used for capital investments. There are two categories of people within an organization: those that serve customers and those that do not. Does information systems prioritize support to those "serving customers"? The choice of categories for information systems is one that management can decide. A second logical criterion for an information systems support priority is for those people within the company that have a profit responsibility.

✦ Is the information systems manager a member of the top management team? Has the information systems executive earned a seat at the corporate table?

♦ What percentage of the operating budget of the business is for information systems? This may not be a precise indication but it can be meaningful.

♦ Are information systems regarded as a core competency by senior management? Have these same systems become a significant factor in running the business both strategically and on a day-to-day basis? The answers to these questions are a good indication of the attitude and priorities given to information systems by senior management within a company.

♦♦♦ THE BEST INDUSTRIES AT USING INFORMATION SYSTEMS TO COMPETE

It is easier to assess specific companies than entire industries in determining which are particularly effective in leveraging the use of information systems to their competitive advantage. However, a good case can be made for both the retailing and transportation industries. Across the entire retail industry—including department stores, discounters and specialty stores—are an impressive number of companies that are excellent examples of successful use of information systems. A short list would include L.L. Bean, Dillards, The Gap, Home Depot, Kmart, Men's Wearhouse, Mervyn's, J.C. Penney, Toys R Us and Wal-Mart.

Comprised of airlines, railroads, freight companies and overnight delivery companies, the transportation industry provides an equally impressive list of companies successfully using information systems. American Airlines, American President Companies, British Airways, CSX, Federal Express, Singapore Airlines, United Airlines, Union Pacific and UPS make a case for this industry.

There are clearly others. The brokerage industry has placed significant emphasis on information systems in recent years. Why have these industries placed more importance on the use of information systems in the core of their business? The amount of information that they need to run their business is a major factor. Both retailers and transportation companies deal with major inventory control challenges. Is there a more perishable inventory than an empty seat on an airline when the flight lifts off the runway? Inventory control has been a prime application since the very beginning of data processing equipment.

At the opposite end of the spectrum are those industries that have not placed a high priority in applying information technology to the overall success of the business. A trailing industry list would include the construction industry, the petroleum industry and the federal government. Part of the explanation for this is less day-to-day applications with inventory control, record-keeping characteristics. More important is the tradition and culture of the people running these businesses, which put higher priorities on other factors. For years computers were viewed by the construction industry as part of overhead—something to minimize or even avoid. Personal computer use on construction job sites has become common, but this still has not made information systems a high-priority business success factor in this industry. In recent years the petroleum industry has increased its use of information systems in sales and marketing, but it traditionally viewed computers as the tools of accountants.

The federal government has a different set of problems. It is too big! Sheer volumes of master records and transactions make many federal government applications unbelievably big to design, implement and manage. It also suffers from having either too many bosses or no one who is actually accountable. Who actually runs the federal government? There are elected officials (the executive and congress) and the bureaucrats. The employees within the bureaucracy may stay around, but the elected and appointed leaders tend to change. This is not conducive to the type of management system and approach advocated by many, including the author of this book.

✦✦✦ CONCLUSION

Information systems—what are they? Are they significant to a specific business? If so, why? What will they do for the good of the business? Who plays a key role within an organization once the decision is made to implement a major, new information system? What skills are needed and what are critical elements to this approach? At what cost? Does this involve a restructuring of current business processes? Once accomplished, will business life be easier, cheaper or at least better? How will this be determined initially and on a continuing basis?

This book will provide answers to these and many other questions regarding the use of information systems within a business. For now, we will conclude by emphasizing that to use information systems to compete requires the integration of these systems with the business management process. That is the only reason they exist and it cannot be done any other way!

RECOMMENDED READING

Ackoff, Russell L., *The Democratic Corporation: A Radical Prescription for Recreating Corporate America and Rediscovering Success*. New York: Oxford University Press, 1994.

The deterioration of the American economy in general and companies in particular has often prompted an oversimplification of the problem and the solutions. This book is an attempt to chart a way out with an understanding that a systems solution is required. The performance of this system is not the sum of the performance of its parts taken separately, but the product of their interactions and interdependence. The challenge is to stimulate the right kind of leadership by confronting the problems with ideas that mobilize human resources into concerted, constructive action.

Drucker, Peter, *The New Realities*. New York: Harper & Row, 1989.

The premise of this book is that the future has already happened. Many factors that will have a profound impact on businesses around the world are already well advanced. Most if not all of these factors were predicted and their significance can be understood and discerned. Unfortunately they bring high levels of uncertainty with them. They set new limits and functions on governments, dictate a transnational economy, suggest that management has new social dimensions and emphasize the importance of a knowledge base.

Scott Morton, Michael S., and Thomas J. Allen, eds., *Information Technology and the Corporation of the 1990s, Research Studies*. New York: Oxford University Press, 1994.

A report on research funded by twelve industrial and government sponsors in the U.S. and the U.K. Emphasis is on innovation in the market and technology in parallel in response to changes in one or both of these business drivers. The book is organized into three sections: (1) The Information Technology Revolution, (2) Strategic Options and (3) The Organization and Management Response.

Scott Morton, Michael S., ed., *The Corporation of the 1990s*. New York: Oxford University Press, 1991.

This is an earlier edition similar in content to the above publication.

Toffler, Alvin, *Future Shock*. New York: Bantam Books, 1971.

This book was the first of many warnings that we are facing an increasing rate of profound, complex changes that involve an interaction of enterprises, institutions and societies.

EXERCISES

1. **The challenges faced in the current business environment prompt the following questions:**

   a. How significant are the changes that are occurring within the business environment?

   b. Are they temporary or permanent changes? Explain and justify your answer.

   c. How much of a challenge will it be for U.S. companies to effectively respond to these changes? Where and how does a company begin to solve its problems?

   d. Provide multiple-company examples in different industries that illustrate both a positive response to the new challenges and a failure to do so. Identify companies that initially failed to respond to foreign competitive challenges but have turned things around and are now successful.

    e. Compare the difficulty for a small company to address the challenges of the new business environment versus that of a larger company.

    f. Is timely and more complete information important for a company to respond to many of the business environment challenges?

2. Simultaneous revolutions.

Use Figure 1-2 to analyze a specific company within its industry to assess the impact of the simultaneous revolutions. Do not generalize but provide specific factors in building this company and industry profile.

3. Using all of the business success factors presented in this chapter:

    a. Evaluate a specific company relative to its strengths and weaknesses for each of the factors. Use excellent, good, fair and poor in arriving at an evaluation.

    b. Be prepared to explain and defend your evaluations.

4. What makes information technology right for a specific company?

Can the information technology be right if:

    a. The business climate is wrong?

    b. The business strategy is wrong?

    c. The business leaders have other priorities?

    d. Senior management is focused on other competitive issues?

5. The three potential major roles of information systems.

Explain the chart in Figure 1-5 relative to the following:

    a. The three potential roles of information systems within an enterprise.

    b. The degree of difficulty for an organization to be a successful user of information systems within each role.

    c. The posture and relationship of the information systems organization relative to users and user management.

    d. The importance of senior management involvement on an ongoing basis in each of the three areas.

6. The importance of information to a business.

Select one of the companies cited as good examples of successful use of information systems in this chapter and be prepared to discuss if the example addresses factors that are important to a sustainable competitive advantage.

SECTION I

THE FIRST OF THREE PERSPECTIVES:
THE BUSINESS ENVIRONMENT

The basic premise of this book is that it is not possible to gain an understanding of the contribution of information systems to the success of the business by looking at either the information technology or the computer-based applications. To understand the significance of the information systems requires an understanding of the company—its vision, strategies and tactics, as well as its management style, including how the company deals with both internal and external challenges, issues and problems on a day-to-day basis. But even this is not enough. To understand the company it is necessary to position it in the industry in which it competes and to appreciate how companies in the industry compete.

This first section starts where one must start—by understanding the business environment in which a company must position itself to be successful. Initial focus is on business success factors, the competitive environment and the competitive forces within an industry.

BUSINESS COMPETITIVE ENVIRONMENT

*The global market will come to you,
if you don't go to it.*

LEARNING OBJECTIVES

Competition can be local, regional, national or international. For the reason indicated in the quote above, the business environment of more and more companies is acquiring a global dimension. This chapter takes a general look at competition, defines it and then focuses on the global landscape. The role that the nation plays relative to the competitiveness of its home-based companies is evaluated. These are basic but important factors in beginning to understand the competitive environment of a specific company.

QUESTIONS

Some appropriate questions regarding competition and the role of the nation in shaping competitive success:

1. How do you define competitiveness?
2. What is a competitive advantage based on?
3. What are the three primary inputs to domestic competitive success?
4. How significant is the role of the nation in today's global business environment?
5. Is management style the key to competitive success?
6. Is there an advantage in "who knows the most" in a business relationship?

✦✦✦ DEFINING COMPETITIVENESS AND A COMPETITIVE MODEL

In 1984 President Ronald Reagan established a commission on industrial competitiveness. The president's commission was a star-studded group of people that included industrial leaders, union leaders and academics. Led by John Young, at that time the CEO of Hewlett-Packard, they were surprised at how easy it was for a fairly diverse group of people to agree on both the competitive issues and appropriate proposals to address them. While it was difficult to determine the direct impact of the commission proposals, this excellent effort produced a logical definition of competitiveness, a very easy-to-understand competitive model and readily agreed-upon recommendations by the commission participants.

The commission's January 1985 report provided the following conclusion in the final paragraph of the cover letter:

> Mr. President, it has been a great honor to serve you and the Nation. *The competitive challenge calls for the leadership only you can provide.* [Italics added.] We thank you for your vision, interest and initiatives in making competitiveness a priority on our national agenda.[1]

Subsequent chapters will address the importance of leadership within an organization when it comes to addressing competitive challenges.

The commission's definition of competitiveness and their competitive model are provided below:

Competitiveness: *The degree to which a nation can, under free and fair market conditions, produce goods and services that will meet the test of international markets while simultaneously maintaining or expanding the real income of its citizens.*[2]

A Competitive Model

As depicted in Figure 2-1, there are three primary inputs to improved domestic performance by private sector companies: human resources, capital and technology. Human resources is a quality not a quantity issue. The education and skill levels of people has become a major competitive factor. Capital considerations include both availability and cost of funds. Savings rates and a consistent, steady supply of capital to the private sector influences the cost. There are multiple forms of technology input ranging from design systems to automated machine tools to information technology. If the right combination of these input factors are available at an appropriate price/performance, then an improved domestic performance should be possible.

---

[1] The Report of the President's Commission on Industrial Competitiveness, *Global Competitive: The New Reality*, 1985.

[2] Ibid., p. 6.

Figure 2-1

Courtesy of the President's Commission on Industrial Competitiveness, *Global Competitive*, 1985, p. 6.

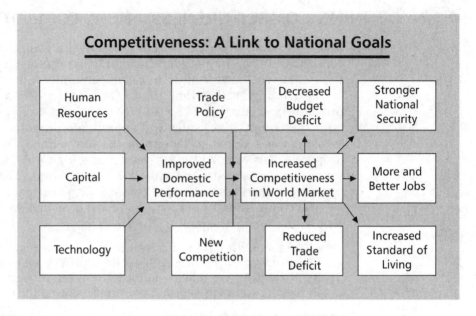

Competitiveness: A Link to National Goals

Two factors can inhibit using domestic success as a platform to expand into world markets. Trade policies like protectionism can become a major hurdle since these often prompt foreign retaliation. Significant new competition can often force companies to spend more of their time and resources in a defensive position within their existing markets in the United States.

Increased competitiveness in world markets can have two very positive impacts within the United States. Increased corporate profits can result in more taxes being paid, which can help reduce the federal deficit. It would also help to reduce trade deficits.

The result of this performance improvement, both domestically and internationally, would start with more and better jobs, which would result in an increased standard of living. Improved revenues and profits result in a corresponding increase in tax payments, providing the financial resources for the government to address its latest priority. At the time that this model was developed, it happened to be military spending. Today these funds would probably go to health care or some other government entitlement program.

In summary, the following are at stake: A rising standard of living, the ability of government to fund domestic programs and the position of the United States as a world leader.

Specific recommendations of the President's Commission included the following:

1. Create, apply and protect technology.

2. Spur new industries and revive old ones.

3. Pursue productivity gains through technology.

4. Reduce the cost of capital to American industry. Increase the supply of capital available for investment, reduce its cost and improve its ability to flow freely to its most productive uses.

5. Develop a skilled, flexible and motivated work force. This requires a strong educational foundation, the reduction of barriers to labor mobility and incentives to work cooperatively toward increased competitiveness.

6. Make trade a national priority. Government policies should encourage trade and industry adjustments to compete more effectively on a global basis.

Who Is Going to Make It Happen?

Government cannot legislate success. The ability to compete, the actual doing, lies with the private sector. This dictates the need for:

✦ World leadership in the commercialization of product and process technology

✦ Raising investment levels in productive assets and the development of employees

✦ Seeking new ways to create a consensus on goals within business organizations

✦ Broadening perspectives to include the possibilities of world markets and the certainty of global competition

Government, however, should take the lead in highlighting the importance of competitiveness and nurturing an effective consensus-building dialogue among leaders in industry. Government can provide the following: a stable fiscal and monetary policy that ensures steady, noninflationary growth; an educational system; protection for technological innovation (property rights); and changes in antitrust and export administration.

Everyone must recognize the competitive challenge and its significance. There is no simple solution that can reverse the competitive erosion that the United States has experienced.

✦✦✦ HOW DOES A COMPANY GAIN A COMPETITIVE ADVANTAGE?

It has been said that if the bottom line to a business is profit, then the top line is providing value to customer. A competitive advantage is gained by a company by providing value to customers. This value can be real or only perceived, but providing value to customers is what competitiveness is all about. Gaining a competitive advantage through the execution of the right strategies must also be both achievable and sustainable over time. Does the following statement represent the best possible strategy?

To produce quality products and services through effective leadership of skilled employees using advanced methods through the innovative use of technology.

This strategy says: Leverage the talents and skills of employees by working smarter. Two other options are always available. You can work longer and harder. You can also work cheaper. It doesn't take long to conclude that working smarter is the better strategy.

A good competitor knows its products and services, knows its customers and knows its competitors. In contemplating whether information systems can help achieve and sustain a competitive advantage, it is appropriate to ask whether there is an advantage to be gained in knowing the most.

✦✦✦ THE COMPETITIVE ADVANTAGE OF NATIONS[3]

There has been a striking globalization of competition in the decades since World War II. This has been accompanied by major shifts in the economic fortunes of nations and their firms. Past studies on competitiveness focused on industries, companies, trade balance of payments and unit cost of labor. The nation was perceived to play a minimal role.

A major study under the direction of Michael Porter involved the following ten countries:

Denmark	Korea	United Kingdom
Germany	Singapore	United States
Italy	Sweden	
Japan	Switzerland	

The focus of the study was on those industries in which that particular country was a dominant or near-dominant global competitor. The study conclusions were published in "The Competitive Advantage of Nations" in 1990. Traditional explanations of economic success credited natural resources, the size of the labor pool, interest rates and currency values and

---

[3] This section draws extensively from the study headed by Michael Porter of Harvard University and the article that summarized the study written by Porter: "The Competitive Advantage of Nations," *Harvard Business Review,* March-April 1990, pp. 73–93.

economies of scale. As the basis of competition has become more knowledge based, the role of the nation has become more significant. National values and histories, cultures, economic structures and institutions have become more significant. The key is to know what works and then apply it.

Nations do not actually compete, companies do. Continuous, ongoing innovation through leadership within specific companies was identified as the key factor to competitive success. However, the way that companies achieve and sustain a competitive advantage in global industries is based on the role played by the home nation in the process. The nation plays a major role by acting as a catalyst in creating an environment in which companies in specific industries have a better chance to be successful.

The Nation and Local Processes

Companies gain an advantage against competitors by responding to pressures and challenges. They benefit from demanding local customers, strong domestic rivals and aggressive home-based suppliers. The Diamond of National Advantage, Figure 2-2, is a model of the complete system. As indicated in the figure, the entire business process starts with "chance" or

Figure 2-2

Adapted and reprinted, by permission, from Porter, "The Competitive Advantage of Nations," *Harvard Business Review,* March–April 1990, p. 77.

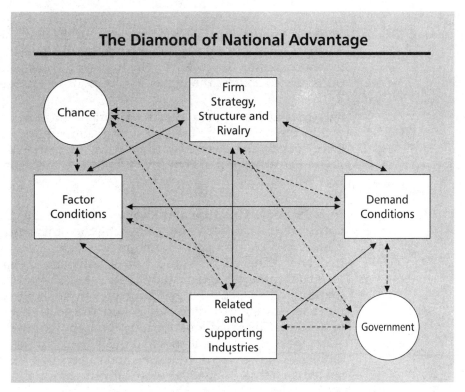

what could also be called business opportunity. Be it domestic or international, a business exists to pursue the opportunity to provide products or services that customers value in exchange for financial rewards.

Government's role varies by country in what it does and the significance of its impact on the private sector businesses. China is the latest interesting example of a country where the role of government regarding business operations is going through a dramatic shift. State-owned companies still accounted for 40% of industrial output in 1994, but this is down from 60% just three years earlier and 80% when Deng Xiaoping initiated reforms in late 1978. From 1992 to 1994 the state-owned companies grew just 6.8%, while in 1994 alone the 25 million companies without state ownership expanded their output by 24%. There is little question that governments play a major role relative to private sector businesses in many countries. A question that continues to be debated is whether this is good or bad.

The four basic elements of the Diamond of National Advantage include:

Factor Conditions   These are the basic factors needed to compete in a specific industry. They include infrastructure factors like roads, communications, and transportation, and logistical support factors. Personnel training and skills as a product of the educational system is often extremely important.

Demand Conditions   The sophistication of the customer demand within a nation plays a major role in determining the level of competition. The more demanding the customer, the tougher the competition if a competitor is able to address the higher expectations of sophisticated customers.

Related and Supporting Industries   Important here are strong suppliers within the nation who are also strong competitors on an international level. Toughening themselves through an international competitive experience makes them more effective suppliers to their customers within the host nation.

Firm Strategy, Structure and Rivalry   This segment of the diamond is to some extent what is left after addressing the other three. It is the circumstances in a country that determine how companies are created, organized and managed. It is also how a company competes in its home market. Contrary to origin study expectations, successful companies were found in all shapes, sizes and structures in different countries. Management styles were very different, as were the goals that companies sought to achieve. The Swiss look for long-term appreciation while the United States looks for new industries and quick financial success. There is also a difference in the type of education and careers that the brightest and best students choose. Individual motivation to work and expand skills was considered important, with the educational system and tax structure acting as important influencing factors.

Nations are rarely the home base to just one industry-dominating company or one competitive industry. The diamond promotes industry clusters and the presence of strong industry rivals within the same host nation. Banks and pharmaceutical companies in Switzerland, commercial aircraft and software companies in the United States, consumer electronics and automobiles in Japan and luxury automobiles and chemical companies in Germany are all examples of this. Nowhere is the role of extremely tough competition within multiple global industries more apparent than in Japan.

Disagreement on the Role of the Nation

Not everyone agrees with Michael Porter that the role of the nation has increased in importance. Kenichi Ohmae, formerly a partner in McKinsey and Company's consulting operation in Tokyo, contends that the multinational company has become the key player in today's borderless world. Nations are less important to companies whether as home bases or sources of identity. He believes that governments build the biggest obstacles to a prosperous, borderless world through protectionism. A major fault on the part of companies is nearsightedness. Multinational companies tend to be dominated by the thinking, likes and dislikes of their domestic customers, which they must forsake. Successful companies will transform themselves into truly global firms. This can mean maintaining a local focus and products but functioning as a global company. See references to two books by Ohmae in Recommended Reading at the end of this chapter.

✦✦✦ THE COMPANY AGENDA

As indicated earlier, only companies can achieve and sustain a competitive advantage. It takes leadership to harness the forces in the competitive diamond to be successful. A logical company action plan would include the following:

- ✦ Creating pressure within the company for innovation.
- ✦ Seeking out the best, most successful competitors as a measure of what it takes to achieve and sustain competitive success.
- ✦ Viewing the presence of domestic competition as a positive factor.
- ✦ Staying alert to customer, market and competitor trends.
- ✦ Emphasizing that competitive success is built within the home market, which becomes a platform to compete internationally.

✦ Selectively pursuing international advantage opportunities.

✦ As a company, playing a role in strengthening the national competitive diamond.

✦✦✦ THE ROLE OF GOVERNMENT

The logical role for government is to serve as a catalyst and challenger. Governments can do a number of things to encourage and even push companies to raise their level of expectations and move to a higher level of competitive performance. Doing anything that would promote unrestrained competition would be appropriate government action. To perform effectively in this role, governments should accomplish the following:

✦ Focus on specialized factor creation for specific industries within the Diamond of National Advantage.

✦ Avoid intervening in currency markets and competing with the private sector for capital. Savings rates, government deficit spending and resulting interest rates all play a part in this critical area.

✦ Promote company goals that lead to sustained investment. Consistent government policies that companies can count on to position long-term investment positions are necessary.

✦ Enforce strict product, safety and environmental standards. Compliance with these standards effectively postures a product in both the domestic and global marketplace.

✦ Limit cooperation among industry rivals. Cooperation can create a market environment that minimizes domestic competition. Governments need to promote host country competition as a launch pad to global competitive success.

✦ Deregulate competitors. Monopolized industries have a history of bloated employee ranks, inflated cost structures and a lack of organizational response. All of these add up to an inability to truly compete.

✦ Enforce domestic antitrust policies. This is similar to the above point. The government should do everything to promote true, open competition.

✦ Reject managed trade. This is simply a way to circumvent legislated trade restrictions and obviously limits competition.

✦✦✦ CONCLUSION

We have defined competitiveness and competitive advantage, looked at a competitive model and concluded that the role of the nation has become an increasingly important competitive factor. An equally important message is that global success is based on the success and strengths achieved in a domestic market. All of this was done with little, if any, mention of information systems. The logical and necessary starting point in understanding the role of information systems within a company is to first understand the environment in which they operate. This has several layers to it: a locale, an industry, a country and a global economy. The use of information systems must be postured within the context of all of these considerations—as the business strategy would be.

In the "Competitive Advantage of Nations" Porter asserts, "Perceive a new basis for competing or find a better means of competing in old ways." Information systems can play a significant role in the process of innovation and improvement. Such innovation is not easy; it is often the result of unusual effort. This demands leadership. Company leaders must believe in change and energize their organizations to innovate continuously.

Once a company achieves a competitive advantage through a new way of doing things or a better way of doing old things, it can sustain it only through relentless improvement. Always remember that a competitive advantage must be achieved and sustained over time. The question that will continue to be addressed within this book is whether and how much information systems can help to accomplish this.

RECOMMENDED READING

Ohmae, Kenichi, *The Borderless World*. New York: Harper Business, 1990.

> A dissenting but worthwhile perspective on the role of the nation. Ohmae argues that multinational companies are the dominant forces in today's global economy. While these companies do play a major role, it is worthwhile to start with an understanding of the role of the nation.

Ohmae, Kenichi, *The End of the Nation State: The Rise of Regional Economies*. New York: The Free Press, 1995.

> The theme of Ohmae's publications have not really changed. As in *The Borderless World*, cited above, he argues that the fate of nations is increasingly determined by economic choices made elsewhere. Four sources are cited that combine to usurp the economic power once held by nations: (1) capital, (2) corporations, (3) consumers and (4) communication. Chief among these forces are the irreversible effects of information technology on the structure of business processes and the values, judgments and preferences of people around the world. Ohmae cites the four I's—industry, investment, individuals and information—that flow relatively unimpeded across national borders. But as he also acknowledges, "in most governments there is a gap of more than a century between the cross-border realities of the external world and the framework of ideas and the principles used to make sense of them." In other words, old ideas, old explanations die hard. This book could have been entitled "Why It Should Be the End of the Nation State as

a Major Economic Force but Probably Isn't for Some Time to Come." It is worth reading this book to reflect on what the role of governments should be within the global competitive environment.

Ohmae, Kenichi, "Putting Global Logic First: Economics, Not Politics, Defines the Landscape on Which All Else Must Operate." *Harvard Business Review,* Jan.-Feb. 1995, p. 119.

An article based on the above book that offers Ohmae's perspective of the nation state in a condensed form.

Porter, Michael E., "The Competitive Advantage of Nations." *Harvard Business Review,* March-April 1990, pp. 73–93.

This is the source of additional detail on the subject study. One might call this the in-between article. You could start with the summary in this chapter, then read this *Harvard Business Review* article and look to the book referenced below for the specific details of the study.

Porter, Michael E., *The Competitive Advantage of Nations.* New York: The Free Press, 1990.

This is the book that describes in complete detail the study headed by Michael Porter. If you are looking for facts, charts and supporting material on this study, this is where to find it.

Potter, Edward E., and Judith A. Youngman, *Keeping America Competitive: Employment Policy for the Twenty-First Century.* Lakewood, CO: Glenbridge Publishing, 1995.

The authors define competitiveness as the ability of companies to sell their goods and services profitably in both domestic and foreign markets. As suggested by the book title the focus is on how employment policy impacts the ability of these individual companies to compete. Unfortunately the conclusion is that many of the employment laws in the U.S., while well intended, often do more harm than good. The cumulative effect of a significant number of government laws and mandates that came into being during the 1960s and 1970s have left U.S. companies among the most regulated employers in the world. The issues addressed are a frequent reminder that governments and politicians play a major role in either helping or hindering the competitiveness of their home-based companies.

President's Commission on Industrial Competitiveness, *Global Competitive: The New Reality.* Washington, D.C.: GPO, 1985.

A well-written report with an excellent executive summary if you are not interested in all of the details. In several respects you can see in this study the germ of ideas that influenced Michael Porter to initiate the Competitiveness of Nations study.

EXERCISES

1. Definition of competitiveness.

Challenge or defend the definition of competitiveness as presented in this chapter.

2. **Global competition and the role of the nation.**
   a. Be prepared to discuss the quote at the beginning of the chapter: "The global market will come to you, if you don't go to it." What are the primary implications of this statement to a U.S.-based company both in terms of threats and opportunities? Identify major U.S. industries that have responded well to this challenge and those that have not.
   b. Use the Diamond of National Advantage to analyze a dominant industry in a specific country.
   c. Contrast the basic premise of the significance of the role of nations to company competitiveness as advocated by Michael Porter with the contentions of Kenichi Ohmae in the publications cited above, which emphasize the end of the nation as a major economic factor. Take a position that definitely favors either Porter or Ohmae on this issue.

3. **A new "Competitiveness of Nations" study.**
   a. If you were to head a new study team to evaluate the competitiveness of nations, identify and explain why you would select three countries that were not included in the initial study.
   b. Complete an analysis of one of these countries using the factors in the Diamond of National Advantage.

4. **The role of government.**

Evaluate the impact of the role of the U.S. government to serve as a catalyst and challenger to the competitiveness of companies within a specific industry using the factors presented within this chapter.

THE PORTER COMPETITIVE MODEL FOR INDUSTRY STRUCTURE ANALYSIS

*Awareness of competitive forces can help a
company stake out a position in its industry
that is less vulnerable to attack.*

Michael E. Porter
Competitive Strategy

LEARNING OBJECTIVES

The objective of this chapter is to provide an understanding of the Porter
Competitive Model. The material in this chapter plus additional information
provided in Chapter 4 demonstrates how the Competitive Model can be used
to analyze a company's competitive position within an industry. Also included
is an introduction of an information-systems-oriented infrastructure that can
be an important factor in a company's ability to be responsive to changing
business conditions.

QUESTIONS

The following questions need to be asked when analyzing an industry in a
structured, systematic way:

1. Are there significant forces in addition to direct competitors and
   customers that impact a company's position within an industry?
2. What basic objectives does a company have relative to the forces within
   the Competitive Model?
3. What are the power implications within the Porter Competitive Model?
4. Identify and explain the two basic strategies and three supporting
   strategies used by intra-industry rivals.
5. Can the Porter Competitive Model be used effectively to analyze all
   industries?

✦✦✦ THE PORTER COMPETITIVE MODEL

Michael E. Porter teaches courses on competitive strategy at the Harvard Business School. He is a consultant to leading companies throughout the world and the author of two highly acclaimed business strategy books, *Competitive Strategy: Techniques for Analyzing Industries and Competitors* and *Competitive Advantage: Creating and Sustaining Superior Performance.* These are the sources of the **Porter Competitive Model** and the **Value Chain** presented in this chapter. The Porter Competitive Model[1] shown in Figure 3-1 is used to understand and evaluate the structure of an industry's business environment and the threats of competition to a specific company. A benefit of its use is that it helps to avoid viewing a company's competitive environment too narrowly. The use of the model duplicates the same logic that an engineer would follow. It breaks an industry into logical parts, analyzes each part and puts the parts back together within the industry's structure.

It should be noted that this model was not developed specifically for analyzing the competitive role of information systems. It is a broad analytical tool used by people who run entire businesses or major functions within a business to assess competitive position. Thinking competitively is essential to assessing the competitive role of information systems, since strategy should dictate how information systems should be used. At the same time, information systems make new strategies and new ways of competing possible.

Specifically the model can be used to identify whether information technology can:

✦ Build barriers to prevent a company from entering an industry.

✦ Build in costs that would make it difficult for a customer to switch to another supplier.

✦ Change the basis for competition within the industry.

✦ Change the balance of power in the relationship that a company has with customers or suppliers.

✦ Provide the basis for new products and services, new markets or other new business opportunities.

Porter tells us that competition in an industry is based on five forces, as shown in Figure 3-1. **Intraindustry rivalry** is the logical and necessary starting point in understanding an industry. It deals with the nature and degree of competition among companies in the same industry. To reach this level of understanding requires an analysis of the industry size, structure, market and financial performance, dominant companies, typical competitive strategies, critical core competencies, global implications,

---

[1] Porter, Michael E., *Competitive Strategy*, New York: The Free Press, 1980, p. 4.

Figure 3-1

Adapted and reprinted, by permission, from Michael E. Porter, "Forces Governing Competition in an Industry," *Harvard Business Review*, March-April 1979, p. 141.

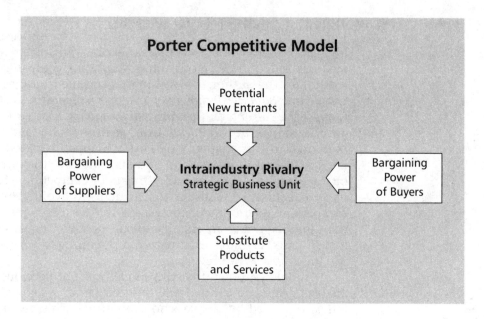

recent or impending trends and anything else that would significantly impact a company within the industry.

The **bargaining power of buyers** comes from the customers of the products and services within the industry. Identifying customers is often easy but sometimes more difficult than might be expected. Is a company truly a customer or an intermediary? Are there multiple tiers of customers, as in the airline industry with its travel agents and passengers? This will be discussed in more detail in Chapter 4. A major consideration is whether the customer has significant power, why this power exists and what benefits this accrues to them. The large volumes that Wal-Mart obtains from its suppliers provides buying power in the form of cost discounts and additional services. In a court case in Arkansas an independent druggist testified that he can buy certain products from Wal-Mart at retail prices that are cheaper than what he must pay his wholesaler.

The **bargaining power of suppliers** refers to the key providers of products and services that contribute to the competitive posture of companies within the industry. Again, it is important to assess any power implications. Does the supplier provide a unique or scarce product or service that cannot be duplicated from another company? Intel is an excellent example of a supplier with power as long as it can continue to provide high-performance microprocessors. This power certainly helps to explain the high profit margins that Intel has realized. Keep in mind that suppliers have motivations to maintain a good business relationship with customers and vice versa. Customers need to work at maintaining a good relationship with quality vendors.

The **threat of new entrants** represents the likelihood that additional companies will start competing in the industry. These can be new companies, existing companies that change business strategies to enter an industry that is new to them, or existing companies that have not competed in the same geographic or product area but decide to do so. Consideration should be given to barriers to entry. Are there factors that would discourage a new competitor from entering the industry or a specific market? These could be high entry costs or high switching costs for an existing customer to change to the new entrant company. Barriers to exit, to stop doing business in an industry, can also serve as a barrier to entry.

The final force in the model is the **threat of substitute products or services** that would be viable alternatives to those offered by companies in the industry. Consideration should be given to the substitutes and why buyers would find them attractive.

To establish a strategic agenda a company, identified as the **strategic business unit**, must understand how the five forces work in the industry and how they affect the company in its particular situation. Assessing the competitive risks is the first step in developing a competitive strategy, which will lead to tactics that will enable the company to realize its goals. Information systems are a potential key ingredient in this process. It is necessary to understand both the industry-level changes that can be brought about by developing information systems and the potential impact on the company.

✦✦✦ AN ANALYSIS OF WAL-MART USING THE PORTER COMPETITIVE MODEL

To further illustrate the concepts of the Porter Competitive Model, an analysis of Wal-Mart within the retail industry is illustrated in Figure 3-2. This is not a complete, detailed analysis of Wal-Mart, but it should help to clarify the forces and the power structure within the industry.

Intraindustry Rivalry

Retail sales in the United States exceed $2 trillion a year. This represents everything that is sold directly to consumers by all retail establishments including restaurants and bars, fast-food outlets, grocery stores and car dealers. Total retailing is too broad and diverse for an appropriate analysis of Wal-Mart. The retailers that represent Wal-Mart's direct competitors need to be identified to evaluate its industry structure. Wal-Mart is a discounter and in this specific industry segment Kmart and Target Stores are clearly direct competitors. But to look at discounters only would also

Figure 3-2

Adapted and reprinted,
by permission, from
*Porter, Harvard Business
Review,* March–April
1979, p. 141.

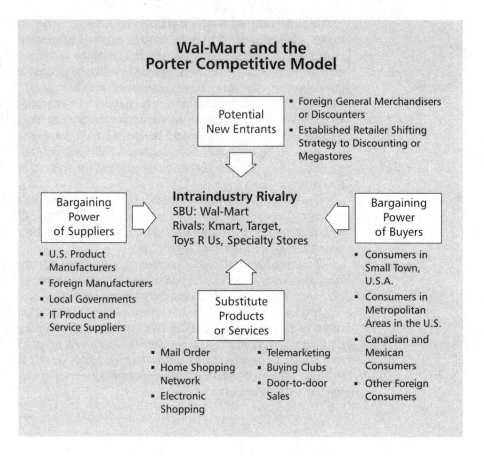

Wal-Mart and the Porter Competitive Model

Potential New Entrants
- Foreign General Merchandisers or Discounters
- Established Retailer Shifting Strategy to Discounting or Megastores

Intraindustry Rivalry
SBU: Wal-Mart
Rivals: Kmart, Target, Toys R Us, Specialty Stores

Bargaining Power of Suppliers
- U.S. Product Manufacturers
- Foreign Manufacturers
- Local Governments
- IT Product and Service Suppliers

Bargaining Power of Buyers
- Consumers in Small Town, U.S.A.
- Consumers in Metropolitan Areas in the U.S.
- Canadian and Mexican Consumers
- Other Foreign Consumers

Substitute Products or Services
- Mail Order
- Home Shopping Network
- Electronic Shopping
- Telemarketing
- Buying Clubs
- Door-to-door Sales

be a mistake. The discount segment is dominated by Wal-Mart, Kmart and Dayton Hudson's Target Stores. These three companies control approximately 75% of the discount business, up from 62% in 1988. Wal-Mart also competes against specialty stores and department stores. This is particularly true when the economy is weak because consumers are more inclined to "down-grade" where they shop. A representative of Mervyn's said, "During good economic times we compete with stores like J.C. Penney. In bad times we compete against everyone." An analysis of Wal-Mart would focus primarily on discounters but would also address specialty stores and department stores. These three categories of stores are grouped into a retail industry segment referred to as general merchandising. For the sake of simplicity, we will concentrate primarily on discounters.

The leanest, toughest companies with the greatest cost advantage have been the most successful in this market segment. Discounters are concentrating on two important trends: a consumer who is becoming increasingly short of time, while also becoming more value conscious. Discounters' everyday low prices appeal to these consumers because they eliminate the time necessary for price comparison shopping.

For many people, shopping has become both a time-consuming and frustrating experience. Discounters are responding by focusing on customer service. They have installed check-out scanning systems and offer more cashiers to minimize the time spent waiting in line. They are also trying to make shopping easier by means of organized displays, clear signage and uncluttered aisles. To also address shopper needs, discounters carry large assortments of merchandise and use computerized inventory control systems to reduce stock-outs.

Bargaining Power of Buyers

In the United States, there is a surplus of retail space. The natural result of this oversupply is the increasing power of the buyer for better prices and value-added services. Individually buyers have minimal power over retailers other than to decide to take their business to another store. Collectively they determine whether a retailer prospers or fails. They are demanding the right combination of quality merchandise, low prices, convenience and service. Retailers must deliver what their customers want or risk losing them to a competitor who does.

Bargaining Power of Suppliers

Large, powerful retailers are changing their relationship with suppliers and manufacturers. Organizations like Wal-Mart and Kmart are gaining more control over their suppliers. Where once suppliers had control, today the retailers with major market share are demanding and gaining concessions in negotiating price, delivery and terms from their suppliers. For instance, retailers are demanding that suppliers accept inventory responsibilities while providing quick response and short lead-time product delivery. Wal-Mart was among the first retailers to insist that all ordering be done through computer-based systems.

Threat of New Entrants

The threat of a new entrant as a discount store start-up is very remote. A start-up would have to compete with three established discounters that have already developed levels of cost efficiency, service and merchandise selection that would be extremely difficult for a new entry to match. Existing retailers that could shift their market focus pose a slight threat. Wholesale clubs like Price-Costco could expand their range of merchandise and increase their service levels and compete more directly with the discounters. Established foreign companies could also decide to invade the U.S. market.

Threat of Substitute Products or Services

Catalog shopping is a convenient alternative for time-poor consumers. The emergence of home-shopping networks and electronic shopping using personal computers in the home also gives consumers more choices as to what to buy and where to buy it. While these are interesting alternatives, they have not captured a large percentage of the retail market. L.L. Bean as a very successful mail-order company has never achieved annual sales of a billion dollars. Contrast this to Wal-Mart's inevitable march to an annual revenue total of $100 billion by or before the year 2000.

✦✦✦ INDUSTRY STRUCTURE AND THE COMPANY POSITION

The retail industry analysis using Wal-Mart as the strategic business unit was provided to illustrate the basic concepts of the Porter Competitive Model. The Competitive Model requires the analyst to pursue the answer to two key questions:

1. How significant is the structure of the industry to existing companies and possible new entrants or providers of substitute products or services?

2. What is the company's relative position within the industry?

These factors are related since positioning a company within an industry requires an understanding of the industry structure. Does the industry structure address a single market segment or is it really multiple subindustries? Are major competitors targeting the same customers? Is the industry dominated by a single or small number of companies or is there no single company with a significant share of the market? Is the industry vertically integrated or does it rely on both major suppliers and distribution channels?

Computer Industry Analysis

Industry structures vary significantly. An industry can be clearly defined and structurally stable. It can also be in a state of transition with an ambivalent structure. The airline industry would fit the first description. It has a structure that makes good use of the model, and is analyzed in Chapter 4 using the Porter Model.

Using the model for the computer industry is more difficult. The problem with the computer industry is that it is changing from a vertically integrated vendor structure to one with multiple horizontal market segments. The "old" industry, shown in Figure 3-3, was dominated by a small number of companies led by IBM. In this earlier era, a computer acquisition was primarily a vendor decision. Layers 1 and 2, which comprised

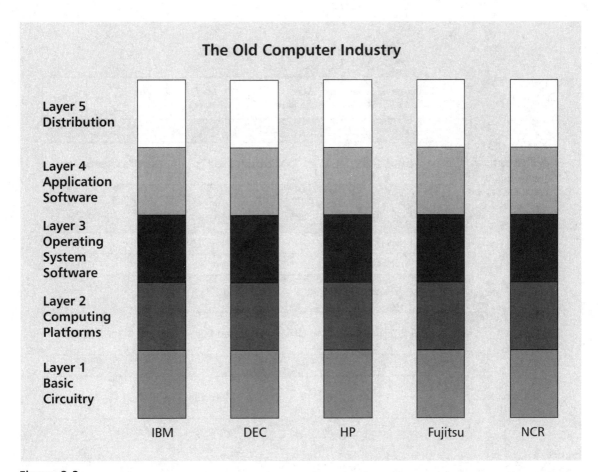

Figure 3-3

Reprinted by permission of Intel Corporation, © 1993.

the basic circuitry and computing platform, was the basic hardware. Layer 3, the operating system software, was an integral part of the computer. If Layer 4, application software, was available that met the company requirements, it was a major consideration. This was often a primary motivation to select a specific vendor since the application software was probably unique to the hardware proposed by that vendor. Layer 5 was a direct field marketing organization of every major computer vendor.

The "new" computer industry described in Figure 3-4 is comprised of thousands of companies, and market strength is a function of the segment being addressed. The industry can be logically segmented by computer processor size. This includes large supercomputers, mainframes, midrange or minicomputers and workstations and personal computers. There continues to be market demand within all of these segments, but since 1993 personal computers have produced the most total revenue. For

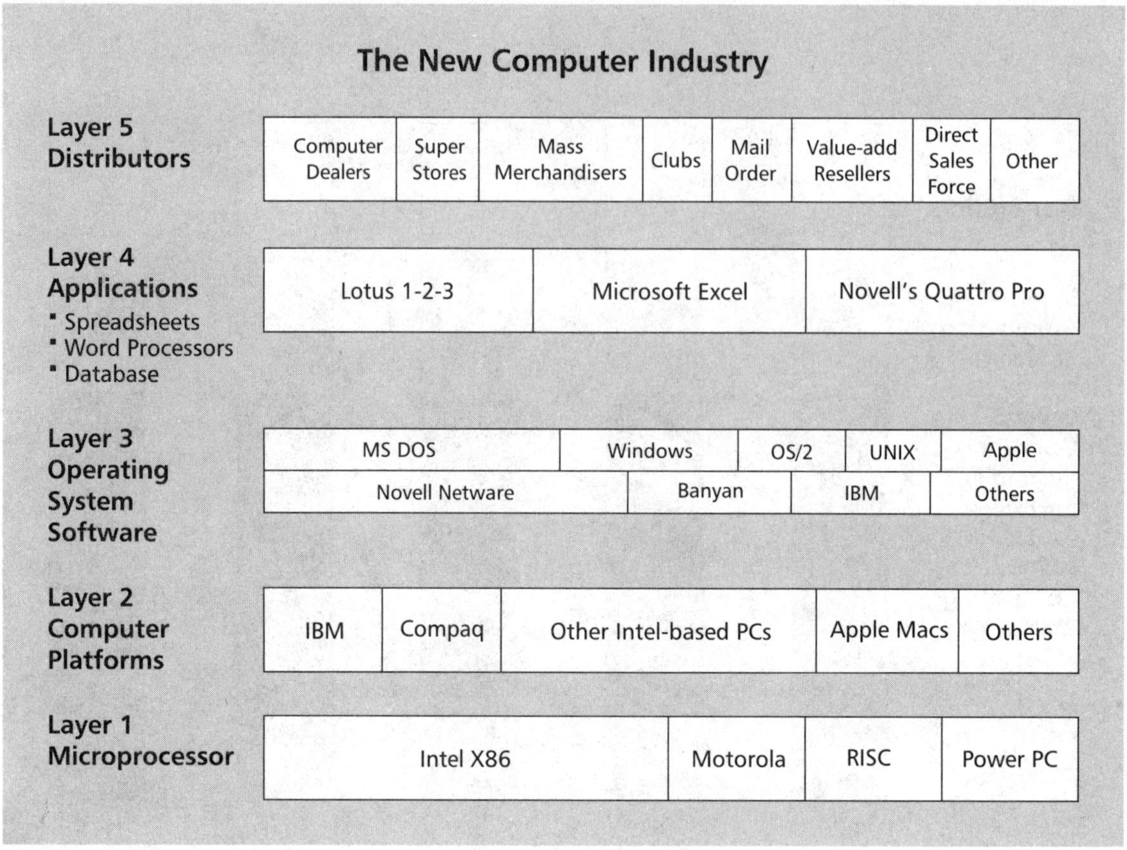

The New Computer Industry

Layer 5 Distributors								
	Computer Dealers	Super Stores	Mass Merchandisers	Clubs	Mail Order	Value-add Resellers	Direct Sales Force	Other

Layer 4 Applications · Spreadsheets · Word Processors · Database			
	Lotus 1-2-3	Microsoft Excel	Novell's Quattro Pro

Layer 3 Operating System Software					
	MS DOS	Windows	OS/2	UNIX	Apple
	Novell Netware	Banyan		IBM	Others

Layer 2 Computer Platforms					
	IBM	Compaq	Other Intel-based PCs	Apple Macs	Others

Layer 1 Microprocessor				
	Intel X86	Motorola	RISC	Power PC

Figure 3-4

Reprinted by permission of Intel Corporation, © 1993.

this reason it is appropriate to view the industry from the perspective of the personal computer segment. It is not only the largest in terms of revenue but it is also influencing the overall approach to customers and the market for computers in general.

A personal computer purchase could start at Layer 1, Microprocessor, with a decision to acquire only a unit that includes "Intel Inside." The actual logo on the unit may be determined more by cost than the specific company that assembled the computer. A major part of this acquisition is the operating system, with MS DOS and Windows being the dominant worldwide choices. Network operating systems can be another important factor, but this can be obtained from a different vendor than the one that provided the operating system. Application packages have become the norm, not the exception, with personal computers. Both individual applications and suites of applications are important and even determining factors in an acquisition. The personal computer made Layer 5, multiple distribution channels, a reality within this industry. This ranges from the traditional direct marketing force to computer stores to mail-order companies as shown.

The major difference in this new computer industry is that competition exists at each layer, and a decision can involve different companies within each layer. Competition can also come from vendors proposing other computer segment equipment (a midrange computer versus multiple personal computers connected with a local area network) from the more traditional companies like IBM and DEC. The Porter Model can be used to analyze this industry, but it gets complicated. A risk is that the complications would tempt a narrowing of the scope of the industry analysis, which could be misleading and probably inappropriate.

While use of the Porter Model is easier for an industry with a defined structure, there are still benefits in analyzing an industry undergoing transition. The lack of structure could be very meaningful in assessing a competitive position and appropriate business strategies.

✦✦✦ THE STRATEGIC BUSINESS UNIT AND COMPETITIVE STRATEGIES

The strategic business unit, the company being analyzed, has two basic objectives:

1. To create effective links with buyers (customers) and suppliers.
2. To build barriers to new entrants and substitute products or services.

To understand the position of the strategic business unit within the industry requires an understanding of the intra-industry rivalry. This dictates an understanding of the strategies of the major companies that are rivals of the strategic business unit. Porter's guidelines identify two basic strategies, differentiation and low cost. Every company *must* pick either one or the other as a primary strategy.

Differentiation Strategy

A **differentiation strategy** separates a company from its competitors by selecting one or more needs that are valued by the customer and uniquely meeting these needs through superior performance. This approach should selectively add cost if necessary to do so. The ultimate reward to the companies that successfully implement a differentiation strategy is the ability to charge premium prices.

The sustaining of a differentiation strategy depends on the durability of the difference as perceived by the customer. Multiple sources of differentiation obviously help. The ability to sustain this strategy also ties to whether the differentiated product has a cost advantage. It is important to remember that a differentiation strategy is usually costly. Common pitfalls in differentiation include:

✦ Failing to meet customer expectations regarding value

✦ Looking too narrowly for sources of differentiation

✦ Charging an excessive price premium

✦ Failing to understand the costs of differentiation

✦ Ignoring changing signals from customers regarding value

✦ Creating differentiation that is easily duplicated by competitors

Low-Cost Strategy

A **low-cost strategy** means that cost is the primary factor on which a strategy will be based. In pursuing this strategy it is important to remember the following points:

✦ There is only one winner in a least-cost competition.

✦ The sustainability of a cost advantage depends on the cost drivers underlying it.

✦ Multiple sources of cost advantage increase its sustainability.

✦ Primary low-cost sources include economies of scale, tight cost control in all facets of the business, proprietary knowledge and processes, unique linkages and alliances that are consistent with this strategy.

✦ Cost reduction must be emphasized in most, if not all, functions within the organization.

✦ Information systems can be exploited to accomplish cost reduction.

A low-cost strategy can be sustained if better than average return can be reinvested in improved facilities, equipment and processes.

Supporting Strategies

In addition to the two basic strategies, there are three strategies that can support them. They are innovation, growth and alliance. A company can elect to pursue none of these, all of them or combinations of these supporting strategies.

Innovation   Differentiation through innovation is a common combination of a basic and supporting strategy. It would be accurate to say that Charles Schwab's strategy was differentiation, growth and innovation. Innovation was based on its ability to provide computer-based applications in support of the other two strategies. *USA Today* sought innovation in both the product it was selling and how it used information technology to manage and distribute the product on a national level.

Growth   Size can be a necessary factor for a company to sustain its business strategies and achieve success. Federal Express is a good example of a company with a strategy that needed to realize package volume growth to justify the large amount of capital equipment involved in its delivery network. *USA Today* and Charles Schwab are two other companies that placed a high priority on growth as a key element in their business strategies.

Alliance   No one says that a company must do everything itself. Alliances that really work are difficult to establish but can be used to support a strategy that otherwise would be impossible to implement. The airlines use alliances to implement and operate passenger reservation systems. British Airways is using alliances to more quickly build a global route system that would otherwise not be possible within the same time frame.

✦✦✦ THE VALUE CHAIN AND COMPETITIVE ADVANTAGE

A second model that is a product of Michael Porter's work is the Value Chain. Unlike the Competitive Model, it focuses internally within an organization. It was developed as a systematic method for examining all the activities a firm performs and how they interact, as a basis for analyzing the sources of competitive advantage.[2] The relevant level for constructing a Value Chain is a firm's activities in a particular industry. A simple version of the Value Chain is shown in Figure 3-5. The complete generic value chain is depicted in Figure 3-6.

The simpler model focuses on the flow of a new product or service within the manufacturing industry from the origination of an idea to delivery to a customer. Four major points need to be made regarding the use of the Value Chain in assessing this new product process. First, the chart as shown in Figure 3-5 is incomplete. It fails to show the ultimate objective of the entire concept, which is providing *value to customer*.

Second, the Value Chain concept says that ideas for products or services pass through multiple functions within an organization. In a manufacturing company they begin in research and progress through product development, manufacturing, marketing, sales and distribution and customer service. The objective should be to *maximize the value-adding activities* while minimizing those that do not add value to the product in

---

[2] Porter, Michael E., *Competitive Advantage*, New York: The Free Press, 1985, p. 33.

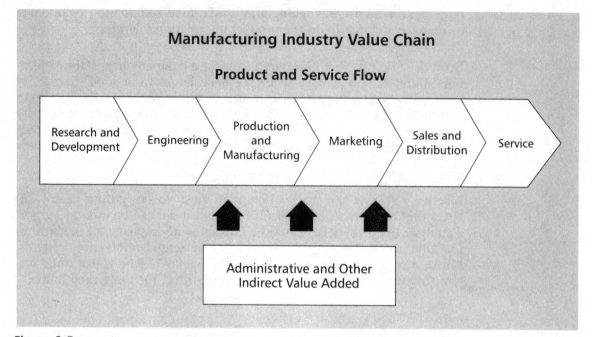

Figure 3-5

Based on concepts presented in Porter, *Competitive Advantage: Creating and Sustaining Superior Performance*, New York: The Free Press, 1985.

the eyes of the customer. It may seem illogical for a company to continue any activities that do not contribute value to the customer, but there are necessary internal procedures and controls that do not meet this criterion. If these cannot be eliminated, the next best alternative is to minimize the activities that do not provide value to customer. A challenge in using the Value Chain is to validate the fact that increasing value within specific functions of the organization results in value to customer.

The third point to consider regarding the Value Chain involves establishing departmental objectives. It is common for medium to large organizations to have functions or departments that establish objectives and measurements dealing with their specific responsibilities. For instance, a major retailer's warehousing operation established objectives for shipping merchandise to its stores as early in the month as possible. It measured its five warehouses and published results on a monthly basis with rewards bestowed on the best operation. This seemed logical and appropriate for those running the warehouses. The problem was that the stores were not able to accommodate the earlier shipments. One store actually rented space to hold the merchandise until it was able to deal with it. The warehouse managers had failed to recognize that when they establish objectives for their operation, *they must be consistent with the ultimate objective for the entire organization*—value to customer.

Finally, it is important to recognize the time dimensions of the entire Value Chain. Since *time is a major competitive factor,* there needs to be a sense of urgency as to how long a new product spends within each of the major functions. Traditionally products were developed by a relay-team approach. Research worked on a new product until it had completed its task and then passed it to product development, which turned it into a marketable product. With the need to reduce a new product's time to market by 50% or more, the relay-team approach becomes infeasible. Instead a basketball-team approach is needed, where each major function has a position on the team. This concurrent engineering process would include customer service as well as sales and marketing people on the team for product development and maybe even for research. This allows these departments to discover any problems much earlier in the development process and thereby save the company time and money.

It is important to remember that the Value Chain is a structure. The actual contents of a Value Chain for a specific company determine a source of competitive advantage. There are five primary activities involved in competing in any industry, as shown in Figure 3-6. Each category is made up of multiple activities that depend on the company, its strategies and the industry in which it competes. The primary activities include:

+ **Inbound logistics** involves receiving, storing and disseminating inputs to the product.
+ **Operations** transforms inputs into the final product.
+ **Outbound logistics** collects, stores and physically distributes the product to customers.

Figure 3-6

Reprinted, by permission, from Porter, *Competitive Advantage*, 1985, p. 37.

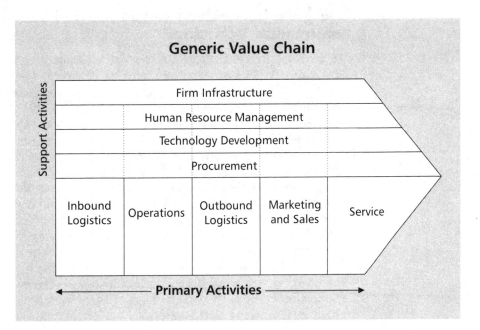

✦ **Marketing and sales** identifies markets and how customers buy the company's products or services.

✦ **Service** deals with customer support and repair service.

In addition to the primary activities there are common support functions. These include:

✦ **Procurement** of inputs used in the firm's value chain.

✦ **Technology development** in every facet of the operation but not limited to information technology.

✦ **Human resource management** involving the recruiting, hiring, training, development and compensation of employees.

✦ **Firm infrastructure** includes planning, accounting and finance, legal, community affairs, government relations and quality management.

The benefit to be gained from the Value Chain, as with the Competitive Model, is to systematically evaluate a company's key processes and core competencies. Attention should be particularly given to strengths and weaknesses relative to the primary factors that would contribute to the company's ability to compete. It is important to identify discrete activities as well as where these activities can be linked. How one activity is performed affects the cost and performance of another. Established effective links among key activities can be a powerful source of competitive advantage.

Using the Value Chain to Summarize Potential for Information Technology

An important point regarding the Value Chain is that it is applicable to any industry. The terminology may be different, but every industry has the same five basic activities and four supporting functions. Figure 3-7 is an example of the value chain for the property and casualty industry. Is there any segment where there is no potential for information technology use for this business that deals with the management of information?

Figure 3-8 is another use of the Value Chain in that it depicts all of the potential technologies that could be applicable to a company in each of the segments. Two conclusions often result from using the Value Chain in this manner. The first is that information technology must compete with other technologies for prioritization, including funding, within a company. The second conclusion is that information technology has become both a prominent and pervasive tool within most, if not all, segments of the Value Chain. A manufacturing example is used in Figure 3-8, but the concept is applicable to any industry. (An example of its use in the airline industry to identify areas of information technology use is provided in Chapter 4 in Figure 4-3.)

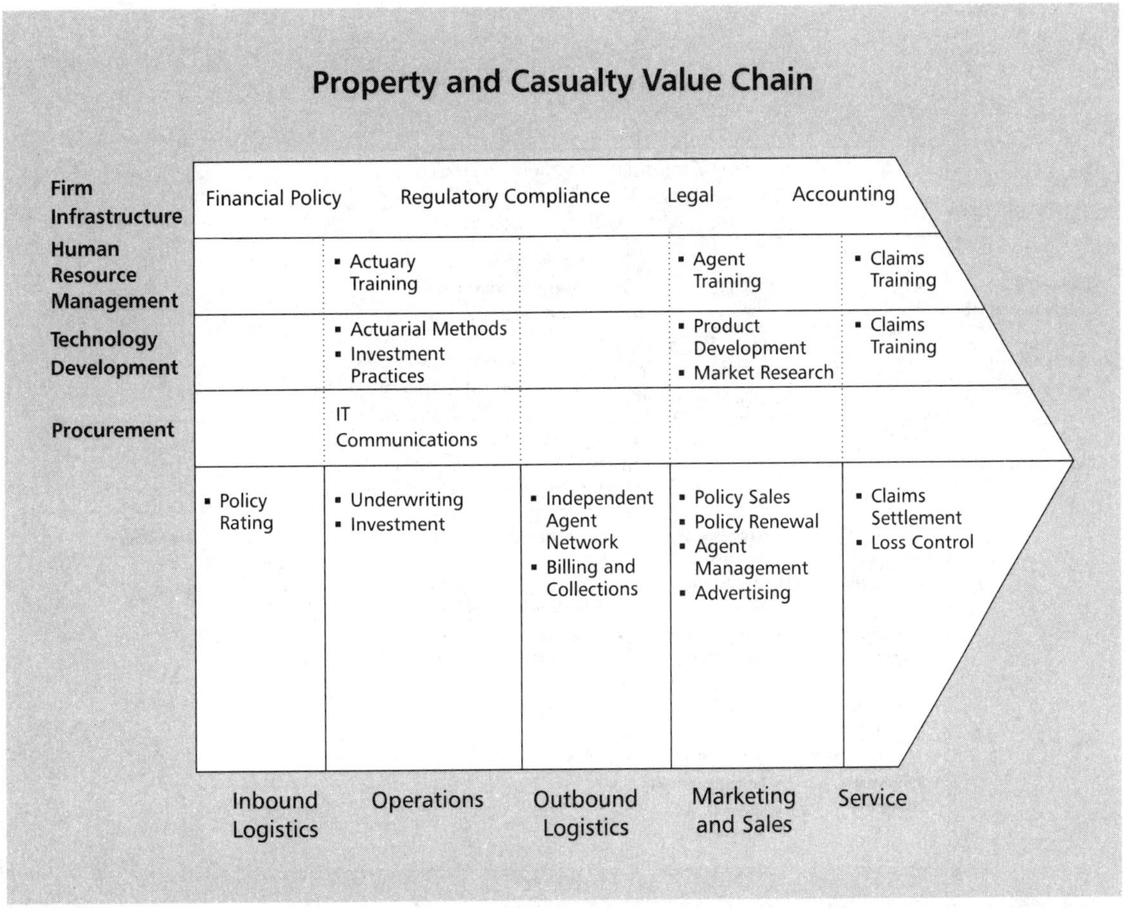

Property and Casualty Value Chain

	Inbound Logistics	Operations	Outbound Logistics	Marketing and Sales	Service
Firm Infrastructure	Financial Policy	Regulatory Compliance		Legal	Accounting
Human Resource Management		▪ Actuary Training		▪ Agent Training	▪ Claims Training
Technology Development		▪ Actuarial Methods ▪ Investment Practices		▪ Product Development ▪ Market Research	▪ Claims Training
Procurement		IT Communications			
	▪ Policy Rating	▪ Underwriting ▪ Investment	▪ Independent Agent Network ▪ Billing and Collections	▪ Policy Sales ▪ Policy Renewal ▪ Agent Management ▪ Advertising	▪ Claims Settlement ▪ Loss Control

Figure 3-7

Included with permission of Michael E. Porter, based on ideas in *Competitive Advantage,* © 1985 by Michael E. Porter.

✦✦✦ CONCLUSION

This could be entitled the Michael Porter chapter. I, like many others, am grateful for the contribution that Porter has made to the teaching of business competitiveness. The Competitive Model has become a standard for a course dealing with the subject of business strategy and information systems. It continues to provide an understanding of an industry and its competitive environment. As indicated earlier in the chapter, it is less effective in cases where industry boundaries are blurring.

Some people are questioning the logic of focusing on the position that a company has within an industry as an indication of competitive strength. Many companies are discovering that an existing position is not to be taken for granted as it can change quickly. It is worth determining the position of a company within an industry (whether well defined or

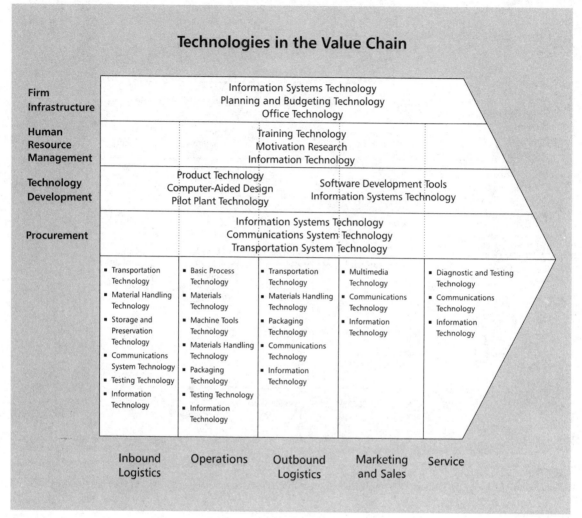

Figure 3-8

Reprinted, by permission, from Porter, *Competitive Advantage*, 1985, p. 167.

not) and its power relative to customers and suppliers. It also guards against taking too narrow a perspective in evaluating the business environment of a company.

RECOMMENDED READING

Boyett, Joseph H., with Jimmie T. Boyett, *Beyond Workplace 2000: Essential Strategies for the New American Corporation*. New York: Dutton, 1995.

This book emphasizes the dramatic change that is occurring within the business environment and what it will take for companies to succeed in such a dynamic world. It suggests that improving quality, lowering cost or doing traditional things faster will not sustain a competitive advantage. The organization of the future must turn to the only remaining source of differentiation: innovation in the design, manufacture and marketing of products that customers will value. Key to innovation will be a new style of leadership, cross-functional teams and empowerment of employees, all leading to customized products.

Porter, Michael E., *Competitive Advantage: Creating and Sustaining Superior Performance*. New York: The Free Press, 1985.

This book introduced the Value Chain, which Porter describes as a tool needed by the strategist to diagnose and enhance competitive advantage. A Value Chain analysis allows the analyst to separate the underlying activities that an organization performs in designing, producing, marketing and distributing its product or service. It is from these activities that a competitive advantage can be realized.

Porter, Michael E., *Competitive Strategy: Techniques for Analyzing Industries and Competitors*. New York: The Free Press, 1980.

This was Porter's original publication that included the Competitive Model. There are critics who contend that Porter's Competitive Model is not as valid as when this book was originally published. While some of the examples in this book are dated, the concepts are still valid and usable.

Vance, Sandra S., and Roy V. Scott, *Wal-Mart: A History of Sam Walton's Retail Phenomenon*. New York: Twayne, 1994.

An interesting account of the success of Wal-Mart but also a very good historical perspective of the history of retailing in general and discounters specifically within the U.S.

Walton, Sam, with John Huey, *Sam Walton: Made in America—My Story*. New York: Doubleday, 1992.

The authorized biography of Sam Walton.

EXERCISES

1. **The Porter Competitive Model and information systems use.**

   a. Use the Porter Competitive Model to analyze the retail industry or an industry of your choice, using a specific company as the strategic business unit. Explain each of the five competitive forces within the Porter model and provide specific examples of each of the forces within the model.

   b. Give examples of how information systems impact the power structure of the major forces.

2. **The Porter Competitive Model and the computer industry.**

Either challenge or defend the logic of using the Porter Competitive Model to analyze the computer industry.

3. **Information systems as a barrier to entry.**

   a. Identify and explain five industry examples where information systems are a definite barrier to entering the industry.

   b. Provide three examples where information systems are not a barrier to entry.

AIRLINE INDUSTRY ANALYSIS

*We must look at the world as it is, versus
how airlines would like it to be.*

Robert L. Crandall
Chief Executive Officer
American Airlines

LEARNING OBJECTIVES

An evaluation of the airline industry using the Porter Model should solidify
the discussion of the competitive model. A number of things about the airline
industry make it a good subject for such an analysis. Its boundaries are
relatively clearly defined and it is a highly visible and well-known industry.
Intra-industry strategies are an integral part of an industry analysis. American
Airlines, British Airways, Singapore Airlines and Southwest Airlines are
presented to provide an understanding of both traditional and changing
strategies within the industry.

QUESTIONS

The following questions pertain to the airline industry and its use of
information systems:

1. How do you explain the poor financial performance of the worldwide
   airline industry during 1990–1994 and its equally poor long-term history?
2. Is over capacity a major burden that will continue to plague the global
   airline industry?
3. Does an "open skies" policy make sense for the global airline industry?
4. Can studying the profitable operations of Singapore Airlines, British
   Airways and Southwest Airlines provide significant insight regarding a
   successful strategy?
5. Is the worldwide airline industry undergoing a major restructuring?
6. Are computer-based reservation systems (CRS) still as important as they
   were in the past?

✦✦✦ THE AIRLINE INDUSTRY AND AMERICAN AIRLINES

An assignment to analyze American Airlines within the airline industry in early 1990 was as easy as a swan dive in an Olympic diving competition. American Airlines was the model of the industry. It was the largest airline in the world in terms of revenue, with a home base in the largest airline market. It had just completed the second of the two most profitable years in its history and its stock had hit an all-time high. Bob Crandall, its CEO, was the spokesman for the industry. American's hub-and-spoke system was lauded as the best route strategy, and it was flexing its international route muscles. Last but not least, it was the originator and controller of the world's largest computer reservation system, the SABRE system. This accomplishment put American at or near the top of most lists of successful examples of how to use information systems to compete.

So who would have expected that the subsequent four years would be so unkind to American Airlines in particular and the airline industry in general? From 1990 through 1993, the U.S. carriers incurred substantial losses. These four years of losses exceeded all profits realized since the beginning of the industry in the United States in 1920. American experienced losses of $1.3 billion during this four-year period. Delta Airlines lost a billion dollars in 1993 alone. An initial reaction to this dismal performance is that it is a definite departure from the past. From 1970 through 1989 the worldwide airline industry achieved a long-term passenger and revenue growth trend. In the United States the period of 1979 to 1983 resulted in significantly reduced operating profits because of the trauma of deregulation, but that can be viewed as a one-time transition period.

In evaluating the industry it is not the short-term performance or periods of transition that really matter. The more important question is whether this is an industry that has achieved good financial results over the long term. The answer is a resounding "No!" In the last quarter century, the U.S. airline industry has had only one year, 1978, in which its profit margin reached the 4% to 5% norm for industries in general. For the ten years immediately preceding deregulation, the profit margins for the airlines averaged less than 2%. In the first fourteen years following deregulation, the industry averaged a negative .7%.

Passenger growth volume projections are very positive. Boeing's analysis indicates that all major travel markets are either growing or beginning to show signs of a strong recovery. Air travel will grow in parallel with economic growth. Travel growth is expected to average 5.8% per year through the year 1999 as the global economy further improves. At this rate passenger traffic will double by 2007 and nearly triple by 2014. While the rate of growth will gradually slow, the number of passenger miles added each year will continue to multiply because of the size of the traffic base. The challenge for the industry is to capitalize on this rate of growth while realizing a profit.

What can individual airlines do to achieve at least an adequate financial performance over the longer term? Passenger traffic growth, rational fare structures, improved revenue yields, lower fuel costs, aggressive cost reduction and other productivity improvements are offered as the key to a return to sustainable profitability. It is obviously much easier to list these factors than to achieve them. A logical solution matches carrier capabilities with market potential. The number of aircraft and their capacity and performance dictate capabilities and strategies. Quick changes in strategy are not very practical because of existing equipment and facility costs.

While suffering the worst financial period in its history, American Airlines continues to be viewed as a leader in the U.S. airline industry. In an annual evaluation done by Wichita State University it was rated the best U.S. airline in overall quality in 1994. Southwest prevented American from winning this award for five consecutive years by finishing first in 1993.

American's Plans to Increase Profits

In 1994 AMR's[1] CEO, Bob Crandall, announced a plan to maximize performance while managing the transition from the growth of the 1980s to a higher level of profitability. The plan has three major parts: (1) to make the airline better and stronger where possible, (2) to withdraw from markets in which it cannot compete effectively, and (3) to expand the profitable nonairline businesses. Does Crandall's indication that American will forego some of its airline plans to shift its focus to information systems business opportunities also represent a possible deemphasis of the airline? The most basic financial analysis concludes that AMR is first and foremost an airline. It must do what is necessary to operate the airline profitably. A $1.5-billion information services business can contribute to, but will not completely offset, a poor financial performance by the $15-billion airline.

Basic premises that help to understand the transition plan are:

✦ Profit is a more important gauge of the success of the airline than revenue. Being the largest U.S. carrier is important since this is an industry that rewards economy of scale. Profitability that is sustainable over time is more important for American as it is for any business.

✦ The international market represents the largest projected growth but poses major challenges regarding access. These factors will not be resolved quickly and could take many years, especially if they are addressed on a bilateral basis between individual airlines as has been the case in the past.

---

[1] AMR is the parent company of American Airlines.

✦ Profit margins are better in nonairline businesses. This is certainly reason for AMR to consider these businesses. A definite benefit is that these information services businesses complement the airline and vice versa. The airline capitalizes on the information services capability, while information services achievements help to strengthen the airline. The consensus is that American is uniquely qualified to successfully run an information-technology-based business since it has developed its computer capabilities so extensively over the past twenty-five years. It has historically set the standard for passenger reservation systems. Capitalizing on this capability American has built a reservation system for the French railroad system and for Aeroflot in Russia.

✦ American is a different business than Southwest Airlines. Southwest is a short-haul, high-frequency, point-to-point, low-cost and low-fare carrier. It makes no sense for American to discard its short and long haul, hub-and-spoke and service strategies to directly compete with Southwest. This is not to say that it must abdicate the short-haul, city-pair (high passenger traffic between two cities) market to Southwest. It can and has implemented some point-to-point routes involving city pairs. There are, however, approximately 500 city pairs with sufficient passenger volumes to adequately support point-to-point service. Using its hub-and-spoke system, American serves over 12,500 origin-destination city pairs.

This leaves us with additional questions that need well-conceived answers. Can the major U.S. carriers realistically expect to expand their international operations and still make a profit? If so, when and at what risk? Will there continue to be major fallout among U.S. and foreign carriers? How does an airline like American differentiate its full-service, hub-and-spoke strategy in an environment where low-cost tickets are a primary strategy for carriers representing one third of the airline capacity in the United States? Is there a short-term answer to these questions? Finally, how significant will information systems be in the future in this industry?

Causes of Poor Airline Profits

Objectively, it is important to point out that American's four consecutive years of financial loss were paralleled by most of the airlines throughout the world. Of the 224 members of the International Air Transport Association (IATA) only four made a profit in 1993. The failure of American specifically and airlines in general to make a profit in the first four years of the 1990s resulted from many factors. The Gulf War and the threat of terrorism caused a major decline in travel to Europe and the Middle East, as did the general decline in the world economy. Aircraft fuel price increases significantly increased operating costs in 1990 and 1991.

A one-cent increase per gallon in aircraft fuel costs American $2.5 million dollars a month. In addition, a combination of wages, work rules and work patterns have added to the financial woes of American. Its relations with employee unions continue to be a problem.

During 1993, 19% of the airline capacity in the United States was controlled by airlines that were in Chapter 11 bankruptcy proceedings. This allowed these airlines to continue to operate without fulfilling their financial obligations to their lenders and other creditors. Since these airlines have problems attracting passengers, their common strategy is to compete on the basis of low-priced fares. Other nonbankrupt airlines have to respond to this form of competition while paying their bills. The common criticism is that the bankrupt airlines are allowed to stay under the protection of the courts too long, often two or three years. Continental Airlines was actually in and out of Chapter 11 bankruptcy twice. Despite its failure to submit a business plan for reorganization, America West was granted six extensions by the bankruptcy judge.

The industry as a whole already has excess capacity both within the United States and worldwide. Despite this some airlines tend to resolve their financial problems by expanding their capacity through the purchase of new aircraft and going further into debt. A logical case can be made that for the foreseeable future, eight megacarriers could satisfy the capacity requirements for air travel for the entire world. The likelihood of this happening, however, is extremely remote. With 224 carriers in the IATA, nationalistic reasons alone are enough to conclude that this simply won't happen.

This is a very capital-intensive business. For safety, noise abatement and fuel-efficiency reasons there is an ongoing need to replace older aircraft. Replacing them is costly but necessary for both operational and competitive reasons.

The international market is another major challenge. The international strength of American is in the Western Hemisphere. It is the leading U.S. carrier in the Latin American market and its Caribbean operation has been profitable for over twenty years. A 1994 code-sharing agreement with Canadian Airlines has also positioned American to effectively serve the Canadian market. While American has a presence in the Pacific Rim, it is not a major factor in that market. It is doing better in Europe, but the negotiations that are necessary to gain access in most European countries make it difficult to compete successfully in that market. Gaining access to foreign routes can often mark the beginning of a new set of problems. How a U.S. carrier is treated in a foreign country can include poor gate assignments, air traffic delays, high landing fees and excessive charges for ground equipment.

Finally, American spent too many years as a regulated airline. Even though the industry was deregulated in 1978, American still carries negative, built-in factors that were products of the regulated era. While it has shed a regulated monopoly mentality among its management and employees, it has not been able to overcome many of the salary and work-rule concessions made before deregulation. As Bob Crandall says, "With competitive labor costs, we can compete with any carrier in the world. Our airlines have great brand identity, widespread networks, modern fleets, leading-edge technology and tens of thousands of dedicated employees. If we can achieve competitive labor costs, those strengths coupled with the success of our nonairline businesses will carry AMR to new heights of achievement." [2] Efforts to accomplish this have been unsuccessful to date with any of their three major unions involving pilots, flight attendants and ground and maintenance personnel. This leaves American at a cost disadvantage compared to post-Chapter 11 carriers like Continental.

✦✦✦ MAJOR LESSONS OF THE CONSISTENTLY PROFITABLE CARRIERS

While the domestic Big Three—American, United and Delta—and foreign carriers like Lufthansa, Air France and Japan Air Lines recorded major losses from 1990 through 1993, there have been four consistently profitable carriers: Singapore Airlines, British Airways, Southwest Airlines and Cathay Pacific. A better understanding of these carriers might suggest what it takes to be successful within the airline industry. The following sections analyze the operations of three of these carriers.

Singapore Airlines

A good case can be made to support the contention that Singapore Airlines (SIA) is the world's most successful airline. It is consistently profitable, often ranking as the most profitable airline in the world. Recipient of countless awards, it has been recognized as the best airline in the world based on an unrivaled reputation for quality service, leading-edge technical operations, innovative financial planning and outstanding marketing. It has also been highly ranked on suitability of destinations served, quality of inflight food and awareness of the needs of business travelers.

As impressive as this list is, you can't ignore the significance of its travel infrastructure. Singapore's Changi International Airport is probably the best in the world. *Condé Nast Traveler,* a travel publication, ranked it as the world's number one airport for six years in a row. One of its innovations is a duty-free shop when you arrive. Transportation from the airport is convenient, safe and economical. Choices of hotels may be influenced by a 1993 survey that ranked three Singapore hotels among the top ten in the world. As several former residents have said, "You may

---

[2] AMR Annual Shareholders Meeting, Chicago, May 17, 1995.

fault their authoritative methods, but things in Singapore work and work very well."

Geographic Location   Every major airline in the world has a domestic market on which it builds a passenger and financial base. The only two exceptions to this position are Singapore Airlines and Hong Kong-based Cathay Pacific. Because of the geography of these two locations—Singapore is a small island republic and Hong Kong is an island colony about to revert back to China—these two carriers function only as carriers beyond their own boundaries. The very nature of the geography that they service makes them long-haul carriers. It has also meant that they have always had to compete successfully beyond their own boundaries.

Singapore is both the business center for Southeast Asia as well as a major tourist attraction. Over 7,000 foreign corporations have operations in Singapore. A 1993 survey of company CEOs ranked Singapore first in the world as a desirable place to locate a corporate headquarters. In 1994 it attracted 7 million tourists, or twice as many visitors as its own population.

National Strategies   Singapore Airlines was formed in 1972 as a result of a split with Malaysian Airlines. The key to its success has been excellent management, a strategic location, modern facilities and the radical free-market philosophy of its government. Although the airline is 54% government-owned, it would be a mistake to conclude that its financial performance has anything to do with government financial subsidies. In fact, it has been paying handsome dividends to its shareholders, the government included. A key point regarding SIA is that it is a direct result of a national strategy to be the gateway to Southeast Asia for both commerce and travel. The airline is an extension of this strategy and benefits from the infrastructure that supports its operation.

Singapore has implemented a national strategy to provide an infrastructure that includes excellent information technology and telecommunications networks, worldwide distribution linkages and a total value chain to support a diversity of manufacturing and service businesses. It wants companies to believe that these business capabilities enable them to function as a strategic partner. Singapore has epitomized multinational-corporation-led development. The government has been extremely aggressive in attracting foreign investment to provide stable and high-quality employment for their people. In no other Asian country do foreign enterprises play such an important role. They number over 7,000, employ 60% of the labor force and produce 80% of the exports.[3]

---

[3] OECD (J.R. Chaponniere), "The Newly Industrializing Economies of Asia: International Investment and Transfer of Technology," *Science/Technology Industry Review*, No. 9, April 1992, p. 102.

This small republic, with a minimal initial domestic market, has been the successful architect of an infrastructure that serves as the basis for a business investment that companies conclude can enhance their business success. The Singapore government has highly realistic aims and a clear understanding of its economic strengths and limits, and has set market-conforming directions to its strategy for development. Based on this strategy, Singapore has successfully planned, implemented and sold the concept that it is the gateway to Southeast Asia. Singapore Airlines is an integral part of this strategy.

A strength of Singapore Airlines is their managing director, Dr. Cheong Choong Kong, who has held this position since 1984. He has proven to be an effective, financially astute executive and the sponsor of their information systems focus. Dr. Cheong works closely with the airline board of directors who are the movers and shakers within the Singapore government. The combination of a logical and clearly understood strategy and a strong supporting infrastructure has enabled the airline to do an outstanding job by a number of different measurements.

Shrewd Management and Leadership in IT   Averaging four and a half years, SIA's fleet is the youngest among major carriers in the world. This was accomplished by its management team through shrewd deal making, clever financing and selling its aircraft at a young age. Modern aircraft, excellent facilities, excellent marketing, including the "Singapore girl" promotions, and outstanding service prompt SIA to conclude that passengers should feel that they have experienced the best possible traveling experience.

Part of the excellent reputation that SIA has earned is based on the leadership role that it has played among Asian airlines. A good example of this is the creation of the Abacus passenger reservation system as a multicarrier, multinational system. SIA had its own computer-based reservation system before Abacus was established. It, together with Cathay Pacific, agreed that a multicarrier computer reservation system similar to SABRE and Galileo was needed to help Asian carriers compete more effectively worldwide. They evaluated existing passenger reservation systems throughout the world and concluded that the TWA system was most suitable for their needs. Abacus as a reservation system and an organization was the outgrowth of this evaluation and implementation in 1988. The system is owned and operated by Abacus Distribution Systems Ltd., a joint venture among eleven Asian carriers and U.S.-based Worldspan Global Travel Information Services.

Worldspan is a system owned in the United States by Delta, TWA and Northwest Airlines. The Abacus system runs on a mainframe in Atlanta, Georgia and supports 7,000 reservation terminals in 3,000 locations. In addition to Singapore Airlines, those that jointly own Abacus are All Nippon Airways, Cathay Pacific Airways, China Airlines, Malaysia

Airlines, Royal Brunei Airlines, Philippine Airlines, Silk Air and Hong Kong Dragon Airlines.

Singapore Airlines is also using an advanced departure-control system to expedite passenger check-in and boarding. Called DCS90,[4] it is a PC- and LAN-based system that augments their reservation system. The use of color and graphics displays speeds check-in and makes it easier to answer passenger questions. Baggage tags are bar-coded to help passengers to more easily reclaim their baggage. The system's user-friendly philosophy is also intended to allow the gate agent to deliver more personalized service.

Outsourcing of major functions within the information systems organization is not a unique U.S. innovation. In 1993 SIA signed a five-year contract with Datamatics, a Bombay, India computer software development company. Datamatics will work exclusively for Singapore Airlines to develop software for reservations, cargo-handling and departure-control applications. The primary explanation for taking this approach is the difficulty of competing for information technology skills in a country that is expanding rapidly in the use of information systems.

Competitive Strategies While acknowledging the strengths that have produced such an enviable record, it is also important to explain that SIA and other regional carriers have not competed on the basis of low-cost fares. The fifteen major carriers who are members of the Orient Airlines Association (OAA) have agreed to compete by other means such as better service, newer aircraft, convenience of flight schedules, more new destinations and, more recently, through alliances with carriers outside of the region. By taking steps to reduce costs, increase productivity and manage capacity and yield, the majority of these carriers have remained profitable.

Meanwhile, the U.S. carriers are looked upon as spoilers of a good thing as they begin targeting the Southeast Asian market with excess capacity and a low-fare mentality. Impediments to U.S. carrier competition remain in place as market entry, capacity, frequency of service and route designations are all tightly controlled by the Southeast Asian governments. Singapore is again an exception to this attitude. It does not seek to impede the entry of U.S. carriers. It has one of the most open aviation policies where U.S. carriers are concerned and is a staunch supporter of the concept of "open skies" for all of the world's airlines.

How does Singapore Airlines feel about its future? It is firmly committed to growth, supported by the fact that Asia has the world's fastest travel growth rate projections—8.5% until the year 2000. By that time Asian travel would make up nearly 40% of the world's passenger traffic. Tangible evidence of their confidence is their ordering fifty-two new aircraft, worth more than $10 billion, from Boeing and Europe's Airbus Industrie with deliveries starting in 1996.

---

[4] *Aviation Week & Space Technology*, November 23, 1992, p. 101.

British Airways

The turnaround company of the 1980s in the airline industry was British Airways (BA). This success story began when the stodgy, bureaucratic, government-owned-and-operated company was technically bankrupt in 1982. It concluded with their becoming consistently profitable as the world's largest carrier of international traffic during a time that almost all major airlines were losing money.

British Airways is the result of the merger and privatization of BEA, a European carrier, and BOAC, a transatlantic carrier, into a single airline in 1987. At the same time Colin Marshall became its chief executive, and he deserves a great deal of the credit for its success. Of the four profitable carriers it is the only one that is both a short- and long-haul carrier. However, it should be remembered that its international traffic, revenue and profits are the key components of its success since its domestic operation is relatively small.

Improved Customer Service The role model for the BA improvement was Scandinavian Airlines (SAS) under the leadership of Jan Carlzon. Carlzon had discovered that the reputation of SAS was not based on aircraft, schedules or baggage handling. It was based on the way that passengers are treated by airline personnel.[5] Airline passengers have learned to expect that things will go wrong. It is how they are treated when this happens that really matters. These experiences are a major factor in formulating an opinion of the airline. More importantly, it is the basis for passenger decisions in terms of repeat business. Marketing becomes an integral part of how passengers feel about an airline, because it is the traveling experience that they actually buy. British Airways took this realization to heart and trained managers and employees how to provide better treatment to passengers. This definitely changed both the culture of the airline and the structuring of the organization.

Use of Alliances Looking back to the early 1990s, the business strength of British Airways was its service across the Atlantic. Its problem was that it did not have feeder flights in the United States for passengers who originated and terminated in U.S. cities that British Airways did not service. If BA cannot pick up passengers where they live and take them where they want to go, then passengers will find someone who can. In such a market this is a big problem. This is an example of how international travel has changed the industry. Like domestic travelers, international passengers want to do business with an airline that can provide access and convenience for their entire travel requirements.

---

[5] Carlzon, Jan, *Moments of Truth: New Strategies for Today's Consumer-Driven Economy*, New York: Ballinger, 1987, p. 3.

This was not a problem in the days when their predecessor company competed against Pan Am, which did not have feeder flights either. The U.S. regulators would not allow it. American, United and Delta were the domestic carriers, and Pan Am was the U.S. international flagship carrier. Only after deregulation was Pan Am allowed to develop a domestic feeder network to support its international operations. Hindsight would suggest that this happened too late to help Pan Am survive in a changing industry.

The lack of feeder routes is not just a U.S. problem, it is universal. Regulations in the United States and many European and Asian countries limit the ability of a nondomestic carrier to operate feeder routes. Alliances have been considered the best alternative to address this problem. The British Airways solution was to buy into a domestic U.S. airline that could feed its international routes. It did this in the United States while actively pursuing a strategy of global alliances. An agreement with USAir was culminated in 1992 and was approved by the U.S. Department of Transportation in 1993. BA and USAir are not only sharing computer reservation systems but also branding and marketing strategies. A similar alliance was established with TAT European in France, Deutsche BA in Germany, Air Russia in Russia and Qantas in Australia. These alliances add up to more foreign city destinations than any other carrier. Colin Marshall has stated that the future will witness a dozen alliances split evenly among Europe, Asia and North America.

The current problem is that the BA partners are doing poorly financially. British Airways invested an original $300 million in USAir and gained access initially to 38 U.S. cities. This has since increased to 65 cities. The access part of the deal is working but the financial performance of its alliance airlines has been poor. The implications have caused BA to back off from a commitment for another $450 million until USAir gets its financial house in order.

Southwest Airlines

Founded by Herb Kelleher in Dallas in 1966, Southwest Airlines flew its first airplane in 1971 as an intrastate airline within Texas. This New Jersey–born lawyer turned Texan still runs the airline. How successful is it? The U.S. Department of Transportation concluded that Southwest is the principal driving force for changes in the U.S. airline industry.

Aircraft Utilization   Southwest is a short-haul, point-to-point carrier with an average flight duration of one hour and 400 miles. It claims high aircraft utilization and labor productivity, which are greatly aided by using only one aircraft—Boeing 737s. While this limits its flexibility regarding longer flights, it has major advantages in terms of crew training, aircraft and crew scheduling, maintenance costs and spare parts inventories. It also results in fewer self-imposed delays and the best on-time performance in the industry. It costs Southwest 7.1 cents to fly each seat 1 mile on a typical 400-mile flight. It is estimated that it costs United, American and Delta more than 13 cents a mile to fly similar routes. These cost savings are passed on to passengers in the form of low fares, helping to make Southwest the dominant carrier in 32 of the 46 airports that it serves.[6]

Focus on City Pairs As a no-frills operation, their strategy is a definite contrast to American, United or Delta. Their flights focus on a sister-city concept (city pairs) and avoid the competitor hub-and-spoke route system. This adds up to passenger convenience since their flights are direct city-to-city while also being low-priced. It also adds up to 30% better productivity compared to American, United and Delta. Southwest aircraft are in the air twelve hours a day, which is 20% more than most major airlines.

Currently doing 25% of its business in California and 50% west of New Mexico,[7] there are still a number of city pairs for which Southwest does not provide service. You can expect them to continue to add two or three new routes a year, with the midwest a likely candidate or a number of possibilities along the East Coast. An interesting question is whether they should deviate from their traditional short-haul strategy and compete on longer domestic and international routes.

Corporate Culture Southwest Airlines has been the center of attention for a number of reasons. Southwest has succeeded in differentiating itself through its focus on service, operations, cost control, marketing, its people and its corporate culture. The best part of all of this is that it has added up to financial success, which has kept their airplanes flying. Its success is further explained by Herb Kelleher's reputation as a maverick and his attitude toward unnecessary overhead. Kelleher's personal relationship with his employees is legendary and has resulted in the best labor relations in the industry. Southwest is known for having a strong culture among its employees and gets high productivity not only from its aircraft but also its people. While its salaries are comparable to the Big Three, its flexible work rules translate into higher productivity and lower costs. Its city-to-city flight schedules result in fewer layovers for crews, which in turn saves Southwest hotel and meal expenses.

Cost Savings in Reservations In the early summer of 1994 three of the four major computer reservation systems stopped listing Southwest flights and fares. Apollo, owned by United, Continental's System One and Delta-owned Worldspan all said, "Either pay for being part of the system or get off." Southwest had never paid booking fees to the owners of any of these reservation systems. It had paid American, and Southwest continues to be part of the SABRE system while offering the explanation that being listed on the world's largest computer reservation system should be enough.

---

[6] "Low Cost Carrier Still Challenges Industry," *USA Today*, July 10, 1995, Money Section p. 2.

[7] Ibid.

Herb Kelleher responded to his exclusion from the other reservation systems with a full-page ad in the *Wall Street Journal* that said, "We decided twenty years ago that paying fees to all the computer reservation systems owned by our competitors would undermine our commitment to low costs and low fares." Where does this leave Southwest? Southwest runs its own reservation system to manage the passenger load for each of its flights. The difference with their system is that it is not tied to travel agents. Only about half of its reservations come from travel agents, compared to an industry average of 80–85%.

Meanwhile Southwest is expanding its own reservation system while also emphasizing ticketless flights for its passengers. The airline industry issues 500 million tickets a year and estimates that it could save $1 billion if it could sell passengers on a ticketless approach. In January 1995 Southwest became the only airline to offer ticketless travel on all of its flights. By July 1995, 30% of its 125,000 daily passengers were flying ticketless, saving the airline $25 million a year.[8] That is half of what Southwest feels it can save when ticketless becomes truly accepted by its passengers.

This approach is typical of the cost-saving mentality within Southwest. It results in the need for fewer reservation agents and can avoid both the computer reservation fees from other carriers and the fees charged by travel agents. Southwest wants you to call them directly, charge the ticket to a credit card and get a confirmation number, and then stand in line at the airport to exchange the confirmation number for a boarding pass for a very competitively priced ticket.

◆◆◆ AIRLINE INDUSTRY ANALYSIS USING THE PORTER COMPETITIVE MODEL

Using the Porter Competitive Model to do the analysis, what can be concluded regarding the industry structure, the competitive strategies and the power structure within the airline industry? If there is an advantage to the airline industry, it is that it has a relatively clean industry structure. This is unlike the financial services industry, where competition can come at you from any number of traditional or new directions. If you are in the airline business you know who your competitors are. An airline is an airline. Beyond that, the analysis gets more complicated.

Intraindustry Rivalry

In this analysis we will use American Airlines as the strategic business unit. The question regarding its intraindustry rivals is not all that clear cut. American Airlines' obvious direct rivals are carriers that are very

---

[8] Ibid.

similar to its operation: United, Delta and Northwest. Like American they focus on major regions, nationwide hubs and a presence in the international market. But what about rivalry with the airlines that do not follow the same competitive strategy? Is it as simple as listing any airline of any size, or have the profiles of Singapore Airlines, British Airways and Southwest Airlines suggested that the industry structure is more complicated?

Business Competitive Strategies   The size of an airline may suggest how competitive it might be, but this does not address the question of rivalry. It is necessary to understand its specific business competitive strategy to determine if it is a direct rival. Figure 4-1 can help in an analysis of the strategy options available to any airline. While the airline industry seems to be evolving to a global industry, it would be premature to conclude that this is the case today. The industry breaks down into four major markets: North America, Europe, the Pacific Rim and Latin America. Within each of these markets there are both short-haul and long-haul opportunities. There are also long-haul opportunities among the four markets.

Integral to the strategy of market focus and routes is whether a hub-and-spoke or a city-to-city (point-to-point) route structure makes marketing, operational and financial sense. For an airline like American with a large, established hub-and-spoke network, there is also the option of selectively offering point-to-point service for city pairs that can be operated profitably. Routes like Kennedy-Los Angeles, Boston-Los Angeles, Washington-Los Angeles and Seattle-Tokyo are examples of point-to-point service provided by American.

Premium service versus low fares is another major decision. Traditionally airlines stressed service. More recently low fares are a primary competitive strategy. The final two factors in the chart deal with implementation of the strategy. Does an airline try to go it alone, limit alliances to code-sharing, or does the British Airways emphasis on equity position alliances make more sense? Finally, how important is the use of information systems particularly in dealing with passengers?

Putting the three profitable airlines into their correct industry structure results in the following examples. Singapore Airlines is exclusively a long-haul carrier that has capitalized on a growing market in Southeast Asia. It has some major market routes to Europe and North America, but its financial strength has to date been based on long-haul routes in its immediate region. Southwest could compete across the board with American, United and Delta, but it doesn't. It is a specialized competitor. It carefully picks routes based on passenger traffic and whether its type of service matches passenger expectations regarding convenience, service and price. As indicated earlier, British Airways has some domestic routes in the United Kingdom but its primary focus is international routes with a major strength in providing trans-Atlantic service.

What does one conclude from this? Airlines like Southwest (specialized short haul in the world's largest airline market) and Singapore (long

Figure 4-1

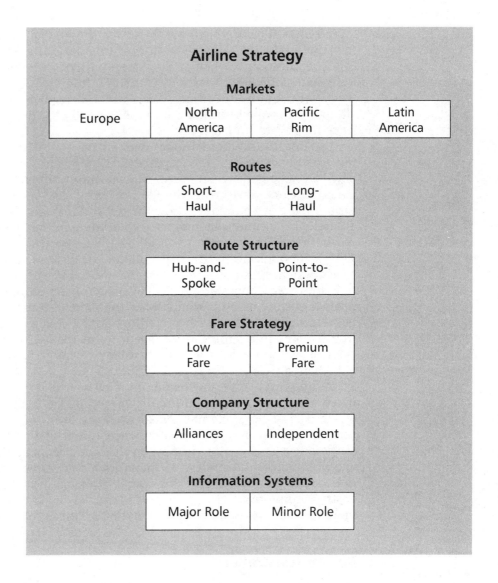

haul but concentrated in a growing region) have done better than the larger national and international carriers. The airline that should impress any airline analyst is British Airways, since it is the only combined short- and long-haul airline that has remained profitable among the world's major carriers. On the other hand, it has accomplished at least part of this success in a more regulated and protected market in Europe.

American, United and Delta are structured from an equipment, personnel and capability standpoint to be what they are—large national and international carriers. They must either succeed in operating successfully as currently defined, or go through what would be a major and traumatic restructuring effort. The deregulation of the U.S. airline industry is often criticized as the core of the problem for these large carriers. The fact is that the market has changed and the structure of the industry is changing. The question is whether these large carriers can also change. United has begun a shuttle operation (United Shuttle or U2) that competes directly with Southwest Airlines. That is what deregulation of the airlines is all about. No one said that Southwest gets to pick the better routes and leave the rest to someone else.

Looking to the international market, the post-deregulation competitive experience has left U.S. carriers lean and mean since they have competed so aggressively on price. This positions them well from a cost structure to compete with the likes of Lufthansa, Air France and Japan Airlines. The key question is how the rest of the world will deal with their airlines. U.S. airlines can compete on an international level; the question is whether other countries will allow them to do so. There is talk and some action regarding the deregulation of airlines in other countries. Worth watching is how the European Union (EU) will deal with their airline industry. Under current EU law, government subsidiaries are illegal unless a private investor would make the same decisions based on potential return. The EU is also expected to adopt a single policy by 1996 that would represent a significant change from the past. They would deal with the rest of the world collectively instead of individually, which should give them a stronger bargaining position.

Airline productivity is frequently cited as a major problem. Unfortunately the norm for most airlines is an occupancy factor of 62% to 65%, which is very close to what it takes to break even financially. Individual companies must deal with their cost structure if they continue to operate at these levels, or figure out how to increase occupancy. It is interesting and undoubtedly frustrating to the airlines that some fairly simple solutions could greatly improve the overall financial performance of the industry. Adding two more passengers to each flight or charging ten dollars more for each ticket would have a dramatic impact on the bottom line.

Buyers (Customers)

The complete Porter Model for the airline industry is shown in Figure 4-2. Once you have thought your way through the rivalry strategy dimensions of the airline industry, the rest of the analysis is relatively straightforward. Customers of airlines are the people who fly for business or personal reasons. These individual customers have little power over the airlines other than picking a competitor. Collectively, customer behavior impacts the carriers, but neither individual travelers nor corporate customers enjoy much bargaining power with the airlines.

Airlines claim to be particularly sensitive to business travelers. While they represent only 20% of the passengers on any given flight, they fly 80% of the total air miles. So what happened when IBM attempted to negotiate special travel rates with the carriers? "No, thank you," was the

Figure 4-2

Adapted and reprinted, by permission, from Porter, *Harvard Business Review*, March–April 1979, p. 141.

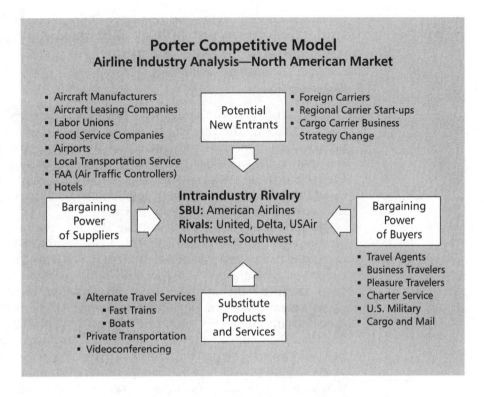

response. (An exception to this policy is the federal government, which is given large discounts on ticket prices.) Businesses may not win special concessions from the airlines, but business travelers will no longer be the customers they were in the past when they traveled with little regard for cost.

Suppliers

Suppliers are a significant competitive force in the airline industry. Three deliverables from suppliers—aircraft, fuel and all labor (from unions)—are the most significant determinants in the operating costs of the carriers. The power implications of suppliers is mixed in this industry. Labor unions continue to have a significant amount of power. A strike can have a devastating impact on a carrier, as American once again realized during the Thanksgiving holiday in 1993 when its flight attendants went on strike for five days. Since aircraft suppliers are solely dependent upon the airline industry for their livelihood, the airlines enjoy some leverage as long as the two major suppliers, Boeing and European-based Airbus Industrie, maintain their "fight to the death" competitive attitude and strategies. Aircraft fuel is more of a commodity, so the power rests with the customer until the next oil shortage. Governments that control airport gates and landing rights and fees have definite power. Supplies like food tend to be a commodity with an ample number of options for the airlines, so the power remains with them.

New Entrants

New entrants are companies that have not competed with you in the past. In this case they are either existing airlines that enter what represent for them new markets, new start-ups or existing companies like cargo transport companies that decide to add passenger service. The likelihood that UPS or Federal Express will decide that they want to carry passengers in addition to cargo seems very remote, but they do represent a potential new entry into the passenger business.

Despite the financial woes of the larger carriers and the large capital requirements to start an airline, there continue to be new entrants into the industry in the form of new start-ups. A major barrier to entry is the capital-intensive aspects of the industry. Expensive aircraft, high labor costs, landing rights and fees, gates, ground equipment and facilities add up to a great deal of money. But if a company times it right they can buy used airplanes for a very good price, hire flight personnel for considerably less than the major airlines and pick routes, landing rights, gates, etc. that in some cases are being left by other carriers. Reno Air is a classic example of good timing, and it is realizing a profit in its first two years of operation as a specialized point-to-point carrier, having moved into a number of markets as American pulled out.

Agreement to true open skies throughout the world would mean more international carriers competing on routes flown by American. This would, however, create similar opportunity for American on international routes.

Substitute Products or Services

Analysis of this category requires an examination of the motives for air travel. People generally choose to travel by air for two primary reasons: (1) because they desire more personal contact than is afforded by telephone and (2) the distance to travel is far enough that a significant time savings justifies the additional expense over alternative modes of travel. In the United States the airlines have a definite advantage. The country is quite large, fast trains do not exist and cars and buses are relatively slow. If the traveler has limited time and must be in the destination city, there really is no substitute for air travel.

However, there is evolving a technology-based alternative that has the airlines very concerned. Videoconferencing is frequently cited by business travelers as a viable alternative that they would gladly accept over a large number of their trips. Trips that require personal interaction between multiple parties will still be made, but ongoing collaborative and status-gathering trips could quickly become a thing of the past. Boeing estimates that intracompany travel (30% of total business travel) will decline by 20% and intercompany travel (40% of total business travel) by 5%. The balance of business travel (conferences and training) will also decline by 5%. Can the airlines fight technology with technology? Inflight entertainment and communications services do not address the basic challenge posed by videoconferencing.

♦♦♦ IMPORTANCE OF INFORMATION TECHNOLOGY

Information technology plays a major role in almost every aspect of the operation of an airline because of the high information content. Volumes of data on passengers, flights, meals, hotels, etc. need to be processed. The Porter Value Chain is shown in Figure 4-3 to graphically explain the scope of IT use.

At the mention of the airline industry and computers, most people think of passenger reservation systems. While these passenger service systems are significant, they are not the only important computer application within most airlines. Sophisticated operational information systems are required to effectively manage equipment, personnel, flight scheduling and contingency planning. Yield management is critical to the profitability of most airlines. This involves analysis of demand versus capacity on every flight with pricing decisions made accordingly. Flight operating systems involve a computer in the cockpit of the airplane that deals with throttle setting for take-off, weather conditions while en route and gate assignments upon arrival.

Benefits of Information Systems to American Airlines

American Airlines has consistently been the industry leader in the use of information systems. It implemented the first computer reservation system, the first frequent-flyer program, which it calls AAdvantage, and airport logistical systems for baggage handling, check-in, etc. All of these were geared to provide passenger convenience. Carriers have also implemented computer-based maintenance systems, including links to manufacturers like Boeing, to aid in diagnosing problems and obtaining spare parts as quickly as possible.

A number of benefits have accrued to American Airlines as a result of its focus and innovation with information systems. These include the following:

Convenience to Customers   This has been the primary motivation for the passenger reservation system. The ability to make a reservation for an entire trip, be assigned a seat, receive a boarding pass to eliminate standing in line, request a rental car and a hotel in multiple cities, arrange for

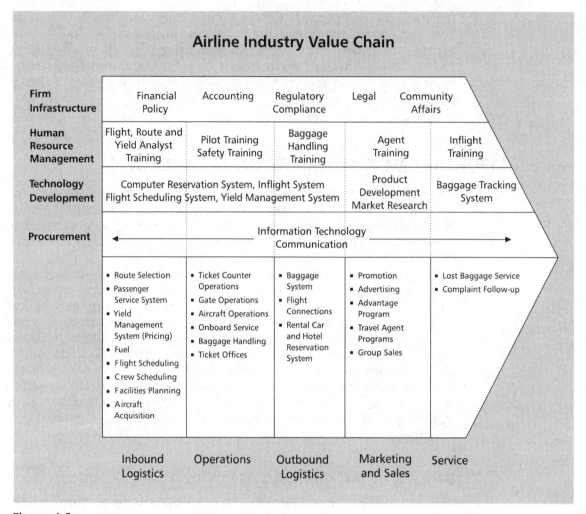

Figure 4-3

Included with permission of Michael E. Porter, based on ideas in *Competitive Advantage*, © 1985 by Michael E. Porter.

a special meal and conveniently change your plans before or during the trip, are all examples of benefits made possible by this type of system.

Knowledge of Customers This benefit was gained through the frequent-flyer program AAdvantage. The airline wanted to know who its better customers were and tried to increase the loyalty of these passengers by rewarding them for the amount of business they did with the airline. From a data-gathering standpoint the program worked very well. Most passengers get upset if they do not receive frequent-flyer points, so they carefully identify themselves when they take a trip. Although a large number of people signed up for the program, the loyalty factor has not been as successful as they had hoped. People who fly a great deal tend to take the first available flight to their next destination.

Providing a Foundation for Other Systems   This was a major benefit of the computer reservation system. The data regarding both the better customers and all passengers is used to analyze the logic of routes, frequency of flights, ticket structure and prices. The yield-management system mentioned previously is a key factor in realizing a profit for the airline. A typical flight can have as many as fifteen to seventeen differently priced tickets. The yield-management system deals with how many tickets in each category should be sold for each flight. A key consideration is how many tickets to hold until the last minute to accommodate business travelers who would be charged at a higher rate.

Building a Base for Other Businesses   "In an age when innovation, efficiency and up-to-date technology are important business success factors, AMR's information- and management-services businesses provide a significant competitive advantage."[9] These information systems capabilities within have been marketed by American to other airlines and businesses in general. They designed and built a reservation system for the French railroad and Aeroflot in Russia. In addition to consulting and systems design they provide telemarketing services, systems training, ground services and investment services.

The challenge for American specifically, and the airline industry in general, as it relates to information technology is to keep pace with data management requirements that are increasing significantly on an annual basis, while maintaining the systems reliability required to compete.

✦✦✦ AIRLINE RESERVATION SYSTEMS: A CHANGING COMPETITIVE RESOURCE?

American's SABRE system was the world's first computer reservation system (CRS). It was a success for a number of reasons. Consumers received faster, one-stop shopping for flights and other travel accommodations. It extended services and improved the productivity of travel agents. It resulted in cost reduction of airline administrative expenses and provided an ability to deal with volume increases that would have been difficult to handle any other way. It also provided a marketing vehicle that was to prove significant over time.

---

[9] AMR 1993 Annual Report, p. 25.

Most important is that SABRE was the core system that became a totally integrated approach to managing a very complex business. The rules are changing based on the attitudes, priorities and preferences of the customer. SABRE is the data source to better understand these changes.

The potential is there for options other than CRS for reservations and ticketing. Alternatives vary from the very specific to very broad in scope. A specific approach would involve ticketing machines in airports. You buy a ticket by inserting a credit card and proceed to the boarding gate. Where this leaves travel agents is unclear. In 1992 the Department of Transportation (DOT) ruled that CRS must consider independent products and services. This included such products as electronic-mail interfaces and remote ticket printers. Since the DOT ruling alternative reservation and ticket distributors have come onto the scene. Changing the foundation of their revenue from the distribution of tickets to the distribution of information puts CRS on the way to becoming more of an information network than a provider of travel agency systems. It also makes it possible for nonairline information servicers to provide this service.

✦✦✦ THE AIRLINE INDUSTRY: DEREGULATED BUT STILL VERY REGULATED[10]

While the perception is that the U.S. airline industry was deregulated in 1978, what was actually deregulated was entry and exit to routes and the pricing of fares. There are still a large number of government-related activities that demand the attention, time and resources of the airline industry. Most of the rest of the world is still operating their airlines in a regulated mode, so matters that go beyond U.S. boundaries are addressed by the federal government. The Department of Transportation and its government counterpart are involved in which airline flies what routes from U.S. cities to foreign destinations. For instance, politics can determine if American Airlines is permitted to fly from Salt Lake City to London.

The federal government also plays an active role in safety factors, has the responsibility for air traffic controllers and is very politically attuned to what airlines do for and to constituents. Similar sentiments exist at a local level, including the cost of building and operating airports and other elements of the transportation infrastructure. When American Airlines announced that it was discontinuing its flights that service Sioux Falls, South

---

[10] The author's perspective of the regulatory aspects of the airline industry was greatly aided by an interview of Congressman Norman Mineta of the Eleventh District in California, who for many years has served on and chaired the Public Works and Transportation Committee of the United States Congress. This committee, which oversees the airline industry, was renamed Transportation and Infrastructure in 1995.

Dakota, it had to deal with congressmen, county supervisors, airport managers, etc. and the political pressures that go along with these decisions.

Some contend that the economic health of the U.S. airline industry cannot be maintained without government assistance. A list of government-related factors that could make a major difference include:

1. Changes in the tax laws as they relate to airlines.
2. Encouraging foreign investment in U.S. carriers by changing the current constraints that do not allow a majority of foreign ownership.
3. Changes in bankruptcy laws to eliminate the ability of airlines to hide from their creditors under court protection.
4. Improving the capacity and capabilities of airports. Airports are owned and controlled by cities and counties, so there really is no national plan.
5. Providing a better air-traffic-control system to minimize flight delays.
6. Helping to negotiate better international rights for U.S. carriers instead of leaving this negotiation to individual airlines.
7. Equalizing the regulatory requirements on U.S. and foreign carriers.
8. Elimination of unnecessary and costly regulatory requirements on airlines within the United States.

These industry and business environment factors at first glance would not seem to involve information systems use. But if they are addressed, an airline needs the ability to respond to possible changes, some of which could be dramatic. It needs information systems that are flexible, that can adapt to new competitive strategies to either pursue opportunities or to defend against threats from competition.

✦✦✦ CONCLUSION

No one would dispute that the airline industry in the 1990s and beyond is a tough business. Can the worldwide airline industry operate profitably as privately held companies at or near its present industry structure? Can the companies accomplish three important goals: (1) realize a profit for stockholders as private corporations, (2) maintain a public service responsibility and (3) provide a potential strategic resource for their home countries in times of natural disaster or war?

The strategic role of the privately held airlines is not generally understood. Under the Civil Reserve Air Fleet provisions of the federal government, approximately seventy-five Boeing 747s from the airlines were used during the Persian Gulf War to transport military troops. The airlines receive a small federal subsidy for this when they purchase their aircraft.

This strategic role is a major influencing factor with both the regulators and Congress on the question of whether foreign carriers should be allowed to buy controlling interest of U.S. airlines.

Critics say that this is an industry built on defying gravity. A common solution to poor performance has often been incurring significant debt by buying new aircraft, adding routes, facilities and people. Many airlines need to rectify their capital structure and profitability problems while also renewing their fleets. With many of their current assets belonging to leasing companies, it is going to be difficult to accomplish this on a short-term basis.

The International Air Transport Association (IATA) is fairly optimistic regarding the future of the industry, predicting that its 224 members will return to profitability. The question is when, at what rate of return and after what restructuring individually or as an industry? For the industry the IATA consistently projects load factors in the 66% to 68% range, with the financial break-even point at 66.5%. Performance at 70% of capacity, a number never achieved by the industry, would produce a $13.2 billion profit.

The U.S. Congress established a bipartisan commission, the National Commission to Ensure a Strong Competitive Airline Industry, to focus on government regulations, pricing/service practices, bilateral agreements, taxes and foreign ownership issues. In addition to addressing these points the commission also raised a basic question: Does the United States have an entire ailing airline industry, or simply a collection of sick, poorly managed companies? Only time will ultimately provide an answer to this question. At the present we can conclude three things regarding the airline industry:

✦ It is a vivid example of the dynamics of the market that it serves.

✦ Establishing strategies dictated by the market is critical.

✦ Once the right strategies have been identified, information systems can play an important supporting role.

RECOMMENDED READING

Carlzon, Jan, *Moments of Truth: New Strategies for Today's Customer-Driven Economy*. New York: Ballinger, 1987.

This is an interesting, personal account of the challenges faced by Scandinavian Airlines and its efforts to change the focus of the organization so that the customer came first. It is available in paperback edition and well worth reading.

Hampdem-Turner, Charles, *Creating Corporate Culture: From Discord to Harmony*. Reading, MA: Addison-Wesley, 1990.

This book contains a chapter that offers a good analysis of the changes made within British Airlines that made them so successful.

Harris, Brian, *Babs, Beacon and Boadicea: A History of Computing in British Airways and Its Predecessor Airlines*. Hounslow, Middlesex, U.K.: Speedwing Press, 1993.

Colin Marshall is quoted in this book as follows: "The application of information technology has, more than any other factor, enabled British Airways to take quantum leaps into the competitive development and overall expansion of its business. Information technology is a vital key to the airline's success." The book goes on to provide background information to explain how Sir Colin Marshall arrived at the above conclusion.

Peterson, Barbara Sturken, and James Glab, *Rapid Descent: Deregulation and the Shakeout in the Airlines*. New York: Simon & Schuster, 1994.

This book offers an excellent review of the companies and the key people that played major roles in the deregulation of the airline industry in the U.S. As the title of the book suggests, the authors are not overly pleased with the results of deregulation. They are critical of the impact on pricing (chaotic), new competition (the lack of) and jobs within the industry (the good old days of fat paychecks and slow-paced workdays are over). On the other hand they conclude that the political clout is not there to turn the clock back to regulation. If you are interested in the airline industry, this is a very worthwhile book.

U.S. Congress. National Commission to Ensure a Strong Competitive Airline Industry, *Change, Challenge and Competition*. Washington, D.C.: GPO, August 1993.

This is the summary of the study completed by the commission. It includes industry data and an analysis of issues and challenges faced by the airline industry. The commission's conclusion was that the industry must be (1) efficient and technologically superior, (2) have the financial strength to respond to rapid change and opportunity and (3) efficiently move people, products and services to markets wherever they exist. To accomplish this the commission recommended that the FAA needed to be reinvented to provide necessary operational efficiencies; factors that impact financial health of the industry must be addressed; and the current bilateral systems must be replaced by a multinational regime to provide access to foreign markets.

Vietor, Richard H.K., *Contrived Competition: Regulation and Deregulation in America*. Boston: The Belknap Press of Harvard University Press, 1994.

A good analysis of the deregulation of the airline industry using American Airlines as the company example.

EXERCISES

1. What does it take to start an airline?

Assume that you are a member of a group of investors who want to start a new airline.

    a. What are the major resources that you will need and what capital will be needed to acquire them?

    b. Why would you want to start a new airline?

    c. What are the major risks in going into the airline business?

    d. What are the barriers to entry to provide route service in the United States and in the European market?

    e. How can information systems increase your chances of realizing a profitable operation?

2. Competitive importance of computer reservation systems (CRS).

    a. How important are computer reservation systems to you personally?

    b. How do typical business travelers feel about the benefits of these and other computer-based systems used by airlines?

    c. How do you feel about the ticketless approach being implemented by Southwest and other airlines?

3. Understanding the competitive role of information systems in the airline industry.

Read the article, "Rattling SABRE—New Ways to Compete on Information," by Max Hopper in the May–June 1990 issue of the *Harvard Business Review* (p. 118). Explain why and how Max Hopper recommended a major change in the way that airlines should develop large, new systems. Is the Hopper approach consistent with or a contradiction of the major contentions suggested by the Porter Competitive Model?

4. Open skies as the trend for the future of the airline industry.

You have been selected to lead a team to negotiate an "open skies" agreement with the Republic of Singapore. You need to brief the members of the team regarding the implications of this negotiation and specific factors on which you will want to gain agreement for this negotiation to be successful. What major factors must be included in this plan?

5. Computer reservation systems (CRS) as data collection devices.

Identify the major type of information obtained through the use of a CRS and how it can be used by an airline to make future business plans.

INFORMATION SYSTEMS CAN REDEFINE COMPETITIVE BOUNDARIES

*Most of the dramatic and potentially powerful
uses of information technology involve
networks that transcend company boundaries.*

James I. Cash, Jr.
Harvard Graduate School of Business

LEARNING OBJECTIVES

The previous two chapters focused primarily on business strategy—how a
company competes. It is also important to understand ways of extending the
capabilities of an enterprise through the use of information technology.
A first approach, interorganizational systems, uses information technology to
cross competitive boundaries into new markets both domestically and
internationally. A second deals with business process changes involving
customers and suppliers, with an emphasis on supply-chain management.
A third option supports multiple forms of strategic business alliances. In
all three situations telecommunications networks and computer-based
systems play significant roles. From a business standpoint it is important to
understand the basic concept of interorganizational systems and to recognize
that this often translates into a new way of doing business, both domestically
and on an international basis.

QUESTIONS

The following questions should be asked regarding how information
technology can extend the reach and capabilities of a company:

1. Which word—global, international or interdependent—best describes
   current markets, products and services, and business relationships?

2. Why is growth such an important part of business success?

3. What is an extended enterprise and why is it an important competitive
   consideration?

4. What role does information technology play relative to an extended enterprise?

5. Do strategic alliances really work and if so, why?

6. What are examples of EDI and an E-mail–enabled application?

✦✦✦ NETWORKS CROSS COMPANY BOUNDARIES TO REAP BENEFITS

Information technology is used not only to create and protect competitive boundaries, it can be used to enhance business relationships and establish strategic alliances. In fact, the most dramatic and potentially powerful uses of information systems technology involve networks that transcend company boundaries. These interorganizational systems, defined as automated information systems shared by two or more companies,[1] can significantly contribute to enhanced productivity, flexibility and competitiveness of many companies. These electronic links can also enlarge a company's strategic options. Driven by the demands of the business environment, information systems used jointly by multiple companies can improve business relationships on a local, regional, national and international level.

The three primary roles of information technology were discussed in Chapter 1. The integration of telecommunications and computers can extend the use of information systems beyond the boundaries of the organization, consistent with all three roles as discussed below.

Efficiency from Interorganizational Systems

Improved efficiency (measured by productivity) can certainly be pursued through the use of interorganizational systems. Much of the paperwork that flows between companies is the output of an internal information system. Studies have indicated that 70% of one computer's input was another computer's output. In the past the output of a purchasing system was printed by a computer. The purchase order was then mailed to a vendor who gave it to a data entry operator who entered it into their computer. This process was both costly and time consuming if both companies were using computers. Transmitting the purchase order electronically eliminates the paper flow and the need to manually enter the data. This can save 25% of the cost of this type of transaction. It also improves accuracy of the data and provides better customer service by speeding up the entire process.

---

[1] Cash, James I., Jr., and Benn R. Konsynski, "IS Redraws Competitive Boundaries," *Harvard Business Review,* March–April 1985, p. 134.

Purchase orders, order acknowledgments and statements are certainly not the only possible areas of efficiency benefits. Any type of information exchange between companies is a candidate for productivity gains.

Effectiveness from Interorganizational Systems

Effectiveness—the broadening of the scope of tasks, activities and even jobs—can be realized through the use of interorganizational systems. By breaking down barriers between companies, those company functions that deal with each other can communicate more effectively, on a more timely basis, and deal with the total picture on what they are mutually trying to accomplish. The well-publicized example of Wal-Mart and Procter and Gamble (P&G) is evidence of this. Wal-Mart provides access to inventory records on their computer to Procter and Gamble. A P&G product representative monitors the movement (sale) of products in Wal-Mart stores. When additional quantities are needed, they write a purchase order to themselves electronically and ship the product to the appropriate Wal-Mart distribution center. P&G representatives are not just sitting on the sidelines wondering whether their product is selling well within Wal-Mart; they are monitoring what is actually happening and managing their product for their customer.

Competitive Advantage Through Better Customer Service with Interorganizational Systems

Competitive advantage can be gained through better customer service that accrues from interorganizational systems. These systems can truly become a link for customer satisfaction, which in turn gains the company a competitive advantage. The system says on behalf of the business:

+ *We are available.* We are immediately accessible, 24 hours a day, 365 days a year through our on-line system.

+ *We are interested in you.* We care enough that we want you to have immediate access to information about us and our products.

+ *We are responsive.* The reduction in the time to access and communicate with us can also reduce the time to respond to your requests and your requirements.

+ *You can count on us.* Our people, products and systems are all of the same professional caliber. We hope that you find us knowledgeable, businesslike and enjoy dealing with us personally.

+ *We want to earn your trust and respect.* Our systems approach indicates not only that we care about you and want your business, but that we deal with you on a factual and professional basis.

Competitive Advantage Through Strategic Alliances and Interorganizational Systems

Strategic alliances have become an integral part of contemporary thinking, and interorganizational systems have changed the competitive ground rules as to how these can be accomplished. The motivation of a company in entering into a strategic alliance is to be able to build a combined capability that makes it a stronger competitor. It wants to be able to say: It is no longer our company competing with a competitor's company, but it is our extended enterprise against the competitor's extended enterprise. Our success in the future will be a result of our combined capabilities against their combined capabilities.

An extended enterprise, by definition, says that you have taken the interorganizational system approach beyond the point of seeking efficiency and/or effectiveness benefits. As depicted in Figure 5-1, approaching this with a competitive advantage objective could involve customers, vendors, support services (legal, tax, security, cafeteria, etc.), business partners (strategic alliances) and even competitors. They can also involve industry associates, government agencies, information service providers and any other entity that is important to how a business operates. Why does a company work to build an extended enterprise? Because it is extremely

Figure 5-1

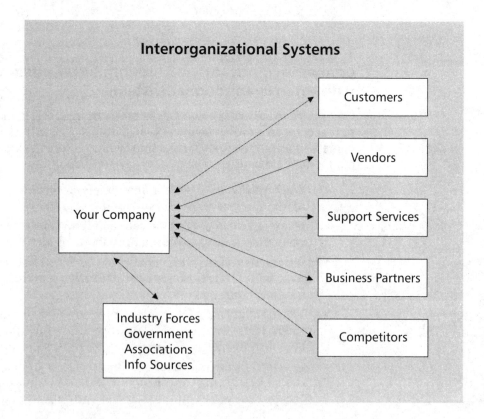

difficult, costly and risky for a company to try to deal with the challenges of a global business environment all by itself.

Strategic alliances between two companies can be structured in a number of different ways. They can involve a cross-equity position, a joint venture subsidiary, technical licenses in research or product development, a joint marketing agreement, a fixed-term contract or a handshake agreement to cooperate and work together. There is no fixed way that companies must agree to work together. A general guideline for an alliance would be to improve a competitive position by accomplishing one of the following four objectives:

1. Providing access to a new product or geographic market.
2. Significantly improving a position in an existing market.
3. Accelerating the time to bring new products to market.
4. Dramatically changing product cost structure.

Do strategic alliances really work? Some do and some do not. Learning to work together is difficult, but consider the alternative of competing against those who have found a way to do so. The value chain is a good place to start to identify areas where an alliance could make a major difference.

Both partners should bring strengths to the alliance table. Playing to the weaknesses of either potential partner makes little sense. Strategic alliances take time and an investment of money and effort by both companies to make them work. For this reason companies should seek relationships that offer long-term strategic advantage versus short-term cost savings. Meshing management style, company cultures, reward systems, business processes and overall objectives are just some of the things that must be addressed within an alliance. The strategic agreement must be clearly defined and agreed upon, but must also be flexible enough to respond to changes within the business environment.

Company Examples of Interorganizational Systems

With the acceptance and growth of Electronic Data Interchange (EDI), addressed in more detail later in this chapter, the number of interorganizational systems has grown rapidly in recent years, although they are by no means limited to EDI. Boeing's 777 design systems has links with subcontractors in Japan and the United States. Boeing also has a parts logistics system, which airlines are connected to, that provides information regarding parts availability to support aircraft maintenance operations. Independent insurance agents are linked to Progressive Corporation's systems for policy quotes, policy information and claims processing. Brokerage firms like Charles Schwab have trading systems that connect on-line to the stock exchange systems to execute trades. Federal Express and UPS have both implemented systems that involve the use of a computer by their customers to track their own packages through the distribution process and to facilitate billing. Visa International is a network-based business that is linked to member bank computers where the data for credit authorization is obtained.

As indicated earlier, crossing company boundaries is no longer unique but is becoming commonplace for a very simple reason—it is a better way to improve business processes, reduce operating costs and deal with customers in a timely, responsive manner.

Payment Process Industry

How payment is accomplished is the basic premise of any business transaction. Without some form of payment there is no business transaction. Conducting business started out with bartering and was replaced by cash, checks, money orders, bank drafts and travelers checks. More recent methods of payment are through the use of credit cards, debit cards and electronic funds transfer. What is unique about credit cards is that they represent the only form of deferred payment. While many companies offer installment payment arrangements, the actual payment options represent an immediate transfer of funds. Is there any wonder why credit cards have become the preferred form of payment in the United States?

Visa International has a goal to be the world leader in the payment process industry by providing multiple products and services to accommodate payment. As noted above, credit cards are the currently dominant instrument that uses Visa's and other network-based payment processes. Visa is a network-based business in support of the payment process industry. As a not-for-profit association owned by member banks, Visa's telecommunications network links 19,000 member banks in 130 countries. This links to 11 million merchants to provide the infrastructure that enables the extensive use of credit cards and a more limited use of debit cards. This three-party relationship created the current payment process industry as a subindustry of the financial services industry. It deals with very large volumes that continue to grow. On a worldwide basis Visa has issued over 335 million credit cards and processes 8 billion transactions worth over $700 billion on an annual basis. Visa projects that these numbers will grow to 15 billion transactions worth over $1 trillion by the year 2000.

How does the payment process industry actually work? As shown in Figure 5-2, in the case of both Visa and its primary rival, MasterCard, the cards are issued by the member banks. The member banks also recruit merchants to accept their cards and maintain the data that is the basis for the on-line credit authorization to approve a purchase. The primary role that Visa plays is in providing the network that serves as the connection between the member banks and the merchants.

In addition to describing business relationships, the solid lines in Figure 5-2 represent electronic links through telecommunications networks. Dotted lines indicate where card holders gain network access to initiate

Figure 5-2

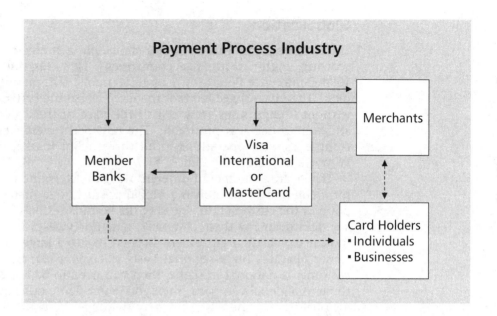

credit and debit card transactions with merchants, or account creation and payment with banks. Visa also does a daily reconciliation of all transactions (charges) similar to the check-clearing process done by banks.

Co-branding is another dimension to the issuing of credit cards. The Discover card is issued by Sears under its own name, but both Visa and MasterCard offer a co-branding service. The AT&T Universal card is an excellent example of co-branding. AT&T owns a bank in Utah that issues both Visa and MasterCard as AT&T Universal cards. A Universal card holder who has a Visa co-branded card can use that card with any merchant that accepts a Visa card. The transaction process utilizes the Visa network or a third-party network like First Data Corporation to accomplish the credit authorization and daily reconciliation. AT&T's motivation in issuing the Universal card was to promote its use as both a credit card and a telephone calling card. AT&T offers a 5% discount on long distance calls made through the use of the card. Experience to date is that the Universal card has been very successful in promoting an increase in long distance service use. As with all credit card issues, they also make money on unpaid balances on the credit card.

✦✦✦ ALLIANCES PROVIDE GROWTH OPPORTUNITIES

A primary motivation to establish alliances with other companies is to drive business growth. The need for businesses to consider growth a high priority is addressed in Chapter 7.

Globalization

"International expansion is not a choice but a strategic imperative for all growing, high-performance companies." This was the conclusion of a 1994 Conference Board study of 1,250 public U.S. manufacturing companies.[2] Their data suggested that the more global the better, since companies without foreign sales grew at half the pace of their global counterparts and were much less profitable. The best performers were multinational companies with operations in all three major markets: North America, Europe and the Pacific Rim.

There are a number of different ways to determine why it is important for a company to establish a global posture. The first is from the viewpoint of the customer. In assessing the boundaries that were a logical market definition for their company, a senior vice president of one bank indicated that their customers dictated this to a large extent. If your customer operates on a regional basis, then you can be regional. If your customer is national in scope, then you need to be national. If your customer is a global company, then you better figure out how to function on a global basis. Otherwise they may no longer be your customer.

A test of whether a company can function successfully on a global basis is its ability to tailor products and services to specific markets. Pepsico feels that it has an excellent opportunity throughout the world since all three of its businesses (soft drinks, snacks and restaurants) cross country borders so readily. While these products may have global appeal, they are still sensitive to taste differences: Frito-Lay chip flavors can vary significantly in different parts of the world.

A successful global business starts by identifying markets that represent good business opportunities but quickly shifts to product measurements, standards, documentation language, vendors, support infrastructure, etc. In many respects it really starts with attitude. Does a company feel that a product that sells well to U.S. customers is good enough for everyone else around the world? Alternatively, do they recognize the differences of other countries' markets and can they gear their products to these characteristics and requirements?

Another major consideration is the foreign competitors that are threatening a company in its home market. When the competition gets tough, it is especially convenient to turn inward to try to protect an existing market share *if* the current market happens to be the largest in the world—the United States of America. The obvious question that this raises is whether it makes sense to fight your competition in your market or to also make them fight you in theirs.

Finally, there is the basic question of skills, capabilities and resources (capital and otherwise) that will greatly influence an ability to compete successfully outside of your existing home market.

---

[2] Conference Board, *International Business*, July 1994, p. 38.

Global, International or Interdependent?

The next time someone starts debating foreign trade balances, try using the term "interdependent" instead of "international" or "global." In many industries interdependent is the correct word to describe the current situation. The difficulty in determining which automobile in the United States has the largest U.S.-sourced component content is an excellent example of this. As the automobile industry becomes truly global, it becomes possible for the Honda Accord that is built in Marysville, Ohio to have the highest U.S. product content of any car made in this country. As another example, try suggesting that U.S. semiconductor manufacturers should be protected by import restrictions or duties, and see how many U.S. computer companies would be negatively impacted by such a move. The U.S. economy is in a win-win, or a lose-lose, situation with other major world economies. The high degree of interdependence of products is both the cause of and the result of this relationship. The historical openness of U.S. markets has actually left U.S. companies in a much better position to pursue additional interdependent opportunities.

✦✦✦ ELECTRONIC DATA INTERCHANGE (EDI)

Systems that transmit data between companies have been around for some time. The grandfather of these systems and the predecessor of today's EDI systems was the American Hospital Supply's Analytic Systems Automatic Purchasing (ASAP) system, which was initially implemented with hospital customers in the early 1960s. IBM punch cards were provided to the hospitals that corresponded to an American Hospital Supply (AHS) product. When the hospital wanted to order that product, they dialed an AHS telephone number and transmitted the information through a card reader to a card punch at the other end of the telephone line. The quantity to be ordered was entered through the numerical keys on the card reader after the card was read. While this fairly rudimentary system falls short of the current definition of an interorganizational system, it had a major advantage—it worked. The hospitals liked it and American Hospital Supply rode its success and realized significant growth. The success of the initial system supported multiple equipment upgrades with a dumb terminal approach in 1977 and the first computer-to-computer order entry system in 1984.

Electronic Data Interchange systems are the most common form of interorganizational systems in use at the present time. The concept of electronically exchanging information in the form of structured trade data between two companies is easy to understand. It is logical to think of EDI as a form of electronic mail. A major difference is that it is a specialized, structured format compared to the open, free form of traditional E-mail. Electronic Data Interchange can be defined as the exchange of routine business transactions in a structured, computer-processable format. It is used for such traditional applications as inquiries, planning, purchasing, acknowledgments, pricing, order status, scheduling, test results, shipping and receiving, invoices, payments and financial reporting. The widespread uses of computers for business applications and telecommunications improvements provide the basis for the successful EDI applications.

Before an *application* can be successfully implemented through the EDI approach, both business and technical issues must be addressed. The word application was emphasized because that is exactly what EDI addresses—the implementation of a computer-based application that is processed on two different computers owned and operated by two different companies.

Even though information technology is involved, EDI is more of a business issue than a technical one. As much as 70% of the decisions involved in implementing an EDI system will center around business issues. This includes legal considerations dealing with such basic issues as, when is an electronic order considered firm so that a vendor should spend money and initiate operations to fill it? The problem arises from the fact that electronic orders can quickly be transmitted and just as quickly canceled, causing possible financial harm to the vendor.

The paperwork savings are minor compared to the opportunity to fundamentally change the business relationship with suppliers and customers. This is what prompts the common use of the term "trading partners." EDI provides an opportunity to change a possible adversary relationship with a vendor to one that is much more of a partnership. This could mean involving the vendor in the design process, seeking their help regarding the difficulty to produce a specific part, negotiating prices versus competitive bidding, committing to order quantities over a longer time frame, etc. All of this would be intended to add up to a win-win proposition—good for the originating company and good for the supplier.

Small companies that rely on business from a major customer tend to say, "If it is what our big customer wants, then we will naturally do it." The customer company should work with the vendor so that they can derive value from the EDI approach. The vendor needs to see how it can change its business relationship with its large customer while also realizing benefits. The attitude of the customer will be a determining factor. If it feels that EDI is a way to offload administrative, clerical and inventory carrying costs, then the term "trading partner" is not appropriate.

Successful EDI Systems Are Logical Extensions of Existing Systems

A valid point can be made regarding successful EDI or any other form of interorganizational systems: They are logical extensions of existing successful applications as shown in Figure 5-3. None of the five applications included in the description of EDI applications was originated by an EDI system, with the possible exception of advanced shipping notices. These

Figure 5-3

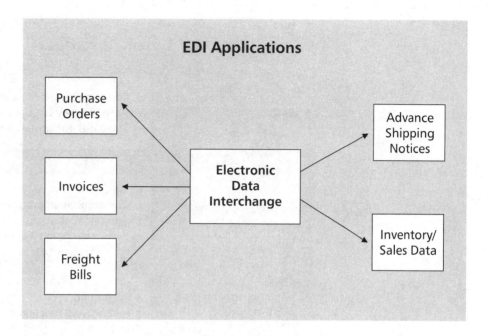

applications may have been enhanced, but the primary thing accomplished by the EDI approach was their integration. A successful purchasing, accounts payable, and warehousing distribution system was just sitting there waiting for the next logical extension. The fact that it happens to be beyond the boundaries of the organization is not proving to be a deterrent to this systems extension.

EDI Implementation Obstacles

In addition to business issues, the challenges to implementing an EDI application include data formats, the timing and scheduling of business communications, telecommunications technical issues and the ability to interface applications. These obstacles are summarized in Figure 5-4.

Data format differences must be dealt with. Purchase orders used in an existing purchasing system do not comply with EDI data format standards. Compliance with the EDI foundation data standards starts by using a common dictionary of terms. A transaction is formed to accomplish a specific trade function. A purchase order, an order acknowledgment, an advance shipping notice or an invoice are examples of EDI transactions. The envelope that contains the message being transmitted is referred to as the "interchange." It contains identifying information but also specific, structured data to support the message to accomplish the specific transaction. Tools in support of the EDI process are specified. Rules explain how to define data and an interchange. Transaction design guidelines are also available to modify existing messages or to design new ones.

Figure 5-4

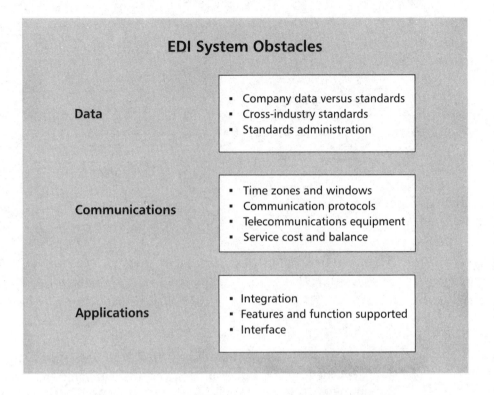

EDI System Obstacles

Data

- Company data versus standards
- Cross-industry standards
- Standards administration

Communications

- Time zones and windows
- Communication protocols
- Telecommunications equipment
- Service cost and balance

Applications

- Integration
- Features and function supported
- Interface

Time zones and business schedules are an operational consideration. A California company that writes purchase orders at the end of their day has missed the closing time of their New York supplier. Even if the California company changed its schedule, it would still miss the order-entry window of the New York company, since it processes all orders from the previous day the first thing each morning. This three-hour time difference and the difference in business schedules is not a unique problem. In using an EDI system, the company in California enters its orders into an electronic mailbox whenever it is ready to do so. At the time that it wants to process new orders, the New York company would open the mailbox and retrieve its orders, overcoming both the time zone and business schedule problems.

Competitive time pressures created the need for information technology improvements. The acceptance of standards and the willingness of companies to work together brought these interorganizational systems into being. Linking computers through the use of telecommunications services provides the foundation for an EDI system. Communication service speeds, costs, reliability and the ability to trace a message through the network are factors that must be considered. Using a Value-Added Network (VAN) Service (described below) minimizes some of the telecommunications issues, but answers to these factors still need to be understood.

To this point no business transaction has been completed. The data records have been properly structured, transmitted across a telecommunications network and received by the trading partner computer. If the trading partner's order-entry application can accurately read the purchase data record sent by their customer, then the process will have been completed. Most EDI systems have application interface software that sits between its own internal application software and the communications network providing access to trading partners. It accomplishes the translation from the EDI data format into one that can be processed by its internal order-entry system.

EDI Value-Added Network (VAN) Services

Implementation of an EDI system can be accomplished directly between the trading partners. For reasons cited below, the use of a Value-Added Network Service, presented graphically in Figure 5-5, should definitely be considered. VANs provide services that address two major elements of an EDI process: a telecommunications network and EDI application translation support. The network connects the trading partners in what can be a broad range of geographic locations and provides network management, including multiple routing paths and security. The application part of the service includes an electronic mailbox where "documents" are deposited

Figure 5-5

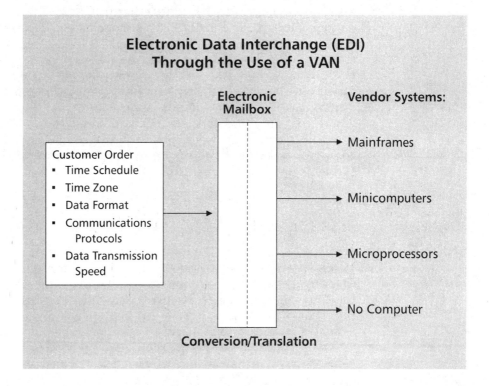

**Electronic Data Interchange (EDI)
Through the Use of a VAN**

Electronic
Mailbox

Vendor Systems:

Customer Order
- Time Schedule
- Time Zone
- Data Format
- Communications
  Protocols
- Data Transmission
  Speed

→ Mainframes

→ Minicomputers

→ Microprocessors

→ No Computer

Conversion/Translation

until picked up (forwarded to) by the trading partner to whom they are addressed. The VAN also does any necessary conversion of the sending company's data protocols and some data formatting needed to accomplish connectivity with the trading partner.

Initiating an EDI relationship does require both parties to have a computer. This can be a personal computer with a modem to provide the telecommunications connection. Hardware and software costs are not prohibitive for a small company to pursue this approach. Several large retailers that are actively promoting EDI as a standard way of operating have support programs for small vendors to help them implement their part of the system, especially if it is their first-ever computer.

The benefits of a VAN in the EDI process include:

✦ Having a 24-hour service on demand.

✦ Gaining access to national and international networks to connect to trading partners.

✦ Support for multiple telecommunications protocol conversions.

✦ Interchange support for multiple document formats.

✦ A cost-effective approach for even a small number of transactions, since you only pay for the services that you actually use.

Most of the more successful VANs have national and international networks. Their success is aided by their ability to provide a service similar to a telephone company, by connecting to any location where a business partner is located. The major EDI VANs are large companies with large networks. They include AT&T, IBM and GEISCO (General Electric). GEISCO has an international network that provides EDI service to seventy countries.

Like most new ways of doing business, EDI-based applications are proving to be very successful at some companies and disappointing at others. Smaller vendors, despite a win-win mentality on the part of their customers, often find EDI complex and cumbersome. This is particularly true if it is their first experience with any computer system. A first-time computer user would also not be in the position to benefit from treating EDI as an extension of an existing system.

EDI at Mervyn's

Mervyn's, a division of Dayton Hudson, is a department store that specializes in family clothing and home furnishings. Headquartered in Hayward, California, they have been both aggressive and successful with EDI. While there are technical issues, Mervyn's would tell you that the major EDI issues deal with business factors. In their case as much as 80% of an EDI system is business-issue related.

Mervyn's initiated their EDI program by conducting one-day vendor conferences to introduce and sell the idea. The first Mervyn's speaker was a senior vice president who talked about how they wanted to fundamentally change the business relationship with vendors. They use the term "business partners." Their intent is to extend their vision into vendor organizations and treat them like they were a department within Mervyn's. The major objective in this case was to reduce the time of the order cycle.

There are three major players in their EDI system: Mervyn's, vendors and freight companies. The importance of the system to a company like Mervyn's and the role of the vendors has already been discussed. The third major participant in their system, the freight companies, represent a major part of the time cycle. Advance shipping notices indicating when the shipment will actually arrive at the warehouse is a key factor in better managing this entire process.

Mervyn's has all of its 6,000 vendors on the EDI system. While they made an effort to sell the merits of the system to their trading partners, they now resort to a penalty if the system is not used: If a supplier sends a printed statement, Mervyn's will deduct $25 per page to process it.

✦✦✦ E-MAIL–ENABLED APPLICATIONS

Practically everyone in a business of any size is using E-mail these days. It is easy to use, a highly visible way to communicate and growing in volumes of use. But is E-mail viewed as it should be? E-mail and voice mail are examples of the benefits of nonsimultaneous communication—the person you are communicating with is not available but communication is still possible. It is also the foundation for further improvement in business processes that can be built on an extension of E-mail. In other words, an E-mail–enabled application! It often takes a culture change or at least a shift in attitude, but there are a number of possible applications that can be done through E-mail extensions.

Sun Microsystems has addressed electronically the age-old process of approving travel plans, submitting and approving expense accounts and reimbursing employees. All but the reimbursement, which is done by electronic funds transfer, is accomplished on what would be considered extended E-mail. An employee requests approval for travel plans by completing an electronic form on E-mail. These are approved by the manager via the same E-mail record. It would be nice to say that the record is then sent automatically to the travel agent, but this is not currently part of the system's capabilities. (Maybe this is being planned as a future system enhancement.) The employee calls the travel agent and requests the necessary reservations. Upon returning from the trip, the employee completes the expense account form on the E-mail system, and it is approved by the manager. It is then electronically processed by the accounts payable department. Receipts from the trip are submitted separately in an envelope, but the payment is not delayed pending the traditional auditing of receipts. It all adds up to an easier process for the employee, quicker submission and reimbursement for travel expenses and everyone likes it—employees, managers and the accounting department.

Hughes Aircraft in El Segundo, California has implemented a similar system for the approval of purchasing requisitions. It all gets done electronically very similar to the process at Sun Microsystems for travel requests. A difference is that certain purchase requests need a higher level of approval based on the total expenditure. These are automatically routed to the higher level manager for their authorization. These applications have the same potential as the EDI examples addressed earlier. Once they work internally, they can be extended to customers, suppliers, etc.

✦✦✦ THE INTERNET

The Internet, often referred to as the "information highway," is already playing a significant role in providing a telecommunications connection between organizations. Use of this network as the electronic link for interorganizational systems will continue to grow for a simple reason: It is already established and can be used to access not only companies but also institutions and individuals around the world. The Internet is described in detail in Chapter 11.

✦✦✦ CONCLUSION

Successful small systems tend to grow into larger systems. As EDI applications continue to accomplish their business objectives, they will also expand into related areas. Advance shipping notices have become a key ingredient to the overall success of a number of order entry-inventory control EDI systems. The entire area of product planning and inventory management is not beyond further improvement. These systems are changing customer relations. Wal-Mart no longer allows vendor sales representatives to call on their buyers in their Bentonville headquarters. They say, "Send your systems people over and we'll see how we might do business."

RECOMMENDED READING

Barnet, Richard J., and John Cavanagh, *Global Dreams: Imperial Corporations and the New World Order.* New York: Simon & Schuster, 1994.

Addresses how global companies are doing things and the changes that they are driving in the business, economic, political and social arenas.

Keen, Peter G.W., *Shaping the Future: Business Design Through Information Technology.* Boston: Harvard Business School Press, 1991.

Peter Keen is one of the best in linking information technology to business issues. This book explains in very clear terms the issues that people who run businesses must address in order to gain a competitive advantage through the use of information systems.

Kristof, Nicholas D., and Sheryl WuDunn, *China Wakes: The Struggle for the Soul of a Rising Power.* New York: Time Books, Random House, 1994.

Whirlpool's global strategy, which is described in detail in the next chapter, includes three joint ventures with companies in China. They had better understand that in redefining the boundaries in which they will compete, they are doing business in a very different world. While many businesses become excited over the idea of 1.2 billion Chinese consumers, it is important to recognize that 900 million of them are peasants with an average annual income of $123 in 1993. There is also the issue of corruption—one of the oldest problems in China. If you want to do business in a certain area it may require paying off the local officials, or all kinds of hurdles will suddenly appear. The question as to whether China is a police state with major human rights abuses is raised by the authors through numerous examples. They do their best to provide a perspective in their final concluding sentence: "There's a revolution going on out there." Based on their five years of working as *New York Times* correspondents from 1988 to 1993, this husband and wife team looks at China politically, socially, culturally and economically. If you are going to China to make washing machines for Whirlpool or any other business venture in the Chinese market, this should be mandatory reading.

Parfett, Martin, *What is EDI? A Guide to Electronic Data Interchange,* 2nd ed. Oxford: NCC Blackwell, 1992.

A basic primer on EDI.

Rogers, David, *The Future of American Banking: Managing for Change.* New York: McGraw-Hill, 1993.

Commercial banking in the U.S. is on shakier ground than at any time since the Great Depression. Increased competition, deregulation, globalization, bad loans and derivative problems raise a number of questions regarding the shape and role of banks in the future. This book is referenced here because banks have the potential to play a major role within the overall scope of interorganizational systems. For instance, banks have always played an integral role within the payment process industry. Yet in recent years a major growth of credit cards within the U.S. has been through co-branded cards. What are the implications to banks of trends within the payment process industry and the role of traditional banking instruments like checks and even cash? This is only one of many challenges that banks face in posturing their role in the banking business of the future.

Simmons, Matty, *The Credit Card Catastrophe: The 20th Century Phenomenon That Changed the World.* New York: Barricade Books, 1995.

This book was written by a man who was in on the ground floor of the "credit card era" as a public relations agent for Diner's Club. It includes vignettes about people with credit card problems, which serve as a reminder that a credit card society still has its difficulties. It also offers an interesting perspective of the beginning and development of the payment process industry and concludes with prognostications regarding the future of the industry from key industry people.

EXERCISES

1. An extended enterprise example.

Evaluate a specific company to assess the value of its extended enterprise approach. What major challenges did it encounter in establishing the alliance? What specific benefits has it derived from this approach?

2. E-mail–enabled applications.

Assess the evolution of an E-mail system from basic messaging through the creation and use of an E-mail–enabled application. Clearly posture the E-mail–enabled application as to where it fits within a major business process.

3. A company based on and threatened by information technology.

Both Visa International and MasterCard are technology-based organizations. If they were built on a technology, could their role in the payment process industry be significantly negatively impacted by a new technology?

4. EDI as a highly visible interorganizational application.

EDI is receiving a great deal of attention as an example of reengineered business processes that have fundamentally changed the management of supply-chain logistics and the business relationships between customers and vendors. Identify two industries where EDI has practically become a standard way of doing business. Document the factors that have prompted this to happen. Identify two other industries where EDI has not become a successful computer-based application.

5. EDI policies and practices.

Identify major policies and practices that need to be addressed in designing and implementing an EDI application with major vendors. Be sure to include the major legal considerations that must be included in such an approach. Considering these factors, can an EDI system be justified by a small company?

Section II

THE SECOND PERSPECTIVE: THE COMPANY ENVIRONMENT

This second section deals with understanding the company. The factors shown below comprise the overall management and control functions of a company. The process begins with a vision (a long-term projection of what the company wants to be) and concludes with the implementation of specific tactics. All companies, both large and small, follow a path like this. Some companies have more formal systems than others, but it boils down to where the company wants to go, how it is going to get there and measuring how well it is progressing. While the process is similar, there is no real standard for how the terms are used within different companies or by those that consult on or teach these subjects. (See Collings and Lazier, *Beyond Entrepreneurship* in Recommended Reading at the end of Chapter 6 for an in-depth discussion of the importance of these factors, their relationships and how to address them effectively.) An explanation of the terms is provided to assure an understanding of their use within this book.

Values, beliefs and principles are basically the same and are the foundation for establishing a mission statement and a vision. They are a guiding philosophy of business and even life that are held to be inviolate. Examples are respect for the individual, best possible customer service, share with those who contribute to the success of the business, be fair with those with whom you do business, do unto others as you would have them do unto you, we expect profit from work that benefits humanity, etc.

Mission is articulated in a statement that outlines the sense of purposes of the organization. It is usually a broadly defined statement ranging from a single sentence to one page. It is appropriate for it to address the company's

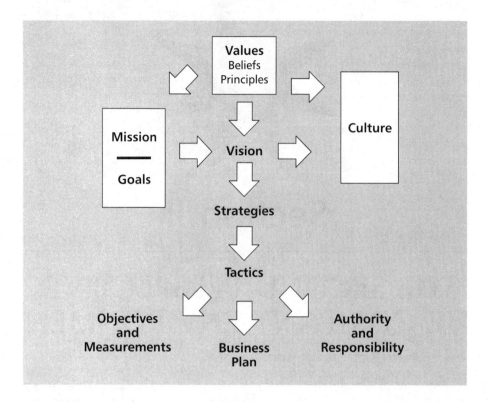

multiple stakeholders with a clear and compelling overall statement of what the organization aspires to be. It also helps to explain why the company does what it does in the manner that it does it. Some contend that a mission statement is timeless, while others argue that it needs a specific time frame for its achievement even if it is 20 to 30 years.

Goals is a broadly used term. They can be what the organization is committed to and what it wants to accomplish as a company in the foreseeable future. They can also relate to both strategies and to tactics, although it avoids some confusion if "goals" is used relative to strategies and "objectives" is used in connection with tactics. The higher level organizational-commitment definition is used within this book.

Vision is an image of what the organization wants to be like in the future. While values form the core of the vision, the mission statement and goals also influence the creation of a vision statement.

Strategies deal with how the organization is going to achieve the long-term goals spelled out in the vision statement.

Tactics are specifically how you implement strategies to achieve goals and make a vision a reality. Tactics establish measurable objectives, spell out authority and responsibility and determine much of what is included in a final business plan.

The business plan describes the allocation of resources (people, capital funds and budget) to achieve both strategies and tactics.

BUSINESS VISION

*To carry out its work, the organization needs
from a leader a clear statement of
its vision and strategy.*

Max DePree
Chairman of the Board
Herman Miller, Inc.

LEARNING OBJECTIVES

The primary intent of this chapter is to position vision as the starting point
in directing, posturing and running a business. It is important for a student to
understand the significance of the vision process as its importance is actually
increasing in today's business environment. Two company examples are
provided to enhance this understanding, in addition to a discussion of the
major elements of a successful vision process. The major point to be
remembered is that vision triggers the entire business and information
technology management process.

QUESTIONS

Questions that pertain to vision and its relationship to other factors important
to the management of a business include:

1. How important is it for a company to have a well-understood vision?
2. Is there something unique about a visionary executive?
3. What factors influence the creation of a vision?
4. What are the logical time dimensions of a business vision?
5. What major challenges frequently accompany establishing a new vision
   within a company?
6. What impact does a vision have on information systems?
7. Relate the concept of a vision to an actual company situation.

✦✦✦ WHAT IS A VISION?

A vision is a photograph of the future. It is a self-image that reveals what the business wants to look like over the long-range future. Business visions are realistic, credible and attractive to people within the organization. We are not talking about dreams, but something achievable. If you expect people to work toward achieving them, visions must be concrete and easily understood. It is difficult to think concretely about something that has never existed, so there is a need for a formal process to build a shared vision, as shown in Figure 6-1. It starts with sensing opportunity and concludes with successful implementation. Central to the entire process is the accomplishment of three things:

1. Establish a clear vision of the future.
2. Provide a basis for sharing values and views (the vision).
3. Send a message regarding the importance of the vision process throughout the entire organization to gain consensus and momentum.

Figure 6-1

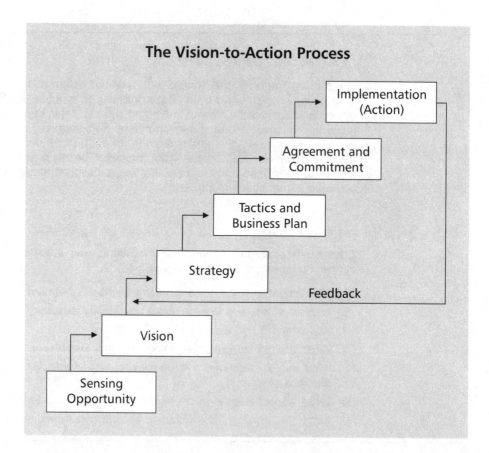

The uncertainties of a vision can be understood by looking at the business driver model in Chapter 1. These uncertainties include:

✦ The dynamics of the market (customers).

✦ Rapidly changing technologies that frequently offer new product life cycles.

✦ The logic and need to address changing employee values and traditional ways that work is done.

✦ The shift from the old to new regulatory practices in many industries.

Two examples of organizations that successfully implemented a vision process are presented in the following sections. The first deals with USAA, a diversified financial services company based in San Antonio, Texas, and their CEO from 1969 through 1993, Robert F. McDermott. General McDermott is an excellent example of a visionary executive. His accomplishments, including a major emphasis on the use of information systems, have been well chronicled but warrant another analysis since these efforts have been successful for more than two decades.

The second example addresses the ambitious efforts by CEO David Whitwam to transform Whirlpool from a company that was basically a North American company to the world's number one manufacturer of large appliances. This was accomplished by a company whose products do not travel well because of their size and structure. This dictated having operations within four of the five major global markets to both manufacture and sell products. A basic theme of a key strategy to implement Whirlpool's global vision was to think global but act local.

✦✦✦ A LEADER WITH A VISION AT USAA

How do you grow a company from $206 million in assets to $31 billion; increase annual revenue from $143 million to $5.3 billion; increase members (customers) from 653,000 to 2.4 million; significantly increase the level of customer service while decreasing the employee annual turnover rate from 43% to 7%; while also broadening the product base by redefining the business from a property and casualty company to a financial services organization? You hire General Robert F. McDermott as CEO and let him apply his visionary and leadership skills.

San Antonio–based USAA did this by convincing General McDermott that he should leave his fourteen-year tenure as the Dean of Faculty for the first ten graduating classes at the U.S. Air Force Academy, retire from the U.S. Air Force and start running the company. He was a man who challenged people to strive for the best while stretching the boundaries on how things have been done. At his first meeting with the managers who reported directly to him in January 1969, he told them, "Our goal is to become a paperless insurance company. We may never get there, but that is where we are going."

USAA is a worldwide insurance and diversified financial services institution. *Forbes* magazine described it as "a place where the financial supermarket—a one-stop shop for everything from stocks to life insurance—really works."[1] Many people have not heard of USAA because they are a company that focuses on a niche market. They market their products and services to active-duty or retired U.S. military officers. Dependents of members are also eligible to become members, and this category is becoming increasingly larger. Happy members suggest that their offspring take advantage of the same good company. Despite this relatively small market focus, they are the fifth largest insurer of automobiles and fourth largest insurer of homes in the United States. They do this as a member association instead of the more conventional stock company approach. Upon becoming a USAA member, you not only acquire insurance coverage but also become an owner of the company.

Robert F. McDermott is a graduate of the U.S. Military Academy at West Point and was a pilot in the Army Air Corps during World War II. He earned an MBA from the Graduate School of Business at Harvard University and taught economics at West Point after the war. In 1956 he became the Dean of Faculty at the new Air Force Academy. Rather than simply borrowing the best from the other two service academies, he carved out a curriculum that was unique to the Air Force Academy. One of his new programs was computer science—the wave of the future. This early experience with computers marked the beginning of efforts by General McDermott to harness the potential of information technology, something that he continued to consider a priority for the rest of his career. Convinced that a move to USAA made sense for himself and the company, he became the president on January 1, 1969.

When he retired in December 1993 after 24 years at USAA, the company had become a model of an excellent organization. USAA is highly rated by customers relative to service and receives superior and excellent ratings by A.M. Best Company for financial performance. Many industry analysts say that USAA is the best in terms of operating efficiency and the effective use of information systems.

In the eyes of its customers (members) USAA is a unique company. There is a mutual trust and respect between the company and members. Fraudulent claims are significantly lower than the insurance industry average for this reason. Quality service and a diversity of products combine to create loyalty among members that is truly enviable. The turnover rate among members going to other insurers is one of the lowest in the industry.

---

[1] Mach, Toni, "They Have Faith in Us," *Forbes*, July 25, 1988, p. 181.

There is also uniqueness in how the company operates. USAA was founded by a group of Army officers in 1922 to provide insurance to military personnel whose frequent moves made insurance difficult to obtain. From the beginning it was felt that the best possible prices could be provided to members if marketing costs were minimized. To this day USAA has no direct-solicitation field marketing organization—no field insurance agents knocking on your door to sell you something. It has salaried sales representatives, not salespeople paid a commission on the amount that they sell. They are basically a mail-order company with much of the interaction with members accomplished through the use of 800-number telephone calls. For a long time this customer service was centralized in their headquarters in San Antonio, but with significant growth regional centers were created to better serve members.

Customer Service Is the Vision Driver

Members started the company and they own it, so USAA exists to serve them. The mission and corporate culture of the company are, in one word, service. The quality dimension of service is based on the Golden Rule—to serve others as you would want to be served. As a company objective, service comes before either profits or growth.

The vision for the company has been to become the very best in providing this service. General McDermott's early efforts were to improve member service through the following four-step process:

1. Automating the policy-writing system.
2. Reducing the number of employees by means of attrition.
3. Upgrading employee quality and enriching jobs through an education and training program.
4. Decentralizing decision making by empowering employees with knowledge and information technology support.

Employees Make a Vision Happen

When General McDermott arrived at USAA, they were experiencing a 40% annual turnover of employees. At that time the word in San Antonio was that you worked for USAA for two years after finishing school and then you got a good job. This level of turnover was a major deterrent in achieving quality customer service. After all, quality service comes from committed people. Satisfaction with the company and the work place was something that McDermott took pains to nurture.

Their headquarters is truly impressive. The 286-acre campus has attractive architecture that is nicely designed, open and well lit. Employee facilities include six cafeterias (three that provide a take-home evening meal service), health and safety services, an employee library, three physical fitness centers, a company store, covered parking, van pools, car pools and recreational areas.

One of the more unique employee practices is their work week. While they are open to customers five days a week, USAA has been on a four-day work week since 1972. This four-day, 9.5-hour schedule has been extremely popular with employees. It is not only an incentive to join the company but is also viewed as having a positive impact on employees' personal lives, since it means 39 extra days off from work a year.

Equally important to the facilities is a working environment that encourages involvement. This includes production goals, self-improvement opportunities, a college degree education program and community volunteer efforts. The end result of all of this is that employee turnover, which was one of the highest in the industry, is now one of the lowest at 8.5%. In 1993 USAA was listed among the top ten in *The 100 Best Companies to Work for in America*, being called "a safe harbor where employees have incredible opportunities."[2]

Vision 2000: Evolution to a Financial Services Organization

In 1985 General McDermott felt that the company was facing a number of challenges because of changes in the demographics of their members and restructuring of their industry. Members were getting older, more had retired and they were more affluent and demanding. General McDermott wanted USAA to think about the events in the life of career officers and work out ways of helping them get through them.

Competition in this industry had always been a challenge, and new competitors were looming on the business horizon. In response to a question I posed to him regarding the possible threat of Japanese insurance companies in the U.S. market, General McDermott replied, "You worry about the Japanese, I'll worry about General Motors." His point was that because General Motors sells and finances cars, it would be logical for them to also sell automobile insurance as part of an overall package. The breakdown of traditional industry boundaries was certainly possible, and this could result in new competitors for USAA.

In response to these challenges he felt that it was imperative for them to address changing member needs while taking full advantage of the new and emerging opportunities that information technology offered. A task force was created to focus on the vision of the company in the year 2000. General McDermott asked Jim Patterson, the Information Systems Vice President at that time, to head this effort and aptly entitled it Vision 2000.

It is difficult to summarize a seven-month effort with a single chart, but Figure 6-2 offers one such attempt. The members have been and will

---

[2] Levering, Robert, and Milton Moskowitz, *The 100 Best Companies to Work for in America*, New York: Doubleday, 1993, p. 456.

Figure 6-2

Reprinted with permission of USAA.

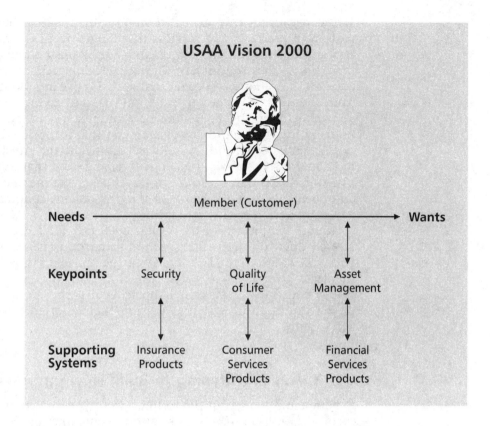

continue to be the primary reason for the existence of the business. These members have needs that become wants, since they are willing to make necessary investments in three key factors: security, quality of life and asset management. The "wants" of members translate to business opportunities for USAA in three major categories:

1. Insurance products, which have been the core of the USAA business.
2. Consumer services products that are traditionally tied to insurance products but could be further expanded.
3. Financial services products that represent new business opportunity while offering one-stop shopping to members for a broader scope of financial products and services.

The development of this new vision confirmed the logic of USAA evolving from a property and casualty company to a financial services organization. The redefined USAA includes property and casualty insurance, life and health insurance, no-load mutual funds, real estate investment opportunities, a discount brokerage service and a bank. The USAA Federal Savings Bank was recognized as the "Best Bank in America" by

Money magazine.[3] This was based on a survey of 428 institutions in a comparison of products and services that ranged from CD rates to checking fees and business hours. Things that *Money* liked about the USAA bank included (1) rock solid safety, (2) free checking accounts regardless of balance, (3) the nation's best credit card deals, (4) five free monthly withdrawals from any ATM, (5) generous yields on CDs and savings accounts, (6) convenient banking by telephone or computer, (7) bargain car loans and home mortgages and (8) a welcome mat that is extended to literally everyone. Such recognition would be significant for any bank. It is even more impressive for USAA when it is remembered that its bank was established in 1983. USAA also has a travel agency, a member buying service and operates USAA Towers, a 23-story retirement community, and USAA Parkland West, a health care facility.

Upon completion of the Vision 2000 task force, General McDermott created a new position and asked Jim Patterson to become the Senior Vice President of Strategic Planning. With the updated vision of the company in place, he needed to make sure that someone concentrated on the things necessary to make it happen. Don Lasher became the President of the Information Systems Division that reported directly to General McDermott.

USAA Uses Prototyping to Build New Information Systems

Experimental models in the form of prototypes are commonplace within manufacturing companies. Automotive companies produce prototypes, as do aircraft manufacturers. It also makes sense for a company like USAA, which is in the business of managing information, to build a document-processing prototype. Consistent with the paperless company vision, they built an image-processing prototype in 1984 and used it for 1–2% of their members on a customer service and claims-processing application until 1987. In evaluating the prototype an image-processing consultant said, "The prototype was technically klugey [not the best combination of technical components] but it worked." In using it for three years they accomplished exactly what they had intended. They clearly defined the requirements for the ultimate system. Despite the objections of the employees who liked using it, they disconnected the prototype and signed a contract with a vendor to build the new system. The manager of the installed system proudly proclaimed that they did a four-year project in one year. The value of the systems prototype was that it provided clear, well-understood requirements that avoided delays and rework and accelerated the implementation of the final system.

The details of the image-processing system are beyond the scope of this book, but a functional summary will be provided. The system

---

[3] "The Best Bank in America," *Money*, June 1995, pp. 126–133.

is presented in Figure 6-3. The image-processing system asbuilt on top of an existing transaction-processing system. The customer master files and customer service applications that utilize the image-processing system already existed. Processing correspondence through images was an extension of what they were already using computer-based systems to accomplish.

Following a transaction through the process would include the following steps:

1. A letter arrives in the mail room, requesting a change to an existing policy. This change needs to be accomplished by a customer service representative and becomes a part of the customer master file.

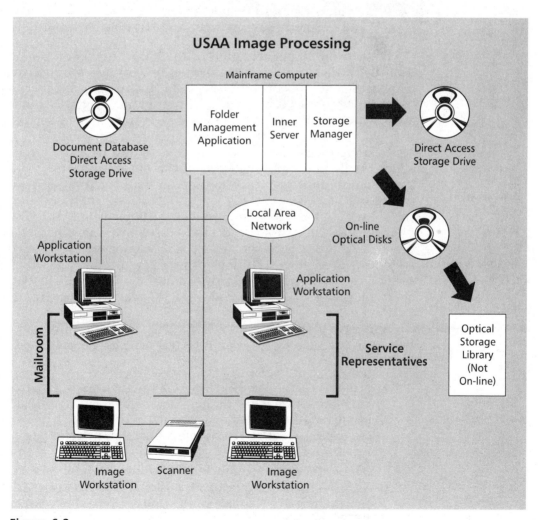

Figure 6-3

Reprinted with permission of USAA.

2. The letter would be scanned in the mail room and indexed to give it a unique identifying number and work priority. The original document is then destroyed.

3. The scanned letter is distributed in digital form to the appropriate customer service representative workstation.

4. Based on the assigned work priority code, the document is processed by a customer service agent and, when finished, is filed (stored) electronically.

5. Recent correspondence is stored in on-line disk files for ninety days. The record is then stored in a magnetic juke box, which can be either on-line or mounted on the system if requested. The juke box involves the use of tape cartridges. Some of the cartridges are mounted within the unit. Others are stored in a cartridge library and retrieved manually when a record stored in them is requested.

Prior to the implementation of the image-processing system, USAA dealt with the receipt and distribution of mail in a more conventional manner. Activities like mail sorting were automated as much as possible, but the total process of receiving and distributing mail lacked the systems approach of the image-processing system. Under the old approach once the mail was delivered to a customer service representative it was processed using the computer-based systems to deal with the specific transaction. With the implementation of the image-processing system they have improved the way they accomplish both the distribution of documents and processing of assigned work. Both capabilities existed under the old approach but were improved by the implementation of the image-processing system. USAA added a third capability, which did not exist under the old approach, relating to the ability to manage workload down to an individual employee. Previously the only way to manage workload was to look at in-baskets on individual desks. By capturing the documents electronically they have obtained the data necessary to manage the workload to process the documents.

A massive project like this is not just an interesting application of information technology; there must be real benefits. Benefits were realized in the form of:

✦ Reduced costs—A net savings of $5 million per year was realized. This was almost equal to the cost of equipment, staff and supplies to operate the new system. Specific savings were gained through the reassignment of 120 people to more meaningful tasks, the saving of 39,000 square feet of office space previously used for files, plus a savings of equipment and supplies used by the old system.

✦ Improved productivity of professional employees—This primary benefit came from automating assignments, tracking work in process and better management control. A 2–5% productivity gain among 2,000 professionals was realized through the use of the new system.

✦ Improved customer service—The information needed to serve a customer is always there under the new system. Additional work flow, privacy and security controls were also gained that were not possible with the paper system.

The Role and Contribution of Information Systems

Five people served as information systems managers under General McDermott. Don Lasher had this responsibility from 1985 until his retirement in 1994. As the President of the Information Systems Group, he headed a large organization both in terms of people and the information technology that they manage. There are 1,300 people in the Information Systems Group. They support five mainframes, 3.8 trillion characters of stored data and 22,000 workstations for 16,500 employees. USAA owns and operates its own communications company, which handles 93 million voice telephone calls a year through toll-free lines that use over 4,300 AT&T trunk lines. An automated voice response system allows customers to conduct business with USAA 24 hours a day, 7 days a week. All of this telecommunications capability results in 90% of all business transactions being conducted over the telephone.

There are a number of key factors relative to the role of information systems within USAA. These include:

✦ A horizontal integration of applications.

✦ An executive partnership.

✦ Technology experimentation and assimilation.

✦ Leveraging their information systems.

✦ Strategic architecture.

At the top of the list is the ability to manage their customer relationship, not individual products. This has dictated a horizontal integration of applications that supports a focus on members instead of products. The logic behind this is that the number of people buying IRAs is of interest to people with product responsibility. The number of total products that a specific member is buying is key to both servicing and marketing to them. For instance, a customer service representative can look at a customer record and see a complete picture of which products they have with the company.

An executive partnership has been a major reason for the successful use of information systems. (See Chapter 9, the Roles, Roles and Relationships concept.) This starts with the role played personally by General McDermott in prioritizing and positioning the importance of information systems. The information systems executive reported directly to General McDermott and functioned as a member of the senior management team. This also recognizes the interdependence between information systems and the USAA businesses. This partnership provides the foundation for decision sharing, which in turn means a sharing of risks, successes and failures. For example, when a major new application project is started a user manager is made the manager of the project team. This puts the responsibility for the success of a new application where it should be—with the appropriate line manager whose business requirements are being addressed by the new system.

Another important factor is technology experimentation and assimilation, which is sustained by a balanced R&D program. USAA executives feel that business and systems plans need not be constrained by current technology. An investment in future technology is viewed as an investment in the future of the company. The image processing prototype project is an excellent example of technology experimentation. The ability to assimilate, accept and utilize information systems is an integral part of the USAA culture.

Leveraging their information systems makes basic sense for USAA as a leader in the use of information technology. Computer and communications vendors are offering sophisticated products and services that often provide economic advantages over similar in-house, custom-built approaches. They actively engage in joint studies and projects in pursuit of technology-based benefits to the company. This represents better customer service opportunities and is consistent with the fact that an increasing number of their members have their own personal computers and modems and would find computerized access to USAA systems a natural way of dealing with them.

Finally, establishing and adhering to a strategic architecture is critical to USAA because of the significant role of information systems and their heavy utilization of telecommunications. A strategic systems architecture is maintained that will ensure uninterrupted capability to support business needs in a very dynamic business environment.

Summary of USAA's Success

USAA runs one of the most sophisticated and successful insurance operations in the world. It is the largest direct-response marketing organization of any kind in terms of sales volumes. It has managed to stay at the forefront of insurance and financial services organizations because it:

+ Provides quality service.
+ Attracts, trains, retains and motivates employees.
+ Aggressively and successfully uses information technology.
+ Provides products and services to address the changing needs of its customers.
+ Maintains one of the lowest operating expense ratios in the industry.

✦ Achieves financial results that warrant excellent to superior ratings.

✦ Makes business, organizational and management changes on a timely basis.

✦ Had an outstanding CEO in General McDermott who, through the right vision and leadership, has left a company that is definitely better off but different in many respects than what it was when he first arrived.

✦✦✦ WHIRLPOOL CORPORATION: THE WORLD'S LARGEST MANUFACTURER AND MARKETER OF MAJOR HOME APPLIANCES

As recently as 1987 Whirlpool was content to concentrate on the U.S. market. Today it is the world's largest manufacturer and marketer of large home appliances. The transformation of this company can be attributed to the following factors:

✦ A successful, well-managed company that is alert to both market opportunities and competitive threats.

✦ A new CEO in 1987 who initiated a global vision in 1988.

✦ A global strategy that emphasized product technology, procurement and information systems.

✦ Strategies and tactics based on "thinking global but acting local," with foreign operations managed whenever possible by nationals within the markets in which products are manufactured and sold.

✦ Having the patience to allow the above strategy to evolve over time.

✦ Becoming the only company with a major or growing presence in the four major regional markets for major home appliances: North America, Europe, Latin America and Asia.

✦ Realizing significant revenue growth, improvement in operating financial performance and creation of shareholder value.

✦ Becoming a "new Whirlpool."

Asking people within Whirlpool who or what is behind this dramatic change in market focus and the related strategies prompts the response: David Whitwam and his global vision. What type of person is this man who has served as Chairman and CEO since 1987? One might conclude that his background includes international experience, diverse experience in multiple functional areas, senior positions in several companies and an engineering degree and MBA. Such a conclusion would be wrong. David Whitwam has no international work or living experience. He was hired by Whirlpool in 1968 following his graduation from the University of Wisconsin with an undergraduate degree in business and two years of U.S. Army service. He had spent his entire career at Whirlpool in sales and marketing positions. His prior senior management experience was spent as Vice Chairman and Chief Marketing Officer for several years prior to being named CEO and President.

All of this makes Whitwam's accomplishments at Whirlpool all the more impressive. It should also offer encouragement to other U.S. companies that international expansion, despite its challenges, can be successfully done.

The effort to globalize Whirlpool was a transformation of a successful company rather than a turnaround of a company in major trouble. Whirlpool did not initiate its globalization under the threat of dire consequences from competitive pressure. As in the past, Whirlpool had the management talent to do the things that made sense for the future as dictated by market opportunities and competitive threats. Whirlpool has had very good CEOs over the years. A mention of Bud Gray, who served as CEO from 1949 to 1971, brings nothing but the highest praise from long-time employees. He made Whirlpool a full-line appliance company and did a great deal to establish a culture that resulted in a common sentiment that Whirlpool was the best place in America in which to work.

John Platts was CEO from 1972 to 1982. He was succeeded by Jack Sparks, who led the company from 1982 to 1987. Sparks reinitiated Whirlpool's traditional strategy of reaching out for growth through acquisitions. He was also the person who groomed David Whitwam to become the CEO. Whitwam is the first college graduate to head the company since Bud Gray. (Both Platts and Sparks rose to the top of the company from positions as employees on the factory floor.)

Whirlpool did not completely ignore foreign market opportunities in the past. They were involved with Nalleys in Australia until that company was acquired by GE. They began operations in Brazil through a joint venture in the 1950s, and this became the base for their current Latin American operation. This earlier foreign experience was minor compared to the scope and magnitude of what they are addressing today.

Successful brands like KitchenAid and Roper in the United States and Inglis in Canada were the result of acquisitions. Whirlpool's history also includes attempts at diversification. This included television, space heaters, electronic organs and kitchen cabinets, none of which are currently part of the Whirlpool product line.

Whirlpool was founded in 1911 in St. Joseph, Michigan by Fred and Lou Upton. The company struggled until Sears, Roebuck started buying their washing machines. By 1924 Whirlpool had become Sears' sole supplier of washers, and this business relationship, based on mutual trust and respect, has continued for over seventy years. The Sears relationship is changing, however. The Sears Brand Central strategy has resulted in its marketing of competitor appliances, so Whirlpool has become less dependent on Sears as a primary business source. In 1970 Sears represented two thirds of Whirlpool's total sales. By 1980 the percentage was 50%, and by 1992 it was 19%, where it has remained fairly constant.

A Global Vision

David Whitwam's vision is for Whirlpool to become an integrated and leading global enterprise that can leverage its talents and capabilities to achieve breakthrough performance in major markets around the world. Realizing this vision is not easy, and Whitwam is quick to point out that even after seven years the transformation is not complete. He feels that there is a big difference between being an international company involved in selling products globally and being a true global enterprise. He says that many companies plant their flags on foreign soil, but few are successful in leveraging their capabilities to create a cohesive, global company.

The Whirlpool global vision is:

> Whirlpool, in its chosen lines of business, will grow with new opportunities and be the leader in an ever-changing global market. We will be driven by our commitment to continuous quality improvement and to exceeding all of our customers' expectations. We will gain competitive advantage through this, and by building on our existing strengths and developing new competencies. We will be market driven, efficient and profitable. Our success will make Whirlpool a company that worldwide customers, employees and other stakeholders can depend on.[4]

Competitive advantage, according to Whitwam, means Whirlpool must have the best technologies and processes for designing, manufacturing, selling and servicing products at the lowest possible costs. This dictates that it take its best capabilities and leverage them in all of its worldwide operations. This requires creating an organization whose people are adept at exchanging ideas, processes and systems across country boundaries.

Why Did Whirlpool Pursue a Global Strategy?

Whirlpool was motivated to pursue a global strategy by both internal and external factors. Internally it needed to find a way to offset cyclical performance while also providing more consistent shareholder value. An integral part of this was to escape the deadly attrition in which cost and quality are the only competitive factors and ever-declining profit margins are the only prize. Accomplishing this in a mature North American market that was experiencing a significant slowing in housing starts represented

---

[4] Whirlpool 1993 Annual Report.

a major challenge. The difficulties that Sears was experiencing as its largest single customer provided cause for added concern.

A consolidation of the industry had been going on for some time. Electrolux of Sweden had gone on an acquisition spree that, between 1970 and 1986, resulted in the acquisition of over 300 companies in 40 countries. Particularly significant was the purchase of Zanussie in Italy in 1984 and White Consolidated Industries in the United States in 1986. Maytag, which started and prevailed as a Newton, Iowa company since it produced its first washer in 1909, in quick succession had bought Hardwick Stove in 1981, Jenn-Air in 1982 and Magic Chef in 1986. Expanding international efforts by Matshushita and Hitachi of Japan and Samsung in Korea simply confirmed a globalization trend within the industry.

Whirlpool was faced with four options:

1. Stick to its traditional core business of large appliances within the North American market and fight for increased market share, with the hope that economic factors would improve its market conditions.
2. Diversify within the North American market.
3. Pursue a global strategy as a conservative player in multiple global markets.
4. Pursue an aggressive global strategy with the objective of leading the redefining of the worldwide large-appliance industry.

Whirlpool chose the fourth option—it would attempt to lead the redefinition of the global large-appliance industry as evidenced by its following mission statement:

> To shape and lead the major home-appliance industry globally, becoming one of the world's great companies while creating value for shareholders, employees, customers, suppliers, government leaders and communities.

Implementation of the Global Strategy

A single acquisition—the purchase of the appliance business of Phillips Electronics N.V. in the Netherlands—was the most important factor in establishing Whirlpool in Europe and providing the foundation for its global expansion. This transaction was actually accomplished in two steps. The initial step in 1989 created a joint venture with Phillips whereby Whirlpool gained a 53% share for $361 million. The agreement allowed Whirlpool to buy the entire company if the transaction was completed before the end of 1991. Whirlpool exercised this option in July 1991 at a price of $610 million.

Of the four major global markets, Asia offers excellent growth potential as the incomes and standards of living of its people continue to improve. Because of a lack of market share concentration among major companies, the industry structure differs from that of either North America or Europe. Matshushita claims the largest current market share with between 12% and 14%. In this respect the Asian market is similar to North America and Europe twenty to thirty years ago in having a large number of companies trying to position themselves to capitalize on the projected growth. Whirlpool realized a 40% growth on a relatively small base in 1993, which represents 1–2% of the market.

Whirlpool feels that the market is actually developing faster and is more accessible than it originally expected. Success in Asia would go a long way in strengthening the realization of its global vision. As in Europe, it is hiring nationals for the company operations in the markets that it serves. Sharing the best practices means sharing the best people, which is the logical starting point for the implementation of its global strategy.

An integral part of the global strategy is quality of processes and products—based on the company vision, value-creating objectives and the Worldwide Excellence System (WES)—which drives measurements, decisions and accountability. Fact-based management includes annual objectives that are set to exceed customer expectations and outperform competitors. Customer satisfaction as an indication of value to customer is the ultimate test of the success of the entire system. Figure 6-4 illustrates the Pyramid of Excellence as a summary of the global approach.

Global Strategies Based on Product Technology and Procurement   Global expansion must be accomplished through significant global leverage. Most of Whirlpool's major product categories do not lend themselves to high-volume export. It would be the equivalent of shipping air because of the size and structure of large home appliances. The exceptions are microwaves and room air conditioners, which are exported to different markets. For the other products Whirlpool feels there is significant business opportunity and benefits to be gained through the design of global platforms. Whirlpool currently has four dishwasher platforms but feels that this could be addressed by one. It has twenty-two washing machine platforms and feels that six could effectively serve its multiple global markets.

Ronald Kerber was hired in 1991 as Executive Vice President and Chief Technology Officer to implement two components of the global strategy: product technology and procurement. This will address the product technology platform issues cited above while also harnessing the strengths of its partners, subsidiaries and suppliers. Since 55–60% of Whirlpool's product cost is purchased, the worldwide responsibility for purchasing was included as part of his responsibilities. Having product technology and procurement together helps decide what to make and what to buy. This will result in consolidating purchases among fewer suppliers and working more closely with suppliers in the design of new products and product

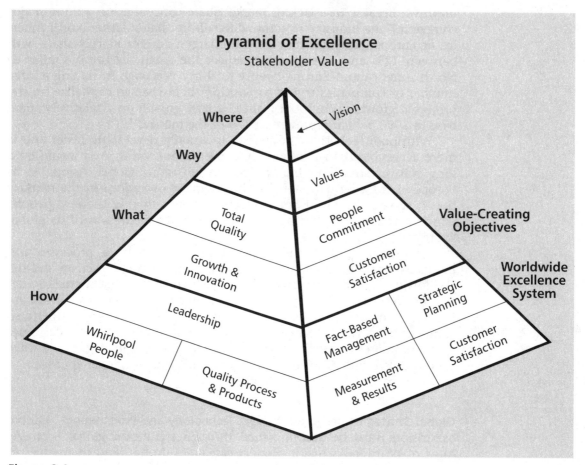

Figure 6-4

Reprinted with permission of Whirlpool Corporation.

components. The goal is fewer risks, more common components based on standard platforms and more of a business partnership with vendors.

The Role of Information Systems in Global Business Strategies

In September 1993 Dan McNicholl was named Vice President of Information Systems. He previously worked for McDonnell Douglas in St. Louis and had been at Whirlpool for three years. His first assignment dealt with strategic opportunity assessment, and he now gets to implement information systems support for the business strategies that he helped develop. While he had been out of information systems jobs for five years prior to his current assignment, he has three degrees in computer science and eight years of information systems management experience. In his current position he reports to the Chief Administrative Officer, Jim Samartini, on day-to-day matters and to the Chief Operating Officer, Bill Marohn, on strategic issues.

When McNicholl was asked to take the information systems executive position, Dave Whitwam told him that he originally felt that the key factors to successfully implement his global vision were product technology and procurement. He later realized that information technology should have been included as a necessary factor. Having mistakenly omitted information technology for several years, it was important to get going as quickly as possible in effectively building the necessary infrastructure to support the global business strategies.

Three business strategies are driving the focus and priorities of information systems within Whirlpool:

1. The global strategy dictates the need for global connectivity of systems and a global communication network. This has resulted in a global network and a standardized E-mail system.
2. The global leverage strategy dictates the need for common technology platforms, common business processes and information systems support of both of these factors.
3. The above two factors dictated a new organizational structure for information systems.

Whirlpool does not believe that a dotted-line reporting relationship works. They use an approach where the information systems managers in the multiple data centers around the world report both to someone within the local line organization and also to Dan McNicholl. It is a matrix management approach versus either centralized or decentralized. A centralized information systems organization is not consistent with the global leverage objective. A decentralized structure emphasizes the regional aspects of the operation and contradicts the need for a global emphasis. The conclusion was that the global vision and strategy dictated the matrix information systems organizational structure.

Information Systems Organization   Whirlpool currently has at least one and in several cases multiple data centers in the major markets that it serves. This includes two data centers in North America and Brazil and single facilities in Europe, Asia and its finance company. The 1994 budget for the worldwide information systems operation was $120 million, with an additional $34 million for capital expenditures. Worldwide information systems personnel number over 900. All of the major data centers have IBM mainframes with smaller operations using IBM midrange AS400s.

The information systems organization was centralized within Whirlpool until 1990, when it was decentralized throughout the line organizations. As noted above, this was not considered consistent with the new business and management strategies. This prompted the creation of the new corporate position, with Dan McNicholl being asked to take the responsibility for worldwide information systems.

While it may not match GE Appliance Park in Louisville as the first commercial computer user in the United States in 1956, Whirlpool is a long-time computer user. This began with extensive manufacturing, product and inventory logistics systems with a first computer installed in 1957. Concurrent with this effort was an emphasis on after-sales (service parts). In the 1990s trade management (sales) became an information systems priority. Product development is becoming more important, and a product data repository has been created to support this.

New Information Systems Through Global Business Process Teams   In evaluating the current role of information systems and making appropriate changes, a balancing act must go on. Elimination of duplicate systems is not the objective. An evolution rather than a revolution should take place. Dan McNicholl refers to this as following a "windows of opportunity model." Within Whirlpool remote locations can no longer autonomously decide to develop and implement a new system. When major changes are to be made to existing systems, or entirely new systems are contemplated, the global system should be implemented if it satisfies business requirements.

The initial global systems focus was on financial data and operational metrics, but it is being expanded to address applications like order processing through the use of global business process teams. They are currently redefining how the company does sales—a new brand-management process and support system. Because of the global business strategy, if a common manufacturing process is developed, then an information system would be developed to support the implementation of such a process.

Challenges to Realizing the Global Vision

Whirlpool clearly understands the challenge that it has undertaken. The following is a summary by David Whitwam of both the challenge provided by competitors and how Whirlpool must respond.[5]

> The market of tomorrow will be huge, filled with tough savvy customers with a wide range of preferences and choices. We must fulfill their needs and meet their expectations in quality and service. We must surprise them.
>
> To meet these challenges, Whirlpool must accomplish the following:
> - Continue to improve its competitive position in Europe and Latin America while expanding its operations in Asia.
> - Support the global strategy with a financially sound infrastructure that prioritizes product technology and procurement and computer-based support for these key business processes.

[5] Whirlpool 1993 Annual Report.

- Realize the theme of "thinking global while acting local." This will require establishing a common culture across the entire organization—the transforming of the old Whirlpool and a blending of the new Whirlpool with their multiple acquisitions.
- Improve thin net profit margins that have been as low as 1.1% in 1990 and improved to 3.1% in 1993—the highest level since 1988, which was the year that the global vision was initiated.
- Manage long-term debt to capital to about 33% over time. This peaked at more than 50% in mid-1991 and was 34% in 1993.
- Successfully blend the new managers hired from outside Whirlpool to help implement the global vision, recognizing that many of the long-term employees are important stakeholders.

The Global Large-Appliance Industry in 2005?

What will the structure of the large-appliance industry be in the year 2005 and who will be the dominant companies in the industry? Projecting the outcome of global industry competition is not without its risks, but logic suggests a company line-up that would include the companies shown in Figure 6-5.

Figure 6-5

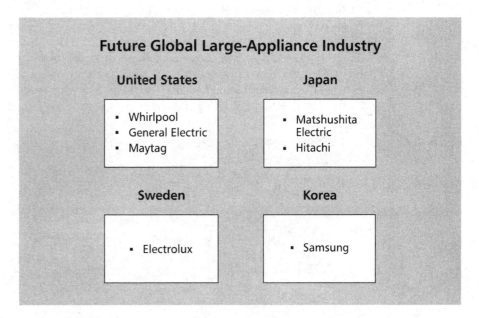

Future Global Large-Appliance Industry

United States
- Whirlpool
- General Electric
- Maytag

Japan
- Matshushita Electric
- Hitachi

Sweden
- Electrolux

Korea
- Samsung

✦✦✦ WHY A VISION?

Why has a vision process become so important for many companies throughout the world? A chief executive can do only a limited number of things to achieve and sustain competitive success. There are only so many ways to restructure a company. You can diversify, downsize, divest yourself of non-core businesses, form strategic alliances, outsource non-strategic functions or do a better job of playing to your traditional strengths. Companies need executives who can do the best possible job of either picking one of the above alternatives or doing something truly innovative and then making it happen.

The best innovators are those who can draw a conceptual road map from where the company is today to some imagined future. They then reinforce this by explaining how to get there. They then motivate people within the organization to buy in to the new direction dictated by the vision. A new vision does suggest change, and in some cases a significant amount of it. Personal traits like self-confidence, personal conviction, staying power, intellectual capacity and team-building skills are words often associated with visionaries. Current visionaries are rejecting the traditional "by the numbers approach" and seeking new paradigms for viewing their company and its role within a global marketplace.

At the beginning of this chapter Figure 6-1 illustrated a logical flow of the vision process, starting with the sensing of a business opportunity through actual implementation. A second perspective is provided in Figure 6-6, which postures vision relative to information technology. It reinforces the logic that the vision of the company drives the selection and prioritization of strategic applications. These applications then dictate the scope and capabilities of a telecommunications network that will meet the future needs of the company.

Determining the scope and support capabilities of the network helps to identify the information technology tools that should be evaluated on an ongoing basis. No organization has the resources to evaluate all new and evolving information technology. Determining the five or six

Figure 6-6

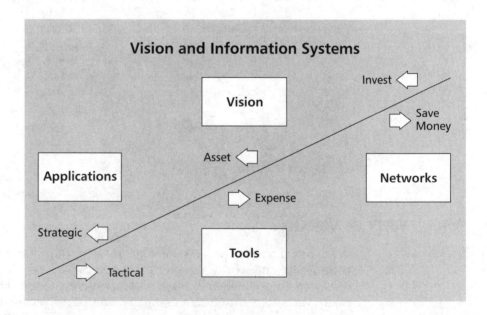

strategic technologies helps to focus this effort. This enables the company to do a thorough, professional job of tracking evolving technologies and in some cases to work with vendors to assure that its specific needs are being addressed.

The Vision Process

Burt Nanus is right when he says that "the right vision is so energizing that it jump-starts the future by calling forth skills, talents and resources to make it happen."[6] To develop the right vision requires a systematic process involving the three perspectives addressed in Chapter 1.

Define the Business Environment Look at the industry and marketplace in order to get a sense of the strategic trends and options. Bring together technical thinkers, who have access to doers, to establish a focus on the competitive context for information technology. The result of this effort would be a concise vision paper.

Build a Company Vision This is based on a thorough understanding of the strengths and weaknesses of the company. The initial vision paper should be used to stimulate discussion. It should be a stimulus for thinking and a force for change. Managers who have product and profit-and-loss responsibility need to play a key role in this effort. Michael Hammer makes a very good point regarding three essential elements of a company vision statement.[7] He feels that it should start by focusing on operations. It should then track progress and provide meaningful feedback by including measurable objectives. Finally, if it is really powerful it will change the basis of competition. The output of this second phase is an extended version of the original paper that makes specific broad recommendations.

Turn the Vision into a Plan Use the commitment to create the necessary plan, make the business case and move on to action. The vision process begins with divergent thinking to open up possibilities and stimulate practical innovation. It has to end with convergence, not on detailed plans but on principles for action.

A Logical Action Plan

The entire process starts with a vision that formulates the future direction of the business. Appropriate and necessary strategies then follow as the means to achieve the vision. Specific, thoughtful tactics provide

---

[6] Nanus, Burt, *Visionary Leadership*, San Francisco: Jossey-Bass, 1992, p. 8.

[7] Hammer, Michael, and James Champy, *Reengineering the Corporation: A Manifesto for Business Revolution*, New York: Harper Business, 1993, p. 156.

time-oriented, measurable objectives to accomplish in support of the strategy. The business plan allocates the resources in support of both the tactics and strategies. Finally, to complete the cycle a theme or a rallying point that provide necessary motivators is needed to make things actually happen. Motivators vary but must fit the style and culture of the organization. Wal-Mart likes buttons for employees. Ford uses banners with "Quality is job number one" prominently displayed. Use what works within the specific organization, but always remember that what you are trying to accomplish is to provide direction to employees to assist them in their day-to-day activities. As General McDermott so aptly said, "How do you know what you should be doing today, if you don't know where you are going?"

✦✦✦ CONCLUSION

A major premise of this entire book is that successful companies are the result of good leadership. This leadership needs to be present in two distinct forms. Companies need to be run well from an operational standpoint. They also need to be well directed. Information systems can play a key role in operational support. If at the same time the company is not headed in the right direction, computer systems might simply enable a company to go out of business faster. When properly directed the use of information systems can be more objectively assessed. The information systems leader then has to provide a vision of the possible impact on the business. Extremely important is how both the business vision and the potential role of information systems is sold within the organization.

RECOMMENDED READING

Collins, James C., and William C. Lazier, *Beyond Entrepreneurship: Turning Your Business into an Enduring Great Company*. Englewood Cliffs, NJ: Prentice-Hall, 1992.

This is an excellent summary of practical experience and scholarship that is very readable. It leaves you with logical, systematic things that need to be addressed to create a great organization.

Collins, James C., and Jerry I. Porras, *Built to Last: Successful Habits of Visionary Companies*. New York: Harper Collins, 1994.

This book is about visionary companies—eighteen of them, including Boeing, Hewlett-Packard, Motorola and Wal-Mart. It discusses how successful organizations achieve their success and how they sustain it over time.

Davis, Stanley M., and William H. Davidson, *2020 Vision: Transform Your Business Today to Succeed in Tomorrow's Economy*. New York: Simon & Schuster, 1991.

This book deals with how information systems are reshaping the basic structure of American enterprise. It explains the principles of capturing, processing and recycling information that can be key to transforming a business. All of this adds up to conclusions regarding the realities of future American businesses.

Davidow, William H., and Michael S. Malone, *The Virtual Corporation: Structuring and Revitalizing the Corporation for the 21st Century*. New York: Harper Collins, 1992.

How virtual is our future world? Davidow and Malone raise a number of valid concerns regarding the old way of doing things and the challenges to be considered in shaping the future organization.

DePree, Max, *Leadership Is an Art*. New York: Dell, 1989.

This is a classic on business leadership.

Drucker, Peter F., *Managing for the Future: The 1990s and Beyond*. New York: Dutton, 1992.

Business visionaries can be aided by those with a broader perspective of things that are happening in the world based on economics, people at work, new management concepts and practices, or the ever changing shape of company organization. Peter Drucker provides an assist in this regard through his analysis of key factors that will make up our future. Important topics include future factors that have already happened, new Japanese strategies, the governance of corporations, permanent cost cutting and trends toward alliances.

Drucker, Peter F., "The Theory of Business." *Harvard Business Review*, Sept.-Oct. 1994, pp. 95–104.

"Some theories of business are so powerful that they last for a long time. But eventually every one becomes obsolete." Drucker backs up this premise with specifications for a valid theory of business. He follows this up with criteria that should be considered in deciding whether it is time to redefine the theory of a business.

Keen, Peter G.W., *Competing in Time: Using Telecommunications for Competitive Advantage*. New York: Harper & Row, 1988.

This includes a good section on vision and the vision process.

Nanus, Burt, *Visionary Leadership*. San Francisco: Jossey-Bass, 1992.

In the view of many people, Burt Nanus is "Mr. Vision." Read this book if you are looking for a good understanding of both the basics and things that work.

Quigley, Joseph V., *Vision: How Leaders Develop It, Share It and Sustain It*. New York: McGraw-Hill, 1993.

The author draws on his personal management experience and more recently his consulting practice to provide a very systematic analysis of the vision process.

Tichy, Noel M., and Stratford Sherman, *Control Your Own Destiny or Someone Else Will*. New York: Doubleday, 1993.

This book addresses how Jack Welch is attempting to make General Electric one of the world's most competitive companies. While GE lost to Whirlpool in its bid to purchase the appliance operation of Phillips in the Netherlands, it continues to be a major player in appliances in the North American market.

Togo, Yukiyasu, and William Wartman, *Against All Odds: The Story of the Toyota Motor Corporation and the Family That Created It*. New York: St. Martin's, 1993.

Before World War II there was an expression in Japan, "Nissan for cars, Toyota for trucks." The success that Toyota has experienced with cars has been a post-war phenomenon. The courage and conviction—the vision—that its leaders demonstrated against very large odds is an interesting story and a tribute to their success. On numerous occasions decisions made by Toyota executives could have bankrupted the company had they been wrong.

EXERCISES

1. The significance of business vision.

Identify a company that has successfully implemented a vision process and prepare an evaluation of the factors that played a major role in its implementation. What were the main inhibitors to successfully accomplish this? What impact did the vision process have on the role of information systems?

2. The use of business management terms.

The Section I introduction stated that terminology relating to vision, mission, goals, etc. can vary from one company to another. To solidify an understanding of the use of these terms, summarize the specific documents and terminology used by a company to which you have access.

3. A visionary executive.

Identify an executive, other than those discussed in this book, who has built a reputation as a "visionary." Document the background, education, experience, management style and, most importantly, why he or she gained a reputation for being a visionary.

4. Vision drives the evaluation and selection of tools.

Using Figure 6-5 as a framework, evaluate if this process was actually implemented by a specific company. If it was followed, then explain how it was formulated and communicated throughout the organization. If it was not followed, what factors prevented the process from being implemented?

5. Peter Drucker's "Theory of Business."

Explain how Drucker's major premises in the *Harvard Business Review* article in Recommended Reading influence the formulation and acceptance of a company vision.

IMPLEMENTING A VISION: STRATEGY, TACTICS AND BUSINESS PLAN

If we know where we are and something about how we got there, we might see where we are trending— and if the outcomes which lie naturally in our course are unacceptable, to make timely changes.

Abraham Lincoln
16th President of the United States

If the strategy is a hammer, the tactic is a nail. The actual end results are accomplished by the nail. If the nail isn't hammered correctly then the battle is lost. Sometimes the hammer also misses the nail.

LEARNING OBJECTIVES

This chapter provides an understanding of how a company makes the transition from vision to action. It deals with strategy, tactics and business plans. Strategy is how a company will achieve the long-term goal of the vision. Tactics are more specific ways to make a vision a reality. Business plans involve the allocation of resources. Progressive Corporation, an auto insurance company, is used as an example of a company that gained success through a combination of innovative business strategies and information systems support. This should provide an understanding of the basic strategy concepts contained within the chapter and an appreciation of the potential role of information systems in support of the business strategy.

QUESTIONS

The following questions are important in understanding the contents of this chapter:

1. Identify and explain the two basic challenges in developing a business strategy.

2. What decisions must be made regarding three common elements of a strategy within any business? Identify a possible fourth option.
3. What factors will influence the selection of the primary strategy?
4. Identify five examples of computer-based business strategies that have proven to be successful.
5. What can be done to facilitate the transition from vision to strategy to tactics?
6. How does an organization identify key, strategic applications on an ongoing basis?

✦✦✦ PROGRESSIVE CORPORATION'S STRATEGIES FIT ITS NAME

Progressive Corporation of Mayfield Village, Ohio (a suburb of Cleveland), under the leadership of CEO Peter B. Lewis, is determined to lead the industry response to a wave of changing consumer expectations regarding automobile insurance. Their vision is to reduce the economic cost and human trauma of automobile accidents and provide services that delight consumers.

Progressive currently represents 2% of the automobile insurance in the United States. Their goal is to reach 6% percent by the year 2000. If their past performance is any indication, they will probably be successful. Progressive has consistently produced excellent results measured by rate of growth, profitability, quality of customer service (especially on claims), and by many other innovations that have changed industry practices and standards.

The Progressive plan for future success is based on rethinking the definition of its business. While it is still an automobile insurance company, some major changes have been made in how it defines and operates the business. Progressive got its start by insuring drivers that other insurers rejected. These drivers were typically called "nonstandard," though companies classify nonstandard drivers in different ways. Nonstandard drivers make up 19% of the total passenger automobile market. In the nonstandard segment of the U.S. market, Progressive ranked fourth in size in 1994. In the total private passenger insurance market, it was the seventh largest company.

One change that Progressive made involves a new attitude towards financial returns. The previous attitude had been "the more profit the better." For two reasons they decided that the 6% financial return on premiums that they had consistently realized was not good for them. Although these high returns made its stockholders happy, they also attracted new tough competitors. Secondly, the high rates of return got them in trouble with regulators in states like California. This is described in more detail below.

To offset the possible loss of both revenue and profits, Progressive recognized the need to pursue additional business opportunities. Instead of focusing on just nonstandard insurance it is broadening its services to include all auto insurance. What it loses in the nonstandard segment it plans to recoup through larger volumes in a broader market.

What motivated Progressive to make these changes? In 1988 voters in California passed Proposition 103, indicating their dissatisfaction with automobile insurers. Proposition 103 was a ballot initiative that mandated lower insurance rates. It set new limits on insurance rates that could be charged and also required insurance companies to pay rebates on previously paid premiums. Because of this Progressive did extensive market research of its own to determine how consumers felt. What they found was not surprising. Consumers indicated that automobile insurance was difficult to shop for and expensive to buy. Then when they needed service from the insurance company, such as a claim, the insurer was slow to react and service was poor.

Also in 1988 Allstate passed Progressive in total U.S. volume in its specialty of nonstandard auto insurance. The big profit margins realized by Progressive attracted Allstate and other competitors to this market. They came into the market by mimicking Progressive's program, operating at lower costs and accepting smaller profit margins. These experiences and the subsequent assessment of the company, its products and services, and its industry environment resulted in the following new strategies for the 1990s:

A new definition of the business: Minimizing human trauma, cost and frustration is the new business definition. With the Immediate Response® claims service, Progressive has created a whole new standard for auto claim service by responding immediately to all claims in ways that delight both policyholders and claimants.

Lower profit margins: Margins greater than 4% are not sustainable and are undesirable for the long term, because good results attract tough competitors who are happy to operate at lower profit margins. Moreover, they encourage onerous regulation and legislation. Progressive now plans to achieve 4% in each program but no more. This will keep prices attractive to customers and make it difficult for competitors to charge less while still making a profit. Lower operating costs will be converted into lower prices, written premium growth and subsequent earnings growth.

Broadened market: The target customer is now all auto owners and operators that can be profitably underwritten. Progressive believes that industry classifications, i.e., standard and nonstandard, are meaningless to consumers. Its standard policy for everyone makes its consumer offering seamless.

Consumer information: In some markets they are offering consumers comparisons of rates from up to three other leading insurers in addition to their own.

Information source: Once insured, customers can call at any time about claims, policy changes, payment status and other services.

Renewal policy: Progressive will accept and guarantee to renew every consumer who chooses to insure with them.

Multiple distribution: More than 30,000 independent agents sell the majority of Progressive business. The company is experimenting by shifting its focus to the consumer and distributing automobile insurance according to how, when and where the consumer wants to buy.

Consumer identity: Because Progressive has been represented by independent agents, it is relatively unknown. They are communicating a unified and consistent image through advertising to develop a brand that reflects low cost and immediate hassle-free service on a 24-hour-a-day basis.

Curtailed diversification: They will focus more on their core business and be more restrained and disciplined in how they develop new businesses.

Expense reduction: Cost reduction by implementing operating efficiencies is a critically important initiative.

Teamwork: Interlocking and constantly changing teams have been established to understand and meet the specific needs of customers.

New compensation system: This is market based with the same standards for all people and more aligned with shareholder interest. Called "gainsharing," it is based on achieving annual growth and profit objectives and is paid to every person within the organization if the company performance warrants it.

Information Systems Support of the Business Strategies

The Progressive commitment to its customers is backed by a number of computer-based systems. Led by CIO Allan Ditchfield, it has implemented the following new programs.

Their Express Quote® service provides rate information to a prospective customer, not only from Progressive but from other insurers within the state. The Immediate Response® claims service program, a 24-hour-a-day, 7-days-a-week claims service, provides fast, fair, hassle-free service when customers need it, particularly at the scene of an accident. Progressive encourages customers to report accidents immediately so that accident investigation and the claims settlement process can begin as quickly as possible. They have specially marked and outfitted vehicles in some cities that proceed to the scene of the accident to provide immediate assistance. A claims representative arrives at the accident scene to answer questions and provide assistance to the policyholder and other parties involved. If necessary, the claims representative can even write a check to cover a loss at the accident scene.

These are relatively new programs, but as early as 1987 the Progressive annual report indicated:

> We revere accurate data. We collect, analyze and make data accessible because we know it will unlock opportunities to meet customer needs. Our marketing strategies depend on having more and better information. We invest significantly in new information systems.

Evidence of this historical emphasis on information systems is their analysis of customer profile data to determine the type of customer that represents a good business risk. For a long time they have been convinced that better analysis of this data produced an understanding of profile differences that separated good risks from a category that would suggest otherwise. For instance, the ownership and use of a motorcycle does not by itself make a person a bad risk. A 48-year-old accountant who rides a big Harley-Davidson is not the same as a 20-year-old who, based on his data, will probably have a difficult time celebrating a 21st birthday.

Information systems that have been in place for some time include a Nationwide Automated Claims Management System that ties 1,800 claims personnel into a central database on a mainframe. Progressive determined that for them to stay competitive, it had to reduce the time for claims settlement from 30 days to 7 days. Its ultimate goal is 24-hour settlement as evidenced by the Immediate Response® claims service program. A rules-based portion of the mainframe settlement system matches the claims information to the coverage in the policy history database and informs the adjuster on anything that needs to be checked or evaluated. This system, which cost over $6 million to design and implement, is processing about 650,000 transactions a day. While meeting its goal of improved value to customers it has also increased data security and eliminated most, if not all, independent agents' cost on claims. These improvements have made Progressive's claims service among the best in the auto insurance industry.

Progressive values its relationship with its independent agents because this relationship has been, and continues to be, essential to its profitability and growth. "We will either survive together or fail together," says CEO Peter Lewis. "Progressive not only wants to survive, but to flourish. We understand how interdependent we and our agents are, so our programs help both of us achieve superiority in the marketplace." A key element in supporting independent agents is keeping costs down. Progressive has invested millions of dollars in ProRater$_{PLUS}$ Automation Software, a system that makes it easy and fast for independent agents to write new business for Progressive without requiring new computer hardware. This program eliminates redundant data entry, most mistakes, mail expense, policy issuance delay, agency checks, many cancellations and rewrites. It can also query customer accounts. This on-line system not only helps independent agents realize profits on their auto insurance business, but can also reduce their operating expense and increase productivity in the long term.

A sales automation software and outbound file transfer system is used to collect information on independent agents and to distribute the information in a timely fashion to the people who need it. Each user can access and update multilevel customer profiles and sales-related information. The software supports better utilization of information throughout the organization. Currently Progressive has a three-tiered database. At its headquarters a sales and contact database resides on a file server. This server in turn communicates with PCs at each of the twelve division offices around the United States. The field salespeople can dial into their respective offices to upload and download to the servers. Progressive has also upgraded its file transfer system.

Summary of Progressive Corporation

To identify an insurance company that is an aggressive user of information systems is not difficult. Insurance is an information-intensive business; it is in the business of managing data. What is impressive about Progressive Corporation is their ability to focus on the bigger picture of their business and accept the fact that they needed to change. They made major changes to the definition of their business and their financial objectives, since they felt that both had to change for the company to be successful over the long term. They changed the market segment they wanted to serve from primarily nonstandard to all automobile owners. They streamlined their internal operation both from a business focus and the effectiveness of internal business processes. Finally, they created unique computer-based applications to support the new business strategies.

In doing this they took two major risks relative to the stock market value of their stock and the possible negative impact on their culture. Both proved to be short-term risks. Initially the stock market did not think well of Progressive's plan and their stock dropped, but it has since recovered as the new strategies succeeded.

✦✦✦ COMPONENTS AND ISSUES RELATING TO A NEW BUSINESS STRATEGY

Business strategies are based on the vision of the company and influenced by internal and external factors as illustrated in Figure 7-1. The strategy-making process should be based on what is learned from both the internal and external sources. That learning is then consolidated into what should be done to achieve and sustain a competitive advantage.

Two challenges are at the core of developing strategies within any business: (1) deciding what things are worth doing and (2) getting them done. These may seem rather simplistic, but arriving at decisions regarding them can be very difficult. It requires spending a great deal of time,

Figure 7-1

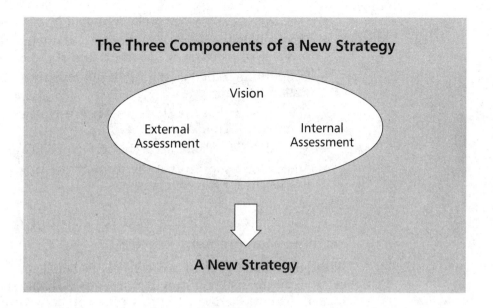

talent and energy within a company. The necessary elements of a business strategy are: [1]

✦ **Competitive framework:** The definition and size of a market including clearly identifying both direct and indirect competitors and their strategies. It is also necessary to know what needs of customers a product or service must satisfy.

✦ **Market target:** A definition of the primary buyer, or customer segment, for your product or service in terms of relevant demographics, purchase or consumption behavior, needs, attitudes and priorities.

✦ **Basis for perceived competitive superiority:** How key customers define superior value of a product or service within a precisely defined competitive framework.

✦ **Key profit drivers:** What factors most affect the profitability of a product or service line?

✦ **Product portfolio:** How to interrelate a product line or service with the other four points.

Additional challenges in making the right decisions regarding a new strategy include:

✦ Whether to be a strategy leader within the industry or to be content to let someone else lead.

---

[1] These elements are based on the strategy options discussed in Chapter 3, the Porter concepts and input from *Unique Value* by Dunham and Marcus cited in this chapter's Recommended Reading.

✦ How aggressively a new strategy should be implemented.

✦ Determining the people skills needed and whether they can be made available to focus on the key elements of the business strategy.

✦ Determining whether the funds are available to implement and sustain the strategy.

✦ Making sure that the strategy does not violate a range of factors from laws to company values.

✦ Maintaining a balance between short-term and long-term objectives.

✦ Addressing issues so that the scope of the strategy produces positive results for the company.

Strategic Management Process

The **strategic management process** described in Figure 7-2 views the process from an internal company perspective. As discussed in the previous chapter, the entire process begins with a company vision. A company's success and failure with strategies in the past have led it to its current strategies. As depicted in Figure 7-1, this has involved an analysis of both the external environment and major internal company factors.

Further development or growth is an important and even essential priority for many companies. Profit growth fuels new product research and development, rewards employees through pay raises for their contribution to the business and compensates stockholders. Revenue growth deals with economies of scale, capacity utilization, unit cost reduction, etc. Profit growth obviously needs to be part of revenue growth. Profits that fuel research and other investments in the future of the company are necessary for a business to not only prosper, but to survive. Is it any wonder that companies are continually looking for growth in the existing business or for new opportunities?

The internal analysis must deal with the structure of the organization. This includes not only how the company is organized but the degree and frequency of change that it has previously been subjected to and its ability to deal with the implications of any new strategies. The culture of the organization, which is based on the values of the company, must be considered. Is the new strategy consistent with the existing culture—the way things have traditionally been done? Extremely critical is the existence and availability of critical skills and the total resources (particularly capital) to implement, support and sustain any new business strategies.

A major consideration for many organizations in the current business environment is the number of employees that the organization can justify and afford. If there has been a common trend in recent years, it has been toward eliminating large numbers of employees. This effort has even resulted in the coining of the term "downsizing." Some contend that downsizing is the incorrect word; it should more accurately be described

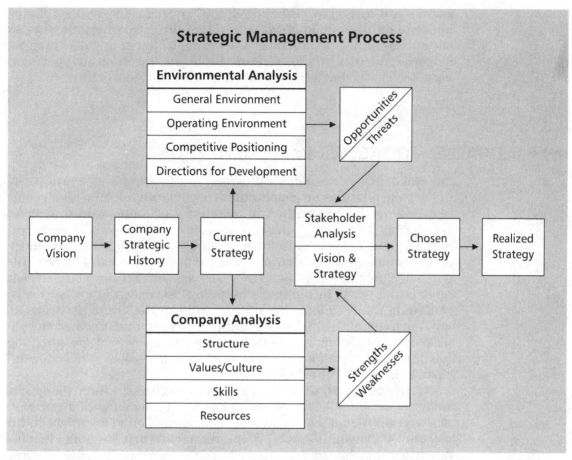

Figure 7-2

Reprinted, with permission, from *The Strategic Management Blueprint*, Oxford, England: Blackwell, copyright 1993.

as dumbsizing, particularly when it is not done as part of a company strategy but strictly as a cost-saving measure with little thought devoted to the longer term implications. The pitfalls to illogical downsizing start with a failure to follow a clear vision for the organization. Ignoring the alternatives to downsizing is a second common failing. Mismanaging the transition can involve a number of problems, but a major one is not providing adequate training for managers to address the issues and deal effectively with employees. Make no mistake about it, size is a strategic decision. U.S. companies are eliminating jobs at startling numbers, but are they doing so consistent with a well-thought-out vision and supporting strategies?

Any new strategies must be held to the test of the strengths and weaknesses of the total organization compared to the opportunities and threats posed by the external business environment. (This part of the planning analysis is discussed in further detail in Chapter 15, Integrating Information Systems into the Business Plan.) All of this is an interactive process, but once again it is important that the formulation of any new strategies be consistent with the longer term vision for the company and make sense for all stakeholders, not just employees and stockholders.

✦✦✦ STRATEGY-TO-TACTICS IMPLEMENTATION

The simultaneous revolutions discussed in Chapter 1 and shown in Figure 1-2 put pressure on organizations to reduce both time and events. They also raise many business uncertainties spanning a broad range of possibilities involving customers, competitors, suppliers and even business partners. To respond to these pressures in an appropriate and timely manner often dictates a change in the vision-strategy-tactics process. This does not eliminate any of these three key elements because all three make fundamental sense in running a business. Vision identifies what the organization wants to look like at some point in the future. Strategies are how to accomplish this. Tactics are the specific, time-oriented ways to make things happen. These often include objectives that measure progress against what was planned. The need to address each of these does not change. The issue is how to do so.

What can and in some companies should change is how the specific strategies are formulated and by whom. The formulation of a clearly articulated and well-understood vision can become more important in this scenario. As shown in Figure 7-3, the vision and what has been identified as a macro-strategy are formulated by senior management. The interpretation of the broader macro-strategies into micro- or specific strategies will be done by empowered implementors. These could be operational level managers or empowered teams of employees. This does not suggest that what has traditionally been called tactics are the same as micro-strategies. This is a delegating of responsibilities for formulating specific strategies to people who are closer to the demands of customers and the market.

In contemplating the logic and feasibility of this approach it is worth restating what is meant by the term strategy. Many people think of strategy as longer term. The compression of time and events that is motivating this entire discussion suggests that long-term strategies are part of the problem. Strategy needs to be viewed as doing those things that will enable a company to win in a competitive situation—to achieve a current competitive advantage and sustain it over time. An important, and often the most important, element of formulating a strategy is defining the range of business that the company will pursue. The source of the proposed competitive advantage must also be clearly identified. Both factors must then logically support how the action plan will achieve the intended results.

Figure 7-3

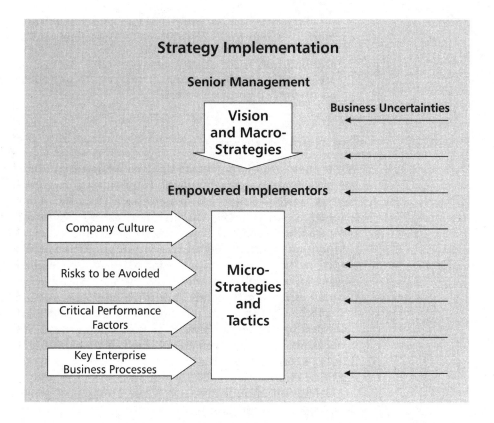

It is very important that the empowered implementors of the micro-strategies understand the new process and are aware of important business uncertainties that have prompted the change in this business process. They also need to clearly understand company culture values and major risks to be avoided. Critical performance factors should also be provided to the implementors as well as an understanding of the importance of compliance with or the need to gain consensus in changing key enterprise business processes.

Ed McCracken, CEO and President of Silicon Graphics, offers the following on how he challenges and coaches employees to deal with the dynamics and pace of change within the computer industry.

> Within Silicon Graphics we say stamp out long-term planning wherever you find it. This does not mean that we do not do long-term visioning. We do a significant amount of long-term visioning based on thinking about where the company will be in the year 2000 or 2005. We just don't lock it in. There is no reason to do operational (tactical) planning for any longer than the amount of time that it takes to implement the plan. If it takes us a year to design new products, we need to do one-year planning. That's it. Any planning longer than that locks us into things that may not be what we want to do. Instead of doing long-term planning we do dynamic step-wise planning. We

do every step that we have to do at the latest possible moment and make sure that every step we take creates new opportunities for the future. We don't try to predict the future but initiate product projects and build on them quickly and profitably. We do better modifying and adapting as we go along than trying to pin down everything in an up-front planning process.[2]

The Issue of Control

While there are many factors that would argue in favor of this approach, the basic issue is one of control. Implied by the word control is also the issue of power—either real or perceived. Is senior management willing to delegate to lower levels within the organization business decisions that have traditionally been viewed as logically and even necessarily made by senior management? Figure 7-4 highlights the factors that can be impacted by this approach. Is senior management willing to at least share degrees of control over these actions with those who are closer to the business uncertainties that prompted the logic of this approach in the first place? On the other hand, there is also a risk that too much will be delegated to the implementors. Senior management must know when it is necessary to lead within the context of this approach. Walking the fine line between empowering people while also leading them is a challenge for those charged with the overall success of the enterprise.

Delegation of authority and responsibility also would impact the traditional flow of information for reporting and control purposes. Figure 7-5 suggests that senior management would want to stay abreast of emerging

Figure 7-4

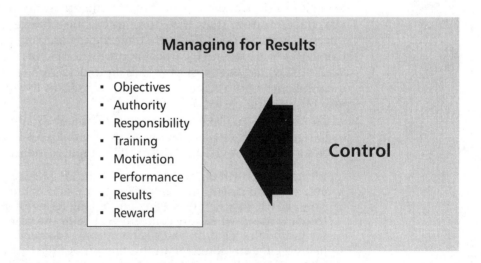

Managing for Results

- Objectives
- Authority
- Responsibility
- Training
- Motivation
- Performance
- Results
- Reward

Control

---

[2] Presentation to San Jose State University College of Business Alumni Association, June 22, 1995.

Figure 7-5

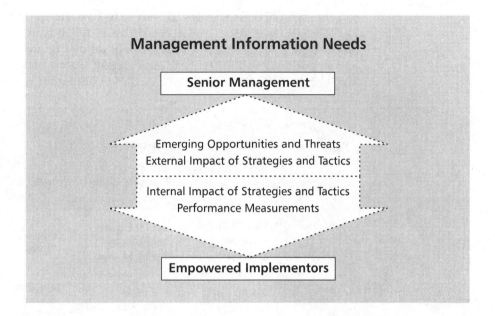

opportunities and threats and continue to monitor the success and impact of strategies and tactics. The flow of traditional performance data would change, as would the interpretation of the impact of strategies and tactics to formulate change in either or both of these factors.

✦✦✦ THE BUSINESS PLAN

The term "business plan" means many things to many people. It spans the range from the document that describes the vision, mission and strategies for the company, to the document that is prepared for bankers or vendor capitalists when a company is trying to raise money. It is used in a less ambitious way within this book: It is the part of the process that deals with the allocation of resources—money (capital and expense funds) and head count (people). In some companies it would be called an operating plan or even a budget. The term is used to reflect the final step of the vision-strategy-tactics-business plan process. Business plans do serve as policy statements because they reinforce or refute the real intentions of those running a business. Where money and head count are allocated reminds people within an organization what is really important.

✦✦✦ INFORMATION TECHNOLOGY-BASED STRATEGIES

A primary focus of this book is on where and how information technology can support successful business strategies. A structured methodology will be addressed in Section III, but it is appropriate and even necessary to highlight successful companies at this point. Business strategies are dynamic and subject to rapid change. The following are offered in support and as evidence of the fact that information systems contribute directly to business success. For a summary of these companies see Figure 7-6.

Figure 7-6

Matrix structure based on concepts presented by F. Warren McFarlan.

IT-Based Strategies		
	Marketplace	**Operations**
Significant Structural Change	Federal Express USA Today Charles Schwab	Whirlpool Xerox
Traditional Products and Processes	USAA L.L. Bean McKesson	Banc One Boeing Frito-Lay Wal-Mart

Significant Structural Change to the Marketplace

There is little question that Federal Express, *USA Today* and Charles Schwab have used information technology to support business strategies that resulted in fundamental change in their respective industries. While the U.S. Post Office has been in the mail delivery business for a long time, Federal Express was the creator of the time-sensitive, air-freight delivery industry. *USA Today* became the first general-interest, national newspaper in the United States. Charles Schwab pioneered the discount brokerage industry and has been its leader in both size and innovative use of information systems since practically its very beginning.

Significant Structural Change to Operations

Whirlpool's global vision, which was addressed in the previous chapter, certainly changed its marketing, product, operational and information systems strategies. The fight that Xerox went through in the 1980s with Japanese competitors, which will be discussed in Chapter 16, was both dramatic and successful. Management by fact became a standard within Xerox, and information systems played a major supportive role in operating in this manner.

Redefining Traditional Products and Processes for the Marketplace

Both USAA and L.L. Bean have placed a major part of their customer service strategies on information technology. L.L. Bean was the first mail order company in the United States to provide 800-number telephone service to its customers. The same can be said for USAA in servicing its members given the fact that it has no field insurance agents. USAA is driving growth through an expansion of products and services versus the traditional approach of attracting new members. It gives a high priority to creating and using information systems that are customer convenient, operator efficient and cost effective. L.L. Bean continues to pursue a strategy of managed growth, continual quality improvement and the best possible customer service. Its information systems play a major role in managing its mailing lists, order entry and inventory management.

McKesson Corporation, the largest pharmaceutical wholesaler in the United States, has been a long-time provider of its Economost order entry system for independent drug stores and, more recently, hospitals.

Redefining Traditional Operational Processes

Banc One has grown significantly as a regional bank from its home base in Columbus, Ohio. This has been accomplished through an aggressive acquisition program and an equally aggressive use of information systems. If there is a new information technology that makes sense for the banking industry, Banc One will be a leader in its implementation and use.

Boeing has a fundamental strategy these days: Beat Airbus! Speed to market, customer-specific product features and cost control are key competitive factors. Sharing R&D risks through alliances with other companies is also key to future product development. Boeing's use of computers to design and build the 777, as described in Chapter 1, had dramatic and significant effects on its battle with Airbus for supremacy in the world's commercial aircraft industry.

Frito-Lay continues to drive growth through an aggressive international expansion program. They have also emphasized reducing costs in the United States to preserve double-digit profit margins. Frito-Lay plans to stay focused on core products while basing competitive strategies at a regional level. It receives a major assist in its marketing, customer service and product management from a route sales representative system that involves a hand-held computer as a major tool to manage products, routes and customers.

For the past two decades Wal-Mart growth has seemed as inevitable as death and taxes. Its current strategy includes expansion in both the U.S. and international markets. It continues to emphasize everyday low prices, "buy American" and innovation in the way it does business.

Quick, decisive execution is then the way that it makes things happen, including its superior computer-based inventory management and distribution system.

✦✦✦ AN INFORMATION-ORIENTED INFRASTRUCTURE IS KEY TO A RESPONSIVE COMPETITIVE STRATEGY

The business environment where many companies find themselves is dictating a need to build an information-oriented infrastructure that will enhance the ability to respond to changing business conditions and market demands. While the specifics of the infrastructure would depend on the particular company, it would include the factors identified in Figure 7-7. There is a definite information technology influence to the factors as they become increasingly vital where companies find it necessary to respond quickly in everything they do.

Figure 7-7

Company Infrastructure

- Data Management
- User Applications
- Voice Management
- Network Management
- Planning Process
- Financial Strategy
- Organization

Data Management

Managing data is what information systems are all about. Providing access to timely, accurate and cost-effective data is the basic reason for most information systems. Business pressures have increased the demand for information (data) in many organizations. An inability to provide needed information, and lengthy lead times required to develop the systems to provide the information, often result in criticism of the information systems organization. Anticipating user information needs has always been a challenge, but decision support systems can be built to at least satisfy some information needs including one-time report requests.

Building "data warehouses" is also often a good hedge against a long lead time to respond to user and management information needs. A data warehouse is a centralized data repository where multiple types of company data are extracted from working files periodically (daily, weekly, etc.) and organized to facilitate user access for queries, one-time reports and other information. Companies such as Intel also include external business information obtained from information service companies as part of this approach.

User Applications

The primary value of information technology is the support of applications for users. These fall into the category of functional support (engineering, manufacturing, accounting and finance, marketing, etc.) or individual support (desktop applications like word processing, spreadsheets, groupware, etc.). Value to customer (users) dictates the significance and benefits of information systems as a support service.

Voice Management

Effective communication, whether it is voice, E-mail, data access, videoconferencing or multimedia, has become an important business success factor. Creating the necessary infrastructure to support this communication is often critically important.

Network Management

When telecommunications, addressed in Chapter 11, become a mission-critical resource within a company, it is necessary to manage it to assure high levels of availability and performance of the network. A company can do this itself or contract with a service organization to manage the network.

Planning Process

Integrating information systems into the business planning process, addressed in Chapter 15, becomes necessary when information systems become an integral part of a competitive strategy. Business strategies dictate information systems strategies, but the planning process can become the glue that keeps the two synchronized.

Financial Strategy and Organization

How does an organization afford, justify and pay for information systems, particularly when the annual cost becomes quite large? Financial strategy, addressed in Chapter 14, is becoming an increasingly important issue in many companies.

Organization includes the structure for the information systems organization that will provide the best results within a company. It also includes the working relationship between information systems organization and user management. A third and very important factor is the company culture and how this influences the use of information technology within the company. This is discussed further in Chapter 13.

♦♦♦ MOVING FROM PLAN TO ACTION

Where possible a strategy should be kept relatively simple. Complex strategies are more difficult to implement, and the ultimate test of any strategy is based on its successful implementation. Implementing a successful strategy starts with gaining understanding, acceptance and support by people within the company. It must then accomplish its objectives by providing direct or indirect value to customers.

♦♦♦ CONCLUSION

Business strategies do not compete with the use of information systems. The goal is for the business strategy to be successful with the support of information systems. Keep in mind that business strategies can work without the use of information systems. Information systems can never be successful as a competitive resource if they do not support the right business strategies.

RECOMMENDED READING

Dunham, Andrea, and Barry Marcus with Mark Stevens and Patrick Barwise, *Unique Value: The Secret of All Great Business Strategies.* New York: Macmillan, 1993.

As suggested by the title, this book focuses on creating unique value as an essential factor for a company to be successful in today's global business world. A unique value strategy focuses the business on five fundamentals required for successful execution as well as profitability. The five fundamentals were discussed on pages 133–134 of this chapter. Done right, this planning process prioritizes the allocation of resources and functional responsibilities to where they are most valuable.

Hamel, Gary, and C.K. Prahalad, *Competing for the Future: Breakthrough Strategies for Seizing Control of Your Industry and Creating the Markets of Tomorrow.* Boston: Harvard Business School Press, 1994.

With downsizing and outsourcing becoming high-priority considerations within many companies, the concept of core competencies becomes a critical consideration. The material on this concept alone would justify reading this book. Added value comes from the discussion of strategic intent and mapping industry evolution.

Hamel, Gary, and C.K. Prahalad, "Strategic Intent." *Harvard Business Review*, May-June 1989, p. 63.

According to the authors of this article, "The lesson is clear: Assessing the current tactical advantages of known competitors will not help you understand the resolution, stamina and inventiveness of potential competitors." Achieving and sustaining competitive success dictates "focusing the organization's attention on the essence of winning; motivating people by communicating the value of the target; leaving room for individual and team contributions; sustaining enthusiasm by providing new operational definitions as circumstances change; and using intent consistently to guide resource allocations."

Nolan, Richard L., and David C. Croson, *Creative Destruction: A Six-Stage Process for Transforming the Organization*. Boston: Harvard Business School Press, 1995.

As suggested by the title, this is a six-stage process to enable a company to change to meet the demands of the current business environment. It identifies a set of twenty management principles to build a network organization to move into the 21st century. Factors like leadership, organization of tasks, cycle time, communication, value creation, and rewards correlate with competitive success and a solid financial performance. The six stages deal with downsizing, seeking a dynamic balance, developing a market access strategy, becoming market driven, developing a market foreclosure strategy and pursuing a global scope. This book is vintage Dick Nolan.

Ohmae, Kenichi, *The Mind of the Strategist: Business Planning for Competitive Advantage*. New York: McGraw-Hill, 1982.

Once again we are reminded that the objective of strategy is to bring about the conditions most favorable to one's own side. Ohmae concludes that successful business strategies result not from rigorous analysis but from a particular state of mind. Successful strategies use analysis to stimulate the creative process, but maintain an intellectual elasticity or flexibility to come up with realistic responses to changing situations. While emphasizing that insight is essential, a successful strategy takes method, mental discipline and hard work. Limits are set by reality, timing and resources. Reality is based on an awareness of customers, competitors and company competence. The timing must be right for a proposed strategy, and a company must be sensitive to its own resource limitations. Although the company examples are a bit dated this book is still worth the time to consider its recommendations regarding the creation of a successful business strategy.

Parker, Marilyn M., H. Edgar Trainor, and Robert J. Benson, *Information Strategy and Economics*. Englewood Cliffs, NJ: Prentice-Hall, 1989.

The source for additional background on the model presented in Figure 7-2.

Ries, Al, and Jack Trout, *Positioning: The Battle for Your Mind*. New York: McGraw-Hill, 1986.

You might have trouble finding this book, but any of the four books by these two authors provides short, insightful business stories that are interesting and helpful if you are looking for a way to add to your understanding of successful business strategies. The authors are advertising executives at their own firm and they do a good job of communicating key factors on competitive battles.

Stalk, George, Jr., and Thomas M. Hout, *Competing Against Time: How Time-based Competition Is Reshaping Global Markets*. New York: The Free Press, 1990.

This does an excellent job of addressing time as a competitive factor. In simple terms it says, "Give customers what they want when they want it." Don't base your performance only on quality and costs, but on quality, costs and responsiveness. The strategic implications of compressing time are productivity increases, an ability to raise prices, a reduction of risks and an increase in market share. Specific material on Wal-Mart provides a perspective of the success of the world's largest retailer.

Trimble, Vance H., *Sam Walton: The Inside Story of America's Richest Man.* New York: Penguin, 1990.

This is actually better than Sam Walton's autobiography. It is objective but presents the Sam Walton story in the positive light that it deserves.

EXERCISES

1. Business strategy model.

Prepare a model similar to the one presented in Figure 4-1 in Chapter 4, that logically structures the major strategy decisions that would need to be made within a specific industry.

2. Business strategies built on information systems platforms.

Identify and document companies that fall within each of the four quadrants shown in Figure 7-6, where a business strategy was possible because information systems played a major enabling role.

3. Strategy implementation, managing for results and information needs.

Use Figures 7-2, 7-3 and 7-4 to explain the challenge of posturing business planning so that it is dynamic and responsive to the competitive business environment. What are the major benefits to be gained and issues to be addressed to realize them?

4. Transition from vision to strategy and tactics.

Evaluate a specific company to determine how they make the transition from vision to strategy to tactics. Which part of this process do they feel they are doing particularly well? Where do they encounter major difficulties and need improvement? Do they feel that the time frame for the entire process is getting shorter?

SECTION III

THE THIRD PERSPECTIVE: THE USE OF INFORMATION SYSTEMS

This third section provides the structure to be used to analyze the use of information systems within an enterprise to gain a competitive advantage. It begins with a model, the Strategic Option Generator, which can be used to gain an understanding of the overall approach. It concludes with the use of the Success Factor Profile to highlight key factors that played a significant role in realizing a competitive advantage through the use of information systems. The Roles, Roles and Relationships and Redefine/Define concepts are at the core of the analysis of factors that can lead to the successful competitive use of information systems. Telecommunications is also addressed as a common delivery process to provide value to customers.

Consistent with the approach used throughout the book, the concepts are presented and then supported by company examples. The specific company examples are provided to help gain a better understanding of the concepts while also supporting their practical use.

The following model, introduced in Chapter 1, is repeated to summarize the five elements (bottom box) that combine to provide a systematic approach to complete this structured analysis.

A Systematic Approach

Vision

Strategy

Tactics

Business Plan

- Competitive Options
- Roles, Roles and Relationships
- Redefine/Define
- Telecommunications
  as the Delivery Vehicle
- Success Factor Profile

EVALUATING BUSINESS STRATEGIES AND THE USE OF INFORMATION SYSTEMS: THE STRATEGIC OPTION GENERATOR

Opportunity: A good chance for progress or success.
Noah Webster

LEARNING OBJECTIVES

This chapter presents the first of the five elements of the analysis structure provided in this book. It is a systematic way to look at the overall approach taken by a specific company in its use of information systems to gain a competitive advantage. The Strategic Option Generator can also be used effectively to identify strategic opportunities. As with all concepts provided in this book, it is helpful to apply the Option Generator to a specific company.

QUESTIONS

Some appropriate questions to consider in evaluating the pursuit of business opportunities and the use of information systems:

1. What was the primary target of the business strategy?
2. What was the primary business strategy?
3. Did information systems support a better implementation of the new business strategy?
4. Was there an advantage in being first?
5. What was the business and technical risk?
6. Who are the actual users of the new information system?

✦✦✦ STRATEGIC OPTION GENERATOR

The **Strategic Option Generator** illustrated in Figure 8-1 is a conceptual model that was developed by Charles Wiseman of Columbia University to identify business opportunities; more specifically, to identify strategic opportunities involving the use of information systems.[1] It can also be used to evaluate organizations that have successfully used information systems to gain a competitive advantage. While not minimizing its value as a vehicle for identifying new opportunities, this chapter will focus on

Figure 8-1

Reprinted, with permission, from Wiseman, *Strategy and Computers,* p. 57.

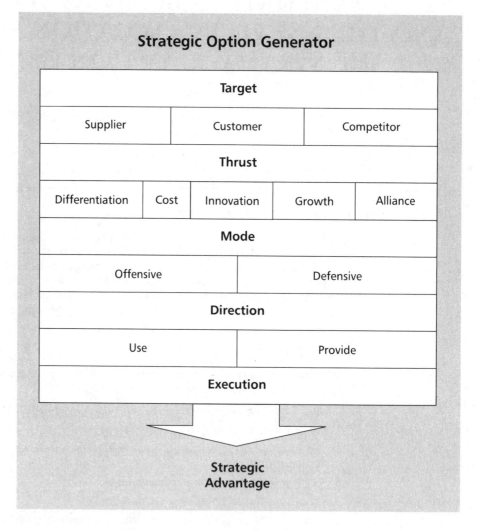

---

[1] Wiseman, Charles, *Strategy and Computers: Information Systems as Competitive Weapons,* New York: Dow Jones-Irwin, 1985.

using the model to understand and explain approaches taken by successful organizations.

The Strategic Option Generator starts by identifying a business target and continues through subsequent layers of thrust, mode and direction. The use of information systems becomes more obvious and more significant as you progress through the model. An analysis of each of the layers builds the case for the combination of factors that made it possible for an enterprise to achieve and sustain a competitive advantage through the use of information systems.

Strategic Targets

There are three possible strategic targets that companies choose when using information systems to gain a competitive advantage. They are customer, competitor and supplier. Some organizations have focused on multiple targets, but it is helpful to identify and understand the primary target. The real value in using the Strategic Option Generator is to understand the focus and logic of a major business strategy that resulted in the successful use of information systems.

Evaluating whether customer or competitor is the primary target can be confusing since most competitive strategies are directly or indirectly focused on competition. In making this evaluation, start with the objective (target) of the business strategy. Also keep in mind how the information systems were used to achieve and sustain a competitive advantage.

An interesting test of this logic is the Saturn operation within General Motors. Why did GM initiate the Saturn project? Saturn, as an organization, was clearly created to beat the Japanese in the small car market. This would seem to make the competitor the target, but what about customers? Weren't Saturn's many efforts targeted at designing, manufacturing, marketing, selling and supporting a product that their customers would buy, like and tell their friends about? Obviously, yes. But the true target, the primary driving business strategy, was to beat the Japanese in the small car market. *Competitor* is the logical choice as the primary target.

Still, a large number of organizations have identified *customer* as their primary target. USAA's image processing system was another step towards providing the best possible service to their members (customers). L.L. Bean's emphasis on 800 numbers as a link to customers along with a computer-based order entry and distribution system was also targeted at customers.

When Federal Express initiated its "absolutely, positively" overnight delivery service, supported by a tracking system through the entire delivery process, who did they target? Since they were the first company to base a business on this strategy, their primary target was *customer*. United Parcel Service (UPS), with all of its success in ground transportation, decided to compete directly with Federal Express in overnight delivery. The fact that it was trying to offset a competitive advantage held by Federal Express dictates that its primary strategy was *competitor.*

Gannett introduced *USA Today* as the first national, general-interest newspaper in the United States. Their business strategy was not to compete directly with local publications, since they did not address local news, but targeted customers who found value in timely, nationally focused articles. Their success with business travelers is well documented.

Singapore Airlines is another interesting evaluation. As an airline with an outstanding reputation for customer service, was their implementation of a computer-based passenger reservation system yet another example of this business strategy? Recognizing that their Abacus reservation system was implemented in 1988, at a time when global competition was increasing, a logical case can be made that this was a response to competitive services from other airlines. Their primary target was *competitor.*

The Boeing decision to design their wide-body 777 aircraft with a paperless, computer-based system was in direct response to the threat of Airbus. Their primary target? *Competitor.*

A logical and simple bit of advice with regard to this evaluation is: "When in doubt, think customer." If the company is an innovator with a new business strategy supported by information systems, then you are probably very safe in concluding that *customer* is the target. If the company is challenging a competitor's strategy and/or success, then the primary target is *competitor.*

What about suppliers? With outsourcing receiving so much attention in recent years, and with the success of Electronic Data Interchange (EDI) in industries like retailing, *supplier* becomes a stronger possibility as a primary target or as a strong second choice.

Thrust

Thrust deals with business strategies. This entire layer is based on Michael Porter's competitive strategy concepts. As Porter advocates, differentiation and cost are the two primary business strategy options that a company can implement. In evaluating a specific company, one of these two factors must be selected as the basis for a competitive strategy. Selecting cost recognizes that least-cost leadership is the primary competitive strategy. Many companies have discovered how many winners there are when least cost is the primary strategy; only one—the company with the lowest cost. Is Wal-Mart out to prove that, as difficult as it is to compete on a least-cost basis, it can be done successfully on a very large scale? Everyday low prices drive many of the priorities within Wal-Mart including the emphasis and focus of information systems.

A company succeeds in differentiating itself from its competitors by uniquely providing value to customers. Sources of differentiation can be product features or functions, price/performance, customer support, repair service, quality, and information content and/or support. One or more of these factors add up to customer value because it lowers the customer's cost or improves performance.

In addition to either cost or differentiation, companies can select none, one or even all three of the other competitive strategy options. Growth is self-explanatory. The important question is whether growth truly played a major role in the formation of a business strategy. It certainly did in the earlier days at Charles Schwab as well as Wal-Mart, *USA Today* and Federal Express.

Innovation is often a primary factor for companies that placed a major emphasis on supporting a business strategy with information systems. These companies clearly avoided implementing status quo systems but took advantage of information technology to support strategies that addressed targets in a unique way.

Alliances come in all shapes and sizes these days. Mergers or equity positions are the most obvious, but they can also take the form of joint research agreements, cross-licensing, marketing partnerships, etc. They can also include not only private sector companies but universities, research organizations, governments and associations.

Mode: Offensive or Defensive?

Did the company lead or did they follow someone else in both business strategy and information systems use? What were the implications of the mode they chose? The risk implications of these questions should not be minimized. There can be both business and technology risk in being the first to offer a new product or service that includes information systems support. The question is, what were the risks involved in being first? If they chose to follow, the technical risks could be less since the approach has been proven by someone else. However, the business risk could be significantly higher with a "me second" strategy.

Direction

Direction is a misleading term for this layer. The most important consideration at this point is identifying the users of the information system. If the users are within the boundaries of the specific company, then the answer is *use*. If the use of the system extends beyond the boundaries of the company that is providing the information system, it is *provide*. As was addressed earlier in the discussion of interorganizational systems, it is common for internal systems to be pushed beyond the boundaries of the originating company. This is certainly true with airlines and their reservation systems. They were originally used by the airline's reservation agents, and later extended to travel agents. Electronic Data Interchange (EDI) systems start as internal purchasing and accounts payable information systems and are extended beyond the boundaries to include vendors. In these cases, both *use* and *provide* aptly describe these companies.

Execution

How does the Strategic Option Generator help to better understand the use of information systems to compete? It systematically walks you through an evaluation process that highlights key elements. First the target needed to be correctly identified. Then the right strategy (thrust) had to be selected. A decision was then made as to whether the organization wanted to be a leader or a follower with a business strategy that included information systems use. Finally, appropriate users of the new system were identified based on the importance, implications and benefits of this choice. Having accomplished all of this, companies were then in the position to make things happen—to execute. Were they successful? If so, why? The marketplace is always the deciding factor as to whether a company gains a competitive advantage. This is the case whether information systems are involved or not.

✦✦✦ ANALYZING FEDERAL EXPRESS USING THE STRATEGIC OPTION GENERATOR

A summary of the use of the Strategic Option Generator is provided in Figure 8-2, which compares Federal Express to UPS. Starting with Federal Express, as the originator of today's overnight air express industry, the primary elements of the Strategic Option Generator include:

Target: For Federal Express the target was *customer* because their strategy was to create a new type of service for the delivery of time-sensitive shipments.

Thrust: Their thrust (strategy) was definitely *differentiation* because their goal was to provide a new, unique service. FedEx is in the logistics business. They recognize that their customers value what is inside of their boxes and packages. They also deal with the movement of and information about shipments from the original source to the ultimate destination. In addition to differentiation Federal Express also pursued a strategy that focused on *innovation* and *growth*. Innovation had a strong presence in both their business strategy and their own design of key information technology. Growth was an essential factor for this capital-intensive business.

Figure 8-2

Adapted from Wiseman, *Strategy and Computers*, p. 57.

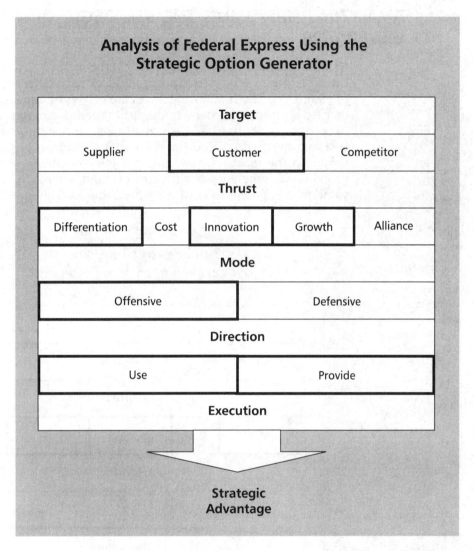

Analysis of Federal Express Using the Strategic Option Generator

Target		
Supplier	Customer	Competitor

Thrust				
Differentiation	Cost	Innovation	Growth	Alliance

Mode	
Offensive	Defensive

Direction	
Use	Provide

Execution

Strategic Advantage

Mode: In both business strategy and the use of information systems, FedEx was on the *offensive*. They have been and continue to be leaders in the offering of new services and the way in which they are supported by information systems.

Direction: As is often the case, the information systems within FedEx were initially developed and used by their own employees, so the direction would be *use*. They subsequently extended the use of their systems (Powership) to their larger and/or more frequent customers, who can request the pickup of a shipment, track it through the delivery process and even "bill themselves" (Powership Plus), so direction is also *provide*.

✦✦✦ ANALYZING UPS USING THE STRATEGIC OPTION GENERATOR

Using the same model to analyze UPS, the arch rival of Federal Express in the air express delivery business, produces very different results as shown in Figure 8-3. The major differences are driven by the fact that UPS implemented a business strategy to duplicate the information content in its delivery processes that had proven to be so successful for Federal Express. UPS had been convinced for years that its industrial engineering efforts produced the most efficient and cost-effective delivery processes. A basic problem stemmed from this attitude and approach. Customers found value in being able to confirm where their shipments were at any point

Figure 8-3

Adapted from Wiseman, *Strategy and Computers*, p. 57.

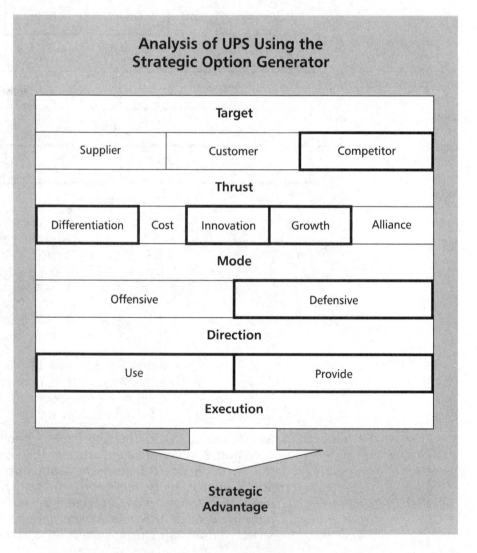

Analysis of UPS Using the Strategic Option Generator

in the delivery process. For this reason FedEx had claimed a dominant position in the overnight delivery market segment.

Target: For UPS the target was *competitor.* They had decided that to command a significant amount of market share in the time sensitive, overnight shipping business, they had to support the delivery process with information content. In other words, they were trying to gain lost market share from Federal Express.

Thrust: While UPS was attempting to provide service support similar to Federal Express, they were implementing a *differentiation* strategy to distinguish them from the many other shipping competitors. They were also trying to say, "We have leap-frogged the capabilities of FedEx." They also emphasized *growth* and *innovation* in support of their differentiation strategy.

Mode: Playing catch-up to FedEx put UPS in a *defensive* mode. Their obvious strategy is to shift from defensive to offensive as they prove their capabilities in the marketplace.

Direction: The current primary users of UPS systems are their own employees, so the direction is *use.* They are also extending the use of their systems to their larger customers, so it is also *provide.*

✦✦✦ CONCLUSION

This chapter will be concluded by pointing out some of the common mistakes that are made in using the Strategic Option Generator to analyze a company. Most companies target customers directly and competitors indirectly, so this part of the analysis is fairly straightforward. A frequent mistake is made in determining the thrust of the company. Differentiation *or* cost can be selected, but not both. According to Porter one or the other must be selected. Beyond differentiation or cost, none or any combination of the other three thrust options can be logically included. Mode is also an either/or determination. The company is either a leader or a follower in using information systems in support of a business strategy. Be sure to make the transition at this point between the business strategy and the use of information systems to support the strategy.

Mistakes are often made in determining the direction. This concerns the use of information systems. If it was for the company's own employees, then the choice is *use.* If the systems use was intended for other than the company's employees, the selection should be *provide.* If the use of the information system is both for employees and beyond the boundaries of the company, it can be both *use* and *provide.*

Effective execution must follow to realize the competitive objectives that are being pursued.

RECOMMENDED READING

Porter, Michael E., *Competitive Advantage: Creating and Sustaining Superior Performance*. New York: The Free Press, 1985.

Provides background for the thrust layer of the Strategic Option Generator in addition to material on the value chain.

Wiseman, Charles, *Strategy and Computers: Information Systems as Competitive Weapons*. New York: Dow Jones-Irwin, 1985.

Useful for background regarding the Strategic Option Generator and its use to identify strategic opportunities.

EXERCISES

1. Company evaluation using the Strategic Option Generator.

Prepare an analysis of a company of your choice using the Strategic Option Generator to evaluate after-the-fact what was actually accomplished.

2. Evaluation of American Airlines and Singapore Airlines using the Strategic Option Generator.

Prepare an analysis of American Airlines and Singapore Airlines using the Strategic Option Generator.

3. Strategic Option Generator as a planning tool for the future.

Be prepared to discuss how the Strategic Option Generator can be used to identify and develop strategies that are based on the use of information systems.

9

THE ROLES, ROLES AND RELATIONSHIPS CONCEPT

Information systems are strategic weapons, not cost centers.

Robert F. McDermott
Former CEO
USAA

LEARNING OBJECTIVES

This chapter provides an explanation of Roles, Roles and Relationships as one of the two core concepts of the analysis structure used in this book. Examples are included to illustrate its use with actual companies. After understanding the concept, a student should be able to use it when evaluating a company to assess the significance of the roles played by individuals in using information systems to gain a competitive advantage. Important concepts related to the role of information systems are the "business within a business" approach for the information systems organization and technology transfer through organizational learning.

QUESTIONS

Appropriate questions regarding the Roles, Roles and Relationship concept to gain a competitive advantage through the use of information systems include:

1. What organizational leadership is necessary to gain a competitive advantage through the use of information systems?

2. How does an organization determine the appropriate use of information systems to gain a competitive advantage on an ongoing basis?

3. Does a specific event, activity or person tend to trigger the start of a program that emphasizes the competitive use of information systems?

4. Can an organization sustain a competitive advantage that is built on an information system?

5. Is this a broad-based approach or is the successful use of competitive information tied to a small number of people playing key roles?

6. Does outsourcing the management of information systems impact its possible use as a competitive resource?

✦✦✦ USING INFORMATION SYSTEMS TO COMPETE DICTATES AN ESSENTIAL PARTNERSHIP

As businesses march towards the 21st century the issue of competing is a top priority for most, if not all, executives. But what about information systems? Are information systems part of the business competitive equation? Should they be? How do you explain the success that specific companies have achieved through the use of information systems? At the same time, why is this same subject a point of frustration for other companies who are not able to harness the competitive use of information systems successfully?

Intuitively one concludes that if information systems are to be used to gain a competitive advantage, those executives charged with determining the business strategies must also determine why and where information systems should be used to compete. This is why it is essential to establish an ongoing working relationship between senior management, who identify the business need, and the information systems organization that implements the systems that deliver the support to meet the needs of the business.

There are some outstanding examples of U.S. organizations that have achieved a competitive advantage through the effective use of information systems. Some, like Banc One, Federal Express, Frito-Lay, Charles Schwab, Visa International and Wal-Mart, have been on the success list for a long time. Others, like American Presidents Companies, Boeing, Blockbuster Entertainment, Men's Wearhouse, The Progressive Corp., Saturn Corp. of General Motors, Singapore Airlines, UPS and *USA Today*, are more recent additions.

A conclusion reached over the author's twelve years of research is that successful companies share common characteristics. It is also a fact that the difference between the organizations that have succeeded in this area, and those that are still not sure if or how they should proceed, is growing larger. This raises several questions, but the most important is: Why and how have the leaders succeeded in applying information technology to their key competitive endeavors?

✦✦✦ ROLES, ROLES AND RELATIONSHIPS

Because of the dynamics of competitive environments, there are distinct differences in the approaches taken by the organizations cited above. Nevertheless, a common theme runs through all of these success stories, which can be explained by the concept of **Roles, Roles and Relationships** described below:

✦ **The role of information systems:** Their role is focused on competitive priorities.

✦ **The role of senior management:** They play a major part in positioning and prioritizing the competitive role of information systems.

✦ **The relationship:** The above two factors confirm that an ongoing working relationship between senior management and the information systems organization is imperative in order to sustain the successful use of information systems to compete.

The Role of the Senior Executive

By no means do senior executives need to become computer technicians. Understanding computer usage conceptually certainly helps, but the key role that the senior manager must play is to provide a long-term vision for the future of the business. This is simply acknowledging the primary responsibility of the senior executive to assure the long-term viability of the business. The communication of this direction to the information systems organization is a crucial starting point. To be able to personally accept the appropriateness of an increased emphasis on the use of information systems, it is necessary for senior management to recognize the value of information to the organization. The importance of data as an organizational resource is at the heart of this decision. If it is decided that it is an important resource, then through words, actions and deeds the senior manager must personally sponsor and participate in selling the importance of information systems within the organization.

Major information systems that address business requirements must be funded and properly staffed. After the above factors have been addressed by senior management, these same executives must realize that this attention to information systems use is not an event, but an ongoing requirement.

When information systems are implemented, the job of realizing the benefits is just beginning. Senior management can make a major contribution through motivating people within the organization to make things happen and managing this effort with an expectation that results and benefits will be achieved.

The Role of Other Senior Management (Managers of Major Business Functions)

In addition to participating in some of the activities cited above, functional management must understand the competitive role of information systems within the organization. It is their job to identify and specify requirements for new systems. In most organizations they must also provide the financial justification. Paying for these systems, through the budget process, usually is the responsibility of these same managers. User or functional managers must also act like they own any systems within their area of responsibility. They must demonstrate this attitude of ownership by sponsoring their information systems on an ongoing basis.

The Role of the IS Executive and the IS Organization

The mission statement below is very consistent with this entire concept and spells out how the information systems organization should posture itself.

Information Systems Organization Mission Statement
To assure that the corporation's present as well as future demands for information, information processes, information systems and computer-based technologies are provided in such a manner that the daily conduct of the business will not be impacted and that the future business opportunities can be capitalized on and managed by the corporation.

As the use of information systems both increases and becomes broader in scope, there is a corresponding increase in contact between the information systems organization and user personnel. This dictates the need for the information systems organization to be postured as a service and support operation in both fact and the perception of user personnel. There is no question that major benefits can accrue to an organization if the information systems executive can function as a member of the senior management team. To serve in this capacity enables the information systems executive to provide an understanding of the realm of the possible, feasible and achievable with information systems through direct, personal knowledge of key business and organizational factors.

The Role of the Users of Information Systems

Operational level people, as users of information systems, make things happen. They are the actual achievers of any competitive advantage through the use of systems. In many cases the users of the systems play a very major role within the entire process. The Roles, Roles and Relationships chart is presented in Figure 9-1.

Figure 9-1

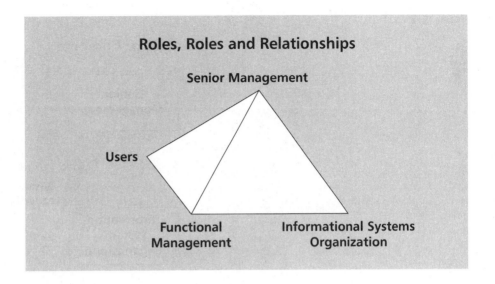

Relationships

Establishing and maintaining an ongoing working relationship between senior management and the information systems executive can be accomplished in multiple ways. It can be integral to the way that the business is managed. Information systems would be addressed as a high-priority resource within the organization and receive appropriate senior management attention. Another option would be a formal, structured approach that would specifically focus on information systems. This could be done by establishing a senior management steering committee. This group would meet on a regularly scheduled basis to maintain a level of awareness of information systems activities and provide advice and counsel to the information systems organization. Steering committees will be discussed further in Chapter 13.

Whether the approach is integral to managing the business or a more formal structure, the objective remains the same: to maintain an ongoing working relationship between those that run the business and those that provide information systems support.

Few executives running companies can provide both business and information systems leadership. Realistically you cannot expect to find clones of Bob McDermott of USAA in a large number of companies. Even today a senior executive who has the ability to envision the future of the business and the role of information systems is unusual. A practical approach is shown in Figure 9-2. Senior management needs to make it a priority to provide business leadership to the information systems organization by communicating business direction and priorities. The information systems organization must then provide information technology leadership to those running the business. They need to articulate the

Figure 9-2

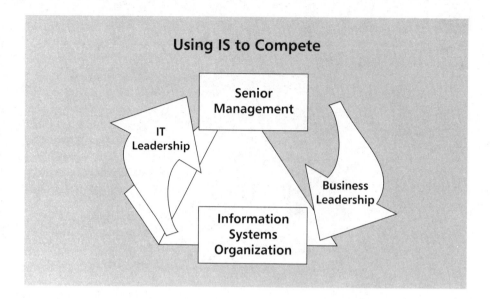

realm of the possible, feasible, implementable and affordable use of information technology to address business needs.

If both of these leadership efforts become an ongoing activity, then the organization has achieved the essential partnership to pursue a competitive advantage through the use of information systems.

✦✦✦ TECHNOLOGY TRANSFER THROUGH ORGANIZATIONAL LEARNING

Educators have studied learning curves for years. This basic concept applies to information systems. An important dimension of the introduction of a new information system is the ability of users to learn how to effectively use it. Both the information systems organization and user management need to understand the following principle, which is the basis for the successful transfer of information technology to users:

There is a direct correlation between the successful introduction of a new information system within an organization and the learning curve of the primary users.

This organizational learning is one of three learning curves that are developing in parallel (see Figure 9-3). A second learning curve deals with the

Figure 9-3

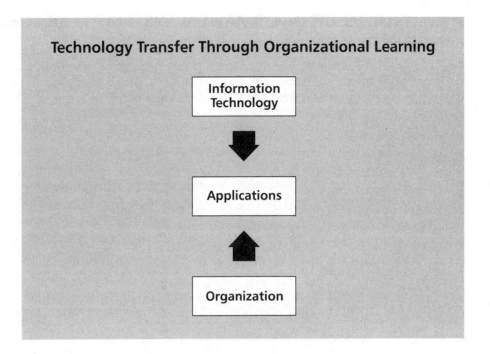

Technology Transfer Through Organizational Learning

design, development and manufacturing of information technology. As with all learning curves, the engineers that are part of this process do not start over when they attempt to design a better product. They build on an existing knowledge base and product capabilities. Some technological products are totally innovative and new, but far more are extensions and enhancements of existing products. Information technology is going through a learning curve.

In addition, while there are times when a new application is completely new, more often new applications are extensions or enhancements of those already in place. They also follow a learning curve. The new applications take advantage of better price/performance of the hardware and software while providing new capabilities and functions.

A concern prompted by these multiple curves is that the technology curve is outdistancing the organizational learning curve. Continual and impressive improvement is being provided by the information technology companies. Things like larger memory and faster internal processing speeds provide improvements in the ease of use of microprocessors. Beyond this, can users keep pace with the technology enhancements, or are they really using a relatively small percentage of the capabilities that they already have? If users do not keep pace there is less reason to pursue application enhancements, which minimizes the potential for new applications even though they might represent significant return to the company.

✦✦✦ PHASES OF INFORMATION SYSTEMS MANAGEMENT

The participation of management is often a function of where the organization is within a three-phase process of direction, conceptual approach and specific approach. Figure 9-4 shows this process based on an allocation of a total of 10 points in each phase in terms of management responsibility.

Figure 9-4

Using IS to Compete: Primary Responsibilities

	Direction	Conceptual Approach	Specific Approach
Senior Management	7	2	1
Functional Management	2	5	4
IS Management	1	3	5
	10	10	10

Direction

Any major new information system must be positioned by the direction (vision and strategy) of the business. There is only one place where you can obtain this and that is from senior management. Logic would suggest that at least 70% of this effort (7 of 10 points) will come directly from senior management. They could seek input from functional management and information systems management, but the primary responsibility and input for determining direction rests with senior management.

Conceptual Approach

If a direction is determined and a project is authorized to address this through the use of information systems, a conceptual approach must be determined. If the new system will focus on manufacturing, then the management of that function will play a key role. Senior management retains responsibility for final approval, and information systems management provides guidance regarding information technology.

Specific Approach

At this point there would be an approved project, so senior management would play less of a role. In this phase the roles of functional and information systems management are subject to some debate. A possible issue is, which group should have the primary leadership role in this phase? The specifics of the project and the organization need to be understood to determine this. A general case can be made in favor of functional management having a primary responsibility for the implementation of a major new system within their area. On the other hand, a strong information systems manager could logically have the primary responsibility while doing a good job of interfacing with the functional management. Either way, a working partnership between information systems and functional management is an important element in successfully implementing major new systems.

✦✦✦ MAKING THINGS HAPPEN: CAPITALIZING ON INFORMATION SYSTEMS OPPORTUNITY

A new emphasis on the use of information systems in an organization does not just happen. Something or someone makes it happen. While there needs to be a receptiveness, a readiness to change, often a specific factor will actually initiate action. These initiators, illustrated in Figure 9-5, can be categorized into three areas: (1) a threat to the business, (2) the personal power of a senior manager or (3) the need for business process improvements.

Figure 9-5

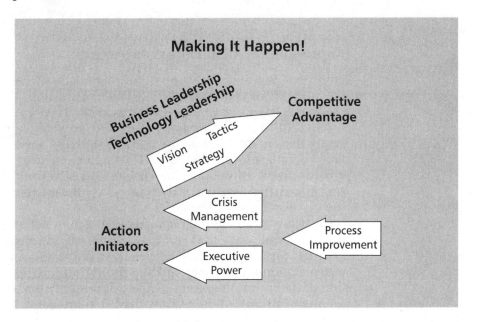

Threat to the Business (Crisis Management)

When Mikhail Gorbachev was trying to sell the people within the Soviet Union on the logic of *perestroika*, he spent a great deal of time emphasizing their problems. Why? Because he was trying to gain their acceptance to the need for change. We even have a management term for this called "crisis management." There are those who say, "If you don't have a crisis within the organization then make one up, because it is one of the best possible ways to get people's attention."

CEO Frank Shrontz, in the midst of the most prosperous time in the history of Boeing, was able to sell his people on the need for a totally new computer-based design system for the 777 aircraft. His explanation of why this was necessary was that Boeing was in a death battle with Airbus, and the new design and manufacturing systems were critical to their corporate survival.

Personal Power

The concept of Roles, Roles and Relationships says a number of things, but probably most important is the role of a senior manager as the business executive sponsor of information systems. Robert McDermott of USAA is a classic example of this type of initiator. Upon being named the new CEO in January of 1969, he met for the first time with the people who reported directly to him. His message included a vision of USAA becoming a paperless insurance company. For the next twenty-four years he was the personal power behind their very ambitious and successful use of information systems.

Improvement of Business Processes

Improving business processes on an ongoing basis has traditionally been the most difficult to accomplish of the three initiators. While this is still the case, the focus on Total Quality Management (TQM) programs and the publicity given to process reengineering have provided a major assist to triggering this approach. As addressed in Chapter 17, information systems can play a significant role with both TQM and reengineering programs. It is a classic win-win situation. The business benefits from the improvements and information systems play a more significant role in contributing to the success of the business.

Pick any company that has gained Malcolm Baldridge Award recognition and you will find good examples of information systems use. Whether this emphasis had efficiency, effectiveness or competitive advantage as a primary objective for the use of information systems is a function of the specific application. You can certainly find competitive success examples within Federal Express, IBM, Motorola and Xerox.

Summary of the Three Options

As indicated above, the most difficult of the three initiators is the improvement of business processes. This is particularly true if the organization has had a period of business and financial success. How do you get employees' attention regarding change when "things seem like they couldn't be better?" Xerox, which invented and owned the technology patents, lost 40% of the U.S. copier market to the Japanese before realizing that they needed to make some major changes in order to remain competitive. Even then it took several years to gain the necessary momentum within the organization to start to effectively address the core problems to turn things around. Xerox is discussed in more detail in Chapter 16.

Threat to the company versus personal power leaves room for debate as to the degree of difficulty in initiating change. In fact you can find company examples that combined all three factors to drive the need for change. Threat is arguably the strongest of the three options for the reasons cited above. On the other hand, the more respected a senior executive, the more likely it is that such a person can get people to accept the need for even significant change.

A Road Map to Business Success

The combination of the initiating event and a receptiveness to change supports a new or in-place vision that drives strategies, tactics and implementation programs. If these factors are valid as determined by the marketplace, then the organization should realize business success. In parallel to this is sustained leadership or, as emphasized in this chapter: roles, roles and relationships that translate to ongoing business and information technology leadership.

✦✦✦ LEADERSHIP PHASES

Bob Townsend, former CEO at Avis Rental Cars, spoke at a conference in San Francisco in 1988. Some of his primary comments are still valid today. His point was that organizations historically go through three phases. Which phase an organization is in has a major bearing on the type of leadership and the risks that these same leaders are willing to take.

The first phase involves the **entrepreneur founder** of the company. These people have everything to gain and not much to lose from a company standpoint. Mr. Townsend had nothing but good things to say about these people because they built their companies from the ground up. The successful ones are legendary. They include people like Sam Walton of Wal-Mart, Charles Schwab of the Schwab Corporation and Ewing Marion

Kaufmann of Marion Laboratories. You can tell they were the founders—their companies bear their names.

Phase two is when the company is run by the successors of the founders, or the **corporate managers.** In Wal-Mart's case this is David Glass. Companies like Federal Express and Charles Schwab are still in the first phase. These next-in-line executives do a credible job because they have a major advantage: They were picked by, worked with and were trained by the founder entrepreneur and still reflect many of that person's attitudes and values.

Phase three is the one for concern. Townsend referred to these executives as **corporate caretakers.** The problem is that they are too far removed from the founder entrepreneur to reflect the founder's values. By this time the companies are large in many ways. They are big in the number of employees, which results in too many organization levels. They are large by financial measurements, which prompts big salaries for executives, posh facilities, lots of perks and even golden handshakes. The problem is that these executives are more motivated to protect what they have instead of building, growing, and developing—all those things that represent risk in today's business environment.

If this truly reflects management attitudes, it certainly helps to explain the woes of some U.S. companies because many of them are in the third phase. It also makes the job done by David Whitwam at Whirlpool, Gil Amelio at National Semiconductor and Al Zeien at Gillette seem even more impressive. They realized the importance of building on traditional strengths while seeking new opportunities for their respective organizations.

✦✦✦ THE IS ORGANIZATION AS A BUSINESS WITHIN A BUSINESS

Is the information systems organization a business within a business? Should it be managed as a business within a business? Would this offer advantages to both the functions that it serves and the people within the information systems organization?

A Principles of Management class will tell you that there are fundamental components that constitute a business. These major elements are shown in Figure 9-6. The only factor in the model that might require explanation is the board of directors. What is the primary role of a board of directors? Is it to represent the interests of stockholders, monitor the financial status, compensate senior management or fire the CEO? All of these are addressed by a board, but their primary role is to act in an advisory capacity regarding the health of the business based on direction and strategies.

Figure 9-6

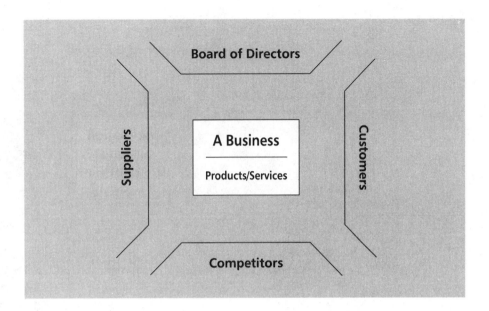

Does the IS Organization Fit Within the Business Model?

Figure 9-7 substitutes the information systems organization for the business model. The question is whether it really fits. Is an information systems organization really a business? An initial reaction would be that it does fit the model. Information systems organizations have customers (users), suppliers and competition. They also have a board of directors, more appropriately called a steering committee. The right kind of steering committee functions in an advisory capacity like a board of directors.

To answer the basic question regarding information systems as a business within a business, it is necessary to get more specific. Factors that are important to the running of a successful business need to be evaluated to see if they also apply to an "information systems business." These would include profitability, market share, amount and type of competition, quality and range of products and services, skills and quality of the people, caliber of the management team, and long-term viability. Figure 9-8 should help in this evaluation.

The area where the information systems organization does not fit the business model is profitability. While money can flow from user departments to the information systems organization for services and support provided, this is not true revenue or profit to the company. How excited would a CEO be if the information systems executive reported that they had made a large profit for the year? The reaction would be that the user departments were overcharged. More on this financial issue will be provided in Chapter 16.

Figure 9-7

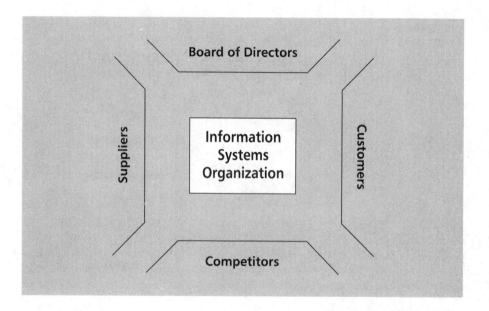

Figure 9-8

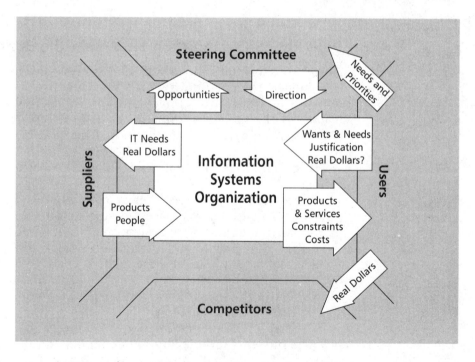

Advantages of a Business-Within-a-Business Orientation

The people who are the customers of the "information systems business" are called users. They really do not mind being referred to as users. In other areas it might be offensive, but not with information systems. If the users do not mind the term, why bother changing it to "customers" or "clients"? The major benefits to calling them customers or clients is to the members of the information systems organization if changing the name changes their attitude towards users. It is possible that a systems analyst could have negative thoughts towards users who are having difficulty defining the specific requirements of a new application. Treating them like customers can be an advantage in fostering a better working relationship. Businesses also seek out new opportunities, pursue new ways to provide value to customers and proactively market their products and services. Why wouldn't an information systems organization want to treat users like customers?

✦✦✦ OUTSOURCING INFORMATION SYSTEMS

Competitive pressures have forced companies to look objectively and critically at everything they do. Functions that are important to the long-term viability of the business are retained and provide the focus and resources they deserve. Functions, activities and people that do not play a strategic role as a customer value-added factor are eliminated or significantly curtailed. Human resources departments have frequently been reduced in size and decentralized into the line organization. Accounting and finance departments no longer hire bookkeepers and they have fewer financial analysts. Those that remain have a job with a major customer value-added responsibility.

What about the largest support organization—information systems? What role does information systems play within the organization? Can this same role be provided to the company by someone else? Can this be accomplished while also realizing a cost savings? What benefits can be realized from this approach? What are the disadvantages?

In evaluating the logic of outsourcing information systems, it is appropriate and even necessary to view the support provided in three categories:

1. Designing systems.
2. Developing and implementing systems.
3. Delivering systems support.

This is saying that the information systems organization is in three different businesses: designing, building and running information systems.

If you ask the questions posed above relative to each of these three different businesses, you will probably come up with different answers. The most important question deals with the strategic significance of each of these three businesses. The answer to this question can in many cases result in three different answers. Determining the requirements for and designing a new information system can definitely be strategically significant to the company. Building the system might be significant, but could be done by someone other than the company's own employees. Running the systems after they are built would not seem to be strategic. What difference does it make who runs the data center?

Company Examples of Outsourcing

The Eastman Kodak decision to outsource to IBM was very consistent with the above logic. While this happened in 1988, it is still looked upon as a hallmark decision. It was the largest outsourcing contract ever signed by a single company at the time and remains one of the largest. It was initially for over $1 billion for a ten-year period for IBM to run their major data center. They outsourced the run portion of their information systems business, which resulted in the consolidation of a number of data centers into one. They kept the design responsibility. Kodak had traditionally had information support people within the line organization. The new arrangement with IBM had no direct impact on the working relationship between information systems and users. They still dealt with the same people that they had worked with in the past. The build activities are determined on a project basis. If they can outsource to a contractor on a cost-effective basis, they do so. Some projects are still developed and built by Kodak personnel.

The early companies that opted for outsourcing did so because they had problems relative to business direction and strategy, were in dire financial straits, or both. This included Kodak and General Dynamics. General Dynamics completely outsourced their entire information systems operation (all three "businesses"). Even considering their obvious business problems as a major defense contractor, this total transfer of its information systems management could be very short-sighted.

As strategic alliances have become more common and at least in some cases very successful, some companies that do not fit the above profile are entering into outsourcing agreements. Xerox made such an agreement with Electronic Data Services (EDS). They approached outsourcing as a way of enhancing their competitive position in both technological and financial terms.[1] The Xerox-EDS transaction is recognized as the largest and most complex outsourcing arrangement to date. Xerox does not feel that they are abdicating all information technology decisions. They have retained the flexibility necessary to take advantage of shifts in either their business or the technology marketplace. Retaining the right to change some of the basic factors in their strategic alliance comes with a price in exchange for flexibility—a commitment that Xerox was willing to make.

---

[1] Halvey, John, "Strategic Outsourcing: No Longer a Last Resort," *Information Week*, August 1, 1994, p. 84.

✦✦✦ CONCLUSION

The lesson learned from organizations that have successfully used information systems to compete is that it is often not so much a matter of embracing new technologies or methodologies as it is a matter of repositioning roles. It is important to clearly change the role of information systems so that it becomes an effective competitive resource. To accomplish this it may be necessary to change the role of senior management to position and prioritize the competitive role of information systems. It is also necessary to recognize that this process is dynamic, so these new relationships need to function on an ongoing basis and become an integral part of a continuing management process.

RECOMMENDED READING

Heller, Robert, *The Super Chiefs: Today's Most Successful Chief Executives and Their Winning Strategies for the 1990s*. New York: Truman Telley, 1992.

There is a new breed of top executives who are practicing dynamic leadership, with results being the ultimate factor determining their success. Included are narratives on Colin Marshall of Bristish Airways, Robert Haas of Levi Strauss, Vaughn Beals of Harley-Davidson, Robert Galvin of Motorola, Bill Gates of Microsoft and many more. The major message is unlocking the power that exists at every level within an organization through leadership and quantifiable objectives.

Morita, Akio, with Edwin M. Reingold and Mitsuko Shimomure, *Made in Japan: Akio Morita and Sony*. New York: Dutton, 1986.

This is an interesting history of the Sony Corporation with a success strategy for both the company and the information systems organization. For the company this entails challenging people to be: (1) innovative in design, (2) innovative in manufacturing and (3) innovative in creating markets for innovative products. With just a slight modification the guidelines for people within the information systems are to be: (1) innovative in design, (2) innovative in development and (3) innovative in creating markets for information technology opportunities within the company.

Slater, Robert, *The New GE: How Jack Welch Revived an American Institution*. Homewood, IL: Business One Irwin, 1993.

GE had long been regarded as almost an American institution. Did "Neutron" Jack Welch, as the new CEO, set the standard for reengineering a major American corporation, or did he tear up a good thing? He created an atmosphere where people could flourish if they had the talent and the will. He argued that managing less is managing better. Finally, he created a blueprint on how to cope with an increasingly dynamic and hostile global business environment.

1. Information systems mission statement.

Evaluate the information systems organization mission statement on page 162 and explain the implication of the major parts of this statement to both the business and the information systems organization.

2. Buying a business.

a. If you were going to buy a business, what factors would be important in determining that it would be a good investment?

b. How would you determine (measure) if the organization was doing well in each of the areas identified above?

c. Would these same factors apply to an "information systems business" within an organization?

3. Outsourcing information systems management.

Using a specific company as the basis for your analysis, would the outsourcing of information systems management be a logical step to take? What major business considerations would prompt an organization to do this? Identify possible advantages and disadvantages in doing so.

4. Making things happen: capitalizing on information systems opportunity.

Using Figure 9-5 as your road map, do an analysis of how a specific company acquired the necessary business and information technology leadership to use information systems to gain a competitive advantage.

5. Technology transfer through organizational learning.

Provide specific examples of how the presence of necessary employee learning regarding information technology enables a company to capitalize on its use. Also contrast this with examples of organizations that failed to gain the necessary knowledge and failed to realize potential benefits from the use of information systems.

6. Roles, Roles and Relationships concept.

Validate or refute the logic of this concept if an organization is to gain a competitive advantage through the use of information systems.

THE REDEFINE/DEFINE CONCEPT AND CHANGE MANAGEMENT

*Equipping a company with the latest technology doesn't
mean a thing if you don't alter how your employees
think and how management leads them.*

Chad Frost
President
Frost, Inc.

*As we change what computers can do, we must
change what we can do with computers.*

Max Hopper
Former Senior Vice-President of Information Systems
AMR and American Airlines

LEARNING OBJECTIVES

The Redefine/Define concept is the second of the two core concepts of the analysis structure provided in this book. It concerns primarily the changes that can be realized through the use of information systems to provide value to customers. Change management is receiving considerable attention because the needs of the business dictate that changes be accomplished in a relatively short time.

QUESTIONS

Some appropriate questions regarding material addressed in this chapter:

1. What is the ultimate objective of business competition?
2. How many options are available to a company to achieve this ultimate objective?
3. Can you provide five company examples where the use of information systems complies with the Redefine/Define concept?

4. How important in today's competitive environment is the product or service delivery process?

5. How significant is change management both in terms of business in general and information systems specifically?

6. Is change management an issue with managers, employees or both?

✦✦✦ **THE REDEFINE/DEFINE CONCEPT**

Redefine/Define is the second of two key concepts in understanding the general approach of successfully using information systems to gain a competitive advantage. The following statement should position one's thinking in tying a business strategy to the use of information systems:

---

*Companies that achieve a sustainable strategic advantage with information systems generally **redefine** the factors of competition rather than use the technology in a traditional way.*

Merriam Webster's Collegiate Dictionary, 10th edition, tells us that redefine is "to define (as a concept) again; to reexamine or reevaluate esp[ecially] with a view to change." The key word here is *change*. Webster goes on to explain that define is "to make distinct, clear or detailed esp[ecially] in outline." Another definition is "to determine or identify the essential qualities or meaning of [something]." This can be summarized with the word *clarify*.

While thanking the dictionary for an assist in understanding this concept, we have simply used the definitions to help us understand the possible impact of the use of information technology on major aspects of the business. Posing it as a question would probably help. How can information systems be used to redefine (change) or define (clarify) the competitive position of the organization? In other words, will it help the organization achieve and sustain a competitive advantage? An integral part of the question is whether the current mode of operation makes sense or whether it should be redefined.

The actual goal of any competitive effort is to provide *value to customers*. We can get more specific by asking how information technology can be used to redefine and/or define value to customer. Three options are available to most organizations to achieve the value-to-customer goal. The company can redefine/define:

1. The business.

2. Products and/or services.

3. Business processes.

The ultimate goal of all of these is to provide value to customer.

The kernel of the idea for this concept came from Peter Drucker's *Innovation and Entrepreneurship* (see Recommended Reading at the end of this chapter). Mr. Drucker states that management is a new technology (rather than any specific new science or invention) that is making the American economy into an entrepreneurial economy. He goes on to describe how McDonald's, under the direction of founder Ray Kroc, built one of the biggest success stories in the last twenty-five years. He concludes that the key to its success was based on their fundamentally changing the traditional mom-and-pop hamburger stand that had been in existence in the United States since the 19th century.

Taking just a few liberties to bridge from Drucker's analysis to the Redefine/Define concept, take note of what Drucker said in his book:

> McDonald's first designed [defined] the end product; then it redesigned [redefined] the process of making it; then it redesigned [redefined] or in many cases invented tools so that every piece of meat, every slice of onion, every bun, every piece of potato would be identical, turned out in a precisely timed and fully automated process. Finally, McDonald's studied what value meant to the customer, defined it as quality and predictability of product, speed of service, absolute cleanliness and friendliness, then set standards for all of these, trained for them, and geared to compensate for them. All of which is management, and fairly advanced management at that.[1]

It would be nice at this point to conclude that this is yet another information systems success story. Unfortunately for our purposes, it is not. The information technology involved in this example is minimal. At the individual restaurant level it was nonexistent. Nevertheless, it is still a good example of how an organization addressed the fundamental aspects of business success by providing value to the customer. It also helps make the point that business management determines the use of technology, because the redefine/define concept can be applied to organizations that lend themselves to solutions that are hi-tech, medium-tech or even no-tech. The challenge for us is to understand the concept, know how to apply it and make the right decisions regarding the technological approach that should be taken.

✦✦✦ REDEFINE/DEFINE THE BUSINESS

In thinking about the three options available to organizations to achieve the value-to-customer objective, examples can be cited in all three categories. Changing the business through the use of information technology is the most difficult example to find because it represents significant

---

[1] Drucker, Peter F., *Innovation and Entrepreneurship*, 1985, p. 17.

and often dramatic change. Still, some good examples can be found. *USA Today* definitely fits into this category. American Airlines and American President Companies are also examples of organizations that have redefined their businesses based on information technology.

USA Today: The First National, General-Interest Newspaper

Critics call it McPaper—fast-food journalism. It is also referred to as the most unprofitable newspaper in the world, but *USA Today* has survived, completing its first profitable year in 1993. Its original business plan projected that it would take five years to reach a profitable level. It actually took a decade to reverse the loss trend that exceeded $600 million and generated significant criticism. Irritated by its size and effect, the critics noted that it is not difficult to run a money-losing newspaper.

Analysts now predict that *USA Today* will remain solidly in the black, with profits inching upward as the decade progresses. For now they are praising how the newspaper has stopped draining money from its parent corporation, the Gannett Corporation. Gannett, known for its high-profit newspapers, is the largest newspaper in the United States. As now-retired CEO Al Neuharth used to say, "The name is Gannett—with two T's and an emphasis on the 'net'!" After more than a decade *USA Today* is living up to that expectation by generating a net profit.

Gannett had been involved in running local area newspapers for decades. Under the leadership of Neuharth, *USA Today* was created as the first national, general-interest newspaper in the United States. Other countries have national newspapers, why not the U.S.? The traditional answer had been that the United States posed too many logistical problems because of its size. Information technology in the form of computers and satellite communications provided the solution to this problem. The newspaper is composed in Arlington, Virginia and transmitted to thirty-two print locations across the country. This has been expanded to include international print locations in Hong Kong, London and Lucerne, Switzerland. A major challenge to the entire *USA Today* distribution process is the time element. The window, from the time that the newspaper is printed until the distribution process must be completed, is three hours.

An irony of the information systems story at *USA Today* is that the business systems were the last to be addressed. It had a computer-based editorial system in place to create the newspaper. It also had automated production systems to print it. What it lacked were business systems to address the distribution process, including mail delivery, home delivery and single-copy sales; and the management of advertising and billing. Under the leadership of Tom Farrell, then General Manager of *USA Today*, and John Palm, Information Systems Vice-President on loan from his job as the information systems executive for all of Gannett, the business systems were implemented with very short lead times. These systems provided the necessary management capabilities for the entire circulation distribution process. Having achieved a daily circulation of 2,055,000, *USA Today* has moved ahead of the *Wall Street Journal* into the number one spot for U.S. publications.

A vision, some guts to try it, innovative journalism, financial staying power and the combination of telecommunications and information systems enabled Gannett to redefine their business in the form of *USA Today*.

American Airlines Is in Two Primary Businesses

Until 1982 AMR (American Airlines' parent company) was also in the food service and energy business. It made a decision to divest itself of these two profitable businesses to concentrate its efforts on two primary businesses: (1) running an airline and (2) information systems. The latter became a very profitable business for American Airlines. CEO Bob Crandall has frequently been quoted that of the two businesses, the information systems business provided the best profit margins and return on investment. This would seem to suggest that it might be well advised to get out of the airline business and concentrate on the information systems business. It would be difficult, however, for AMR to offset the $15 billion airline business with a $1.5 billion information systems business even with the better profit margins and significant growth. Despite difficult times with the airline, AMR will continue to operate the two businesses with the strategies and strengths of one playing to the strategies and strengths of the other. A logical conclusion is that information systems redefined (changed) the businesses of AMR.

American President Companies

Oakland-based American President Companies Ltd. (APC) and their subsidiaries provide container transportation, distribution and logistics service within and between Asia and North America. It has built an intermodal system that combines ocean, rail and truck transportation to become one of the largest transportation companies in the United States. As with other forms of transportation, this is a very competitive industry. APC faces vigorous competition, primarily on the basis of price and service, from twenty-two other U.S. flag operators plus foreign flag companies, with some of them being government owned and operated.

APC became a publicly owned company in 1983 and under the leadership of CEO Bruce Seaton set about redefining the business from a containerized shipper to the distribution company that it is today. In the 1990s they positioned themselves as a leader in the container transportation and distribution business in three distinct markets: Trans-Pacific, North American and Intra-Asia. To gain a competitive advantage they built the industry's most extensive satellite telecommunications and computer information systems, linking all service points in Asia and North

America. The information systems provide operational efficiencies and information-based services that cannot be accomplished any other way.

Seaton believed that APC's future success depended on its ability to compete with information systems. Their information technology infrastructure provides real-time access to data supporting a range of value-added services that compliment its intermodal transportation package. APC enables their customers to track their shipments through a PC linked to the APC system. They can also obtain the anticipated time of arrival of their shipment and cargo availability through a touch-tone telephone connected to the APC computer's voice response unit. APC also has a cargo-tracking system that identifies the contents of a container without opening it and manages it during the entire distribution process. The combination of shipping technology, management systems and information systems attracts higher margin cargoes. This enables APC to realize economies of scale that make it difficult for competitors to imitate.

While he has now retired, Bruce Seaton's vision and commitment to information technology was a key factor in implementing the strategy that used information systems to help redefine APC from a shipping company to an intermodal distribution company.

✦✦✦ REDEFINE/DEFINE PRODUCTS OR SERVICES

Examples of organizations that have used information technology to redefine products and/or services are fairly numerous. Banks like Bank of America, Citibank and Banc One, through use of ATMs, fit this definition as do many of the organizations that have implemented interorganizational systems with their customers.

A Change in Business Strategy at Charles Schwab

Charles Schwab & Company, operating out of its San Francisco headquarters, is the largest discount broker in the United States. Initially founded as a full service broker in 1971, Schwab pioneered the discounted commission era following deregulation in 1975. In the earlier days of Schwab's operation, their business strategy was geared to growth with the goal of becoming the largest discount broker in the United States. Promoting the savings to be gained by dealing with a discount broker enabled Schwab to achieve this goal. Following the stock crash in 1987, Schwab diversified into new services and continued its emphasis on new accounts. It continues to expand its network of branch offices, now over 200, and spends heavily on advertising to expand its customer base. Schwab's current goal is to improve the value, price and selection of services to an increasingly diverse customer base. It tries to offer investors the best selection of investments at reasonable prices regardless of the size of their portfolio. A key part of this strategy is to have helpful, knowledgeable representatives provide client service without the commission-based sales pressure of traditional brokers.

To meet its strategic and financial objectives, Schwab invests heavily in new services, information technology and training to differentiate itself from its competitors. Information technology acts as an enabler in improving service quality, service delivery, internal business processes and product development. Information technology plays such an important role that Schwab has had a policy since almost its very beginning of only offering products or services that are computer based. It has built its business by using information systems to continue to redefine its delivery process of products and services. Its brokerage trading system has defined the standard for timely execution of trades. Made possible by an advanced computer-based transaction system, confirmation of a trade can occur most of the time while the client is still on the telephone. Street-Smart and Equalizer are PC programs that offer clients on-line access for stock quotes, Dow Jones news, analysts' opinions and trading opportunities marketed to "help investors help themselves." These two programs also enable clients to execute their own trades. Telebroker is a convenient method for investors to conduct transactions via an integrated, automated, voice/data system accessed by a touch-tone telephone.

This represents a shift in strategy made possible through the use of information systems. The Schwab television ads no longer say "we save you the most money on brokerage commissions." Instead they emphasize the best overall service and a wide range of investment opportunities.

A Change in Products and Services at Banc One

Banking was once about managing money. Today it is about managing information about money. Banks offer products and services that require knowledge of the consumer's special wants and needs. Information systems play a major role in determining the right mix of products and services and delivering them to customers. There are few if any banks in the United States that have been stronger believers in the power of information systems than Banc One, based in Columbus, Ohio. It operates sixty-one affiliate banks in eighty-five cities in the Midwest and Texas, which provide banking services ranging from loans, leases, and deposit accounts to money market accounts. It also operates companies that are involved in data processing, venture capital, investment and merchant banking, trust, brokerage, investment management, equipment leasing, mortgage banking, consumer finance and insurance. Since 1935, when John McCoy began the family dynasty, a McCoy has served as CEO. John McCoy was succeeded by his son, John G. McCoy, in 1958, who turned over the corporate reins to his son, John B. McCoy in 1984.

Banc One includes information technology as one of its three major strategies, which are to:

1. Serve retail and middle market customers through community banks, which operate with significant local autonomy, coupled with central and credit controls.

2. Invest and implement technologies that enhance retail products, create competitive advantages, provide operating efficiencies and general nontraditional banking revenues.

3. Treat banking acquisitions as an ongoing line of business, requiring rigorous pricing and management disciplines which permit market expansion and provide economic diversification.

Information technology is specifically identified in the second strategy but it is also prominent in the other two strategies. Banc One has grown dramatically over the past twenty years, and information systems have played a prominent role in its acquisition strategy. It buys another bank, immediately implements its information systems and consistently reduces operating costs while gaining control over key operations.

Beginning in 1986 Banc One redefined the way it does business and began building the new support systems. It decided that it was no longer a transaction business but one that dealt with service "products" and business processes. This resulted in the development of the Strategic Banking System (SBS) in a joint effort with Electronic Data Services. SBS eliminates a significant amount of paperwork and, more importantly, time delays to process loan applications. It also consolidates information about a customer, which can be accessed for customer service and marketing purposes. SBS helps Banc One build a loyal customer base. For instance, if a customer comes to a branch to make a deposit and does not have a Banc One credit card, the system will prompt the teller to offer the customer a credit card with a preapproved limit. If the customer has been with the bank for a long time, the system would authorize waiving the annual fee for the first three years. The system also provides simple, colorful charts to help a customer service representative analyze and the customer visualize different investment scenarios. SBS will eventually replace fifteen major transaction processing systems designed to support the redefining of Banc One's products and services.

✦✦✦ REDEFINE/DEFINE BUSINESS PROCESSES

The redefining and/or defining of business processes is the area that many organizations have addressed. This concerns the internal processes of the business. The answer to the question of who is the customer of the organization's product or service is often that there are multiple levels or tiers of "customers." This concept also applies to the customer of the support or service being delivered by the information systems within the organization. Charles Schwab delivers brokerage product support to its own brokers, who in turn make this service available to Schwab clients. Frito-Lay delivers products from manufacturing plants to distribution centers, from distribution centers to route sales representatives and from route sales reps to retailers. That is three tiers of customers without having sold a product to the customer who actually consumes it.

Boeing Redefines Its Design Process for the 777

Boeing has made the first major change since World War II in how they design an aircraft. The 777 is the company's first airplane that is 100% digitally designed and preassembled through the use of a computer system. The motivation behind the use of this system was design quality, design schedule integrity (staying on schedule) and manufacturability (minimal difficulty to manufacture the final product). All of these factors are critical to Boeing's efforts to fill a product gap that was already addressed by their primary competitor, Airbus.

The design system enables Boeing engineers to design parts as three-dimensional, solid images. By simulating the assembly of the parts they can find and easily correct misalignments and other interference problems. The finished design then bypasses the traditional paper drawings and prototype by going directly to manufacturing from computer images. This saves time and the cost of fixing design problems that typically do not show up until production is in full swing, or even after an airplane has been delivered to the customer.

Boeing's design system is based on a software package licensed by IBM and developed by Dassault Aviation in France called CATIA (Computer-Aided Three-dimensional Interactive Application). The CATIA system originally ran on eight mainframes that operate like a single computer with over two thousand engineering workstations. The bulk of the workstations are in Seattle with additional on-line units in Wichita, Philadelphia and Japan. The workstations in Japan are used by Boeing program partners.

Boeing has had 7,000 people working on the 777 project. About half of them were in 238 design/build teams. These teams worked on over 132,500 unique parts of a total of 4 million parts for the 777. It is also important to remember that no two aircraft are identical, as the final configuration depends on the intended use of the airplane by the customer.

This new approach with the 777 has resulted in a significant improvement of the entire design and manufacturing process. It has meant better quality, reduced design costs, fewer changes and errors, and less paperwork while still staying on schedule.

L.L. Bean: From a Mail Order to an 800-Number Order Process

Founded as a mail order company, L.L. Bean has been in business in Newport, Maine since 1912. The story of their initial product, the Maine hunting boot, is legendary. Leon Leonwood Bean, as the founder of the business who personally designed the boot, had them manufactured, sold 100 pairs, and in so doing started his mail order business. When 90 of the boots fell apart, L.L. returned the customers' money. His philosophy was "sell good merchandise at a reasonable profit, treat your customers like human beings, and they will always come back for more." The character and culture of the company was thus established and remains much the same to this day. Leon Leonwood Bean died in 1967 and was succeeded as president by his grandson Leon Gorman.

The company has clearly benefited from the leadership of Leon Gorman. When he became president the company did $4.7 million in annual sales. Despite an intended slowing in revenue growth in 1990 and 1991, L.L. Bean did $743 million in sales in 1992 and reached $974 million in 1994. From the initial Maine hunting boot the company has grown to where it now markets 6,700 items through 30 different catalogues.

Gorman has also led the company in introducing information technology within the organization. The first computer application handled mailing lists of customers and has since expanded into every major company operation. The technology itself has not been the real secret. It is the creative and practical ways in which it has improved internal processes through effective information systems support that has been so successful. Customer information was used to identify and understand the different customers to directly target them. The company realized that customers want individual attention and current information, so they developed order entry systems that allow them to provide this. L.L. Bean was the first mail order company in the United States to implement the use of an 800 telephone number in 1983. Today approximately 80% of their orders are received from 12,000 daily telephone calls. Operating year-round, 7 days a week and 24 hours a day, during their peak Thanksgiving to Christmas shopping period they have 1,500 customer service representatives answering telephones to service customers. The customer service representatives are backed up by Merchandise Information teams that can advise customers on specific merchandise and on questions such as what to take on their first fishing trip to Alaska.

L.L. Bean as a company, and Leon Gorman personally, are highly acclaimed and frequently recognized with awards. A more recent success was its winning the Malcolm Baldridge National Quality Award in 1993. Gorman received the Master Winner Entrepreneur of the Year Award and was inducted into the Direct Marketing Association Hall of Fame. The success of L.L. Bean is largely due to the integration of fundamental beliefs and attitudes of its founder, the modern business management that Leon Gorman brought to the company and the support of business strategies and operations by information systems.

✦✦✦ THE PRODUCT AND SERVICE DELIVERY PROCESS

Consider the following question: When you make a purchase decision does the delivery process become more important than the product or service? In other words, do you buy a product or service because you want the thing being purchased, or is the purchase decision greatly influenced by the delivery process? It is almost illogical to suggest that the answer is anything other than because you want the product or the service. But is that actually the case? For the sake of discussion we will use the model shown in Figure 10-1 to evaluate this question. In this model what a customer buys has been separated from the delivery process. The question is whether the delivery process actually provides value to a customer such that it becomes an important part of the buying decision. Even more important from a business management standpoint is the decision from whom to make the purchase.

Figure 10-1

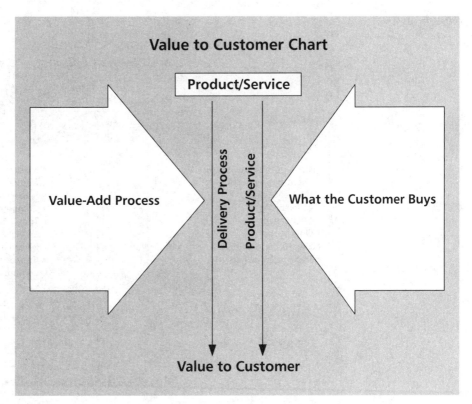

Using Charles Schwab as the example, Figure 10-2 examines a typical customer relationship. On the right side of the model are the things a customer buys from Charles Schwab. Some are specific products and services, others are related to them. Is there really anything unique about this list of factors? There must be a dozen or more companies in any major U.S. city that can duplicate this list. Why would a customer choose to do business with Charles Schwab instead of one of its competitors?

On the left side of the model are the factors in Schwab's delivery process that distinguish it from its competitors. At one time Schwab was unique in being able to confirm a stock trade while the customer was on the telephone. They can still do this 90% of the time, a capability that has been duplicated by some competitors. This service is equal to any major broker in getting customers the best possible price on listed stocks. It also gives an investor much better control over their investment decisions. Contrast this to the alternative: A "buy at the market" order results in a notice arriving in the mail several days later or a follow-up call with the broker. This capability clearly makes a difference in the eyes of Schwab clients, as do the other delivery process services.

Using Mervyn's as another example, as shown in Figure 10-3, leads to a similar conclusion. The delivery process can make a major difference—

Figure 10-2

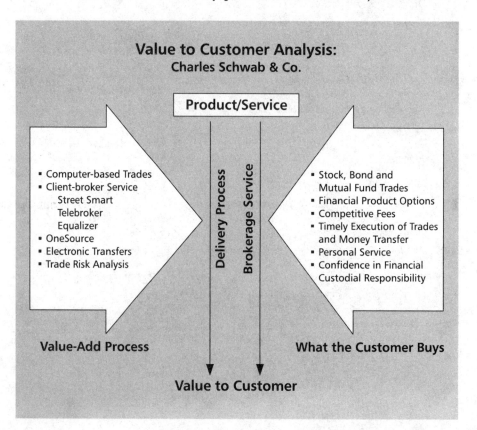

Value to Customer Analysis:
Charles Schwab & Co.

Product/Service

- Computer-based Trades
- Client-broker Service
   Street Smart
   Telebroker
   Equalizer
- OneSource
- Electronic Transfers
- Trade Risk Analysis

Delivery Process

Brokerage Service

- Stock, Bond and
   Mutual Fund Trades
- Financial Product Options
- Competitive Fees
- Timely Execution of Trades
   and Money Transfer
- Personal Service
- Confidence in Financial
   Custodial Responsibility

Value-Add Process

What the Customer Buys

Value to Customer

Figure 10-3

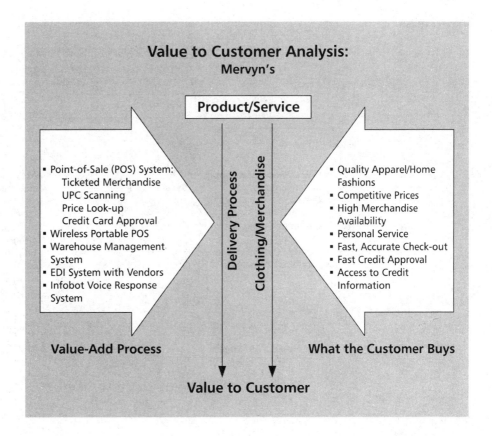

Value to Customer Analysis:
Mervyn's

Product/Service

Delivery Process

Clothing/Merchandise

- Point-of-Sale (POS) System:
  Ticketed Merchandise
  UPC Scanning
  Price Look-up
  Credit Card Approval
- Wireless Portable POS
- Warehouse Management
  System
- EDI System with Vendors
- Infobot Voice Response
  System

- Quality Apparel/Home
  Fashions
- Competitive Prices
- High Merchandise
  Availability
- Personal Service
- Fast, Accurate Check-out
- Fast Credit Approval
- Access to Credit
  Information

Value-Add Process

What the Customer Buys

Value to Customer

certainly not with all customers, but enough to make a difference in the competitive success of Mervyn's.

It is much easier to make a case regarding the delivery process value with service industry companies than with manufacturing companies. The Boeing Commercial Airplane Group is depicted in Figure 10-4. You have to work harder to conclude that the delivery process is a major factor, but the case can be made that the customer buys both the product and the delivery process. You can be confident that Boeing works very hard to make sure that its customers understand the delivery processes that are in place and what these can mean in terms of added value over and above the purchase of the aircraft.

✦✦✦ CHANGE MANAGEMENT: A MAJOR MANAGEMENT CHALLENGE

We live in a world of change, yet we act on the basis of continuity. People basically do not like to change. They sleep on the same side of the bed, park their car on the same side of the garage, drive the same route to

Figure 10-4

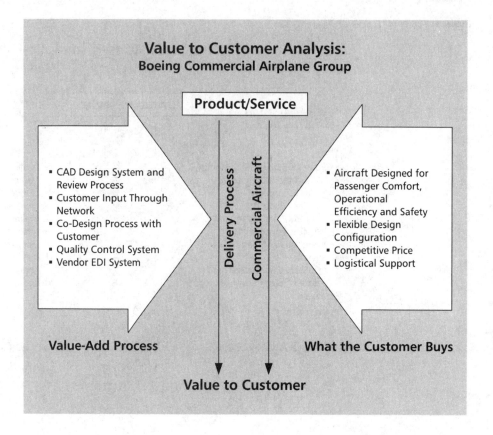

work, etc. Unfortunately these same people are employees who do not like to change how they do things at work. Someone should write a law that summarizes the challenge of making a change. Newton on gravity, Gresham on bad money versus good money, and Parkinson on what can go wrong, will go wrong achieved lasting notoriety this way. We remember their names and laws like they were indelibly written on our brain. The change management law would read:

The Law of Change
Achieving change, of any significance within an organization, is in inverse proportion to the success that it has had up to the time that management feels a change is needed. The greater the success of the company, the less likely it will change.

People are brought into an organization, are oriented to the business culture, trained to do a job, gain experience, succeed within the environment and grow and prosper career-wise. It all seems very logical and worthwhile. Then someone comes along and suggests that things need to change and change dramatically. If change has not been viewed as logical (vision), necessary (strategies), and an ongoing part of the operation (culture), then get ready for major resistance.

This is not to suggest that managers like change while other employees do not. The TQM story at Xerox discussed in detail in Chapter 14 is a classic example of management resistance to change, despite efforts by the people at the very top of the business stressing its importance. Change does not happen unless actions are rewarded. Managers do not change unless their rewards dictate that it is important. Senior management can also be leery of being punished by Wall Street if change impacts short-term earnings.

Four factors contribute to the challenge of change management within a company. These have been addressed earlier but can be summarized as follows:

1. The pace and time pressures of change in business.
2. Financial controls that do not allow the increase of employees within a specific function despite significant growth.
3. The shifting of productivity and other operational objectives to information technology.
4. Dramatic improvements in information technology price/performance and function.

Translating these factors into a simple statement, we could say that companies need to make change happen faster for business reasons, and information technology is a vehicle to do it if the changes can be successfully made.

IS Change Management at Hewlett-Packard

Skip Ross, Director of Information Technology for Hewlett-Packard's Worldwide Customer Support organization, has addressed the change management challenge. He created a position with a primary responsibility for change management within his IT organization. Ross has a technical background with a degree in electrical engineering. His previous assignments within Hewlett-Packard were in instrumentation hardware development and computer software development. It is interesting to hear him say, "The tough stuff with information technology is the soft stuff." In other words, the bigger issues involve people and not technology. Nancy Calcese is the "manager of change management." She is not a technologist but has a human resources and management background and spends half her time consulting with line managers on how to manage change. She feels that the following are key organizational factors needed to deal with change management:

✦ **Sponsorship.** Management must feel strongly enough about the change so that they know what needs to be done and what they personally need to do as sponsors.

✦ **Know and understand the difference between change and transition.** All changes include a period of transition. Why does transition take so long? It concerns the shift from the current to the desired state. This impacts how people feel about themselves, their personal identity, how they behave and how they change.

✦ **Assessment of the organization's history of change management and action planning.** Some organizations are flexible and adaptive while others resist change. It is important to understand the challenges and risks associated with the people within the organization. This includes their ability and willingness to accept the need for change before initiating a program to make the actual changes.

A Little Creativity Can Go a Long Way[2]

A new beginning, innovation, creativity, fresh ideas and avoiding the status quo still translate into a single word to many employees—change. To foster the willingness to be creative, to take risks and to be receptive to change, the following factors should be considered:

✦ Employees need a sense of freedom in their jobs. The role of management is to set the direction, share ideas regarding possible alternative approaches and get out of the way.

✦ Employees need to be challenged. This means to address them personally, as members of work groups and the entire organization.

✦ Resources needed to do things better must be provided. This includes enough people, funding, staff support and in some cases direct, visible management support.

✦ Management must provide an environment where it is understood by employees that they are encouraged to take risks. This cannot be just talk. It must be reality. Who gets promoted in an organization: the people who are willing to try new things and take risks or the ones who play by the traditional book?

Learning from the NUMMI Approach

The NUMMI joint venture between Toyota and General Motors in Fremont, California has received a great deal of publicity on how American workers were successful within a Japanese-run operation. What did they do and why did it work? Two things influenced the people at NUMMI and their initial approach. First, they felt that the starting point was to make sure that there was harmony in the work force. This involved simplifying and consolidating the job classifications. It also included

---

[2] Gryskiewicz, Stan, "A Little Creativity Goes a Long Way," *Information Week*, June 27, 1994.

designating assembly-line workers as team leaders so that people on the line took their lead from peers instead of salaried supervisors. Second, for an assembly-line operation there must be discipline within the work place. People need to know what they are doing and how to best accomplish it. Significant time and effort was invested in training and practice for the assembly-line workers to accomplish this. Only after these two factors were in place could they successfully automate any of the processes.

✦✦✦ A VEHICLE FOR CHANGE: AUTOMATING AND INFORMATING

In her lengthy analysis of the history of work and the role of technology, Soshana Zuboff in her book *In the Age of the Smart Machine* offers us an interesting perspective. Terminology in this business is difficult enough without creating new words with new meanings, but in this case it is justified. Zuboff offers a contrast between automating and "informating." Automating is introducing technology to the work area to control processes for some basic reasons. They include safety, elimination of boring, repetitive tasks, to achieve consistency in quality and cost reduction. "Informating" is the information content of this process. It is an extension of automating. While accomplishing the objectives of automating, does it make sense to capture information pertaining to these tasks? She contends that a company can automate without informating. The opposite is not possible.

When informating is part of the process, an important question is for what reason and for whom is the data being collected? Relative to a manufacturing operation, the traditional answer would have been for use by the production control department. Foremen or supervisors certainly have a need for data on operations for which they are responsible. The recipient of this information could also be the plant manager in a summary format or as part of a decision support system. Has anyone been forgotten? What about the operators? An automated manufacturing process can result in a single operator having responsibility for multiple machine operations. Does this suggest the possibility of a traditional operator running and managing this type of operation? The next time a business process is evaluated with an objective of improving it, consider automating and informating for the people who have traditionally done the actual work.

✦✦✦ CONCLUSION

Information technology has the potential to be a catalyst for significant change within an organization. It can change business processes, products and services and can even influence a fundamental change of the business. The business need that justifies the use of information technology can warrant and even necessitate change. The issue is whether the people within the organization, both employees and managers, understand and accept the need for change. Are they also willing to personally do the things that are necessary to successfully implement "the new way of doing things?"

RECOMMENDED READING

Boone, Mary E., *Leadership and the Computer*. Rocklin, CA: Prima Publishing, 1991.

There is a particularly good chapter entitled "Battle of the Bags," which addresses the shift by Frito-Lay to a culture and management style that stressed entrepreneurship. Significant is the role of a decision support system made possible by a route sales information system that collects product and customer data on a daily basis. This is an interesting discussion of a management style where a president has access to detail information that would prompt him to take action. The issue is that he has delegated authority and responsibility to people who can also have access to the same information.

Champy, James, *Reengineering Management: The Mandate for New Leadership*. New York: Harper Collins, 1995.

This is a sequel to the earlier book, *Reengineering the Corporation*, by Champy and Michael Hammer. This one starts by stating that "reengineering is in trouble." It asserts that reengineering works up to a point, and only if management reengineers itself will the entire effort be successful. The loud and clear message is that this form of revolutionary change depends as much on reengineering management processes as business processes. It is like reading a second edition of a book that says, "These are the important things that we forgot to tell you in the first book."

Davenport, Thomas H., *Process Innovation: Reengineering Work Through Information Technology*. Boston: Harvard Business School Press, 1993.

In the global business environment it is essential that business processes be designed that will assure the implementation of strategies. This begins with a commitment to the vision of the company and cascades down to strategies, tactics and business processes. A key factor in this entire endeavor is information technology playing the role of enabler of process innovation.

Drucker, Peter F., *Innovation and Entrepreneurship: Practices and Principles*. New York: Harper & Row, 1985.

This book represents innovation and entrepreneurship as purposeful tasks that can and need to be organized as systematic work. It goes on to say that the emergence of a truly entrepreneurial economy in the United States is the most significant and hopeful event to have occurred in recent economic and social history. Mr. Drucker concludes that entrepreneurship is neither science nor an art, but a practice. He then adds that innovation is the specific tool of entrepreneurs to exploit change as an opportunity for a different business or a different service. Integral to all of this is technology, which can and does become a primary vehicle for some profound change in attitudes, values and above all, behavior.

Drucker, Peter F., "The Information Executives Truly Need." *Harvard Business Review*, January-February 1995, p. 54.

This article discusses the tools that managers require to generate the information they need to run the business. As one would suspect with an article by Drucker, it addresses the concepts underlying those tools. What matters in the marketplace is the economic reality, the costs of the entire economic process, not who owns it. The article identifies information that is important for understanding the current business and enabling the creation of wealth. This starts with traditional financial data, which Drucker refers to as foundation information. It also includes productivity of key resources, core competencies that create value to customer and both capital and personnel resource allocation. In addition to this primarily internal information, organized information is needed for strategy development. This includes information about both customers and non-customers, markets, technology, worldwide finance and the changing world economy. The article concludes with the point that the information needs are not new. What is new is the information technology to do quickly and cheaply what only a few years ago had been laborious and very expensive.

Kanter, Rosabeth Moss, *The Change Masters: Innovation and Entrepreneurship in the American Corporation*. New York: Simon & Schuster, 1984.

The pace of change continues to accelerate, and although this book is becoming a bit dated it still deserves readership. It defines the circumstances under which innovation can flourish, including a number of major factors that have not changed since this book was written. It contends that innovation, entrepreneurship and the development of participative management skills are key factors for new ideas, new approaches and new successes to happen within a company.

Serling, Robert J., *Legend and Legacy: The Story of Boeing and Its People*. New York: St. Martin's, 1992.

A thorough background on Boeing including a perspective on the 777 aircraft. Included are the historic and the ongoing challenges faced by the world's leading manufacturer of commercial aircraft.

Zuboff, Shoshana, *In the Age of the Smart Machine*. New York: Basic Books, 1988.

Computers are more than tools; they are revolutionary forces altering nearly every aspect of organizational life. This book covers it all—the history, psychology and politics of work; the promise, threat and challenge of computers. Particularly interesting is the relationship between automating and "informating." The latter term, coined by the author, addresses the information content, objective and role relative to the automation of work.

EXERCISES

1. Redefine/Define concept.

Identify companies other than those addressed in this chapter that meet all three of the options of the Redefine/Define concept.

2. Value to customer model.

Prepare a model similar to the one shown in Figure 10-1 based on an analysis of a company. Stay consistent with the concept by emphasizing specific information systems that play a major role within the company.

3. Change management.

How important is change management when contemplating a major new information system? What approaches would you recommend to address any issues that could arise when introducing this type of change within an organization?

4. Automating and informating.

Using the basic ideas provided by Soshana Zuboff regarding automating and informating, identify specific company examples where providing information to those responsible for actual work paid major benefits.

TELECOMMUNICATIONS AS THE DELIVERY VEHICLE

No field in the world offers more promise than the twin technologies of computers and telecommunications.

Telecommunications can be a link to customer satisfaction.

LEARNING OBJECTIVES

This is a challenging chapter given the scope and technical aspects of telecommunications. On the one hand it provides a basic perspective of the significant role that telecommunications plays to support the data access and communications requirements of an enterprise. On the other hand it attempts to provide an understanding of the use of telecommunications in a world that is increasingly more global, where employees are more mobile and where business dynamics dictate the need for both flexible access to a broader range of information and support for collaborative work groups. Before proceeding with the material in the chapter it would be helpful to review the contents and structure of how telecommunications is presented in the table of contents and the chapter comments in the preface.

QUESTIONS

Questions regarding the significance of telecommunications within an enterprise:

1. Why is the combination of computers and telecommunications an increasingly important organizational resource?
2. Why is building an enterprise-wide telecommunications network a bigger challenge than most organizations realize?
3. Is there a definite trend in the way that organizations are designing and implementing telecommunications networks?

4. How important are management style, management technology experience and company culture to the success of a distributed system? Who wins and who loses, if anyone, with this approach?

5. Are open systems a practical solution to the telecommunications connectivity problem?

✦✦✦ THE INCREASINGLY IMPORTANT ROLE OF TELECOMMUNICATIONS

The integration of computers and telecommunications is becoming increasingly important to the business enterprise. The compression of time and events is bringing new pressures for more effective communication at all levels of an organization. For example, to improve its ability to respond quickly and accurately to customers regarding the availability of products, Intel Corporation developed an integrated sales order system that takes advantage of telecommunications technology to link computers around the world. A customer order can be entered from any of approximately fifty sales locations throughout the world. The system first checks to determine if the order can be filled from inventory from one of seven facilities. If the order cannot be filled from inventory, the system looks for available manufacturing capacity and schedules it in a facility in Malaysia, Puerto Rico, the Philippines, Ireland, Arizona, Oregon or California. Having an almost instantaneous access to a complete picture of the company's entire global inventory status and manufacturing capacity, as opposed to a view of these same factors at a single location, provides an important competitive edge for Intel.

Design and implementation of the Intel system represented major challenges to the information systems organization. It needed to connect existing systems from multiple vendors, presenting a major connectivity challenge with two dimensions: first, the physical connection of computing and telecommunications devices, and second, the interfacing of computer applications across the communications network.

To appreciate many of the information systems in use today requires an understanding of both computing and telecommunications. As in the Intel example, the integrated use of both technologies is commonplace in companies that have used information systems to gain a competitive advantage. Providing a necessary perspective on telecommunications also involves walking a fine line between business and technical issues. This chapter will address the bridging of the use of technology to business requirements. Important fundamentals which provide a basis for understanding the potential that telecommunications offers to a business will be addressed.

The Mission of Telecommunications Within an Organization

The mission of telecommunications is to provide effective and efficient movement of all forms of information between various combinations of people and business equipment. Telecommunications is both voice and data communication by electronic means. It also includes the delivery of textual (formatted) data, computer-generated graphics, scanned images, and full motion video. More recently it also includes multimedia. It is not enough to deal with the technical aspects of this transmission. Telecommunications must support business strategies and accommodate organizational growth and change with increasing flexibility.

The Four Modes of Telecommunications

The four modes of telecommunications—how it is used today and will be used in the future—are shown in Figure 11-1. This is a simple model of the uses of telecommunications, but it covers all four of the possible options. The most obvious example of telecommunications use is voice communication—people to people. This can also be accomplished through nonsimultaneous communication with the use of voice mail.

Since the mid-1960s people have frequently communicated with business machines (computers) through the use of time-sharing and on-line systems. As enterprise-wide networks have become more common, there is growing communication between machines: computers processing applications by transmitting data to each other. Voice synthesis, the audibilizing of data, provides the capability to have machines communicate to people audibly. Applications include reminder telephone calls for overdue bills, or your broker's computer calling to inform you that the financial

Figure 11-1

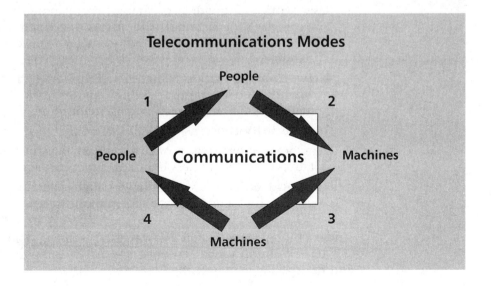

conditions of the buy authorization that you had agreed upon now exist, then asking if you want to execute the trade. If yes, you can simply press 1 to execute the trade, or press 2 to talk to the broker.

✦✦✦ BUILDING TELECOMMUNICATIONS NETWORKS

A Profile of Telecommunications User Requirements

One of the challenges in providing telecommunications support within an organization is to determine a profile of user requirements. Common points of evaluation around which network plans are made include the following:

User connectivity needs either vary over time or are very consistent, dictating a fixed or flexible way to address them.

Network access and use is either continuous or on demand, which dictates the type of connection and helps to determine the capacity of the network.

Response time (system performance) needs to be fast for a person to continue to work, or system requests can be staged while the person is doing something else, allowing slower response time.

Information (data and voice) volumes that need to be transmitted dictate large, medium or small communications capacity (bandwidth).

User work is individual or shared. If collaborative work within an employee's department and across the enterprise is becoming more common, there is a need to support this communication requirement.

Network-based work is sometimes critical enough to the business to warrant fault tolerant capabilities and to justify redundant equipment or a major network management effort.

Data security concerns, if high, dictate the need for encryption.

The location of use is at one or multiple locations, which could dictate a need for wireless communication devices.

Technical skills of users are low or high, which influences network design criteria and dictates user support requirements.

Understanding these factors is a necessary starting point in determining the telecommunications resources needed to support the organization and the specific design of the network.

Additional Considerations in Building a Telecommunications Network

Once the user profile is in hand, there are important factors from a network standpoint that influence the specific approach taken by a company:

Telecommunications Networks Have Traditionally Been Application Specific but Need to Be General Communications Highways

Telecommunication networks have traditionally been designed and built to address specific applications. This was the case with data communication applications, and the factors that influenced this approach also caused companies to maintain separate voice and data networks. The goal of companies today is the creation of flexible, general purpose networks that can handle voice and data transmissions for multiple applications, without losing any ease of access to applications supported by the network from within and outside the enterprise. Outsiders accessing the network include customers, suppliers, business partners, and mobile and telecommuting employees. Quite commonly the networks also need to connect to each other.

The Pace of Technological Change Is Accelerating How Frequently an Enterprise Changes Its Network

As with computer-based systems, frequent technological advances compel the change of networks for a business to remain competitive. It is very likely that a business will make at least two fundamental changes to its network in the 1990s. These changes would follow an evolutionary process that began when large companies initiated networks for use with their mainframe computers, in many cases in the late 1960s to mid-1970s. This was followed by a LAN (local area network) and WAN (wide area network) cycle in the mid-1980s. A third generation of network technology will include high-speed, digital capabilities like frame relay and Asychronous Transfer Mode (ATM). A fourth cycle of network development is the addition of wireless communication capabilities.

Telecommunications Networks Change by Evolution, Not Revolution

The technology may seem revolutionary, but most major network changes are made incrementally because the often large investment in the existing equipment argues against replacing it in its entirety. It is also important to remember that not only are existing networks already paid for, but they are also installed and they work. Any network change can have a traumatic effect on an organization if it entails learning new ways of doing things. The desirability of a major network overhaul is often in inverse proportion to the number of experienced users. The more users of the current approach, the less likely you are to change it. Balanced capabilities across the network must also be maintained. If a company needs high-digital bandwidth transmission, then the equipment throughout the network must be able to support transmission speeds and capabilities that make both technical and business sense.

Is Today's Hot New Technology Here to Stay?

New technologies are being developed at a pace never before experienced in the telecommunications industry. Picking the future winners from an increasingly larger list has become a challenge. A logical approach for the information systems manager is to do trials of a new technology in the early part of its life cycle. Implementation would be made when it has begun to gain general acceptance following the initial trials. As it starts trending down towards the end of its life cycle an evaluation of possible replacements would begin.

Facility Wiring Choices Continue to Be Important

Facility wiring is an important element of the telecommunications capabilities of an enterprise. Getting it right in the first place is not as big an issue today as it once was. In most cases there are two primary choices: (1) unshielded, twisted-pair copper wire for slower transmission and (2) fiber optics media with 100-megabit transmission capability. A combination of media within a building is very common. If the question is how to retrofit an existing building, the cost to replace what is already installed can exceed the cost of the new media. This is enough of a stumbling block that vendors will often make it possible to use what is already installed. This often means that twisted-pair copper wire is used because so much of it is already in place.

The Changing Carrier Service Landscape

Long-distance carriers have completed the conversion of their networks to fiber. Their objective is to maximize performance out of the network. They will work very hard to recapture the sizable amount of business lost to private networks, which should result in lower long-distance rates and bundled network services to their customers. They also want to be able to compete for local services with the Bell Operating Companies (BOC). While control of its business is changing, much of what the Bell Operating Companies do is still regulated by state public utility commissions. This says that the regulators still play a major role in determining what a BOC can offer as a service. The BOCs will be able to offer long-distance service when the long-distance carriers are allowed to compete for local service.

Open Systems Make Sense Philosophically, But Do They Really Meet Business Needs?

The basic premise of open systems—that everything can "plug and play" with everything else—makes eminent business sense. Getting from this philosophical point to the reality of an installed open network is currently a challenge. Open systems are discussed in more detail later in this chapter, but several points need to made about the concept in general and telecommunications standards specifically. The success of open systems is predicated on the existence and acceptance of standards by user organizations. The development of these standards progresses very slowly, being the product of multiple standards organization committees made up of people representing companies with their own vested interests. Open systems also tend to reduce everything to the least common denominator, which does not necessarily provide the best possible price/performance. For both of these reasons, de facto standards often dominate over the official, de jure standards.

Having said all of this, it is interesting that telecommunications standards for the transmission of data have been developed and more widely accepted than standards for data use and management. Telecommunications connectivity has always required some level of standardization. While there are different telecommunications protocols, there are fewer choices than in the past and these can be reconciled. The major issue remains as to how data will be managed, stored and retrieved, accessed by and presented to users and the operating system platforms. Any hope for a solution to this that makes both technical and business sense will probably come from a vendor consortium and not from a standards organization.

Understanding Vendor Compliance with Standards

There are two dimensions to understanding standards. One is the actual official status of a new standard. The other deals with a vendor's true compliance with the standard. Did the vendor design its product before the final standard was completed, or does it have a product that is really built according to the approved standard?

Crazy Things Happen in the Telecommunications Industry

"Bypass," the creation of a private network by a company, is still a reality even though long-distance and local service carriers are working hard to recapture revenue lost to this approach. If a company is really determined to have its own network to bypass the local service provider or the long-distance carrier, then these same companies will sell the equipment needed to bypass them! Options available to user organizations still include: (1) carrier-based services, (2) BYOB (Be Your Own Bell) or (3) a combination of both, which is normally the case.

The coming together of computing and telecommunications is also prompting some interesting mergers or company alliances both within the United States and between U.S. and foreign companies. This trend should continue in the future.

In the Final Analysis, the Needs of the Business Determine What It Can Afford to Do

Networks cost money and must be justified like any other major expenditure. The value of enhanced communication has always been difficult to assess. Adding additional modes to communicate will further complicate determining its value.

✦✦✦ DATA MANAGEMENT CONTINUES TO BE A CHALLENGE

Since the beginning of any and all endeavors to automate information processes, there have been issues as to how to best accomplish the "management of data." That is what data processing, information systems, distributed systems, image processing or any attempt to systematize the use of information is all about. While a great deal of progress has been made, the "management of data" continues to be a challenge because it is a moving target. To make sense out of all of this necessitates both looking at the basic steps of the processes of dealing with data, and remembering what an organization is trying to accomplish.

Basic Data Management Functions

The specifics of any one step will vary, but there are logical functions within any information systems process. This includes:

Data Capture   Automating the initial capture of data into electronic form at the source of the transaction minimizes data errors, is cost effective and results in the data being more timely. For total cost reasons capturing data at the source of the transaction is a high priority.

Indexing the Data   Unique identifying numbers are an integral part of most information systems. Every effort is made to index the data when it is captured to avoid the cost of doing it manually, which can be prohibitive.

Data Definition   Calling the same type of data by the same name seems like a reasonably easy thing to do. Is there a problem in doing this? As a matter of fact, there often is. Companies have "a paper data dictionary." It exists on paper but no one uses it. There are also CASE (computer assisted-software engineering) data dictionaries. They are used by programmers but not by users. Organizational success in defining (naming) data requires a commitment, discipline and motivation throughout the organization.

Data Compression and Storage   Data storage capacity continues to follow an impressive growth curve with good price/performance. Despite this there is still a strong motivation to develop and take advantage of data compression techniques. There are benefits to be gained both in storing data and in reducing the time to access it and transport it over telecommunications lines.

Access and Retrieval of Data   Accessing data ties back to both indexing and data definition. If this is not done accurately and consistently in the beginning, then the entire process falls apart. The time to retrieve data is still a major factor in on-line applications. Optical disks have large storage capacity but can fail to meet performance expectations, particularly if data cartridges and an electromechanical juke box is involved. Magnetic disks are still the primary storage device when access time is an important factor.

Data Transport   Capacity (bandwidth) for telecommunications transport facilities is a function of the number of bits that can be transmitted per second. Very affordable rates for modems used with PCs in homes is 9,600 or 14,400 bits per second. A large company communication backbone would entail a capacity of multiple lines with a rate of 1.544 million bits per second. Meanwhile there is talk of gigabit transmission capabilities. Ten megabits to a workstation will adequately handle all of the needs of most individuals until multimedia becomes more common.

Data Presentation   Accessed data can be presented in a number of different forms. More is being displayed on monitors of workstations, but the days of the paperless office do not appear to be likely anytime soon. Documents from printers and plotters are still a major source of information.

Agreement regarding these functions would be highly likely although there could be some debate concerning the most logical sequence. The challenge of managing data is complicated by cultural and technological factors that can dictate the actual approach. These can include:

1. Organizational structure, management style and assignment of authority and responsibility.
2. How well the MIS organization works with user departments.
3. The level of centralization or decentralization of computer systems.
4. The organization's experience with technology and related methodologies.
5. The willingness to make the necessary investment of time and money in data management processes.
6. The direct cost of many of the factors mentioned above.

✦✦✦ BUSINESS CRITERIA FOR TELECOMMUNICATIONS

Peter Keen provides the following criteria to be used in assessing the feasibility of new telecommunications' capabilities and their potential impact upon an organization from strategic, operational and financial standpoints: [1]

- ✦ **Connectable:** The ability of employees, customers, vendors and business partners to transfer data and access applications within and outside the organization.

- ✦ **Flexible:** Responding quickly by adding, deleting, changing, expanding or doing whatever is dictated by the needs of the business. Organizations often have a difficult time anticipating the "what if" aspects of their business. But when "what if" happens, they need to be able to respond quickly. This requires telecommunications flexibility.

- ✦ **Phaseable:** An architecture that can add capacity and function to grow with the needs of the business with minimal disruption from the change.

- ✦ **Available:** The systems and the network support are available when needed, which means all the time in most organizations. This also says that business strategy, tactics and plans have been implemented on a stable technological platform.

- ✦ **Reliable:** The systems and network work as designed. Hardware has become more reliable, but software is usually the culprit when a telecommunications system does not work.

- ✦ **Manageable:** As a telecommunications network becomes more critical to both business strategies and day-to-day operations, the ability to manage it becomes equally important. The architecture of the network must lend itself to being managed, and the necessary tools must be available to enable the company to do so.

- ✦ **Maintainable:** A discussion of the maintainability of a telecommunications network starts with how critical the major system and network components are in terms of running the business on a day-to-day basis. Backup of some or all of the system is an option. Emergency power supply and disaster protection also deserve consideration. How quickly it can be fixed and the service capabilities of the vendor are also important considerations.

---

[1] Keen, Peter G.W., *Competing in Time: Using Telecommunications for Competitive Advantage*, New York: Ballinger, 1988, pp. 26–27.

✦✦✦ LINKING USERS WITH INFORMATION FROM APPLICATIONS ON NETWORKS

Figure 11-2 illustrates a typical enterprise telecommunications environment. This environment has four basic elements: **users** make use of **information** within **applications** that are **network-based**. As illustrated, each of these have several possible levels. For instance, the information can be traditional data, text, image, graphics, video, voice or multimedia records. The network can be, and often is, a combination of a local area network (LAN) and a wide area network (WAN) and a mix of public and private networks. It is important to remember that users for specific applications can be individuals, entire departments, the total organization or a multiple-location enterprise. Applications are implemented for personal use, to address organizational processes or major functions like engineering, manufacturing, marketing, etc.

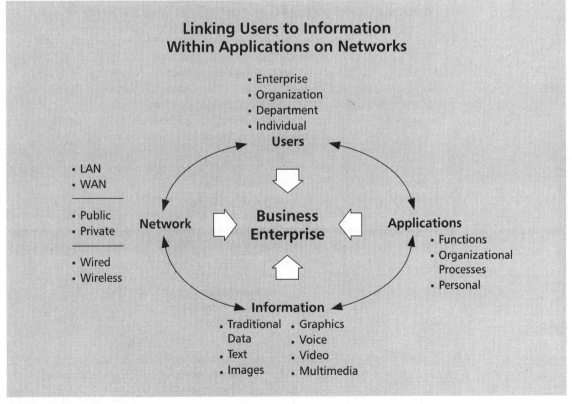

Figure 11-2

✦✦✦ A TELECOMMUNICATIONS ROAD MAP

Figure 11-3 provides a perspective on where most organizations are today and where they would like their information systems to evolve to in the future. A combination of business needs and strategies, financial justification, and management and people skills will determine how and when this will actually happen.

Multi-Vendor and Multi-Product Connectivity

In any evaluation of the contribution of information technology to the success of the business, the starting point is the business environment. The dynamics of the business environment and the changing information technology were addressed in earlier chapters. Addressing the multiple levels of business communication needs—departmental, organization-wide,

Figure 11-3

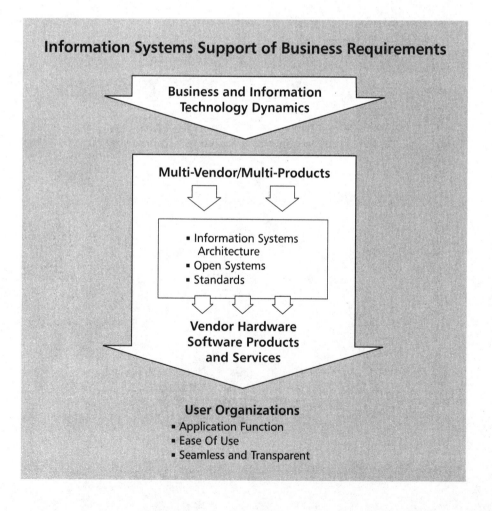

enterprise-wide and interorganizational—with a cost-effective network represents a number of challenges.

In most companies the problem starts with the fact that existing systems (computer applications, voice mail systems, etc.) are from different vendors. These various systems lack the ability to either transfer data or voice messages, or are unable to interface applications with a degree of connectivity that is acceptable to users. You do not even have to buy products from different vendors to have this problem. Incompatible systems from a single vendor is a common complaint.

This problem prompts the question of how these islands of automation were allowed to be created in the first place. The answer is very simple. In the 1970s to the mid-1980s no one foresaw that the ultimate objective was to have integrated systems across the entire enterprise. Even if they did, the computer and telecommunications capabilities and price/performance were not available to support an enterprise-wide approach. Earlier systems were implemented to address specific problems, and they succeeded in this. Information systems managers and professionals received accolades, promotions and salary increases for creating the same systems that are now criticized. The fact that they are so different makes it difficult, and perhaps not even affordable, to integrate them with other systems within the same company.

Information Systems Architecture

If you do not want to repeat the sins of the past and wish to avoid the problems of systems connectivity, then a systems architecture is necessary that addresses the fundamental guidelines around which future systems are designed and built. A systems architecture is a blueprint of the future. It depicts how things are to be accomplished so that information systems professionals and users can create new systems around the same base line. Such an approach requires that the various components of the process be explicitly differentiated and rigorously defined. Particular care should be taken to make sure that the architecture is understood by the people who will be most affected by it, both from a business and a technical standpoint.

It helps to remember that an information system is like a manufacturing operation. In fact, an information system *is* manufacturing. Input (data), process (data manipulation) and output (printed reports, documents, workstation displays, etc.) are the common elements of a manufacturing operation. As a manufacturing operation information systems create complex products. As they become enterprise-wide systems they become even more complex. Effective enterprise analysis is essential to plan, implement and use integrated information systems. The need to do this is driven by the accelerating rate of change of the business environment and enabled by the price/performance improvements of information technology.

A systems architecture is not an end point but a direction. It is important that each decision be made in the context of that direction. While the direction will change, even radically over time, if everyone is pulling in the same direction major benefits can be achieved. The issue is one of implementation while continuing to use existing systems that are necessary to run the business. It is the classic "fixing the battleship while it is at sea."

Distributed Systems, Cooperative Processing and Client-Server

Distributed systems are pushing processing to the desktop of individual users. The term central processing unit (CPU) for a mainframe is obsolete in this context; central storage unit (CSU) would be more appropriate. The role of the mainframe is being shifted from a primary use for processing transactions to one of maintaining large master files, with PCs, workstations and servers taking on more of the actual processing of applications.

To understand distributed systems, cooperative processing and client-server, it is logical to start with distributed systems. A distributed system can be defined as multiple processors that share a communications network. Important is the varying degrees of sharing of data, applications, processing, functions and telecommunications resources.

A wide range of choices is available in planning and implementing a distributed system. The following decisions need to be made:

1. Where to put computers and with what performance capabilities and capacity.
2. Where to store data and how data ownership will be accomplished.
3. Where to process the applications.
4. Where primary users should be located.
5. Where communications functions should be provided and with what capacity.
6. Where the network control should be placed, including whether it should be a single, centralized operation or split among multiple locations.
7. Where both technical and business authority and responsibility should be placed.

Constraints on these choices are both technical and economic. The primary cost constraints are a function of the costs of communication lines versus processing power and storage. Less obvious but growing in importance is the impact of slower response time on user productivity. Also to be considered is the value of having local processing capabilities to address requirements that are unique to the remote location, and the cost of staffing local application development. Central support to remote locations must also be carefully considered.

Cooperative processing is a subset of distributed systems, where application processing is done on multiple systems while appearing to the user to be on a single system. Where and how data is accessed and the application is processed is transparent to the user.

A **client-server** system can be defined as a network shared by multiple user processors involving split processing with specialized purposes. Client-server computing is normally a subset of cooperative processing. The user may know that the data being requested is on another system, but how this is actually accomplished is transparent to the user. Many client-server systems are designed and constructed with three layers or tiers. Application processing presentation is through the user's PC or workstation. A second tier server processes the application or deals with distributed data, while the database application and master data files are on a powerful, centralized database processor.

Benefits of Client-Server Computing   What advantages can client-server computing provide compared to LAN-based PCs with gateways to other systems or traditional on-line systems? The most significant overall advantage is the flexibility to acquire the best and most cost-effective technology for each function. In most PC file server environments the entire database program is downloaded from the file server and sent across the network to the requesting PC. With client-server systems the client formats a compact SQL (Structured Query Language) request, which is sent across the LAN to the data server. The server processes the user request and sends back only the results of the processing initiated by the client request. A summary of the benefits of client-server computing includes:

✦ Achieving ease of use for the end-user through seamless access to data and computer resources made possible by multi-vendor, multi-platform interfaces.

✦ Adding capacity in a modular form.

✦ Enabling applications to become scalable.

✦ Enabling the information systems organization to respond quickly to business change.

✦ Maintaining an emphasis on data integrity and concurrency.

✦ Minimizing communication transmission volumes.

Possible Disadvantages of Client-Server Computing   Going from a traditional system to client-server computing involves a number of potential risks. These can be political, technical, cultural and financial. A client-server system does not eliminate the need for professional information technology skills or for intelligent planning, nor does it reduce the need for user systems-related sensitivity. Specific systems disadvantages include the fact that performance analysis is very difficult. It is hard to model client-server systems and understand why performance is what it is and what can be done to affect it. It is necessary to understand the relationships between the client processing speeds, the network bandwidth, other usage on the network, etc. In the "good old days," this type of problem was solved by installing a faster computer in the centralized data center. Disaster planning is both difficult and not well understood in a client-server environment. It is no longer a matter of taking backup tapes to another processing center. Recreating a system involving shared processing across a LAN and WAN environment brings with it a number of new challenges.

Open Systems and Standards

Connecting systems within an organization and particularly with other companies minimally involves adherence to standards and gives added impetus to the need for open systems. Open systems, when and if they are perfected, will allow various software applications to run on a wide range of computers tied into multiple communication networks. The ultimate goal of an open system would be to support the ability of (1) any user to (2) use any workstation and (3) any application on (4) any system on (5) any network. A decade ago even the most basic of open systems was a fantasy. Much has happened to change the outlook so that the concept is at least being looked at as something that might be feasible. Customers have led the way in telling vendors that is what they want. Responsive vendors that recognize the necessity for open systems have helped, as have government purchasing policies.

Realizing an open systems environment is no simple challenge. The ability to transfer data between systems, to interface applications on different systems and to move application software from one computer to another is much easier said than done. What this means is that all major software components provide or support the same function with the same results. For years software associations and standards groups have debated what function goes into an operating system versus a database management system versus the communications network control programs, etc. Unfortunately the debate continues because of the potential negative impact on vendors and those customers with major investments in software developed according to a vendor's specifications.

To look at the challenge of this effort, the DMR Consulting Group developed "Strategies for Open Systems" to describe where standards are required.[2] Shown in Figure 11-4, there are six major areas that must be addressed.

Operating Systems   Software in general, and operating systems specifically, is where open systems standards are most important. Operating

---

[2] Tapscott, Don, and Art Caston, *Paradigm Shift: The New Promise of Information Technology,* New York: McGraw-Hill, 1993, p. 144.

Figure 11-4

Courtesy of Tapscott and Caston, *Paradigm Shift*, 1993.

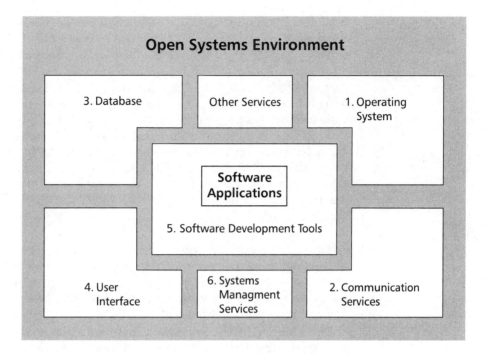

systems are the platform on which application software is based. In addition to a difference in how operating systems actually work, there is the question of whether they support the same type and range of functions. The difference between the functions supported by an operating system on a minicomputer or a mainframe compared to a PC was significant at one time, but this difference is narrowing. Open system proponents cite UNIX as the operating system most likely to be used to realize open standards. In recent years UNIX has experienced significant growth, but it still represents a relatively small percentage of installed operating systems worldwide. Microsoft NT is a challenger to UNIX as an open systems platform.

Communication Services Telecommunication highways are possible only through the use of standards. As indicated earlier, more progress has been made with telecommunications standards than with data. On the other hand personal computers, which have become the dominant workstation throughout the world, were not built initially with any expectation of the demands that are now being placed on them as nodes within large networks. This is changing rapidly, with software enhancements and communication interfaces becoming an integral part of PC microprocessors.

Database Management Systems Database management products for personal computers did not live up to their name for a long time. They were basically file managers. That also is changing—and must change—for open systems to become a true reality, because managing data is at the heart of any enterprise-wide systems approach. The combination of relational databases and high-level query languages has provided better ways to store, manage and access data consistent with open system objectives.

User Interface   Graphics User Interface (GUI) standards are a requirement for open systems. This facilitates the use of new systems by users while also increasing programmer productivity. Definite progress has been made in this area. Microsoft's Windows has been widely accepted, as was the Apple Macintosh operating system. They are very similar in look and feel, so similar that Apple sued Microsoft over this issue. As operating systems become more like each other the battleground for vendors will be the user interface, but it must remain consistent if open systems are to become a reality.

Software Development Tools   If the software is to be portable and/or interoperable, the development tools must be used to build this consistency according to standards and guidelines. Open systems must extend to the tools used to define, design, build, test and maintain applications.

Systems Management Services   These are the management tools of systems and networks, and include systems and network management; performance monitoring, measurement and accounting; problem analysis; and restart and recovery.

Standards in Other Areas   There are systems and network considerations that are not addressed by the above six factors. Things like on-line transactions processing (OLTP), document architectures, multimedia and systems security need standards if they are to be part of an open systems environment.

It is important to remember that all of the above factors can be addressed on a nonstandard basis. It is also possible to have multiple combinations of standards-based open systems and proprietary approaches. These various combinations include:

Proprietary and closed: At one extreme is vendor proprietary and totally closed, which is how the current multi-product, multi-vendor situation happened in the first place. Competitor company engineers did not spend very much time worrying about how a DEC minicomputer was going to interface with an IBM mainframe and an Apple Macintosh. Operating systems from IBM (MS DOS being an exception), Apple, HP and DEC are examples of products in this category.

Public domain and open: On the other end of the spectrum is a product that is completely in the public domain and totally open. The frequently mentioned example is the UNIX operating system. Initially developed by Bell Laboratories, they basically gave it away in the days when they were not allowed to sell it because of a consent decree constraint that forbade their being in nonregulated businesses. The problem with UNIX, which developed over a period of time, is that there are multiple versions from different sources. You really cannot be sure that you will truly have connectivity.

Proprietary but published: The in-between is proprietary but published, and therefore open. One of the key words associated with open systems is "published." Have the specifications for a product been published so that others can build either hardware or software that is consistent with it? A fairly large number of products fit in this category. This is how vendors try to get their way of doing things into at least the category of a de facto standard. IBM's publishing of its PC specifications was a classic example of an open systems mentality. This clearly helped to drive the dramatic growth of the PC with 90% of the world's PCs being IBM compatible. If IBM was so smart in doing this, why at last count were they claiming less than 10% of the PC market? Therein lies the dilemma for a vendor. Does it gain more by making the specifications for a product available, or does this simply mean "giving away the store?" Critics have been very vocal on how IBM put Microsoft (MS DOS) and Intel (microprocessor for its PC) on the map as successful companies and retained the low-margin, commodity components for itself. Sun Microsystems says that it gains more by being a smaller player in a larger market involving standardized products, so they are strong proponents of open systems.

Consortium proprietary but published: There is a growing presence of a fourth category, which is a spin-off from proprietary but published. This is a vendor consortium proprietary-but-published approach. The consortium is not functioning as an official standards body but in their collective proprietary interests. A good case can be made that this could be the winning combination on the data side of the equation. Unfortunately this could mean that user companies will continue to be their own systems integrators. On the other hand, they will benefit from products that are available earlier to address their business needs. While these products will not have an official "open system seal of approval," they will plug and play in a wide enough range to realize many of the benefits of true open systems.

Open Systems Conclusion   Expect the U.S. federal government to continue to push for open systems. This does influence vendors because the federal government is a very large information technology user. On the other hand, how many companies are going to decide that what is good for the federal government also makes sense for them? This decision will be strongly influenced by their existing investment in information systems. Few if any companies have the luxury of starting from scratch. Like most business decisions the cost implications will carry the decision. Will an open systems approach result in cost savings relative to hardware, software, systems and network management, systems change management, and user training? Are there additional savings to be realized from reducing a dependence on a specific vendor, migration to new technology, software integration and gaining a wider range of packaged software choices?

These possible benefits look promising. Despite considerable effort in support of open systems by both vendors and user organizations, a cynic would probably come to the following conclusions regarding the current status of open systems:

✦ No one's complete definition of open systems is acceptable to anyone else.

✦ Vendors are open only when they have to be.

✦ Vendors are closed when they can get away with it because of their constant attempt to carve out competitive uniqueness.

✦ There is no such thing as a true open system.

Whether close is good enough will depend on the specific situation of a particular company.

Distributed Data Management

Distributed database systems would appear to consist of two diametrically opposed approaches to data processing, because they involve a marriage of database systems and telecommunications systems. The logic of early database approaches was based on the premise that data was defined and administered centrally. This resulted in data independence, whereby the application programs were immune to changes in both the logical or physical organization of the data and vice versa. This was viewed as a major advantage, as was the controlled access to the data.

On the other hand, telecommunication networks promote a mode of work that goes against centralized efforts. How can two contrasting approaches be synthesized to produce an approach that is more powerful and more promising than either one alone? The key to answering this question is in the realization that the most important objective of a distributed database approach is not decentralization, but integration. It is possible to achieve integration without centralization, and that is exactly what distributed data management attempts to do.

Why Distribute Data?   Some would offer the sage advice that if you have a choice of whether or not to distribute data management, don't. A centralized database approach is not easy. If you complicate this by creating multiple copies of the database across a telecommunications network, you have minimally multiplied the problem by the number of sites that will have copies of the database. If you go even further and involve different operating systems from different vendors, then you have added further complications to managing the entire system. It is also possible that an organization will want to pursue a distributed approach by integrating existing different database products. In this latter case it will be necessary to provide a translation mechanism between databases. Does this sound fairly challenging? It should, because it is. However, it is possible if the benefits justify the effort. Arguments in favor of a distributed database approach include:

1. Responds to a decentralized structure and culture of the organization.
2. Provides a practical way to address today's big and complicated problems.
3. Addresses the fact that capacity limits for a single processing element are being approached.
4. Disciplines the cost of software development by attacking smaller elements of the total requirement.
5. Because distributed systems are a logical trend, for people reasons if nothing else, it is a way to start building an appropriate infrastructure for the future.

Other advantages of a distributed database system could include local autonomy, improved performance, improved reliability/availability, economics, expandability and shareability. Disadvantages center around reasons such as lack of experience, complexity, cost, distribution of control, security and the difficulty of making the change.

✦✦✦ INTERNET—THE INFORMATION SUPERHIGHWAY

A mention of the Internet conjures up images of a worldwide E-mail network, on-line access to the world's libraries, electronic shopping malls, electronic newspapers and a future of entertainment sources. The believers say that the Internet is all of these and more as it will be constrained only by people's imagination and willingness to try new ways of capitalizing on the information superhighway. Skeptics cite security and cost structure issues as well as technical constraints like bandwidth speeds that are required for quality graphics and certainly for most of the envisioned entertainment. In addition capacity issues will deter progress and acceptance as more users discover the existing capabilities of the Internet. This is an increasingly broadening topic with a significant number of factors that could be addressed. It is appropriate for this segment to deal primarily with the basics of the Internet. The focus will be on explaining what it is and the implications of its use to both individuals and businesses. For an explanation of specific factors that play an important role within the Internet, see the Internet Glossary at the end of this chapter.

An April 1995 article in *Business Week* described the Internet, global and universal, as something that offers the best of the past and a nearly limitless future. It went on to say that it is the biggest thing since the IBM

PC.[3] While the Internet is in a dynamic, developing stage one thing is certain—it is already big, very big. It is big in terms of the size of the network (computer nodes and links), its global scope, the number of users and the number of daily transactions.

What Is the Internet?

The Internet consists of interconnected networks owned and operated by universities, government entities, scientific institutions and business enterprises on a worldwide basis. It is not a single network but a collection of networks that are connected through the use of standards and a cooperative effort on the part of the participants. The National Science Foundation manages the national backbone for the Internet (NSFNet), which is subdivided into regional networks. Recent years have witnessed the democratization of the Internet. Today it connects businesses, research centers, universities, libraries and even elementary and high schools throughout the world. The Internet is a collection of networks in 154 countries. In January 1995 it included 46,000 networks, 4.8 million host computers and an estimated 25 million users.[4] The Internet Society in Reston, Virginia estimates that the number of host computers will grow to 9.2 million by January 1996 and to 124 million by the year 2000. The number of networks is expected to double in a single year to over 100,000 by January 1996. It will then double again with over 200,000 networks by the end of 1996 with a significant amount of the growth coming from outside the United States. At this rate of growth the estimates are that there will be 50 million users sooner than many people expect. This is a classic example of how multiple networks can be connected if they conform to the use of basic standards.

To get onto the Internet requires a personal computer, a modem and communications software that includes TCP/IP protocol capability.[5] You then need an access capability, which is available through an Internet account or an on-line service like America Online, CompuServe or Prodigy. The telecommunications protocol is TCP/IP with information transmitted through the use of packet switching. The common link of the multiple networks is through the use of routers.

Key Players in the Internet World

The beauty of the Internet in the eyes of many people is that no one controls it. There is no Internet Inc. that owns the network and dictates how

---

[3] "Planet Internet," *Business Week,* April 3, 1995, pp. 118–124.

[4] Determining the size of the Internet is a challenge. Confidence in the accuracy of the estimates at any point in time is low because the numbers in all categories are changing rapidly.

[5] See Internet Glossary at the end of this chapter for an explanation of TCP/IP.

things will be done. Coordination is probably a better word to describe how the Internet is administered. There are multiple groups that are both active and influential. The National Science Foundation operates the NSFNet, which is part of the backbone of the Internet in the United States. Through grant funding it has authorized companies like AT&T to provide an Internet directory service. Using the same approach MCI has provided enhancements to the performance of the backbone. It is somewhat confusing at times as to where responsibilities begin and end, but that is the way it is with the Internet. Most of the technical and financial responsibilities rest with the owner of the network that is being connected.

The Internet Society, as an international body, plays a number of roles. It is the parent of the Internet Engineering Task Force, which develops and maintains the communication protocols. It also appoints people to the Internet Architectural Board, which is the main group concerned with all technical issues. Anyone can join the Internet Society. It exists not to control but to coordinate and communicate appropriate information about the Internet to promote its use and success.

How the Internet Got Its Start

Like many networks, the Internet had a humble beginning. Initially it was a single network called ARPANET, used primarily by several thousand computer scientists to access computers, share files and send electronic mail. The original major intent of sharing supercomputer resources very quickly came second to electronic communication as a reason for the network. E-mail had arrived and would be a major driving force behind the growth of the Internet.

This all started as a U.S. Department of Defense project that began operation in 1969. The fact that the military played a major role in the design of the network is significant relative to the architecture of the network. In the midst of the Cold War the military was concerned with how they would be able to communicate within the United States following a nuclear attack. A single command center was ruled out because it would be a primary target. It was also obvious that the wires and switches of a network could not be protected from a nuclear explosion. The solution was to build a network with no central authority that could operate in pieces if something happened to part of the network. These two design principles have enabled the Internet to become the global network that it is today. The network could accommodate different computers and communications equipment as long as they used the standard protocols. TCP/IP was in the public domain, and no one really wanted to stop others from linking to the network. Connecting to the Internet was also practical because each node was independent and responsible for its own technical issues and financing. A military-motivated solution in 1970 provided the basis for what became the Internet.

Early use of ARPANET was limited to the military, defense contractors and universities doing defense department research. A major milestone in Internet history was the creation of the National Science Foundation Network (NSFNet) in 1986, which linked researchers across the country with five supercomputer centers. It was subsequently expanded to include mid-level and statewide academic networks that connected universities and research consortiums. Because the NSFNet was replacing the ARPANET, the latter was dismantled in March 1990. At the time that the NSFNet was built, the Internet we know today started becoming a reality. International networks sprang up rapidly all over the world and were connected to the U.S. network.

Current Uses of the Internet

Despite all the hype about the Internet some basic considerations determine whether the Internet makes sense for a specific individual or organization. E-mail is still a big reason people use the Internet. This can take the form of messages or discussion groups. Remote computing and file transfers—the original reason for creating the network—is still being done. Information access has become a major network use factor. This logically gets broken into current local and world events and library and other data source retrieval. Transaction processing on the Internet is on the rise. Such things as order entry through EDI systems that use the network are increasing both in number of systems and transactions.

The current approach regarding charges for Internet use is what gets people excited. There is no measured use of the NSFNet backbone (long-distance transmission) so there are no charges for its use. Organizations pay for an Internet account and for a communications line to the nearest Internet access node, but these costs are seldom charged out to specific users or user departments. This leaves the typical user with the feeling that the Internet is free, so they can send E-mail messages anywhere in the world without being concerned about charges.

The ultimate commercialization of the Internet is inevitable. The question is whether commercialization will lead to privatization so that "free" use will not last into the future. The first thing that could drive privatization is the cost to continue to improve transmission rates and other services on the Internet. Bandwidth and security are two areas of concern. A second factor is that long-distance telecommunications carriers see the Internet as direct competition, and they are not very happy that the federal government is subsidizing this competitor in the form of the NSF-sponsored backbone within the United States.

The Future of the Internet

To say that the Internet of the future will be different from what it is today is a needless observation. The Internet is changing daily. New services are offered every day. Estimates are that a million new users join the Internet *each month*. While a significant amount of Internet use has been focused in North America, this is also changing. Although some countries have limited Internet use to universities, it is becoming easier for users outside the United States to gain access to the Internet.

An increase in the number of users does not go unnoticed by the business world. Using the Internet to communicate with an advertisement to the 30 million people has clearly caught the attention of many businesses. Some companies are offering services to other businesses on how to best use the Internet. Call them advertising or electronic publishing, they exist to provide a service to companies that need help in capitalizing on a very large but in some cases an uncertain business potential.

But this is not just something for the future. It is happening today. It is easier to ask what industry is not at least experimenting with the use of the Internet. Service companies find the Internet particularly intriguing as a way to communicate with customers, with the potential of creating new ways of doing business. Advertising agencies, law firms, accounting firms, brokerage houses and banks are just a few of these. Specific examples include Wells Fargo Bank (regional bank), J.P. Morgan (trading house), the Chicago Mercantile Exchange (futures exchange), Cohen and Grigsby P.C. (law firm), MCA/Universal (entertainment), the *San Jose Mercury News* (newspaper), Burlington Coat Factory (catalog), Reebok (sportswear), DIALOG (information retrieval service), Hyatt Hotels, etc. This is not to say that manufacturers are not also pursuing the Internet as a marketing and service support channel. General Electric, GM Saturn, Intel, IBM, Apple, Digital Equipment, Xerox and Hewlett-Packard are a few of the companies that have initiated efforts with the Internet. There are approximately 25,000 commercial accounts ("com" domains) on the Internet.

Some of this is through the access of a company's system on its own network, which is linked to the Internet. In many cases it is through the creation of a World Wide Web home page—a series of hypertext documents or "electronic yellow pages"—that can be accessed through the Internet. Making the World Wide Web even more appealing to many users are multimedia capabilities that include audio and video in addition to graphics. Because of tools like the World Wide Web and the graphical browsers it is becoming much easier to use the Internet. As indicated above, Internet entrepreneurs have already blazed a trail into on-line banking, publishing, marketing and database access.

While many companies are anxious to take advantage of these business opportunities, the results to date have been mixed. Some companies are very pleased with the results they have achieved, while others are still waiting for the flood of responses from their prospective Internet customers. There is also a continuing concern regarding a lack of security in general on the Internet and risk related to computer hackers and the problems they might create. Commercial solutions are available that provide encryption capabilities that make it relatively safe to process transactions.

The Internet is obviously here to stay. It will continue to be a part of how many people work and live. In what form and with what capabilities and services will it exist in the future? That is one of the more interesting aspects of the Internet. If no one was able to predict it would be where it is today, how can anyone project with certainty what it will be like (and cost) in the future? There are challenges on both the provider and user side. Companies must provide services and support that individual users and organizations will value. Users face a challenge in grasping all that is available on such a vast network, learning how to effectively access it and then taking advantage of its availability. As the commercials often say, "Stay tuned—it is going to be interesting!"

✦✦✦ INTEGRATED VOICE-DATA APPLICATIONS

For almost sixty years telecommunications meant only voice communications. (That is, unless you accept that the first data communications were done in the 1930s by the U.S. Army.) It was not until the 1960s that data communications became other than a novelty. During the time that voice was the primary mode of communications, managing it meant focusing on the availability of a dial tone and trying to reduce the per unit cost. As illustrated in Figure 11-5 voice communications have progressed along a path similar to and parallel to data communications. The objectives for both evolved from efficiency to include effectiveness, and then they both added competitive advantage. The next step? Can voice and data systems jointly address these objectives, and do the strengths of both add up to improved processes, better value to customers and an enhanced competitive advantage?

Voice applications continue to fall within four basic categories:

1. Voice mail.
2. Least-cost routing—the ability to select the best routing for a call at the time that the call was made. This was the first major CBX (computer branch exchange) voice application.
3. Automatic call distribution (ACD)—the bank of operators at an airline reservation center where "your call will be assigned to the first available agent."
4. Call detail reporting—"If any of the calls on this list that were made from your extension were for your personal use, please write a check to ... ."

When voice applications extend beyond the above four examples, it means a marriage with data. This marriage is far from intuitively obvious because too many years have been devoted to keeping them separate. As

Figure 11-5

A Telecommunications Perspective

Objective	Voice	Data
Efficiency	Voice Message Volumes	Transmission Volumes
Effectiveness	Voice Applications	PCs and Application Packages
Competitive Advantage	Voice Applications Plus Linkage	Systems Linkage
⟹	Integrated Voice /Data Applications	

banks have discovered with their 24-hour banking service, the integration of voice and data applications can go a long way in producing customer satisfaction.

✦✦✦ GROUPWARE—A MAJOR NEW ERA FOR COMPUTING

As is often the case with any new major form of computing there is debate over a correct definition. Such is the case with groupware. It is a broad collection of technologies that includes E-mail, calendaring and scheduling, collaborative document handling, group decision support, conferencing, audio/video/desktop and meeting room conferencing, group application development tools, work flow and project management. Selecting from this menu is a function of specific need. It begins with understanding why groupware might make a fundamental change in the approach taken within an organization to realize more benefits from its information technology.

Groupware is well on its way to becoming the next major computer-based accomplishment because it links colleagues in the same or different locations in ways that vastly improve the efficiency and speed of collaborative projects. It addresses the two primary ways that work groups share their work: (1) sending things to each other and (2) sharing information by putting it in a central document database. The basic foundation for groupware already exists in the large number of installed PCs connected by local area networks (LANs). In addition a significant number of people are experienced in using PCs, E-mail and electronic bulletin boards. For these reasons groupware may prove to be a very strategic technology that should show results within a short time.

Groupware at UB Networks

At a national meeting of sales representatives in Atlanta in 1991 Ralph Ungermann, the founder and then president of UB Networks, Inc., a division of Tandem Computers,[6] concluded that the traditional way of disseminating information to sales representatives was not timely and effective in their dynamic industry. Relying on meetings to accomplish this had obvious built-in time delays and clearly did not provide the information to the sales representatives when they needed it. Ungermann's vision was that his sales representatives would be more successful if they had access to product information when they needed it through the use of an on-line computer-based system.

A telephone call from Ungermann to Tom Waitman, the Group Director of Information Technology, triggered an evaluation that resulted in the selection of Lotus Notes as the most effective way to implement the necessary system. It is important to note that Lotus Notes is not an application that arrives in a box and is then implemented. It is a graphical, client-server application platform that is tailored to the needs of the organization. For this reason the implementation of Lotus Notes can vary dramatically among different companies.

The implemented system supports 1,400 workstations around the world through the use of 69 servers linked through a private network. That this network was already in place was a definite advantage to UB Networks, and helps to explain how the equivalent of six full-time people were able to implement more than thirty applications in one year using Lotus Notes.

The best way to appreciate the success of the support provided is through an understanding of how the field sales organization uses the system and the impact it has had on their jobs. It is the platform for the E-mail systems and the source of all product announcements, sales successes, analyst reports and sales reports. For a specific sales situation a sales representative can use the system to check UB Network prices and the status and availability of products. White papers on products and presentation material is also provided. Literally all product information other than printed material that would be given to a customer is distributed via this system. The competitive database includes information on products, prices, possible competitive strategies in specific situations and an information feed from Business Wire on newsworthy events during the past thirty days. It is also used for administrative tasks like travel authorizations and expense reporting.

The Lotus Notes system has addressed the need that prompted its implementation. A general conclusion is that the field sales force is now more current, better informed and much more productive. The following

---

[6] Ralph Ungermann resigned in 1993 from the company that he founded in 1979. Ungermann-Bass was acquired by Tandem Computers in 1988. The name of the company was changed to UB Networks in 1994.

sentiment is indicative of the value of the system to the field sales force. Mark Weiner, the manager of the Competitive Marketing organization, received an E-mail message that said:

> I am sending you this to tell you what an asset the competitive database is to my efforts as a field sales rep. In my previous position with another company in the telecommunications industry we did not have anything that compared to what you are providing. We would get updates on competitors that were faxed or mailed to us—but we were personally responsible for sorting, filing and making sure that we were up-to-date. For a busy salesperson this was impossible, so most of the information went unused. Your database is a powerful tool. I check it every day just to stay in touch with what is happening in the industry.

When integrated with a data warehouse the Lotus Notes system also supports (1) a summary database for all revenue information on a worldwide basis, (2) a common set of decision support models for analyzing the data and (3) an ability to address ad hoc reporting needs.

Access to timely information by sales representatives and others within an organization and the ability to share this across the organization is often critical for a company like UB Networks. As the above examples indicate groupware is one of the hottest new IT tools around. How else can you explain IBM's paying $3.5 billion to buy Lotus primarily to get the rights to Notes?

✦✦✦ CONCLUSION

This chapter opened with the statement that no field in the world offers more promise than the twin technologies of computers and telecommunications. An interesting dimension of this statement is that it is becoming more difficult to separate the two. One complements the other. Each triggers the use of the other. Data needs telecommunications to broaden the ways to access it. Telecommunications often needs data and voice records to prove that it can deliver something of value to customers, which is what business competition is all about.

INTERNET GLOSSARY

Archie A system that finds files on the Internet and downloads them by using File Transfer Protocol (FTP). It provides the address of the remote server including the directory of where the file is located.

Browser   A hypertext viewer that is used with the World Wide Web (document manager). A browser establishes contact with a server, reads the file and displays it on a personal computer. Mosaic (see below) has become synonymous with the World Wide Web, but there are other browsers like Netscape that are very popular. These two are the best known, but the number of browsers is increasing. The issue for most users is not whether to use a browser with the World Wide Web, but which one. A browser makes it much easier to use the Web by pointing and clicking instead of entering computer commands, which many users find difficult.

Domain   The nodes in the Internet are divided into six domains: "gov, mil, edu, com, org and net." The first three designate the early pioneers and current major users of the Internet (government, the military, and educational institutions). "Com" is used for commercial organizations, with "org" retained for nonprofits. "Net" computers serve as gateways between networks. One of these six domain designations is used as the last part of an address in sending a message on the Internet.

File Transfer Protocol (FTP)   A popular feature of the Internet is the ability to obtain files from other computers, which is accomplished through the use of File Transfer Protocol (FTP). Protocols are rules that ensure the transfer of a file from one system to another. In this case it is implemented primarily as software to accomplish the file transfer.

Gopher   Gopher is a client-server system menu that facilitates finding information on the Internet without having to use hard-to-understand computer commands. It arranges information in a hierarchy rather than with the dynamic links used by the World Wide Web. A Gopher server is software that runs on an Internet host computer and points to the location of information. The Gopher client is software that runs on a user's PC or the local system's host computer.

Home Page   A hypertext document with links to other points on the World Wide Web. It is the first page that is seen when a World Wide Web resource is encountered. It is usually part advertisement, directory and reference library. Universities, institutions, businesses and individuals can have their own page or pages.

Hypertext   A system that links documents stored in multiple computers in multiple locations even though they are not part of the same file. Hypertext was originally envisioned as text only but came to encompass any information that can be stored in digital form, including images, sound, video and any forms of data.

Hypertext Markup Language (HTML)   HTML is used to create pages on the World Wide Web. It embeds commands in a text file to control the appearance of the page and establish links to related articles throughout the Internet.

Internet   Internet is a network of networks. Regional providers have played an integral part in the Internet since its inception. These include SURAnet,

CICnet, NEARnet, BARnet, NorthWestNet, MIDnet and Sesquinet. Although it is often referred to as an ad hoc network, major groups manage its existence. The Internet Architecture Board addresses technical changes to the Internet. MCI, which manages the NSF backbone through a grant from the National Science Foundation, is dealing with the need for increased bandwidth through very high-speed Backbone Network Services (vBNS). The InterNIC (see below) coordinates the issuing of Internet accounts. User groups include the Internet Society headed by Vinton Cerf, who is considered by many to be the father of the Internet.

InterNIC The directory of directories that enables references to be obtained to information resources, products and services on the Internet. This facility is currently maintained by AT&T through a grant from the National Science Foundation.

Mosaic A graphical browser (viewer) that allows users to travel through the World Wide Web on the Internet using a point-and-click interface. The original Mosaic was developed by the National Center for Supercomputing Applications (NCSA) at the University of Illinois. Enhanced versions of Mosaic are sold by companies that the original developers joined after leaving the university. This includes Spry and Netscape Corp.

National Information Interface (NII) Business, technology and political aspects of a National Information Interface (NII) are emerging. There seems to be confidence that this infrastructure will develop. Is the Internet the foundation for this, or will it take on an entirely new form and structure? The second issue concerns who will actually bring it into being. The first choice is between government and the private sector, with cost suggesting that it must be done by the latter. Within the private sector there are multiple candidates to lead the way: cable TV companies, telecommunications carriers, consumer electronics companies, computer companies or combinations of several or even all of them.

TCP/IP This is really two protocols. Transmission Control Protocol (TCP) converts messages into streams of packets at the source and then reassembles them into messages at the destination. Internet Protocol (IP) deals with routing the packets across multiple nodes within a single network and across multiple networks.

Telnet Once a user has logged onto the Internet, Telnet provides the ability to dial directly into a remote computer without having to call that particular computer. In other words, a user dials into the nearest computer and through the use of Telnet connects to a computer in another part of the country or around the world.

Veronica There are hundreds of Gopher servers on the Internet. The one developed at the University of Minnesota, sometimes referred to as Mother Gopher, just happens to be the one that is best known. Veronica (Very Easy Rodent-Oriented Netwide Index to Computerized Archives) can be used to find the information for which a user is searching. It is actually a database that is self-updating with headings for most, if not all, Gopher servers on the Internet. A Gopher client must be used to take advantage of Veronica.

WAIS   There are many databases, and the access methods are not the same. The Wide Area Information Server (WAIS) allows users to search different databases. WAIS also allows searching for information in multiple databases at different locations.

World Wide Web (WWW)   The World Wide Web could be called the glue that makes finding and accessing documents on the Internet possible. It was developed by a group of programmers at the European Particle Physics Laboratory in Switzerland to create a unified hypertext network for high-energy physicists working in a diverse international environment. Rather than attempt to impose standards on the software or the hardware, they defined standards for the data. They created self-organizing hypertext software, which has standardized the way that documents can be indexed, addressed and linked. The beauty of this approach is that it allows maximum openness and flexibility. It established two standards: Hypertext Transfer Protocol (HTP) and the Hypertext Markup Language (HTML). A Universal Resource Locator (URL) is the address that ties the two together into a hypertext view of on-line documents. A URL reference can point in the same document, or to another document in the same file, or to another file on the same or another network.

Worm   A program that "worms" its way through the World Wide Web, searching thousands of home pages for links to other pages. It then compiles the Universal Resource Locator (URL) and the title of each page into a searchable database.

Yahoo   Rapidly becoming the most popular Gopher on the Internet. Developed by two graduate students at Stanford University, it has more advanced capabilities than the earlier Gophers. It also functions on the World Wide Web as a search server. As such it will seek out keywords or other criteria in tens of thousands of documents over the net.

RECOMMENDED READING

Gray, Pamela, *Open Systems: A Business Strategy for the 1990s*. London: McGraw-Hill, 1991.

A thorough analysis of the merits of open systems.

Keen, Peter G.W., *Competing in Time: Using Telecommunications for Competitive Advantage*. New York: Ballinger, 1988.

This book is about business, not technology. It concentrates on organizational issues and not technical ones. Its major value is the material on telecommunications. Peter Keen has an excellent grasp of management issues and does a commendable job, saying "Telecommunications is about competition, innovation, risk and uncertainty. It opens up entirely new ways of thinking about customers, markets, productivity, coordination, service, competitors, products and organization."

Kehoe, Brendan P., *Zen and the Art of the Internet: A Beginner's Guide.* Englewood Cliffs, NJ: Prentice-Hall, 1992.

> While a book describing the Internet can become outdated fairly quickly, this is a good basic introduction. This is available on-line through the Internet.

Orfali, Robert, Dan Harkey, and Jeri Edwards, *Essential Client-Server Survival Guide.* New York: Van Nostrand Reinhold, 1994.

> This book covers all aspects of client-server computing. It addresses how every major facet of computing is changing, from operating systems and communications to database, transaction processing and groupware; from middleware and network operating systems to systems and network management.

Tapscott, Don, and Art Caston, *Paradigm Shift: The New Promise of Information Technology.* New York: McGraw-Hill, 1993.

> This book is an attempt to help see the logic and necessity of making the shift from the old to the new based on the need to create high-performance teams, an integrated organization and an extended enterprise. The major enabler will be information technology in general and network computing specifically.

Vaskevitch, David, *Client-Server Strategies: A Survival Guide for Corporate Reengineers.* San Mateo, CA: IDG Books Worldwide, 1993.

> The Director of Enterprise Computer for Microsoft, David Vaskevitch provides advice on how to take control of changing information technology within an enterprise. The book explains how managers should empower employees with the information needed to do their jobs more efficiently, effectively and competitively, with a client-server architecture providing the platform to accomplish this.

EXERCISES

1. Personal uses of services based on telecommunications networks.

Be prepared to discuss personal uses of services that are made possible by telecommunications networks.

2. Telecommunications road map.

Use the telecommunications road map chart, Figure 11-4, to profile an organization. Be very specific regarding the computing platforms that exist in the major functional areas within the company. Pay particular attention to information systems architecture, open systems plans and major systems and telecommunications standards.

3. Integrated voice/data applications.

Identify existing examples of integrated voice/data applications or possible applications that would benefit from the integration of the two technologies. How do the combination of both technologies benefit an organization over and above the use of data or voice systems?

4. Electronic delivery versus newspapers.

Contrast the traditional role of newspapers with that of the services available over the Internet. Compare the Internet as an information source with a local newspaper, *USA Today,* the *Wall Street Journal* and the national edition of the *New York Times.*

5. Internet business proposal.

Prepare a proposal for a business that would be based on the Internet. Focus on the uniqueness of such a business approach over a more traditional approach. Are there major technical issues that might prevent your proposal from being successful?

USING INFORMATION SYSTEMS TO COMPETE: A SUCCESS FACTOR PROFILE

Success is doing the right thing, not just what the past dictates.

LEARNING OBJECTIVES

This chapter examines the factors that were the major contributors to companies' successful use of information systems to compete. The Success Factor Profile is used in the chapter to analyze the strengths of specific organizations.

QUESTIONS

The following questions deal with the Success Factor Profile:

1. Is there a common pattern to the organizations that have successfully used information systems to compete?
2. In what three modes (time frames) can the Success Factor Profile be used?
3. Why are there so many factors in the Success Factor Profile?
4. Is it possible for an organization to address all of the success factors simultaneously?
5. Is there a single factor that dominates the explanation for the successful use of information systems to gain a competitive advantage?
6. Choosing between senior management, functional management and information systems management, who should have a primary responsibility for each of the success factors?

✦✦✦ THE SUCCESS FACTOR PROFILE

The Success Factor Profile shown in Figure 12-1 is a compilation of the strengths of more than 150 organizations. Information systems executives were interviewed to gain a better understanding of the following questions regarding their strategic use of information systems:

✦ Why and how they used information systems to try to gain a competitive advantage.

✦ Whether they were successful.

✦ The major reasons for their success both within the organization and relative to their competitive environment.

The Success Factor Profile can be used in three ways at three different points in time:

1. As the basis for an **initial planning process** to focus information systems on competitive issues.

2. As an **assessment of the progress** of new systems and how they are meeting competitive objectives.

3. As an **audit device for mature systems** to make sure the company has not missed a shift in the dynamics of the organization's competitive environment. This could prompt a systems change or even a major new approach.

The Success Factors

In evaluating the factors in the profile as they relate to a specific organization, three questions should be addressed corresponding to the three columns on the right of Figure 12-1. First, how important are each of these factors as they relate to gaining a competitive advantage? All of them may be viewed as important, so they should be prioritized based upon which are mandatory, which are worth the investment, and which simply are not important enough to warrant initial attention. Second, who should play a key role? Specify the answer in terms of senior management, functional management or information systems management. When it has been determined what is most important and who must play a key role the final question is, where are the current strengths and what areas must be improved? The answers to this evaluation should serve as the basis for an action plan to gain a competitive advantage from information systems.

The sixteen factors included in the profile are as follows:

Business Vision This is the vision for the future of the business. It should be a documented outlook addressing logical and achievable goals that can be both understood and accepted throughout the organization. Emphasized factors would include market opportunities, product and

Figure 12-1

Success Factor Profile

Management	Importance	Responsibility	Assessment
Business Vision			
Culture			
Risk Management			
Plan Implementation			
IS Integral to the Business			
IS Justification Mgmt. Process			
Executive-IS Mgr. Partnership			
Executive IS Experience			
Operational Automation			
Linkage to Suppliers			
Linkage to Customers			
Linkage to Customer Service			
Pervasive Computing Literacy			
IS Architecture			
IS Marketing			
IS User Relations			

services trends, business risks, geographic focus, organizational trends, possible alliances, and any other high-priority determinants of the future of the business. In other words, what will the business look like in ten, twenty or even thirty years in the future and what things must be accomplished to sustain the long-term viability of the business?

Culture   Culture is simply "the way we do things around here." It is not a grass-roots endeavor evolving through the efforts of employees, but a senior management, value-driven factor. Employees can and will respond positively to cultures that emphasize customer service and quality products or services—two key ingredients to any competitive strategy. Culture has become an increasingly important factor as computing has become more pervasive within organizations. This pervasiveness says that getting employees to accept the use of competitively focused systems can become a critical success factor. A strong culture is often a major benefit in getting people within the organization to recognize and accept the need for a new information system, even though it will change how they personally do things.

Risk Management   Key business success factors are identified during the organization's planning process. Within the context of accomplishing this, a decision can also be made as to where the organization is willing to take risks. There are major options in today's environment. In addition to financial as the most obvious business risk factor, is the organization willing to take a risk in acquiring and marketing products? Knowing the answer to this can help to prioritize the information systems focus and the implementation approach. This risk assessment should include information systems exposure and impact on the business.

Plan Implementation   Planning becomes meaningful when it drives execution. Effective planning represents a significant amount of work for people running the business. Planning must be viewed as a process and not a document driven by calendar dates. This suggests a willingness to change the plan when the dynamics of major business factors make it logical to do so. Once in place the strategic, operational and financial plans should drive the priorities of the information systems organization.

Information Systems Integral to the Business   How integral to the business is the use of information systems? A simple way to formulate an answer would be based on what would happen to the business if the information systems suddenly stopped working. What is the answer to this question for five to ten years in the future? What are the product, service and organizational ramifications of the answers to these questions?

Information Systems Justification Process   This addresses the financial strategies so important to any information systems effort, from saving money to making money so that you can continue to grow the business. The most important dimension to this process is that it provides a response to senior management when they ask: What are we getting for our ever-increasing financial commitment to information systems?

Executive and Information Systems Management Partnership   It is essential that senior management and the information systems manager develop an open dialogue and an ongoing working relationship. Senior management must have confidence in the credibility of information systems as a viable competitive resource. For this partnership to become a reality, information systems management must understand the business including directions and priorities.

Executive Information Systems Experience   Senior executives often lack experience in dealing with many of the information systems-related management issues. They simply did not grow up with the computer being a key part of their earlier business experience. While not wanting to turn senior management into technicians, it is important that they understand the key management factors of information systems. People who manage production operations do not necessarily understand all of the technical details of manufacturing, but they do understand the key factors. The same can be said about financial managers, marketing, product development, etc. Therefore it is appropriate to suggest that people who manage knowledge workers (people who create, use and distribute data) should also understand the key factors relative to the effective use of information systems.

Operational Automation   This is one of the major opportunity areas for the effective use of information systems. Internal operations is where emphasis has traditionally been placed by many organizations. An appropriate question is whether the current expenditure on information systems resources is on the right factors as they relate to the competitive advantage of the organization.

Linkage to Suppliers and/or Other Business Partners   Many organizations have emphasized systems use in this area because of just-in-time inventory systems. Linkage with suppliers can address more than just delivery schedules. This assessment should take a broad look at the value and use of more, better or more timely information in the entire spectrum of the business relationship with suppliers or other business partners.

Linkage to Customers   Much of the interest in using information systems to compete has been concentrated in this area. While important, the other operational areas should not be overlooked. A key question in considering electronic links with customers is whether it is possible to redefine the value of products and services to the customer through more, better or more accessible information. Once this is determined, the frequency of use and the mobility of the marketing representative or the customer will dictate the device to be used to gain access to the information. The various approaches with an objective of redefining the delivery process should also be considered. Can the way that products or services are delivered become as important as the actual products and services because of the enhanced information content?

Linkage to Customer Service   There are at least three levels of information systems use as it relates to customer service. As with customer linkage the validity of the approach is driven by information value and accessibility. In this case the important factor is also how this relates to fixing the problem—the repair service side of the business. The challenge is to take a broad approach. The linkage can be the traditional one between an information system and the company's service personnel. Another approach links the system directly with customer personnel with the assumption that they can fix the problem. A third approach ties the vendor system directly with the product for on-line diagnostics and in some cases actual repair. The more advanced approaches in this area often dictate that on-line diagnostics must be engineered into the product.

Pervasive Computing Literacy   Who in the organization has a job with high information content and can also enhance their efforts through a better understanding of how information systems actually work? How do you prepare your employees to effectively use systems that are intended to provide a competitive advantage? Said another way, is the computer literacy of the people in the organization good enough to effectively utilize more advanced systems that have a competitive advantage objective?

Information Systems Architecture   Information systems to address the requirements of many businesses have a very broad design scope, increasing levels of complexity and involve large total costs. At the same time there is a need for both systems flexibility and quicker response to business needs. These factors dictate the use of a logical architecture to define and control the interfaces and integration of all of the components of a system. A systems architecture has become a crucial part of the necessary infrastructure. It is needed to hedge long lead times which are often unacceptable to senior management's immediate need to address a business issue. To have an appropriate systems architecture requires an architect. This is someone who can understand the vision of the organization and put in place a logical, long-range plan that has high odds of being able to respond to future business requirements.

Information Systems Marketing   The acceptance of information systems within an organization is critical to gaining a sustainable competitive advantage through the use of these same systems. This is acceptance at all levels within the organization, from senior management to employees using the systems. The information systems organization must do a marketing job not only to provide an understanding of their products and services, but also to establish information systems as a value-added resource. This marketing effort should include all of the same factors that any marketing organization would address in dealing with and servicing a customer.

Information Systems and User Relations   While this is a by-product of information systems marketing, it is important enough and different enough to be addressed as a separate topic. If information systems marketing gains internal acceptance, then this must be followed by effort to build and maintain a good, ongoing relationship between the information systems organization and users.

Why So Many Factors?

The number of factors within the profile has often been questioned. The question would suggest that the reason companies are successful in using information systems to compete is not all that clear. Logic dictates that the list should not be consolidated. The five or six strengths of Wal-Mart can be completely different from those of McKesson, Boeing or Visa International. Why? Because they are different businesses in different industries. A list comparing Mervyn's to Dillards could also be different. They have different management, different strategies, operate in different locales with a different product mix—they are different! Each of the factors in the profile was influenced by specific or multiple organizations. The key is not to streamline the list, but to understand the multiple factors and pick the ones that are truly strengths of successful companies.

✦✦✦ COMPANY SUCCESS FACTOR PROFILES

The Success Factor Profile is used in the following examples to identify the four or five major strengths that enabled the organization to achieve and sustain a competitive advantage through the use of information systems.

Federal Express Success Factor Profile

Federal Express redefined the delivery business by capitalizing on the needs of businesses for a time-sensitive, overnight delivery service that they could truly count on. What better evidence is there of an ever-increasing compression of time and events than the very existence of Federal Express with over $8 billion in revenue in 1994? FedEx literally changed "normal" leadtimes for companies. It used to be "three days and hope" based on U.S. Postal Service delivery schedules. Today it is based on the time of the last pickup by Federal Express for next-day delivery.

Federal Express began operations on March 12, 1973, shipping eleven packages that first night. It did not experience a profitable month until July of 1975 and its first profitable year until 1976. A recap of the first three years reads like a soap opera—it was touch and go whether the company would make it because cash flow was a continual problem for this capital-intensive business. From the meager eleven packages the first night, the daily volume of shipments now averages 2 million to all U.S. locations and 186 foreign countries.

The major factors that led to the success of the company whose name has become synonymous with overnight shipment include the following:

Vision Fred Smith, the founder and CEO of Federal Express, had a vision that was initially described in a term paper while he was an undergraduate at Yale University. The fact that the paper received a "C" grade amuses people. More important is that he continued to believe in the idea that there was an excellent opportunity for a company that could provide reliable overnight delivery of a time-sensitive package or document. The priority given to information technology was based on this vision. Smith's commitment to this vision was clearly necessary for Federal Express to survive its early years and to grow to the organization that it is today.

Culture   Fred Smith also deserves a great deal of credit for the extremely strong culture within Federal Express. This internal culture is very customer focused. Smith's emphasis on excellence is evident in the commitment that FedEx employees have made to "absolutely, positively overnight service." This goal of providing a reliable, overnight service unparalleled in the industry resulted in an entire company's acceptance and use of information systems as a better way to achieve their customer service objectives.

Executive and Information Systems Management Partnership   There has been an ongoing working relationship between Fred Smith, as the business visionary, and those charged with designing and implementing the information systems that make the entire FedEx distribution system work. Chief Operating Officer Jim Barksdale and Ron Ponder, Information Systems Vice-President, worked closely with Smith and played key roles. Barksdale has remarked, "Smith would say we need to climb that hill, and Ponder and I would make it happen." When they both left for opportunities with other companies, Dennis Jones became the Chief Information Officer. Jones had previously managed information systems within the sales organization, which was a major driver of information systems requirements. He has a strong information technology background and he maintains a close working relationship with those charged with the daily operations of Federal Express as well as the person who still sets the directions for the company—Fred Smith.

Information Systems Integral to Business   Federal Express is synonymous with reliable, quality service because of state-of-the-art information technology used to develop an innovative distribution system. The hub and spoke system was designed to handle reliable distribution of packages and documents. Information systems were used to automate the distribution process. This approach provided benefits in all three possible roles of information systems which were discussed in Chapter 1. It improved efficiency and the reliability of the process as well as the **effectiveness** of Federal Express employees. All of this was critical to the successful operation of the company, allowing it to claim a **competitive advantage** by providing reliable, timely overnight delivery that customers valued.

Linkage to Customers   The ability to provide information to a customer on the status of a shipment has been an integral part of FedEx service since the very early days of the company. Initially this information was available by contacting a Federal Express agent. More recently FedEx has provided customers with Powership, a personal computer capability that enables them to obtain their own shipment information. This improves the service to customers and also reduces agent costs for Federal Express.

British Airways Success Factor Profile

British Airways is the largest international carrier in the world. It has consistently earned a profit for the past ten years, at a time when many other carriers were losing money. This current success defies understanding by those familiar with its performance in the early 1980s. In 1981 this airline was basically bankrupt. Only the fact that it was owned by the British government kept it alive. Several important things happened that enabled the carrier to make the transition from BA standing for "bloody awful" to the success that it is today. The first was the hiring of Sir John King as Chairman of the Board who initiated the necessary downsizing of the airline. He also deserves a great deal of praise for hiring Sir Colin Marshall as the CEO in 1983. Marshall is arguably as important to this success story as Sir John King. A final major piece to this puzzle was the privatization of the airline in 1987 while Margaret Thatcher was Prime Minister.

The major factors that made this success possible include:

Vision The management team of King and Marshall brought a fresh wind that swept through the company with a new vision, mission statement and well-articulated strategies. Customer service became the driver of British Airway's vision. The vision was to build profitably the world's premier global alliance, with a presence in all major world markets. Realizing this vision involved major challenges but it clearly spelled out to employees where the carrier intended to be in the future.

Culture British Airways culture changed dramatically during the 1980s. It had to! In addition to being financially bankrupt the employee morale was at an all-time low, and customer service was even worse. Using Jan Carlzon's success at SAS as a model, a major employee retraining program called Putting People First (PPF) was implemented. As service improved so did business. Employees began to believe in the value of good customer service, and success bred additional success.

Information Systems Integral to the Business Information systems is integral to the business of British Airways. Running an airline is based on a high amount of information content. Information systems play a critical role in such key functions as the passenger reservation system, yield management system and flight operations system. It also provides links with both customers and suppliers. Colin Marshall said it best: "The application of information technology has, more than any other single factor, enabled British Airways to take quantum leaps into the competitive development and overall expansion of its business. IT [information technology] is a vital key to the airline's success."[1]

Executive and Information Systems Management Partnership   Colin Marshall clearly identified and supported the major initiatives undertaken by John Watson as the Director of Information Management. This definitely helped make Watson's job easier in dealing with others throughout the organization. Watson worked equally hard at understanding the business vision and strategies to ensure the best possible implementation of new systems. A dimension of BA's success with information systems is their stress on hiring people into multiple functions within the company. These "hybrids" have both business and information systems capabilities.

Information Systems Architecture   John Watson realized that forming an executive partnership was a vital factor in his endeavors as Director of Information Management. He also understood that to be effective, a robust systems architecture was required. Watson successfully incorporated the company vision into the design of an infrastructure that had to respond quickly to current and future business requirements. To accomplish this he stressed anticipating future trends in technology, as well as creating a superior technical capability that would provide a secure technical platform for future business development.

✦✦✦ CONCLUSION

The Success Factor Profile is the fifth and final part of the structured analysis process. It can be used as a planning vehicle to identify key factors that must be addressed for an organization to use information systems to gain a competitive advantage. It can also be very effective in summarizing the reasons why a specific company was able to gain a competitive advantage through the use of information systems.

RECOMMENDED READING

The following is good background material on Federal Express:

"Now More Than Ever, Time is Money." *Air Transport World*, March 1, 1993, p. 56.

---

[1] Harris, Brian, *Babs, Beacon and Boadicea: A History of Computing in British Airways and Its Predecessor Airlines,* Hounslow, Middlesex, U.K.: Speedwing Press, 1993.

Sigafoos, Robert A., *Absolutely, Positively Overnight: Wall Street's Darling Inside and Up Close.* Memphis, TN: St. Luke's Press, 1983.
A good early history of Federal Express.

Trimble, Vance, *Overnight Success: Federal Express and Frederick Smith, Its Renegade Creator.* New York: Crown, 1993.

The following can help in better understanding the success of British Airways:

"Air Raid: British Air's Global Push." *Business Week,* August 24, 1992, p. 55.

Corke, Alison, *British Airways: The Path to Profitability.* New York: St. Martin's Press, 1986.

"Firms Take IT to Heart." *Management Today,* February 1989, pp. 137–138.

"From Bloody Awful to Bloody Awesome." *Business Week,* October 9, 1989, pp. 97, 101.

"Grouches Need Not Apply." *Forbes,* December 10, 1990, p. 162.

"King of the Jet Set." *Business-London,* February 1989, pp. 46–54.

Kotter, John P., and James L. Heskett, *Corporate Culture and Performance.* New York: The Free Press, 1992.

Labich, Kenneth, "The Big Comeback at British Airways." *Fortune,* December 5, 1988, pp. 163–174.

"The Privatization of British Airways." *Harvard Business Review Case Study,* March 20, 1990, Case no. 9-390-079.

EXERCISES

1. **Innovative uses of information systems require a systematic approach.**
    a. Explain the logic behind the above statement.
    b. What are the primary objectives of the top box of the systematic approach chart?
    c. What are the primary objectives of the bottom box?
    d. What key factors must be addressed to assure compliance with this entire concept?

2. **Success Factor Profile.**
    a. What is the Success Factor Profile?
    b. How might the Success Factor Profile be used within an organization?

    c. What value can be derived through its use?

    d. Provide an example of a specific company using the Success Factor Profile.

3. **Corporate culture.**

    a. What is corporate culture?

    b. How important is it relative to achieving business success?

    c. How important is it relative to implementing new information systems?

    d. How long is it likely to take and how difficult is it to change the culture within a specific organization?

SECTION IV

MAJOR INFORMATION SYSTEMS MANAGEMENT ISSUES

This section builds on the Roles, Roles and Relationships concept by exploring in depth four factors that play a key role in the successful use of information systems to gain a competitive advantage. These are:

+ The structure of the information systems organization, including some personnel considerations.

+ Issues and challenges affecting ability to articulate the value of information systems within an organization and the formulation of a necessary financial strategy.

+ The importance of integrating information systems into the organization's business plan.

+ The relationship between Total Quality Management (TQM) and information systems.

13

INFORMATION SYSTEMS ORGANIZATION AND PERSONNEL CONSIDERATIONS

Throughout recorded history, it is rare when those in power have the wisdom to lead, not oppose, fundamental change. It is equally rare when they are not overwhelmed by it.[1]

Dee W. Hock
Founder and CEO Emeritus
Visa International

LEARNING OBJECTIVES

This chapter provides an understanding of the major issues and challenges confronting the information systems organization and its personnel. This includes a perspective on the current and possible future information systems organization and its relationship with senior management and the users of the systems support that it provides.

QUESTIONS

The following questions relate to an information systems organization and its personnel:

1. What is the logical skill profile for the person that heads the information systems organization?
2. How difficult is the information systems manager job compared to other major functions within a company?
3. To whom should the information systems manager report?

---

[1] *Nature of Beasts (Out of Control and into Order),* © Dee W. Hock, 1995.

4. If the information systems manager reported to you, what major factors would you like to review with this person on a regular basis to assure yourself that the information systems organization is being well managed?

5. Is there something unique about information systems that necessitates a steering committee that spans the organization?

6. Is there a logical alternative to having a steering committee?

7. It is not unusual to find people who feel that information systems employees are different from other employees. Is this actually the case? If so, how would you suggest that they be treated and managed?

8. What will the information systems organization look like in the future? What are the primary reasons that it is changing?

9. Are there major issues to be addressed in establishing the information systems organization of the future?

10. Does the current information systems environment call for the creation of newly structured jobs and skill profiles?

✦✦✦ BUSINESS STRATEGY AND ORGANIZATION DRIVE THE INFORMATION SYSTEMS ORGANIZATION

How often has a statement like the following been made: "Let's fix things around here—let's reorganize!" Reorganization is seldom the solution to a major problem within a company. It can contribute to the solution to a problem if it is the result of a new business strategy, but it is seldom the only solution. The form of an organization more logically follows function (strategy and tactics) than the other way around. The same business strategy requirements that provide the justification for information systems support also influence, or in some cases dictate, an organizational structure for the information systems organization. It is necessary to understand how these business strategies influence the business organization, and then look at the alignment of information systems support through an appropriate structure.

No matter what final structure is selected, the basic functions found within an information systems organization must be addressed. Whether centralized, decentralized or distributed (a combination of both), the functions to design, build, implement and operate information systems *must be addressed*. The information systems organization can be the beneficiary of effective business strategies and good organizational structure, or it can become the victim of an outdated, outmoded enterprise. One possible result of information systems support of poor business strategies and ineffective organizational structure is to help run the company into bankruptcy at computer speed.

How Effective Are Current Business Organizational Structures?

In today's environment business organizations need to create the right concepts and best possible conditions so they have the mechanisms for continual learning, adaptation, flexibility and evolution. Information systems can support many of the mechanisms needed in this type of organization but need to follow the direction set by those running the business. The major issues are not information systems or the structure of the information systems organization, but company vision, values, strategies, policies, tactics and processes.

What is the effectiveness of current business entities? Dee Hock, CEO Emeritus of VISA International and VISA USA, offers the following observations: [2]

"It doesn't take much intelligence to realize that we are in the midst of a global epidemic of institutional failure. The signs are everywhere if one cares to look. People are increasingly alienated from the organizations that employ them. There is often a chasm between how institutions profess to function and how they actually do. The problem is pervasive despite the attention that has been given for many years to issues of organization structure and control. Although their size and complexity have vastly increased, there has been virtually no new concept of organization since the notion of corporation and nation-state emerged several centuries ago.

"For two centuries we have structured our thinking, believing that with ever more scientific knowledge, efficiency and mechanistic, hierarchical command and control, we could learn to engineer organizations in which we could pull a lever at one place and get a precise result at another, and know with certainty which lever to pull for which result. For two centuries we have been designing these organizations and pulling the levers. Rarely have we gotten the expected results.

"The important thing to remember is not that we have become a world of expert managers, but that the nature of our expertise became the creation and management of constants, uniformity and efficiency, while the need has become the understanding and coordination of variability, complexity and effectiveness. Command and control organizations, whether commercial, political or social, are neither agile enough to fly in an atmosphere of micro- and nanotechnology nor fleet enough afoot to outrun the flood of social change.

"The epidemic of institutional failure has much to do with the compression of time and events. Some of you may recall the days when a check might take a couple of weeks to find its way through the banking system. We called it float and many used it to advantage. Today we are all aware

---

[2] Excerpts from a presentation by Dee W. Hock to Financial Executives Institute, Information Management Issues Conference, March 27, 1995, San Jose, California. © Dee W. Hock, 1995.

of the incredible speed and volatility with which money moves and the profound effect it has on all of us. However, we ignore vastly more important reduction of float such as the disappearance of information float. When man set foot on the moon, it was known and seen in every corner of the globe 1.4 seconds later. No less important is the disappearance of scientific float—the time between the discovery of new technology and its universal application. This endless compression of float, whether money, information, technology or anything else, can be combined and described as the disappearance of change float; that is, compression of time between what was and what is to be; between past and future. Everything is change, with one incredibly important exception. There has been no loss of institutional float.

"Is it possible that your organization could be the next to be overwhelmed by technical innovation and social change? Is it possible your competitors may be more perceptive about that change than you imagine? Is it possible new markets never before conceived are patiently waiting for your wits to grow sharper? If so, have you in the deepest, most fundamental sense, examined the nation of your institution; understood precisely what is form and what is function; developed a clear vision not only of what it might become, but what it ought to be? Do you have the courage to let things get out of control so they can get into order? Do you understand and are you prepared to lead the massive conceptual, cultural and institutional change required?

"A corporation or any institution is absolutely nothing but a mental construction—a concept to which people and resources are drawn in pursuit of a common purpose. All institutions are merely conceptual embodiments of a very old, very basic idea of community. They can be no more nor no less than the sense of purpose and the strength of belief which binds people together. Without the moving force of the mind and spirit of people, all assets are just so much inert chemical, mineral and vegetable matter steadily decaying to a natural state. Without question, the most abundant, least expensive, most underutilized and frequently abused resource in the world is human ingenuity. The source of that abuse is archaic, Industrial Age institutions and the management practices they spawn.

"Those with power and position have the most to lose. It is understandable that they cling tenaciously to the present order of things long after it has become obsolete. They attempt to perpetuate the form of things long after form no longer serves function, a certain formula for failure; for if there is anything approaching a law of nature in the commercial world, it is that form has an affinity for expense, while function has an affinity for income.

"Power needs to be distributed, human ingenuity released and the full power of information technology unleashed. Business leadership much provide an alternative approach to outmoded management methods of suspicion, conformity, control and uniformity, emphasizing instead trust, personal initiative and diversity. The simple truth is, that given the right circumstances, from no more than dreams, determination and liberty to try, quite ordinary people consistently do extraordinary things.

"What does all this mean to the work that you do? Your work is at the very heart of the institutional change required and you are in the enviable position to lead it. Gregory Bateson may have said it best: 'Information is a difference which makes a difference.' As we approach the point [where] the collective memory of the world is no more than a few keystrokes away, how do you insure that the difference which makes a difference for each individual is available and discernible to them? How do you insure that your organization allows them to act on it promptly, in coordination with others and consistent with the purpose and principles of the organization? How do you insure that their acts are instantly communicated to all others whose work those acts will inform? If we take the essence of the word 'inform' to be that which creates within, what does that mean to the structure and culture of your institution and the people you employ?

"Have we, at long last, evolved to the point of sufficient intelligence and will to create the concepts and conditions for the evolution of institutions which have inherent in them the mechanisms for their own continual learning, adaptation, order and evolution; and the capacity to coevolve with other living things to the highest potential of each and all? At such times, it is no failure to fall short of realizing all that we might dream. The failure is to fall short of dreaming what we might realize."

These pressures cited by Mr. Hock demand that companies respond in an ever shorter amount of time, and this can amplify organizational weaknesses. It is exciting to realize that the opportunity exists to play an important role in dealing with these challenges. Information can be the enabler to make the difference. The challenge is to ensure that information that can make a difference is available and discernible to people with the right business organization and information systems support. The information systems organization must help create an information infrastructure that allows people to act on information promptly in coordination with others and consistent with the mission, vision, values and strategies of the organization. It must assure employees that their actions will be communicated to others when appropriate to do so.

As noted earlier the functions must be addressed, but there is no specific, best way to structure the information systems organization. Important factors that will influence the structure of the IS organization include:

✦ Management style and attitude regarding centralization or decentralization of authority and responsibility.

✦ Whether operating units are profit centers (discussed in Chapter 14).

✦ The information technology knowledge and skill levels within the line organization.

✦ The actual information systems implemented.

✦ Whether the IS organization is in a cycle of a significant amount of new application development or is maintaining what has already been implemented.

With respect to the profile of information systems, planning applications are more easily centralized, while operational applications are often implemented where the activities occur.

A qualifier of this entire discussion is that information technology does not dictate the structure of the information systems organization. Although there are economy-of-scale considerations, the technology exists to support multiple organizational approaches. The needs and desires of the business will be more influential in determining the structure of the information systems organization.

✦✦✦ A SUCCESSFUL INFORMATION SYSTEMS ORGANIZATION

A successful enterprise has been defined as an organization that is based on a clear and simple theory of business with clearly understood objectives. An appropriate next question is whether the traditional information systems organization as depicted in Figure 13-1 complies with the definition. A traditional organizational structure is evaluated first with consideration to how such an organization has already changed in some companies and second, how it could change for others in the future.

The major functions within this information systems organization, which must be addressed regardless of the actual structure, include:

Computer Operations: The management of the data center operations or the centralized part of a distributed systems approach.

Network Management: A responsibility for the operations and performance of the communications network.

Database Administration: A combination of data management and data admininistration responsibilities.

Finance and Administration: This information systems controller is a necessary function, because the number of hardware units and the amount of software has significantly increased while also being dispersed throughout the company. This involves such things as dealing with PC purchases for the entire organization, maintaining inventory records of where equipment is located and the

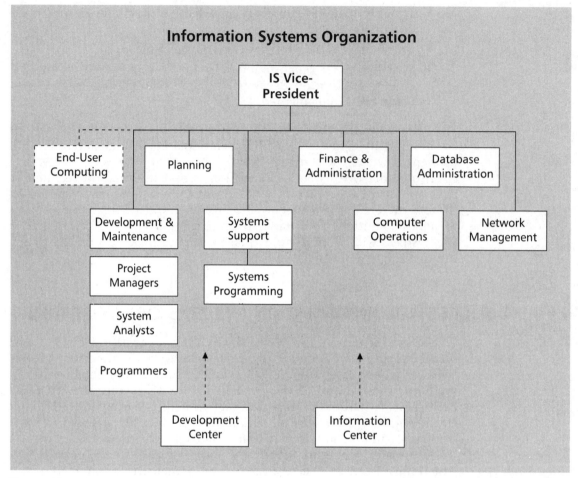

Figure 13-1

implementation of an information systems financial strategy within the organization.

Planning: Whether this is a separate position or addressed by the managers within the information systems organization, the amount of planning-related activity has definitely increased. This would range from the positioning of information systems with an appropriate architecture to bridge its use, to support business strategies and tactics.

Systems Support: This responsibility deals with the technical aspects of operating systems including systems configuration and performance.

Systems Development and Maintenance: New application development is addressed by project teams that include systems analysts and programmers.

End-User Computing: A planning, development and implementation group to address office systems, engineering and scientific workstations, voice applications, etc. This could be an information systems organization function or a user project team with a representative of information systems functioning as part of the group.

Information Center: A one-stop shopping support organization whose activities include user education, application software demonstrations, a help-line and technical support. A primary objective of an information center is to eliminate confusion over where a user goes for information systems help given the nature of the problem.

Development Center: This is a small group of top-notch information systems professionals whose goal is to enhance the efficiency and effectiveness of the information systems organization. They evaluate tools, techniques, methodologies and anything else that can improve the capabilities and performance of the organization. This needs to be a full-time responsibility. This would preclude the day-to-day demands that would otherwise be placed on these people to do the type of evaluations that are necessary to realize possible improvements.

The Evolution of the Information Systems Organization

The size and scope of the typical information systems organization has changed over the years. The earlier, smaller data processing department was fairly easy to understand. Subsequent growth in the number of applications and staffing often prompted its elevation to a management information systems (MIS) department. Continued information systems growth resulted in the creation of a corporate information systems organization, which may have any of a number of names: Information Systems and Technology, Information Services, Management Support Services, Information Systems and Services, etc. Decentralization of the IS function or a distributed systems approach has changed the alignment and location of both people and activities. What has not changed, as noted earlier, is the need for the same functions to be addressed.

The jury is still out on the absolute best structure for an information systems organization. Centralized versus decentralized mainframe data centers versus distributed systems continues to be the basis of the debate. When Eastman Kodak signed their outsourcing agreement with IBM it resulted in the consolidation of sixteen data centers into one. The nature of the data being managed also influences the structure of information systems. American Airlines is very centralized in Tulsa and Dallas. Federal Express has a primary operation in Memphis and a software development team in Colorado Springs, Colorado. Prudential Insurance decentralized their systems analysts and application programmers and ran its data center like a utility. Xerox has received attention for having not only a CIO but a DIO (divisional information officer) at multiple division operations having their own computer operations. The assignment of authority and responsibility has a great influence on the information systems structure as does how well the company uses network-based systems. Frito-Lay decentralized their management into four geographical areas but kept their information systems centralized by providing on-line decision support systems to the regional operations.

✦✦✦ INFORMATION SYSTEMS MANAGER SKILL PROFILE

If a company found it necessary to go outside its own organization to find someone to manage its information systems, what would be the major qualifications for this job? Assume that you run a manufacturing company with $1 billion in annual revenue and an information systems organization with 250 employees. It is important to prioritize the qualifications. Consideration should be given to manufacturing industry experience, management experience, general technical qualifications, specific vendor technical experience, political, organizational and communication skills.

If the executive search firm that is handling this assignment for you concludes they cannot find a person matching the specific qualifications, which qualifications would you be willing to reconsider? For instance, would someone with excellent technical qualifications be acceptable if they have minimal management experience? Is manufacturing industry experience actually required or are basic business skills acceptable?

Difficulty of the Information Systems Manager Job

Just how difficult is the information systems manager job? It is often the largest staff function that provides both products and services. It interfaces with numerous, if not all, functional groups within the organization. It must often contend with users who might know just enough about information technology to be dangerous. The rapid technological changes border on frightening. Last but not least, it is a dual personality job: the information systems executive needs to be a business executive to senior management, knowledgeable and conversant regarding each major business function, and a technology leader within the IS organization.

It is a tough job, but is it any tougher than other functional management positions? How would you like to be vice-president of engineering with marching orders to halve the time to market of a new product that must also be best of breed versus anything offered by a competitor? How about the manufacturing job that is supposed to meet six sigma quality targets? Does the chief financial officer feel that raising $200 million to fund work-in-process is a walk in the park? Where is the marketing vice-president going to find customers that will generate the projected 16% sales increase?

To Whom Should the Information Systems Manager Report?

Where the information systems executive position fits within a company structure has received considerable attention over the years. A common criticism has been that too often the information systems organization reports to the chief financial officer. The sentiment is that it should be placed within operations or report to the executive who has day-to-day responsibility to run the entire business. The ultimate decision rests on three considerations:

1. The importance of information systems to run the business.
2. The interest of senior management, both collectively and individually, in information systems.
3. How formal the organization is regarding reporting structure.

While the reporting structure of the information systems organization is an indication of its importance, this has not been proven to be the determining factor for the successful use of information systems. There are excellent company examples where the information systems manager reports to the chief financial officer. There are disappointing examples where it reports to the president. If the management style within a company is very open and senior executives are very accessible, what difference does it make to whom the information systems manager reports?

If the Information Systems Executive Reported to You

If the information systems executive reported to you, what factors would you want to review on a quarterly basis to assure yourself that the information systems organization is being managed well?

The most obvious would be the status of major projects, both those that have been approved and those under consideration. Of particular interest would be problems, issues and schedule delays.

A second factor would be a future capacity projection of both systems and the communications network. This is like job insurance, because capacity-related problems can get an information systems executive in trouble very quickly. When utilization suddenly increases unexpectedly, negative things happen to users. Response time becomes longer, productivity is affected and user complaints increase. The solution is often a capacity increase at a considerable price. If the increase was not projected and was not part of a financial plan, then someone will have some explaining to do. The request to fund the solution to this capacity problem will more than likely be approved. It will also probably prompt the suggestion to hire someone who knows how to better manage the information systems organization. The retort to the above criticism is that in an on-line systems environment it is very difficult for the information systems organization to anticipate user demand. But its importance dictates that the information systems executive implement a way to accomplish this, because no one else will do this job.

A third factor would be the information systems executive's assessment of how well the IS organization is providing support to key users. A common response is, "Don't ask me, ask them." In most organizations this is probably being done. A comparison of how the information systems executive feels they are doing versus feedback from major users has definite value in determining how close the information systems executive is to their major customers.

A fourth point is the personnel productivity efforts and programs within the information systems organization. This is not unique to information systems but a goal for all functions within the company. Information systems needs to be accountable for the same productivity objectives as everyone else.

A fifth and final consideration is how well information systems is contributing to the competitiveness and profitability of the company. The information systems organization is very much involved with day-to-day activities, but are they also stepping back from the details and focusing on both the competitive strategies and financial implications of running the business?

Additional factors could be addressed, but any information systems executive who can provide good responses to the above questions would certainly be considered an effective manager.

✦✦✦ SUCCESSFUL INFORMATION SYSTEMS ARE A PRODUCT OF GOOD WORKING RELATIONSHIPS

More important than the reporting structure are the working relationships that the information systems organization establishes within the company. There are a number of reasons why this is important and numerous ways to accomplish it. The most fundamental reason for its importance is that information systems is a support organization. The more that it can do to interact with and understand its customers (users), the better job it should do. It is important to recognize that these customers fall into three categories: (1) executives who run the entire business, (2) functional managers who run major parts of the business, and (3) actual users of the systems on a day-to-day basis. There are both formal and informal ways to address building positive relationships within each of these three categories of people. The more successful approaches include the following:

Information Systems Steering Committee

Leading this list with steering committee will probably prompt some criticism because many companies have not been successful with this approach. Steering committee failures are often attributed to the right people not participating on a regular basis or a lack of understanding of the primary purpose of the committee. On the other hand some companies have used them very well. The successful ones avoid the mistake of treating a steering committee as though its job were to run the information systems organization by making every major decision. Instead the committee functions at a policy and priority level like a true "board of directors." The biggest value of an information systems steering committee is what it accomplishes in raising the level of awareness among senior management of information systems plans and activities. It does this by communicating these on a regular schedule.

If the purpose of a steering committee is to focus on the total organization, then the executives who have major functional responsibilities should be on the steering committee. Mervyn's senior management steering committee meets quarterly. It is made up of the CEO, the senior vice-president of merchandising, the chief operating officer and the information systems vice-president. They review the status of major information systems projects and determine the range and the scope of support to be provided. They agree on new technologies to be utilized and establish criteria for information systems investment.

Steering committees are often used when major new systems are being introduced that cross multiple or even all departmental boundaries. The steering committee focuses on status, problems and resource issues but also benefits from the communication accomplished and the policies that are put in place.

Functional Interface Managers

If information systems is viewed as a major organizational resource by senior management, it is very likely that a steering committee is not needed to assure effective communication. Nevertheless there is still a need to address the working relationship between the information systems organization and major functional groups within the company. Using manufacturing as an example, the vice-president of manufacturing would head a functional interface group and chair a steering committee with information systems. They would meet regularly, probably quarterly, to discuss the status of systems, problems, suggestions for improvement, etc. The primary reason for formalizing this relationship is to guard against letting too many other activities preclude both groups from meeting periodically to address areas of common importance. If done right this should build the basis for more effective use of information technology within the organization.

Functional End-User Coordinator

In addition to the functional interface manager there is a need for someone to provide user support within each major function. This could be provided directly by the information systems organization, but can be effectively done by someone within the user organization. This would be a manager picked on the basis of management experience and personal credibility. It is a part-time job; in a busy week it would probably entail about four hours of the manager's time. The coordinators function as a link between the people within their own function and the information systems organization. If a user in their group has a problem with information systems, the coordinator is the first line of support. The person with the problem takes it to someone that they know, respect and work with on a daily basis rather than someone in the information systems organization. The coordinator is much more likely to understand the person's problem and is better able to visualize a solution.

The end-user coordinators provide a link between the business plan and systems strategies, maintain knowledge of existing applications, coordinate activities relative to new applications, coordinate equipment requirements and authorize IDs for access to systems.

Service Level Agreements

Service level agreements, like steering committees, can help to improve communication and build better working relationships with user departments. They can also fit into the category of meaningless or even irritating topics depending on how they are used. Service level agreements are often concerned with an availability percentage or response time performance objectives. They can certainly be broader than this and can and probably should deal with factors that users feel are important in supporting their ability to better serve customers. The information systems organization would be well advised to follow this line of reasoning in establishing service level agreements instead of using them as a defense mechanism when confronted with user complaints.

User Training and Education

User training is often essential to the effective use of installed systems. It should also be viewed as time spent with customers of the information systems organization. Positive rapport can be built during training sessions if the information systems organization views this as an opportunity to do so.

Application and Technical Consultation

The information systems organization can benefit from what the airlines have learned. Users realize that systems, like flight schedules, are not perfect and that things can and will go wrong with both hardware, software and the network. What is important is how their problem gets addressed and how they are personally treated in the process. How many times is the person answering the support hotline telephone a part-time college student who knows less about the problem than the person looking for help?

Joint R&D Projects

The information systems organization needs to be in a position to pursue innovative approaches by working jointly with the user organization. This needs to be a proactive effort on the part of the information systems organization. It also needs to be able to respond to user requests by providing the necessary staffing for information technology R&D projects.

The Working and Personal Posture of the IS Manager

The working posture of the information systems executive is often a key factor in building credibility for the entire information systems organization. Information systems executives need to effectively sell themselves, their organization and its ability to support the strategies and tactics of the business to executives, functional managers and major users. They also need to make sure they have spent enough personal time with each functional vice-president to maintain good personal working relationships.

✦✦✦ INFORMATION SYSTEMS PERSONNEL CONSIDERATIONS

The pace of technology change, the increasing popularity of distributed systems and a client-server architecture, the pressures to respond in less time to changing business needs, and general company downsizing all add to the challenge of managing an information systems organization. It raises the following questions regarding information systems personnel:

✦ Does the organization have enough qualified people?

✦ Do their skills address both current and future needs?

✦ Does a migrant worker mentality exist among the information systems professionals?

✦ Is the best way to grow a strong information systems organization by hiring and developing your own people?

✦ Can an information systems organization promote long-term career growth?

✦ Are the above questions outdated, and is the right future information systems organization a small core of people with the rest subcontracted to outside companies?

Experience, qualifications and specific technical skills all relate to the professional aspects of an information systems employee. In this respect some feel that information systems employees are different from other employees. They are often compared to engineers in being more loyal to their profession than to the company for whom they work. One would ideally hope to have high-caliber information systems professionals who are loyal to the company.

Managing information systems employees involves many of the same requirements and considerations as managing other employees. You start by hiring people who fit the profile of a job. Managing them then involves training, supervision, counseling, motivation and development as a career professional or a potential manager. It also involves dealing with possible job burn-out, reassignment within the information systems organization or possible promotion to another function within the company. How many of these personnel management activities are unique to information systems? None. If information systems organizations have experienced problems in managing people in the past, is it because the people were information systems employees or because they were not well managed? Gordon Moore, Chairman of the Board of Intel Corporation, once said that Intel needed to be concerned about making bad managers out of good engineers. The same applies to information systems. There have been enough examples of good personnel management within information systems to conclude that there are major differences that preclude doing a good job. The following guidelines would help in this regard:

✦ Treat new hires for information systems the same as any new employee within the company.

✦ During their first five years emphasize the value of different experiences by not allowing an employee to stay with the same manager for longer than eighteen months.

✦ Work to establish parity in the perspective of information systems employees towards jobs in operations, applications development and systems design/support. The challenge here is to discourage a perception that operations involves jobs with the lowest stature.

✦ Promote information systems people into other jobs within the company. At a later date bring them back into the information systems organization with another promotion.

✦ Spend more time on identifying and developing people with management potential within the information systems organization.

✦ Work to eliminate a mentality that job burnout is inevitable with information systems employees. In this regard, pay special attention to the dangers of excessive overtime.

✦ Make sure that the work environment is as good as that of the rest of the company.

✦ Recognize and reward employees who make major contributions.

Finally, have fun within the information systems organization. No one ever said that information systems jobs have to be dull and constantly stressful!

The Chief Information Officer

The chief information officer job title has been around for probably eight or ten years. It is yet another example of something that prompts both negative and positive reactions. *Business Week* suggested that CIO meant "career is over" in discussing the rapid turnover of people in this capacity.

A CIO is, or at least should be, the information technology conscience of the company. This means that a CIO needs to sit at the corporate table along with the executives running the business. To do this requires an understanding of the industry, the business and the organization. Chief information officers must also be able to hold their own politically. They must understand IT but project an image of a business-oriented person. They must be able to project the longer term implications of any major new technology and put it into a logical, organizational framework.

Information Specialist

A position rarely found within companies but very logical and probably necessary is an information specialist. This person is part of a user department whose objective is to improve the capabilities of the employees in the department to use information systems. Installed, existing systems tend to be underutilized because the employees for whom they are intended do not understand them well enough to truly maximize their benefits. Realistically a company probably could only justify this type of person on a ratio of one to fifty employees, but the specifics of the company and the number of systems would determine this. What would an information specialist do? The following is a list of activities that could be addressed:

✦ **Elbow-to-elbow assist:** Provide assistance to people who need to do something relative to their job with a computer-based system.

✦ **Single focal point:** Any doubt as to whom an employee within the department turns to with an information systems problem is completely eliminated.

✦ **Gather requirements:** This can span a wide range of possibilities but includes both hardware- and software-related improvements.

✦ **Interface to support groups:** Interface with the information systems organization with a combination of knowledge of the department and information technology.

✦ **Provide education:** This can be in a formal class environment or one-on-one but tailored in content and time schedule to the users' needs.

✦ **Consulting and assistance:** Anything falling outside of elbow assist that users need to get their jobs done through the use of information systems.

✦ **Promotion:** Proactively push the existence and capabilities of new applications, new releases and new tools that can be used by people within the department.

✦ **Maintain equipment:** Interface with repair service people and do anything else involved with setting up equipment for a new employee, etc.

✦ **Track progress:** Track the progress and proficiency of users of major systems within the organization.

The Importance of Education and Training

Education and training continue to be key activities in gaining effective use of information systems and related tools. No one would debate whether the objective should be to educate the right people. Sometimes who the right people are is not all that obvious. Is it the users, user managers, information systems professionals or the user department information systems "guru"?

The very large volumes of people that need to be trained on a system sometimes dictates that formal classroom training is not practical. Systems-based training that can be done at the employee's convenience makes a lot of sense. Training department gurus and letting them pass the knowledge along to others in the department has also been known to work very well.

✦✦✦ THE FUTURE INFORMATION SYSTEMS ORGANIZATION

Recognizing that the future is often now, what is the logical structure for an information systems organization? The structure shown in Figure 13-2 was originally based on the assumption of a traditional, hierarchical, centralized mainframe data center. It is interesting that this same organizational structure could also be used for a distributed-systems, client-server approach. The same major functions must be addressed even though the configuration of processors throughout a network can vary significantly.

This conclusion has been validated at a number of companies including Sun Microsystems (running Sun with Sun), Hewlett-Packard Worldwide Customer Support organization (installed client-server system) and National Semiconductor (evolving to client-server).

As with any organizational structure there can be variations and modifications. It is important to remember that the same major information systems functions must be addressed. This can be done by either a centralized but modified information systems organization or by a decentralized information systems group within the line organization.

An Information Systems Executive and a CIO

The role of a CIO has already been discussed. Figure 13-2 has the CIO position separate from the information systems executive. For a number of years the Duke Power Company in North Carolina kept the two jobs separate. Why would a company separate the two jobs? For one thing, doing

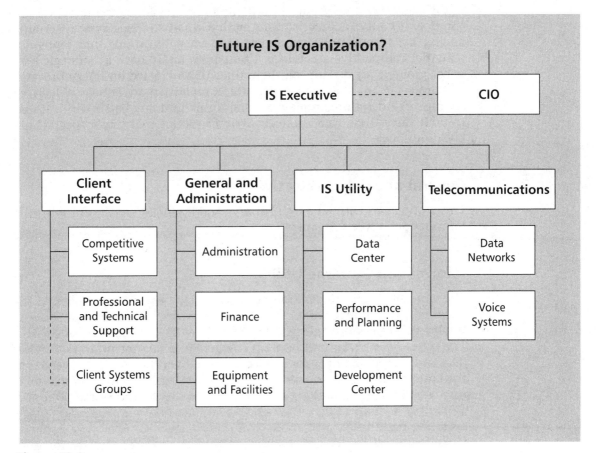

Figure 13-2

both jobs may be too much for a single person. A number of factors would influence this, but it is highly possible. Another reason could be to enable the CIO to maintain a very objective position regarding specific information system activities. It would not be the CIO's job to defend the information systems organization. There would be a strong working relationship between the two positions, but it could make sense to have two people.

Client Interface

The combination of the client interface and the information systems utility are two of the major differences of this approach as compared to traditional organizations. Because of size or the use of a distributed-systems approach, most application-related people and activities would be the responsibility of the client systems groups. Each major function within the company would handle its own application needs, with the client systems people being part of the department they support. The dotted line to the client interface group is primarily for professional and technical assistance. It could include working with a small strategic systems group, having the responsibility to concentrate on applications that represent potential competitive advantage. Companies rarely have a "strategic systems" group; they do not call them that. USAA created an image-processing project team that had a definite competitive advantage objective. Boeing's 777 design team played a major role in doing battle with Airbus. In both cases these were strategic systems groups that had a specific application focus.

General and Administrative

This group deals with all administrative and financial aspects of the entire information systems organization.

Information Systems Utility

The concept of an information systems utility can be best explained by likening it to a public utility. The utility provides basic electrical service. What the buyers of the electrical service do with it is their responsibility. The buyer pays a standard hookup charge and a rate for minimal service plus any charges incurred for service received over the amount covered by the basic rate. The information systems utility parallels this approach. A user would pay for attaching a workstation to the central system and pay a monthly hookup charge. The central computer utility provides data management, basic tools, and access and presentation services. Any applications desired by the user would be developed by the user organization and run on their workstations or use the central computer utility. All systems analysts and application programming would be done by user personnel. The information systems utility operates the data center, has responsibility for systems planning and performance and could have a development center for the improvement of the data center operation.

Telecommunications

This part of the organization, which is responsibile for both voice and data communications, could be placed under the information systems utility. The size and significance of the telecommunications network would dictate whether it would be a separate part of the organization.

✦✦✦ CONCLUSION

Information systems organizations will certainly change in the future, but distributed systems do not eliminate the need for a central organization. The challenge will be to determine which kind of IS organization will gain the best possible results for the enterprise.

RECOMMENDED READING

Fried, Louis, *Managing Information Technology in Turbulent Times.* New York: Wiley, 1995.

The author looks back on thirty-five years of information systems experience and provides a road map for the next ten years on how this increasingly critical resource needs to be managed. He deals with topics like the role of the CIO, business process redesign, user satisfaction, new technology introduction, downsizing, outsourcing and computer security.

Wang, Charles B., *Techno Vision: The Executive's Guide to Understanding and Managing Information Technology.* New York: McGraw-Hill, 1994.

The author is the CEO of Computer Associates International, a major U.S. software company. This book is his attempt to bridge the gap between business executives and information technologists. Wang suggests that this is a two-way proposition. The executives need to include the technologists on business issues, and the technologists need to educate them in return on how IT can contribute to the success of the business. Much of what is described as a disconnect problem is attributed to a communication problem. The book describes key technologies in a business context in an attempt to demystify them. In addition to addressing most if not all of the latest "buzz-word" technologies, it also offers ten steps for improved CEO/CIO relationships.

EXERCISES

1. **Basic information systems functions must be addressed whether the information systems organization is centralized, decentralized or distributed.**

   Validate the above premise with examples of actual information systems organizations based on each of the three approaches.

2. **Future information systems organization.**
   a. Would it make sense to separate the information systems executive job and that of the CIO?
   b. Explain what is meant by "information systems utility."
   c. Why would general and administrative activities be included as part of an information systems organization?
   d. Should a dedicated "competitive group" be included within the information systems organization?

3. **Information systems steering committee.**

   Evaluate the role, objectives and primary responsibilities of a steering committee for information systems. Provide specific examples of company experiences with the use of a steering committee.

4. **Information systems organization personnel management.**
   a. What recommendations would you make regarding the hiring, training, development and personnel practices of information systems employees?
   b. From a personnel management standpoint, what logic supports having information systems professionals within the line organization as opposed to remaining part of a centralized information systems organization?

5. **Chief information officer (CIO).**
   a. Would you personally like to become a chief information officer? What is attractive about this position? Are there also unattractive aspects of the job?
   b. What are primary qualifications for a CIO position?
   c. Why do you feel that the turnover in these jobs has been so high?
   d. Do you feel that the CIO position will continue to increase in importance and more companies will have someone doing this job?

INFORMATION SYSTEMS VALUE AND FINANCIAL STRATEGY

You have got to get me a lot more comfortable with the fact that you are spending $400 million a year on information systems. Meanwhile, you are not getting any more money.
A CEO to an information systems vice-president

There is no universal formula for determining the business value of information technology that can be applied in every company—and value can change over time.
A consultant to an information systems vice-president

LEARNING OBJECTIVES

This chapter examines the issues involved in determining the business value of information systems. Possible financial strategies are then presented that can be implemented to better manage the increasing amounts of money being spent on information systems.

QUESTIONS

Some frequently asked questions regarding the value of information systems:

1. "What are we getting for that?", with "that" being the total amount spent for information systems.
2. Is there a process in place that monitors and tracks the effectiveness of information systems?
3. Does the statement "Information systems costs are all charged out to users" satisfy senior management?

4. Is information systems justification judged in terms of cost, efficiency, effectiveness, current competitive advantage or contribution to the long-term viability of the business?

5. Does the information systems justification process hold managers accountable?

6. Does information systems have parity with other investment decisions?

7. Is what we are spending for information systems at the right level? What is "right"?

8. What is representative of the spending on information systems within our industry?

9. Who is really responsible for information systems benefits and costs?

10. Is it cost effective to chase the benefits of information systems?

✦✦✦ NEEDED: BETTER ANSWERS REGARDING THE VALUE OF INFORMATION SYSTEMS

As information systems spending continues to increase, in some cases at an alarming rate, the inability to articulate the value of information systems within a specific organization becomes an increasingly important issue. The payback exercise was difficult enough when information systems were centralized in a data processing department. It has become even more formidable as information technology has become more disbursed throughout the entire organization. In the current environment some organizations have a hard time just determining the total amount being spent on information technology throughout the entire company.

The inability to articulate the value derived from the use of information systems can become an inhibitor to information systems growth. Other primary inhibitors of information systems growth are the following:

The implementation of new applications *takes too long and costs too much*. Although the time to implement new applications can be and often is shortened, particularly if third-party application packages are used, the time pressures on the business have also shortened user expectations—they need the new systems support now! Additional factors include the need to coordinate projects that are broader in scope, have the potential of impacting organizational structure, necessitate process reengineering, and cross not just departmental but company boundaries. It may be possible to complete the technical activities in less time, but it takes much longer to agree on the definition of the system for business reasons.

Major *connectivity problems* among the installed systems provided by different and even the same vendors, both within and outside of the enterprise, also inhibit information systems growth. Although it is improving, there is still *a lack of "ease of use"* of installed systems, causing a slowing in the learning curve among users. More information systems application integration is not necessarily making it easier to use.

These issues contribute to a general *inability to articulate value* derived from both installed and proposed information systems. The situation with the first three factors has improved in recent years from a technology standpoint. Each factor also has a cost/value dimension. The value issue is an umbrella hanging over the entire use of information systems. The three factors can be and are being addressed, but at what cost and with what commensurate business value?

What Is the Basis for Determining Information Systems Value?

The value issue is certainly not a new problem. It has received considerable attention both in the private sector among major user organizations and consultants, and by academic researchers. To date these efforts have generated more controversy than consensus. If beauty is in the eyes of the beholder, so too are measures of information systems value. Measures of bigness and total spending are relatively easy to identify. Measures of value are much harder to define. Before progressing any further on this topic, it is important to remember the following:

The heart of the matter is not how to quantify the contribution of information systems, but how to satisfy management that this support resource is contributing to the success of the business.

The topic of information systems value is not lacking in focus, but it is lacking an approach that has general applicability. Organizations that have been successful in addressing the information systems value issue are still few in number, even though some of them implemented successful approaches eight to ten years ago. The best answer to the information systems value question lies not in the hands of financial or computer experts. It must be found within the context of business management and contribution to the success of the business. If the business is productivity driven, then the focus should be on measuring efficiency. If the organization has a high customer value priority, then the measure must address this area.

Taking a broad look at the potential impact of information systems on a business involves looking at a number of factors. These represent a hierarchy that begins with the specific information technology and cascades through a Value Chain that includes, in a logical sequence, tasks, activities, programs and organizational goals. Which of these four factors provides the best basis for determining the business value of information systems? Is it at the task level? Does the impact of information technology on a specific task provide a value measurement that would offer senior management an acceptable answer to the question, "What are we getting for that?" If a measurement of the impact on tasks does not provide a good answer, is it necessary to look at activities, programs or even goals?

An entirely different approach would be to use a benefits Value Chain that focuses on systems, individuals, departments, organizations and enterprises. (A company with a single operation is considered an organization, and a multiple-location operation is an enterprise.) Relative to this approach, it would be helpful to remember that, as you progress up the benefits Value Chain, the potential exists for the following:

✦ Financial benefits would be greater but more difficult to measure.

✦ The time horizon to implement a new application would be longer.

✦ The organizational level at which the project would be approved would be higher.

✦ The management direction and coordination would be greater.

✦ The amount of risk in implementing the application would be greater.

✦ The correlation of benefits with information systems would be less.

What Is the Average for Information Systems Spending in an Industry?

Practically everyone wants to know what the average information systems costs are for their particular industry. The answer to this question is at minimum not very meaningful, and at best very misleading. The best company to compare with is your own. How has information systems focus, use and spending evolved and grown over the years? Is the role and effectiveness of information systems what it should be? If it is not, what should be done to improve or correct the situation?

Industry averages can be misleading because the survey validity can easily lack credibility. In conducting a survey of the amount being spent on information systems, who is the logical person to contact? Most people would call the information systems executive. If the executive is out or is having calls screened, the secretary is the one asked the question regarding how much the company spends on information systems. The reply will be one of three possibilities: (1) "I am sorry, I do not know," (2) "That is confidential information," or (3) "Our information systems budget is x amount." What does the number that has been provided really represent? Is it the total for the entire enterprise or is it (which is more than likely) the annual budget for the information systems organization? Since expenditures that are not included in the IS organization's budget are the increase, average information systems expenditure numbers obtained through a survey can be very misleading.

High IS Costs Get Senior Management's Attention

As the significance of information systems has increased within many organizations, there has been a corresponding growth in the financial commitment. Large financial expenditures draw the attention of senior management, who have a tendency to ask questions like, "How can we pay for all that?" The answer that it is all charged out to users, although palatable to some executives, is unacceptable to others. But even the most supportive executives have a "pain threshold" that prompts them to question the return on investment in information systems. In one large West Coast financial services organization, the pain threshold of the president was reached when the budget request from the information systems organization exceeded the profitability of the entire corporation!

As information systems have become a more accepted and entrenched resource within many organizations, three trends have become clear:

1. There is a growing dependence on information systems to run the organization.

2. Information systems expenses and capital funding have become quite large.

3. For these reasons senior management has become more active in managing the role and importance of information systems. They pay more attention to both its impact on the short-term profitability and the long-term viability of the business.

Three Factors in Determining Value

Figure 14-1 suggests that a process to address the value issue could logically be broken into three parts. The first would address the value of an enterprise-wide infrastructure. Factors such as a communications network, a standardized data management approach and an information systems architecture impact and benefit the entire organization and must be evaluated in this context. This is one of the more difficult things to evaluate because benefits stem not from a network but from the applications it supports. Second are applications implemented to support specific or multiple functions within an enterprise. The value of these must be addressed by the people realizing the benefits—the users. Information technology does not directly produce value. The value of information systems is in its impact upon the organization.

The third area of concentrated information technology support is at the individual employee level. This area continues to grow in many organizations. It can also be very diverse in terms of the amount of use and the ability of the user to take advantage of the type and amount of available computer-based support. This diversity makes assessing the value of information technology use very complex. The temptation is to use a more general approach in determining its value—but will this provide an acceptable answer to the value question?

Figure 14-1

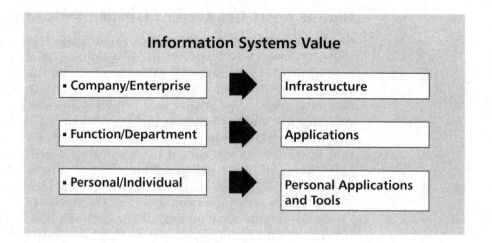

✦✦✦ THE EVOLUTION OF INFORMATION SYSTEMS JUSTIFICATION

The above scenario is increasingly common and is often accompanied by a need to focus on how to justify spending on information systems. Some attention to this issue is clearly warranted, and we will begin with a look at how information systems justification has evolved over time. This is graphically shown in Figure 14-2 as the four stages of data processing growth.[1] It is important to remember that the basic underlying issue being addressed is how to provide credible answers to questions regarding the value derived from information systems. Related to this are the strengths and weaknesses of the approach implemented to manage it.

Stage I: In the Beginning There Are Budgets

In Stage I or the initiation stage most organizations simply include funding for information systems as part of a departmental budget, often within the finance department. The funds involved are not particularly large, but there is a challenge to manage the information systems expense within the budget while providing support on a noncharge basis to user departments.

Stage II: With Growth Comes the Need for a Business Case

Stage II is characterized by significant growth of information systems budgets, and with the rapid acceleration of the use and cost of data processing comes a sentiment that there is a need for prioritization of proposed

---

[1] The chart and the stages concept are based on material drawn from "Managing the Four Stages of EDP Growth" by Cyrus F. Gibson and Richard L. Nolan in *Harvard Business Review*, January–February 1974, pp. 76–88. The financial strategy material is modification primarily from the author.

Evolution of Financial Strategy

	Initiation **I**	Expansion **II**	Control **III**	Maturity **IV**
Application Support	Single Area	Proliferation	Containment	Organization Strategy
Motivation	People Displacement	Cost Avoidance	DP Efficiency	Competitive Advantage
Financial Justification	Budget	Business Case Installation Audit	Charge-Out System	Management Process
DP Planning	Little	Reactive	Directed	Proactive
Organization	Finance Dept.	Multiple Dept.	Centralized	Centralized Decentralized Distributed

Figure 14-2

Based on material from Gibson and Nolan, *Harvard Business Review*, January–February 1974, pp. 76–88.

new information systems. This is often accompanied by an attitude that only those applications that are financially justified should be implemented. A proposal or business case process asks nominating managers to rationalize the financial logic of a new application. The primary items addressed in the business case document are cost avoidance or displacement, data processing development costs, operating costs of the new system and the benefits to be derived from the new approach. Verification of the validity of the initial justification is often accomplished through a post-installation audit. The primary challenge of this stage stems from the fact that business cases are based on one-time evaluations. These evaluations are normally projections over many years, but the question remains as to whether they reflect ongoing value to the business.

Stage III: Departments Should Pay for the IS Support They Receive

Stage III is a period that emphasizes control, and with this comes an endorsement of the idea that people (departments or functions within the organization) should pay for data processing support and services.

Charge-out procedures become the norm and vary from very simple and straightforward to fairly sophisticated processes. Many organizations embrace a charge-out approach as an integral part of their Stage III organizational learning process. This is where a majority of the organizations find themselves today, and many feel that this approach is a satisfactory way to manage information systems resources. The objectives of a charge-out system remain the same: to put the burden of financial responsibility on the people who are using the information systems resources. However, some are finding that it is difficult to specifically identify who should pay for things like corporate databases and information systems R&D projects that are conducted for the general good of the business. Some of the historical challenges remain regarding charge-back systems: Can the end-user understand the bill? Even more important, is it possible to anticipate with a reasonable degree of consistency how much the monthly or annual charges will be?

Charge-Out Decisions   An early decision regarding a charge-out system is whether the information systems organization will be a cost center, a profit center or a service center. A **cost center** operates with a zero-sum budget, and everything is charged out. What it costs to run the information systems organization for the entire year is charged to someone down to the last penny. A **profit center** is similar, with an uplift to the charges so that a profit will be earned over the entire year. It seems illogical to inflate charges to users within the same company, particularly if management wants information systems to be more proactive in support of major business strategies, but there are companies that use this approach. A **service center** approach has definite merit, with approximately 80% of the costs of running the information systems organization charged to users. The information systems manager has some discretion regarding what happens with the remaining 20%. Doing joint studies or creating prototypes without charging the user organization are possibilities. The service center approach enables the information systems organization to be proactive in identifying applications that can be a positive contribution to the success of the company.

The next decision deals with the support for which user departments will be charged. A decision to be a cost center or a profit center simplifies the problem, but a service center approach will dictate the need for decisions regarding the following information systems support:

R&D projects	Data storage	Program maintenance
Feasibility studies	Telecommunications	Program development
User training	Transaction processing	New applications
User support		

It is relatively easy to determine if users should be charged for some of these. Transaction processing for an application done for a specific department, the data storage to support the application and any new development or program modifications should be charged to the user department. Telecommunications costs need careful evaluation. Should a remote facility be penalized for being further from the computer facility than other operations? Some companies average telecommunications costs for the entire company to determine the charge-out rates while others charge on a regional geographic basis.

Careful consideration should be given to the question of charging users for functions that the information systems organization does in order to play an active, participative role in user departments. Is it in the best interest of the information systems organization and the company as a whole to charge for user training, user support, R&D projects and feasibility studies?

Once decisions are made regarding what the user will be charged for, it must be determined how these charges will be priced. A number of pricing methodologies are possible, including:

Memo	Bundled pricing	Break-even annual
As incurred	Algorithm	Break-even product life
Estimates	Standard costs	

A memo approach is not really pricing, but a logical step before initiating a new charge-out system. The memo would be prepared monthly and delivered to the user department as if the user was being charged. The idea is to get users prepared for the day when they will actually be charged. Unfortunately most users pay no attention to "memo bills" that have no real impact on them. Something must be done to ensure that the message intended by the memo is getting through to the users.

An as incurred or estimates approach can make sense for a department that infrequently uses information systems support. Bundled pricing has a major advantage—the users understand it. A single hourly use rate for all charges is very easy to understand. Break-even annual can produce higher user charges and discourage systems use when a new system is installed and there is excess capacity. Break-even systems product life would avoid this problem. Algorithms are very common for determining the rates that users should be charged, but they are complex and frequently defy understanding. They are often developed by a systems programmer who understands how many disk reads and writes occur when a program is executed, but users seldom do. A very good case can be made for a standard cost approach. Users understand it and find it a logical way to anticipate their monthly charges. A standard cost system also serves as an incentive for the information systems organization to meet or beat the standards.

As long as 80% percent of the information systems costs are charged out, there is usually a feeling that this approach still accomplishes its basic objective. Contrary to what many people feel, the major challenge in this stage is not the fairness and clarity of the charge-back system. What is more significant is whether transferring charges from the information systems organization to user departments justifies the total amount of information systems spending to senior management. At a number of companies the answer has been no. A CEO of a large midwestern insurance company expressed this feeling very succinctly: "Transferring money from my left pocket [the information systems organization] to my right pocket [the user department] does not leave me feeling good about the fact that we are spending $50 million on information systems!"

Stage IV: Time for a Management Process

As organizations find that they are faced with the developments described earlier—organizational dependence on information systems, rapid growth of information systems costs, and increasing senior management involvement—it becomes more important to evolve from justification techniques to a management process of broader scope. This is not a unique situation but what one would expect with any major organizational effort involving large financial expenditure.

A possible management process is described in Figure 14-3. The logic of this approach is prompted by business requirements that can be addressed by a broader information systems role in the Stage IV environment. This stage would be characterized by:

1. Application support prioritized by a business strategy.
2. A major focus on using information systems to compete.

Figure 14-3

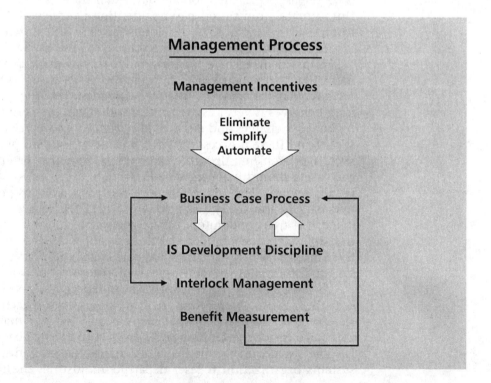

Management Process

Management Incentives

Eliminate
Simplify
Automate

Business Case Process

IS Development Discipline

Interlock Management

Benefit Measurement

3. A proactive role by the information systems organization in the enterprise's planning process.

The key elements of this management process are:

✦ **Management objectives (incentives)** that drive the entire process by indicating what is important to accomplish for the organization to be successful.

✦ A **formal business case** procedure that articulates where and how information systems can contribute to business success.

✦ **Information systems development discipline** and the resources necessary to implement new applications according to the schedule. This would have been agreed upon by both the users and information systems management when the business case was prepared.

✦ An **interlock management process** that collects the benefits identified in the business case procedure.

✦ Ongoing information systems **benefit measurement**, because this entire process will be repeated in the future.

The following sections examine these in more detail.

Management Objectives   Most, if not all, major functions or activities within an organization are motivated by senior management priorities. It is therefore logical that management objectives should also drive information systems management. Specific objectives must be logically thought out and, once identified, clearly communicated to the appropriate managers within the organization. The focus could be on productivity gains that can be stated as revenue growth per employee, or a combination of revenue per employee and number of units produced, sold, serviced or administered. The best approach is one in which these objectives motivate managers to do a better job in managing their area of responsibility, but without dictating specifically how to do things.

Formal Business Case   Within the structure of a management objective process there are a number of options available. These can be grouped into the following categories:

✦ Elimination of unnecessary effort, activity or functions.

✦ Simplifying or streamlining existing business processes or procedures.

✦ Reorganizing.

✦ Looking for a new approach through the use of information systems.

If the last is deemed appropriate, then a formal business case process is used. This involves a business case nomination process that provides an understanding of what is expected in terms of justification criteria and the mechanics of the approval process. This does not have to be complex, voluminous or bureaucratic. For example, the approach has been used successfully with a single-page form in which the sponsoring managers communicate their intentions very concisely. To a management review committee they simply say, "Here is what I want to do. This is my business case to justify it. Sign here!"

Information Systems Development Discipline   This is where the process can break down. If the information systems organization does not have the resources to meet the schedule dates that were a key part of the business case, then the necessary integrity is lacking to support the business case. What logically follows is that achieving the results and benefits from the use of the proposed information system may not be possible. Delayed schedules and missed target dates have a way of excusing the business plan sponsor from realizing the benefits. It is an enlightened senior management that is willing to say to their information systems manager, "We take risks in many areas of our business, but we do not want to take risks with information systems that will impact our ability to run the business. Therefore one of your major responsibilities is to communicate to us what is needed in terms of resources to support the integrity of the business case process, while also not negatively impacting the day-to-day business operations."

Interlock Management   The term interlock management means that a department gives up something in return for information systems benefits. If the business case said that the implementation of a new information system can save money by eliminating thirteen full-time positions, then the management process should collect this personnel savings. Many senior managers adamantly insist on the use of a charge-out system, believing that departments should pay for what they get in data processing support. What they do not require is that projected cost savings used to justify a new application are realized and collected through a logical and necessary management process. The key word is "necessary." The need to include interlock management as part of the management process can become very necessary to assure the logical and justified growth of information systems. Interlock management is one of the more demanding processes to implement with consistency. The most frequent criticism of this approach is that the business environment changes while the new information systems are being developed. The personnel time savings realized through the implementation of a new application that were included in the business case are now needed to address new business requirements.

Over the long term, for information systems to maintain a justified, supportive growth, it makes sense for interlock management to be an integral part of this entire process. The interlock process must be driven by senior management, with the financial organization normally charged with "making things happen." This does not make a charge-out system obsolete. The fundamental reason most organizations have charge-out systems is that they feel it is the best way to establish a value for the information systems services provided. While there are clearly challenges to realizing the successful implementation of such a system, it is the best available alternative, particularly in large organizations or where information systems cost is growing at a very rapid rate.

Benefit Measurement As the use of information systems increases and becomes integral to more functional areas of the business, it will become necessary to focus more management attention on cost-benefit factors. This is particularly true in areas like office administrative services where it is not intuitively obvious that an information systems cost is necessary to sustain efforts that are critical to the success of the business. This is the least implemented part of this entire management process. Yet one can easily conclude that information extracted from a benefit measurement process facilitates going back to the business case procedure to start the cycle all over again.

We will put this into a proper perspective with the following example. The senior management of a well-known insurance company approved the expenditure of $8 million for office automation. The implementation of the approved systems had an immediate, successful impact. The following year the functional manager responsible for the implementation of these systems felt that an additional $7 million was both needed and justified. This second time around the requesting manager was able to say, "Here was my business case a year ago. This is what we accomplished based upon our measurement of realized benefits. We want to do more of the same. Here is my new business case. Thank you for your support and approval for something that will bring so much value to the organization."

Few organizations are actually measuring benefits on an ongoing basis. This raises three points with respect to benefits measurement. First, no single measurement tells the complete story. A combination of measurements is desirable, among them counting transactions, industrial-engineer-type evaluations and interviewing those who are actually involved, including both direct and indirect personnel and managers. Second, one must concede that these measurements may not be precise from an accounting standpoint, although they represent information that can be used to satisfy senior management. The lack of accounting preciseness comes close to explaining why most organizations do not measure information system benefits. The two groups to be challenged to develop and implement an effective measurement approach—information systems and financial organizations—are both products of a precise environment. People who live in a world of preciseness easily find fault with approaches that are not consistent with their way of doing things.

Finally, the more difficult a benefit is to measure, the more important it probably is to measure it. Therefore it takes dedication to make this process work.

✦✦✦   IS THERE A BEST WAY TO MANAGE LARGE IS EXPENDITURES?

A number of aspects of the management process described above arouse controversy among senior management and information systems executives. Some claim that too much emphasis is placed on formal processes. Others feel that it requires additional effort and expense to verify benefits that one intuitively understands are necessary to run the business. (The president of an insurance company likened it to "justifying the air conditioning in my car—and I live in Arizona!") On the other hand there are organizations with multimillion-dollar systems that see the logic and necessity of continuing to justify large systems costs, for two fundamental reasons: (1) they are very expensive and (2) the dynamics of their business environment prompt management to want to periodically reassess the benefits of these systems.

The basic challenge in the fourth stage is sustaining a business process that can drive the realization and recognition of value to the business, given the much broader goals of information systems in this stage. They now include efficiency, effectiveness and competitive advantage. Defining and measuring value in the area of competitive advantage is clearly difficult, but responsible senior managers are not going to allocate large sums of money to information systems if the only answer to "What are we going to get for that?" is "It's good for the business."

It is still rare to find a company that has in place a management process based on measuring efficiency as described above. A financial strategy that focuses on the contribution of information systems to the products and services delivered to customers has also been successfully implemented by some organizations. This approach recognizes that four key elements in the process contribute significantly to the overall success of the organization. First is commitment planning that identifies specific goals and accountable managers. Using an information systems service level agreement, it is possible to monitor the factors that user management feels are important to the attainment of their product and service objectives to their customers.

Another key to this process is an effort to minimize user emotion while establishing reasonable expectations regarding information systems support. Levels of performance based on what information systems is able to provide and what the user organization feels is economically feasible need to be defined.

Equally important is an emphasis on an entrepreneurial attitude and approach within the information systems organization and the company as a whole. This includes performance appraisals and bonuses for information systems managers, with a chance to gain a significant amount of money if they meet or exceed the performance objectives spelled out in the service level agreement. The program should reward information systems people for results that are tied to business objectives.

Finally, and perhaps most important, is the regular communication of information systems performance, measured against the goals negotiated with user management, to the appropriate senior management responsible for that part of the business. This measurement of benefits and the communication of this information on a regular basis are key factors in a company's ability to manage very large information systems expenditures consistent with business strategies and objectives. This is not in lieu of but in addition to budgets, business cases and a charge-out procedure. The significance, size and scope of information systems clearly prompts this evolution in the management approach.

An Alternative: A Cost Accounting System

A major accounting firm devoted two years to a project with an objective of defining and developing a cost accounting system that takes into account the demands and realities of the current competitive world. Not suprisingly, after two years they gave up their attempt. Is a cost accounting system really an appropriate solution to the problems that have been addressed in this chapter? Is information systems justification precise enough that a new cost accounting approach is the right answer? The cost accountants are not giving up on their attempts to address this problem. Some people suggest that activity-based costing (ABC) could be used. In contrast to traditional job cost approaches, ABC focuses on an entire economic process to assign costs to cost objects like products, services or customers. The rationale is that if it works for external customer services, it should also work for internal information systems support.

Managing Information Systems as Two Concurrent Businesses

What adds credibility to the argument for a better financial strategy for information systems is the answer to the following question: Is information systems a single business or is it really two concurrent businesses? It is easy to conclude that a key job of information systems is to help *run* the business by providing ongoing support. A second and very important job is to help *improve* the business by introducing change.

As noted earlier questions regarding information systems costs invariably are distilled to, "How can we justify, afford or pay for that?" No matter how it is said, "that" is a large and ever-increasing information systems budget. It is normally viewed as a single number that demands explanation and is subject to attack from many directions, and often from the top of the business. If reductions in "that" occur, and they often do in these situations, where is the impact felt the most? The answer is in the second of the two information systems businesses—improving the business. This is because it is more difficult to reduce expenditures in the role that information systems play in running the business. In addition, the business applications are the result of earlier management decisions and are often an integral part of the business. Financial reductions in this area, although possible, are often difficult to realize.

Unfortunately, when senior management insists on reductions in the information systems budget, they are in reality asking that efforts to improve the business be curtailed. One company determined that running the business represented 64% of the annual information systems expenditures, while improving the business was 36%. Each of these two businesses are profiled over multiple years with data that addresses contribution to the business, functional performance (productivity and quality) and organizational health (vitality and maturity). This has definitely helped senior management to better understand that the information systems organization is indeed two concurrent businesses and should be managed accordingly.

✦✦✦ CONCLUSION

The issue of information systems value is being addressed by an increasing number of organizations. The answer will not come from new and better techniques and methodologies. These will certainly help, but this is a fundamental management issue that can best be resolved by processes similar to those described above.

RECOMMENDED READING

Carlson, Walter M., and Barbara C. McNurline, *Uncovering the Information Technology Payoffs.* IS Analyzer Special Report. Rockland, MD: United Communications Group, 1992.

This document summarizes fourteen strategies for measuring the value of information systems. Included are methods advocated by Peter Keen, Paul Strassman, Charles Gold, Paul Berger, Peter Sassone and commentaries on their findings.

Drucker, Peter F., "The Information Executives Truly Need: Redesigning the Corporation Requires a New Set of Tools and Concepts." *Harvard Business Review,* January–February 1995, p. 55.

Once again Peter Drucker challenges you to look at an issue with a very broad and historic perspective. He states that the corporation that is now emerging must be designed around an information skeleton. This new approach will define a business as an organization that adds value and creates wealth. The article addresses activity-based accounting as a necessary way to cost an entire economic process. It also discusses price-led costing, value-added analysis, core competence and benchmarking as important business management (wealth creation) tools.

Framel, John E., "Information Value Management." *Journal of Systems Management,* December 1993, pp. 16–41.

Mr. Framel provides a methodology entitled Information Value Management Implementation Steps (IVM/IMP). This approach is based on the premise that everyone within the organization is personally committed to maximizing the value of their operation by managing the value of the information assets that they use. It starts with management's understanding of the role of information systems and systematically follows a process that is very similar to the approach advocated in this book.

Meyer, N. Dean, and Mary E. Boone, *The Information Edge.* New York: McGraw-Hill, 1987.

The major focus of this book is the defense of the premise that the strategic use of information systems can be quantified. Methods to quantify value-added applications are provided and supported by company case studies.

Parker, Marilyn M., and Robert Benson, *Information Economics: Linking Business Performance to Information Technology.* Englewood Cliffs, NJ: Prentice-Hall, 1988.

The primary emphasis of this book is to thoroughly explore the meaning of value in information systems. The authors contend that "the heart of Information Economics is change," and that "a business must change to achieve real, enduring value from information technology."

Saunders, Carol Stoak, and Jack William Jones, "Measuring Performance of the Information Systems Function." *Journal of Management Systems,* Spring 1992, pp. 63–82.

This article is based on the premise that measurement of the information systems function is a critical issue facing today's executives. It goes on to say that "value is reflected in the ability of information systems to satisfy individual managers' information requirements. It is the assessment issue, not the theoretical model, that dominates current concerns of both managers and evaluators." Unfortunately, the measurements vary over time. This article does a competent job of assessing many of the alternatives and factors that can be considered in formulating an approach to address the information systems value issue.

Strassman, Paul A., *Information Payoff: The Transformation of Work in the Electronic Age.* New York: The Free Press, 1985.

Strassman contends that information value is a product of management. One might want to debate whether this can be consistently measured, but the author clearly supports this as the major focal point in addressing the value of information systems.

Among the many additional articles on this subject are:

Clemons, Eric K., "Evaluation of Strategic Investments in Information Technology." *Communications of the ACM,* January 1991, pp. 22–36.

Schwartz, A. Perry, and Peter G. Sassone, "Cost Justifying OA: A Straightforward Method for Quantifying the Benefits of Automated Office Systems." *Datamation,* February 15, 1986, pp. 83–88.

Steiner, Thomas D., and Diego B. Teixeira, *Technology in Banking: Creating Value and Destroying Profits.* Homewood, IL: Business One Irwin, 1990.

Weill, Peter, and M. Olson, "Managing Investment in Information Technology: Mini Case Examples and Implications." *MIS Quarterly*, March 1989, pp. 3–18.

EXERCISES

1. Financial strategy.

Addressing the "IS value issue" through a logical financial strategy continues to be a problem for most organizations.

   a. What is the "IS value issue"?

   b. Name three ways a company derives value from information systems.

   c. Explain how a charge-out system works and the logic behind its use. Include a discussion of its positive and negative aspects.

   d. What problems exist with using a budget in Stage I and a business case approach in Stage II as the primary factors of a financial strategy?

   e. Identify and explain a specific, logical management process that could be used in Stage IV.

2. Activity-based costing.

Does this relatively new cost accounting approach provide a logical solution to the problem of determining the cost and related value of information systems support?

3. Information systems cost allocation in a client-server environment.

Many companies have had difficulty in satisfactorily allocating information systems costs to users in a traditional, centralized information systems operation. They are concluding that this becomes even more difficult in a client-server environment. As computing resources are moved closer to users a new metric is needed to assess the value of information systems. Prepare a recommendation showing what factors should be used to assess the value of client-server systems support.

4. Information systems financial strategy evaluation.

Identify a company that has implemented an information systems strategy that you feel meets the criterion of a "management process" that is beyond the scope of a charge-back system. Focus on what prompted the implementation of this process and discuss its benefits.

INTEGRATING INFORMATION SYSTEMS INTO THE BUSINESS PLAN

The objective of planning is not to control but to guide and direct.

For information systems to be strategic, they should directly support the creation, modification and implementation of an organization's strategic plan.

LEARNING OBJECTIVES

This chapter focuses on understanding the importance of integrating information systems planning into the business planning process so the two become one and the same: a business plan that includes information systems support of strategies and tactics. A successful approach involves making this a priority within a company while implementing a necessary process to make it happen.

QUESTIONS

The following are necessary questions regarding information systems planning:

1. Is information systems a legitimate, high-priority consideration in the developing of business strategic plans?
2. Who needs to play a key role in integrating the role of information systems with the business strategy?
3. Why is there a possible lack of support from senior management for planning in general and for integrating information systems into a business plan?
4. Why are some organizational environments hostile to their own planning approach?

5. What are major barriers to linking information systems with the business strategies?

6. What would be an ideal role for an information systems executive to play relative to business strategies?

✦✦✦ IT ALL STARTS WITH BUSINESS PLANNING

The traditional questions regarding planning are still very appropriate in today's business environment. They are:

1. Why plan?
2. What to plan?
3. How to plan—what is the best methodology to use?

While the questions have remained the same, their significance and implications to the business have changed. Business planning should no longer be viewed as primarily a control function, a way to avoid risks. Too often in the past planning really meant financial budgeting and related controls. The challenges of today demand that planning should be used as the way to communicate the vision of the organization (the direction) and to accomplish the realization of the vision through the formulation of the best possible strategies and tactics.

We have heard the issues raised so often that it is starting to sound like a broken record. Technology and the global economy are changing the business environment at an accelerating and alarming rate. It is logical to refer back to the Business Driver Model in Figure 1-3, and remember the four major factors that are driving (challenging) organizations to achieve and sustain a competitive advantage. The market, enabling technology, the significance of regulation, and the work environment and employee values play major roles in influencing how a business addresses requirements through effective organizational processes.

Business Drivers Influence Planning

Figure 15-1 depicts examples of responses to these business drivers. While not intended as an all-inclusive list, it does reflect a number of possible reactions. For example, to pursue new markets and opportunities while also achieving a competitive cost structure, companies are resorting to decentralization of authority and responsibilities, downsizing, outsourcing, business partnering and corporate alliances through mergers and acquisitions. Business processes are being reengineered, redefined or improved through an emphasis on quality. Companies are frequently rethinking the responsibility and accountability of employees and resorting to cross-functional teams, quality circles and other forms of empowerment. The

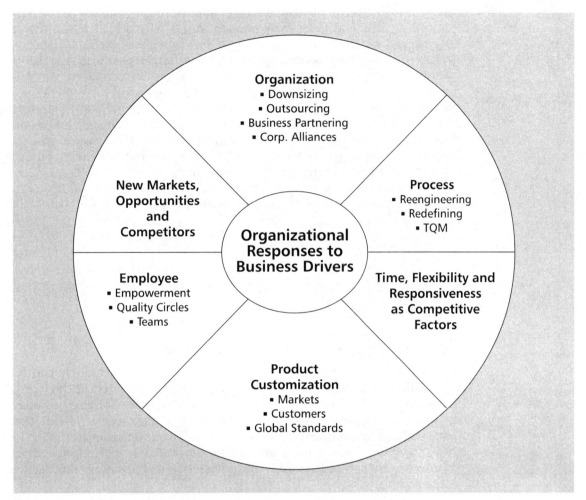

Figure 15-1

ability of each employee to exhibit a particular skill or capability may be seen as necessary to respond to market conditions. Business and societal pressures are also making temporary or contract employees a permanent fixture in work force restructuring. Products are being customized to markets and specific customers and designed to meet global standards, with a major emphasis on programs that provide value-added services. Micro-marketing, the ability to identify that set of potential customers who represent the biggest opportunity, has become an important dimension of this approach.

All these responses add up to attempts to find better ways to compete by decreasing time cycles, improving organizational flexibility and improving responsiveness to customers. Key to accomplishing this is getting the right message to the right people and providing the necessary resources to implement and support both strategies and tactics. A key question in discussing the why of planning is whether all these factors have tipped the scales in favor of short time schedules, flexibility and responsiveness so that business planning is no longer practical, feasible or effective. Have we reached a point where things are happening so fast, product cycles are so short and the need to respond to customers on a specific basis so imperative that planning just gets in the way? Planning advocates are adamant that because of the pace you have no choice—an organization must do an effective planning job or get lost in the maze of increasing complexity. However, this planning job must be true business planning and not a budget or financially driven effort.

The example of Ed McCracken and Silicon Graphics was discussed in Chapter 7. They feel that traditional planning processes have been challenged by the dynamics and pace of change within the computer industry. They do long-term visioning based on where the company will be in the year 2000 or 2005, but they do not lock it in. Under the circumstances they feel that they do a better job by modifying and adapting as they go along rather than trying to pin down everything in an up-front planning process.

The Two Major Challenges of Planning

Organizations have two major challenges. They must decide what to do and then make it happen. An interesting question is, which of the two is more difficult? How do you know what you should be working on today if you do not know where you are going as an organization? How do you make day-to-day decisions in a vacuum? You need to accomplish both of these objectives based on an understanding of directions and guidelines that derive from the clear and well-understood vision, strategy and tactics of the company.

The "making it happen" part of a company's plans has received a great deal of attention in recent years. This was necessary because of the difficulty of changing things, especially in long-time, successful organizations. Two points need to be remembered. Empowering employees, team building, etc. need to be done within an overall context of what is consistent with an organization's strategies. Moreover, the importance of talent and skills to successfully execute these same strategies must not be overlooked. People are often a company's best and most important competitive resource. There are situations where changing or improving the skills and capabilities of a large number of employees is an essential long-term strategy. Transforming the baseline skills of a large number of employees can be as significant as any major product development/launch effort. The challenge faced by AT&T to change its culture from a regulated monopoly to one driven by entrepreneurial, customer-centered thinking is a good example of this. Gaining a competitive advantage through the use of information systems by people is a theme that a number of individuals, including the author, have pushed for a long time. On the other hand when you encourage people to do great things, you are not suggesting that they do so in a vacuum.

Employee downsizing, rightsizing or dumbsizing (take your choice) should not be based solely on cost cutting. This needs to be done in a way that is also consistent with the vision and strategies of the organization. It should be done in such a way as to help build the future strengths of the company while streamlining or eliminating unnecessary processes and functions. Major reductions in personnel are too big a price to pay for anything less than this. The loss of experienced personnel, and younger employees with good long-term potential who jump ship because they lose faith in the company, as well as the negative impact on corporate culture because of layoffs, can cause major damage if not handled logically and consistently. The costs that are being dealt with through illogical downsizing often could and should have been dealt with through a healthy and attentive planning process and a management willing to make necessary and tough decisions.

So what does one conclude from all this? Business planning at a high level is more critical than ever. Leaving room for local adaptation and specific implementation is equally important. Doing great things within the context of a strategy is what you really want. If information systems are to be an integral part of the implementation, then they need to be addressed at the same high level, at least in terms of the role they will play.

✦✦✦　STRATEGIC PLANNING

According to George A. Steiner, strategic planning is the systematic examination of opportunities and threats in the business environment so that you are in the position to identify those opportunities that should be exploited and the threats that should be avoided. This puts you in a position to make better current decisions.[1] N. Les Clark of Hoechst Marion Roussel, Inc. says that strategic planning allows one "to create opportunity that can be leveraged to create differential advantage in the marketplace." He then adds, "Strategic planning's first job should be to identify opportunities to leverage existing efforts. Can incremental differential advantage be created in the marketplace? Although threats are something that you need to keep an eye on, you cannot allow yourself to become preoccupied with them. If you do, you may fail to move the business forward incrementally."[2]

The traditional approach to business planning is shown in Figure 15-2. Information systems planning should parallel this, and the more integrated it is to the process, the better. This suggests a top-down approach,

---

[1] Steiner, George A., *Top Management Planning,* New York: Macmillan, 1969, p. 50.

[2] Internal company documents and interview by author.

Figure 15-2

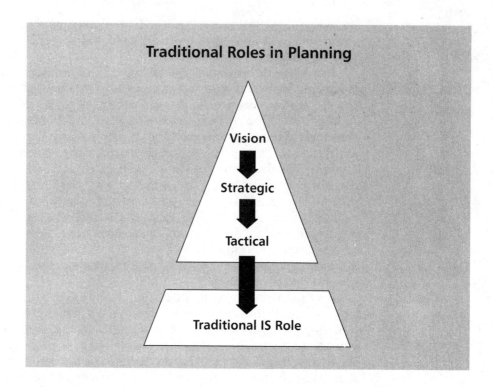

which many organizations are wrestling with. Top-down is often not the real issue. It is what is passed down from the top and how effectively the arrows between each of the levels are managed that are key considerations.

A commonly used strategic planning model is depicted in Figure 15-3. It is the classic SWOT (Strengths, Weaknesses, Opportunties and Threats) model cited by Kenneth Andrews [3] and others. Whether you prefer SWOT or WOTS as an acronym is not the point. It makes basic sense to evaluate strengths, weaknesses, opportunities and threats as they apply to the enterprise. A strong case can certainly be made for an organization to maximize its strengths and minimize exposure from its weaknesses. External opportunities should be exploited by internal strengths. Threats need to be identified and understood, with every possible effort made to improve or to circumvent internal weaknesses.

The True Beneficiaries of Good Business and IS Planning

It is too general to simply say that the company benefits from an effective job of integrating business and information systems planning. More specifically

---

[3] Andrews, Kenneth R., *The Concept of Corporate Strategy*, Homewood, IL: Irwin, 1987, p. 50. Figure 15-3 is consistent in concept but uses terms in the manner presented by the author throughout this book.

Figure 15-3

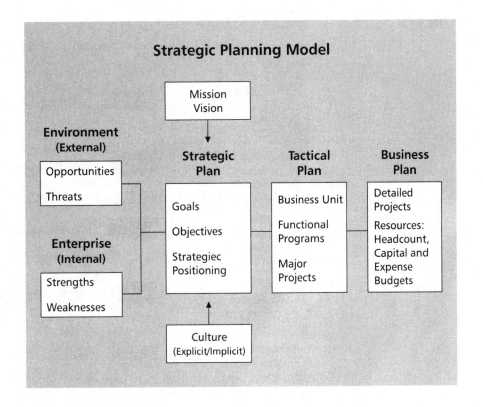

it is important to be able to say that those who are shaping the future of the business benefit by better understanding the business changes that technology will drive. Those with profit and loss responsibility should be better able to exploit current capability and build critical tactical programs. While this is integral to their jobs, an effective planning process should contribute to an enhanced ability to address these efforts.

What to Plan to Link Information Systems to Business Strategies

Information systems planning should be integral to the business planning process. As shown in Figure 15-4, the entire process starts with the creation of a strategic business plan. An information systems plan is then based on the major elements of the business plan. In today's dispersed computer resource world, an information systems architecture has become both necessary and significant. It is a blueprint of the future with guidelines on how data management and telecommunications networks will be designed, implemented and managed. Tactical information systems plans logically follow. These include time targets, budgets, skills requirements

Figure 15-4

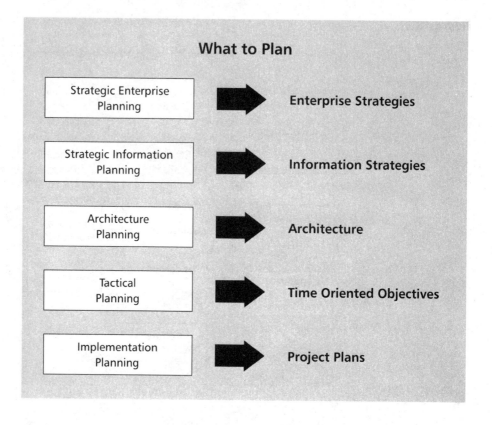

and authority and responsibility. The information systems planning process concludes with an implementation plan for specific projects.

✦✦✦ BARRIERS TO ALIGNING INFORMATION SYSTEMS WITH BUSINESS STRATEGIES

Aligning information systems use with the strategies of the business has many dimensions and possible challenges. Nevertheless we can identify two fundamental factors that may be either the foundation of success or its major deterrent. Depicted in Figure 15-5 is a cause-and-effect model of this endeavor. The two key factors are senior management perception of information systems and the executive skills of the information systems executive. Examining the possible competitive role of information systems, senior managers may be justifiably concerned. Their information systems organization may already have a hard time doing accounting and financial applications on schedule and within budget. Therefore putting the company's competitive strategies in an information systems basket would not seem like a very smart thing to do.

Figure 15-5

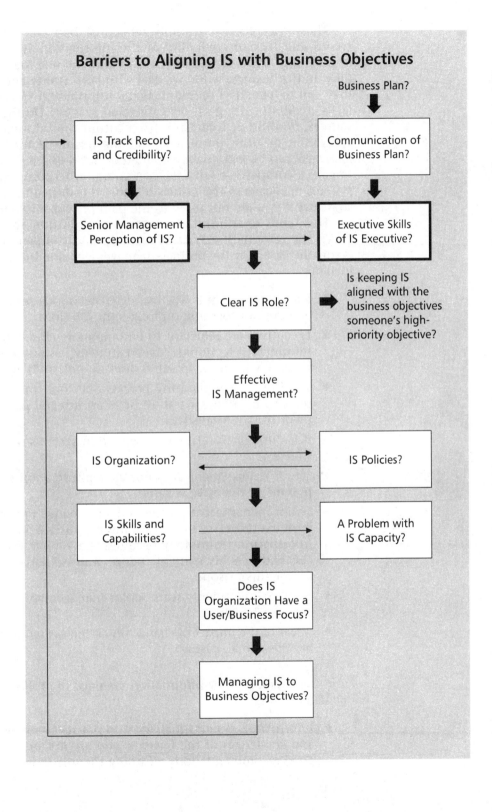

Barriers to Aligning IS with Business Objectives

Business Plan?

IS Track Record and Credibility?

Communication of Business Plan?

Senior Management Perception of IS?

Executive Skills of IS Executive?

Clear IS Role?

Is keeping IS aligned with the business objectives someone's high-priority objective?

Effective IS Management?

IS Organization?

IS Policies?

IS Skills and Capabilities?

A Problem with IS Capacity?

Does IS Organization Have a User/Business Focus?

Managing IS to Business Objectives?

These executives are simply reflecting their perception of the track record and lack of credibility of the information systems organization to get things done. *Perception* is a key word and one that was chosen carefully. In the business world we deal with both reality and perception, and they can be equally important. If the information systems organization lacks credibility, a logical next question is why? Do they lack skills, resources, funding or leadership from within the information systems organization or from those who run the business? Information systems managers can be legitimately accused of not doing a good job of helping to gain a competitive advantage. A common response from information systems managers to this criticism is that it is difficult to support business strategies if you are not privy to the plan or play a role in creating it.

This tends to confirm a lack of communication and partnership between the information systems manager and company executives. Why is this the case? On the business management side the explanation could include:

+ Executives are in a reactive, defensive mode to business problems and are not focusing on long-term solutions.

+ Executives are reluctant to become more closely involved with an information technology-based strategy because they are not comfortable with it, or in some cases do not really understand it.

+ The long-range planning process does not force information systems to be addressed at all or as an integral part of the development of new strategies.

+ It is difficult to relate an information systems role to the business strategy.

+ Senior management does not view information systems as an important competitive weapon.

+ Senior management pursues a major change in philosophy and/or business processes by embedding it in a new information system. Information technology becomes the vehicle for significant process and possibly cultural change, and is viewed negatively by users for this reason.

+ High IS investments scare senior management when they cannot see clear benefits.

+ A fear of the impact of change on an increasing number of users has become a major issue.

From the perspective of information systems, the following could be influencing factors:

+ Information systems managers do not really understand the issues and challenges of the business and are not in a position to make good recommendations regarding the role of information systems.

✦ Information systems is not being sold proactively within the organization.

✦ Little or no previous computer-based systems within the organization could mean that using information systems to make a major contribution to the business would be both costly and time consuming.

✦ Many information systems failures have their origins in discounting or underestimating the degree of IT skills and capabilities needed within the entire company to successfully implement a new system.

✦ No logical information systems infrastructure has been built to offset long lead times to provide information systems solutions.

✦ Information systems as an organization, or the information systems manager specifically, lacks credibility for a number of reasons. Because of this the IS manager has not earned a seat at the corporate table where business decisions are being made.

✦ Information systems is viewed as and acts like a cost center, which prompts an attitude of making what already exists run better and cheaper. This results in a measurement of managing expenses based on efficiency instead of supporting new ways of doing things in support of business strategies.

✦ The dispersion of information technology is not being managed well. Turf battles, low user awareness of changing responsibilities and a lack of a defined approach (architecture) cause many problems.

✦ Technology limitations are always a possible but seldom major cause for an inability to link information systems to business strategies.

✦✦✦ BUSINESS AND INFORMATION SYSTEMS PLANNING FRAMEWORK

The planning framework described in Figure 15-6 is basic, logical and representative of a traditional approach. It correctly states that the business strategy directs the information systems strategy. This in turn guides the selection of information technology, which when properly implemented produces benefits in support of the business strategy. This is still a valid concept but falls short of what can and probably should be accomplished.

The added dimension in Figure 15-7 suggests that the corporate vision, when combined with the technology environment, represents business opportunities. These are influenced by the existing information systems strategy and the in-place systems technology. These lead to the need to address how information technology can create strategic business

Figure 15-6

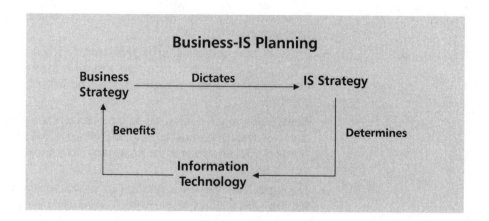

capability. A second dimension of this is how technology could or even will drive business change.

Addressing these factors clearly puts the information systems organization into a proactive, leadership role within the business. The IS organization becomes a technology conscience for the business and a key player in the strategic planning process. The time implications of this responsibility to the information systems executive are significant. To function effectively in this expanded role, an information systems executive could expect to spend half of his or her time in planning-related activities. Who would then run the information systems organization to accomplish the

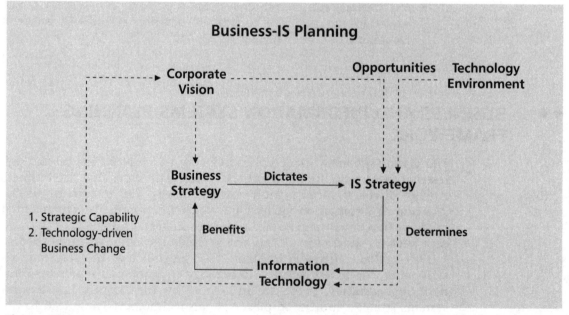

Figure 15-7

day-to-day operations? The answer is, the managers who report to the information systems executive.

✦✦✦ DEVELOPING NEW STRATEGIES AND SUPPORTING THEM WITH INFORMATION SYSTEMS

The Strategic Planning Process Model shown in Figure 15-8 provides a structure and raises questions that can be used in developing effective business strategies and the necessary information systems to support them. It clearly identifies the relationship between the business and information technology domains. Specifically it deals with how the business strategy influences business processes and organization. These then prompt an alignment with the information systems architecture and organization. The combination of three of these factors provide opportunities for information technology to address the needs of the business.

Figure 15-8

Adapted, by permission, from Parker, Trainor and Benson, *Information Strategy and Economics,* Englewood Cliffs, NJ: Prentice-Hall, © 1989, p. 5.

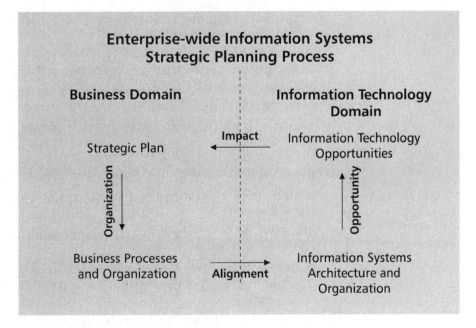

Strategic Planning Questions

The following questions warrant consideration in developing strategic plans.[4] Undoubtedly additional questions could be considered based on

---

[4] These questions have been adapted with modification from Parker, Trainor and Benson, *Information Strategy and Economics,* Englewood Cliffs, NJ: Prentice-Hall, 1989.

products and services, the competitive environment, the organization structure and the leadership style of the company.

Strategic Plan

Vision: Do we have a clear vision of where the organization is going?

Decisions: Do we make major decisions based on our vision and strategies?

Innovations: Do the values and goals of the organization call for innovation?

Risk Taking: Does the reward system support employee and management risk taking?

Change: Do we respond quickly to changes that affect our organization?

Customer Segments: Have we identified and do we understand the needs and each type of customer and how they define products and service value?

Competitors: Are our strategies based on market intelligence and competitive information?

External Factors: Do we regularly review the economic, social and demographic trends that can affect our performance?

Management Teamwork: Are our interactions characterized by openness, candor and teamwork?

Quality: Do we emphasize and measure quality throughout the organization?

Business Processes and Organization

Culture: Does the company have a strong sense of mission and shared values?

Productivity: Is productivity measured and are ambitious but achievable goals established?

Empowering People: Are employees encouraged to get involved in multiple aspects of the business and do they readily accept accountability?

Management Support: Does management openly and enthusiastically support the ideas and efforts of our employees?

Structure: Does the current organizational structure logically and effectively support the business strategies?

Bureaucracy and Complacency: Are unnecessary overhead and bottlenecks being eliminated while being careful not to take things for granted because of past success?

Operational Systems: Are the best possible systems in place to address operational needs?

Decision Support Systems: Do existing systems effectively support multiple levels of decision making?

Communications: Do people openly communicate across the organization, or is a "chain of command" adhered to in most cases?

Experimentation: Does management encourage new ideas, provide funding for trying new things and tolerate mistakes and failures?

Information Systems Architecture and Organization

Existing Information Systems: How critical are existing information systems to our operation?

End-User Support: Does the information systems organization provide a broad range of services and support to end-users within every major function of the company?

Information (Data) Access: Is data available and easily accessible when users need it?

Network: Are information services delivered on a common network to those with a need to have it where and when they need it? (This includes customers, suppliers, business partners and employees.)

Charges: Are users charged fairly for information systems support?

Relationships: Does the information systems organization see itself as an enabling resource with the users viewed as the driving force?

Information Systems Management: Is information systems run like a business within a business, benefiting the entire organization?

Information Systems Role: Is information systems focused and positioned as a competitive resource within the organization?

Strategic Planning Process: Does the strategic planning process ensure that the right things are being supported by information systems?

Distributed Systems: Have the appropriate resources been moved to where they make the most sense from a financial, management and technical standpoint?

Information Technology Opportunities

Industry Impact: Does our industry depend heavily on information technologies to achieve business success?

Competition: Do our competitors frequently use information systems to differentiate their products and services?

Education: Is our management familiar with the potential opportunities for information technology within our industry and company?

Customer Expectations: Do our customers react well to innovative approaches with information technology and will they pay for its added value?

Strategic Impact: Are our business plans directly influenced by potential new uses of information technology?

Opportunity Window: Would we be likely to lose market share if a competitor announced new systems-based services?

Vendors: Do we have a good working relationship with information technology vendors to aid in our planning for potential use of new systems?

Prototypes: Is it likely that we would authorize the building of an information systems prototype to prove operational and/or competitive feasibility?

Joint Development: Are users actively involved with information systems to reduce the risk of failure of new information technology use?

Visualization: Is anyone charged with the responsibility to make sure that time is devoted to brainstorming how the organization might look in the future considering the impact of information technology?

Some Planning Guidelines

The definition of a good plan is not based on quantitative accuracy, i.e., realizing 100,000 units when the plan projected 97,000. A good plan projects trends and directions that influence decisions, which later prove to be correct. The fact that a decision to increase production capacity was justified by market demand is far more important than the preciseness of the numbers. Because of the scope and frequency of change in the business environment, incremental change is often not worth much. It takes major shifts in strategies and approaches to improve or even protect a company's competitive position.

✦✦✦ PLANNING METHODOLOGIES

It is not the intent of this book to cover the many planning methodologies in detail, but to provide a basic understanding of the general types and characteristics of the methodologies that are successful in the current business environment. How many different planning methodologies are there? At least as many as there are major consulting companies. Influencing organizational ways of doing things and developing a plan to change is what a great deal of consulting activity is all about. There is little likelihood that a consulting company would decline an opportunity to assist a company in almost any planning endeavor.

One of the criteria that should be used in selecting a consultant is to understand the specific methodology the consultant uses. This is not force-fitting solutions to a problem, but it is force-fitting a planning methodology. It is possible to associate different planning methodologies with a number of successful consultants. If you like a "vision-driven process," then you will like Peter Keen. If the concept of "critical success factors" fits your and your organization's thinking, then John Rockart could be the right person. Richard Nolan spent a career using the "stages process" as the basis of a consulting practice before returning to the Harvard Business School faculty. Reengineering is a hot topic these days, so an organization interested in that might look to James Champy or Michael Hammer to accomplish good things. These are just a few of many methodologies being used today.

The interest in reengineering confirms that circumstances and attitudes can dictate the acceptance of planning approaches. As a methodology reengineering has been around for a long time. IBM internally developed what it called Business Systems Planning (BSP) in the 1960s. While the basic philosophy of BSP was that data is a corporate resource, it focuses on key processes. The approach develops an enterprise model that assesses the relationships between processes, business strategies, organizational structure and responsibilities, and key data (entities). Senior management sponsorship is emphasized, and a study is accomplished by a team of users and information systems people through an interview process. The end result is recommendations and an action plan for new information systems, guidelines regarding the management of data and in some cases a new information technology architecture.

Although developers and proponents argue the advantages of their approach over others, methodologies are seldom the difference between success and failure within an organization. Most if not all of these methodologies have worked when they have been effectively sponsored by senior management, properly introduced, accepted and leveraged throughout the organization. The two primary objectives remain the same, as discussed earlier in this chapter: Deciding what to do and making things happen. A major issue is how to accomplish both of these in the most effective manner with the highest degree of success.

While simplifying what can become a complex, time-consuming process, it is also important to remember that any planning methodology has three basic components. Using systems terminology these are input, processing and output. Input is how you collect the necessary information that is pertinent to the issues being addressed. Processing is how you make sense out of what is often a large amount of often conflicting information and develop a logical, cohesive set of recommendations. Output is determining the final product of this effort based on the desired results.

Planning in essence is communicating with people who can provide information that will be the basis for a new way of doing things. The new approach will improve key factors that contribute to the success of the organization. This input can be gained through traditional planning sessions involving senior management. Conducted at remote sites to avoid interruptions and distractions and run by a professional facilitator, this approach works well and continues to be used to formulate higher level strategies. At the micro-strategy or tactical level a current trend is to involve line managers or professionals directly involved in key processes. In 1994 National Semiconductor formed a task force of manufacturing managers and supervisors from eight facilities around the world to evaluate how it was dealing with key manufacturing processes. For the first time they brought together a group of people who were directly responsible for making products and asked them to determine how to do things in the best manner possible and to do so consistently around the world. The end result of this one-year effort was the recommendation to implement specific manufacturing application software throughout the company.

Collecting the necessary information and formulating it into a documented proposal is a demanding, time-consuming and often intense effort. But it is not the most challenging part of the process. Getting people (i.e., line management) to accept the recommendations of the plan is usually the biggest hurdle. It is not that they do not want to do what is best for the organization, but without being part of the input and evaluation process they have not benefited from the time spent looking at the many alternatives. They also frequently have different agendas and evaluation criteria for which they are being held accountable, which seem in conflict with significant change. After all, they have a business to run!

✦✦✦ WHY DOES BUSINESS AND INFORMATION SYSTEMS PLANNING FAIL?

If general business planning can fail to produce the desired results, the same can be said for trying to integrate information systems into a business plan. Failure regarding information systems planning falls into two general categories: (1) information systems and general business-related issues and (2) management authority and responsibility. In the first a risk of failure is related to the outcome being stated in technology terms and not business terms. People in the organization either do not understand it or simply do not accept the stated objectives and/or approach. Some plans fail because they tend to place blame on today's environment, rather than project the company to a new and better way of doing things. A third reason for failure can be related to a lack of risk taking based on an incremental approach that, while logical, fails to motivate people to invest the effort to realize the desired return. Management authority and responsibility factors are often the cause for a lack of planning success. These include a failure to support the final plan through actual implementation. Another dimension of this failure is what happens when an unexpected event occurs that was not anticipated by the plan. Is the plan ignored as the new problem is addressed, or is the plan modified to reflect a necessary response?

A failure earlier in the process can be a lack of support of the planning process. Participation and involvement of key management is essential to arrive at a plan that will have a significant impact on the business. Attitudes towards the importance of the entire process are important and obvious to the planning process participants.

Within the planning process too much time can be spent deciding who is to guide, direct and control the outcome instead of determining the most important focus and contents of the plan itself. A broad-scope plan takes time to implement and even more time to achieve results. A lack of organizational patience can do in the best of business plans. If early implementation falls short, all credibility can be lost.

✦✦✦ CONCLUSION

Planning is a tool to be used by an organization to identify the right things to do, and to initiate action programs to accomplish the things identified. A good plan with no execution is simply that—a plan that consumed time, energy and resources with no noticeable impact. What might be perceived as a weak plan, but one with a few strong thoughts supported by tenacious implementation, can produce very positive results for a company.

The challenge is not to slip into an engineer's mentality where you spend a great deal of time analyzing problems, analyzing structures, elements and cause and effect. Always remember that success is measured by satisfying requirements dictated by the customer, market and competition. From an information systems standpoint, satisfying the customer and the client are not the same. External customers buy products and services while internal customers of the information systems organization have profit and loss responsibility.

There is clearly a need for a partnership between the people with profit and loss responsibility and the people who can support them with information systems resources. This should be reinforced by a process that helps identify risks and then enhances success probability by appropriate rewards.

Finally, in today's business environment there is a need for information systems managers who can make tough decisions on resource allocations to pursue new opportunities and orchestrate structural change.

Faced with limited resources, these can be tough decisions. Like the business managers that they support, they must be right more often than wrong in the areas that they agree to support.

RECOMMENDED READING

Ackoff, Russell L., *A Concept of Corporate Planning.* New York: Wiley-Interscience, 1970.

> One of the early classic efforts regarding the concepts and importance of strategic planning. While many things have changed in the business world since 1970, Ackoff is still very correct when he says, "Planning is the design of a desired future and of effective ways of bringing it about."

Ansoff, H. Igor, *Corporate Strategy.* New York: McGraw-Hill, 1965.

> A second hallmark publication that in 1965 was a major event in the world of business management.

Jelinek, Mariann, *Institutionalizing Innovation.* New York: Praeger, 1979.

> An insightful analysis of the role of formalized strategic planning.

Mintzberg, Henry, "The Fall and Rise of Strategic Planning." *Harvard Business Review,* January-February 1994, p. 107.

> This article is adapted from the book with the same title cited below. As in the book, Mintzberg argues that planners should not create strategies but feed data to help managers develop visions and to think strategically.

Mitzberg, Henry, *The Rise and Fall of Strategic Planning.* New York: The Free Press, 1994.

> Mintzberg traces the history of strategic planning from its origin, to prominence, to a subsequent fall. He claims that the processes through which strategic plans are developed must change to emphasize informal learning and personal vision. He argues that the current process can narrow the vision of a company, discourage change, breed a political atmosphere and destroy commitment. This is not to say that planning is no longer a valid and even necessary activity. Planning and planners need to take new roles in posturing plans that make sense for an organization in today's business environment.

Rockart, John F., "Chief Executives Define Their Own Data Needs." *Harvard Business Review,* March-April 1979, p. 81.

> This original publication on Critical Success Factors (CSF) details this simple-to-understand and successful concept. It identifies the four primary sources of CSFs as the structure of the industry, the competitive strategy and industry position of an organization, environmental factors and temporary factors that become critical and demand the attention of management. It elaborates on the importance of CSFs and the fact that different managers have different critical success factors and therefore need different information. This and other related CSF articles plus a primer on the concept can also be found in *The Rise of Managerial Computing: The Best of the Center for Information Systems Research,* Sloan School of Management, MIT, edited by Rockart and Christine Bullen and published by Dow-Jones Irwin in 1986.

Rockart, John F., and Adam D. Crescenzi, "Engaging Top Management in Information Technology." *Sloan Management Review,* Vol. 25, No. 4, 1984, pp. 3–16.

This article presents a three-phase process for management involvement in information systems. This starts with linking information systems to the needs of the business through the use of the Critical Success Factor methodology. It then turns to using decision assist techniques to deliver necessary information to support key decisions. The third part of the process involves building low-risk but managerially useful prototypes to better understand the features, functions and implications of possible new information systems. This approach makes it easier to make the decision to build the ultimate and complete system. One can think of these three factors as individual modules or as related, logical components of an overall approach. (This article is also included in the above referenced *Rise of Managerial Computing* publication.)

Steiner, George A., *Strategic Planning: What Every Manager Must Know.* New York: The Free Press, 1979.

A traditional book that takes you through every stage of the strategic planning process from idea to execution to evaluation.

EXERCISES

1. **Information systems planning.**

   a. In the dynamic business environment of today, is business and information systems planning more or less important?

   b. What are the primary objectives of business and information systems planning?

   c. What major two conclusions do you derive from the chart in Figure 15-5?

   d. Why does information systems planning often fail within organizations?

2. **Business and information systems planning.**

   a. How do you personally feel about planning in general and the need to integrate business and information systems planning? If you have not had personal experience that would enable you to answer this question, then seek out those who have and provide a perspective on this topic.

   b. Is it necessary, feasible and practical for information systems to be integrated into a strategic business plan?

3. **Planning, planners and plans.**

   Strategic business planning came into prominence in the 1960s with the creation of central planning groups. Is the issue faced by many companies today one that deals with planning, plans or planners?

4. Planning response to business drivers.

Tailor the factors identified in Figure 15-1 to a specific company to determine how it actually responded to the demands of the current business environment.

5. Planning successes and failures.

Identify examples of successful planning efforts both from a business standpoint and where it was effectively used to link information systems support to business strategies. Why did the approach work and what were the major challenges in achieving the desired results?

TOTAL QUALITY MANAGEMENT AND THE ROLE OF INFORMATION SYSTEMS

*To compete and win, we must redouble our efforts—
not only of our goods and services, but in the quality
of our thinking, in the quality of our response to
customers, in the quality of our decision making,
in the quality of everything we do.*

Edgar Woolard
Chairman and CEO
E.I. DuPont

LEARNING OBJECTIVES

The relationship between Total Quality Management (TQM) and the role of information systems is examined in this chapter. The material presented deals with how a TQM effort impacts the use of information systems and how the information systems organization supports TQM. There is a general consensus that Motorola was the first large U.S. company to realize major benefits through the implementation of a TQM program. Xerox was in the next wave of companies to emphasize such a program. Xerox is used as an example of a company that went from near disaster to a strong global competitive position by embracing the principles of TQM, an endeavor that included a major assist from information systems. A major lesson to be learned is the difficulty that can be encountered in changing the priorities within a large company that has been very successful in the past.

QUESTIONS

The following are important questions regarding both TQM and the role of information systems:

1. Does information systems help an organization achieve the objectives advocated by a TQM program?

2. Does a TQM program help information systems support the objectives of an organization in a more effective way?

3. What are the fundamental factors that drive the success of a TQM program?

4. How valid is the statement, "If it cannot be measured, it cannot be managed"?

5. How much change within an organization does TQM represent?

6. How long should it take for an organization to realize benefits from a TQM program?

✦✦✦ A CASE ANALYSIS: LEADERSHIP THROUGH QUALITY AT XEROX[1]

The Xerox 914 copier was possibly the most successful product ever built. Introduced in 1959 it was the first plain-paper copier ever produced. A copier is a complex piece of equipment. It has major parts that are chemical, optical, computer and mechanical to move paper. The more function and speed that is built into a copier, the more likely there will be operational problems requiring repair service. This means that copiers require very large R&D funding, are expensive to manufacture and are very labor intensive in terms of field repair service. It is a tough but very good business.

On the positive side copying is a very user-friendly technology. It is easy to use and provides clear value. By making copies quickly information can be disseminated rapidly and widely in an inexpensive way. It is a wonder how businesses survived before Xerox made copying the easy and convenient task that it is today.

Xerox knew only success in the 1960s, but by 1982, it was in danger of going out of business. The company that invented xerography and dominated the U.S. copier market with a 95% market share in 1970 was in serious trouble. The Japanese were selling better quality products for what it cost Xerox to make them. Their product line was lacking, and bad feelings existed between the company and its customers. The only hope for survival was to commit to vastly improving the quality of products and service. This meant changing the culture of Xerox, a company with over 100,000 employees worldwide, from the ground up. This was certainly no easy task.

---

[1] The analysis of Xerox is based on three primary sources: the perspective provided by David Kearns, the CEO, and David Nadler, an outside consultant, who both played key roles in the TQM effort as described in *Prophets in the Dark: How Xerox Reinvented Itself and Beat Back the Japanese* (see Recommended Reading); an internal Xerox presentation on its TQM program; and personal interviews with Xerox employees.

Seven years later, in 1989, Xerox won the Malcolm Baldridge Award for outstanding quality. More importantly the factors that earned it the award resulted in competitive success. Xerox products had become leaders in all seven copier categories. This enabled them to regain installed market share from a low of 12% in 1984 to 19% in 1989. Its copier quality had become so good that it implemented the Xerox Total Satisfaction Guarantee. If a copier did not function to customer satisfaction it would be replaced by Xerox up to three years from the date of purchase.

This is an interesting story of the struggles of a company that knew only success during the 1960s but found that it had to change many of the ways that it functioned. The leadership of CEO David Kearns played a major role in the entire effort. In 1990 he relinquished the CEO position to Paul Allaire, another early advocate of the value of their quality program. He has continued to provide the executive leadership that was needed to sustain the quality program within Xerox.

Early in the effort to address Xerox's business problems, the following policy statement was established as a company guideline:

Xerox is a quality company. Quality is the basic business principle for Xerox. Quality means providing our external and internal customers with innovative products and services that fully satisfy their requirements. Quality is the job of every Xerox employee.

Adoption of this policy was followed by defining measurable-quality targets and setting performance standards based on customer requirements.

Leadership Through Quality

The time schedule of this story is shown in Figure 16-1. In general the 1960s were the golden years, the 1970s were the lost decade, and the 1980s were the comeback years. Fuji Xerox's winning of the Deming Award in Japan in 1980 was ironic. While the U.S. company was suffering because of poor quality, its joint venture company was receiving Japan's award for highest quality.

"Leadership Through Quality" was Xerox's strategy to reinvent the company. The strategy to improve competitiveness was initially based on employee involvement and benchmarking. Xerox defined benchmarking as the continuous process of measuring products, services and practices against the toughest competitors or companies renowned as leaders. The goal was superiority in all areas—quality, product reliability and cost. The advantage of benchmarking is that it challenges an organization to be as good as the best, not just in the company's industry but in any industry. A good example of this was Xerox's focus on mail order company L.L. Bean's warehousing operation. A possible disadvantage of benchmarking

Figure 16-1

Reprinted by permission
of Xerox Corp.

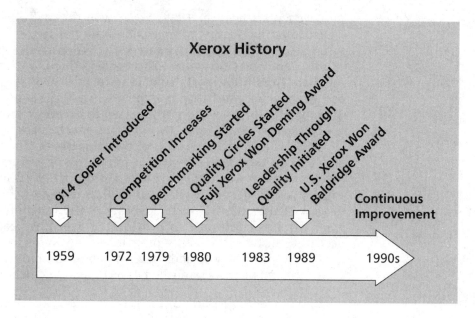

is that it narrows the evaluation to what is already being done. A better solution may exist in an approach that is innovative and new.

Early benchmarking in 1979 and 1980 resulted in shock, disbelief and anger within Xerox. It discovered that it was off the performance of the benchmark company by as much as ten times in some areas. The benchmark comparisons included the following:

	Off the Benchmark
Indirect/Direct Ratio	2×
Production Suppliers	9×
Assembly Line Rejections	10×
Product Lead Time	2×
Defects Per 100 Machines	7×

Meanwhile bad quality was costing Xerox $1.4 billion a year.

The Original TQM Implementation Plan

For an organization with 100,000 employees worldwide, the magnitude and scope of the proposed quality program was very large and had many challenging elements. A plan was developed with the following objectives and milestones:

1. 1983—the year of start-up activities: Guidelines to implement the strategy would be finished.

2. 1984—the year of awareness and understanding: 4,000 senior and middle managers would be trained.

3. 1985—the year of transition and transformation: Most of the managers and half of the employees would be trained.

4. 1986—the year when significant results would be achieved.

5. 1987—the year of approaching maturity.

A nice plan, but they never came close to meeting this schedule. The difficulty with this type of program is getting things to actually happen. Employees were grumbling that all the emphasis on quality was getting in the way of doing business. Instead of realizing results managers were using the amount of training on quality as a measurement of progress.

To get things moving they pursued a management process and cultural changes that included:

✦ Creating dissatisfaction with the current culture.

✦ Training managers and employees in the tools and skills needed to work and manage continued quality improvement.

✦ Establishing good communication to support the quality effort.

✦ Developing standards and measures to use as the basis for management decision making.

✦ Rewarding and recognizing quality-oriented performance.

The Role of Information Systems Within Xerox

Xerox continually strives to improve the way it collects and uses information to effect quality results. Comprehensive information systems and analysis are the foundations for continuous quality improvement. Xerox has over 375 major information systems supporting the total business. Over 175 of these systems relate specifically to the management, evaluation and planning of quality. The validity, accuracy and timeliness of information systems are assured by the use of a Data Systems Quality Assurance process during the design, construction and major upgrade of each information system.[2]

Xerox users require that data be both available and accessible. This is supported by a worldwide network that is operational 24 hours a day, 7 days a week. Two computer-based systems directly support the TQM program: (1) the Quality Improvement Process, a program for planning, organizing and monitoring quality improvement and (2) the Problem Solving Process, which is used to determine problems, develop countermeasures and verify the effectiveness of the countermeasures.

David Kearns provided leadership to the TQM program but was also a strong proponent of the strategic use of information systems. Computer-integrated manufacturing (CIM), Electronic Data Interchange (EDI) and computer-aided design (CAD) systems were an important part of the

---

[2] Xerox Corp., *A World of Quality: The Timeless Passport*, Milwaukee, WI: ASQC Quality Press, 1993, p. 96.

Xerox restructuring. Its worldwide dispatch system for service representatives played a major role in its ability to better service customers while controlling costs. CAD accomplished design improvement and provided improved communication within the engineering community. EDI was used as part of a major new vendor program. A telecommunications network provided the link for their worldwide R&D operation. In summary, information systems was a key part of its strategy across the entire organization.

In recognition of the role that he played relative to the use of information systems, David Kearns received the Excellence in Technology Award from the Gartner Group in 1990. Strong information systems leadership has also continued with the current CIO, Patricia Wallington, who was recognized as the Information Systems Chief of the Year by *Information Week* in 1992. Wallington, who reports to the CEO, joined Xerox in 1989, the year it won the Baldridge Award, replacing Patricia Barron, who became the president of the Office Document Products Division.

The TQM program complemented an existing emphasis by the information systems organization on customer service and managing the life cycle of computer-based applications. What it changed was the level of detail associated with these efforts and the degree of sharing with senior management. The service level to customers (users) was evaluated through (1) satisfaction surveys taken specifically of IS employees twice a year, (2) round-table meetings conducted quarterly by the IS executive, which solicited feedback from systems users, and (3) the overall company employee satisfaction survey. This third evaluation determined whether the information systems organization was providing job satisfaction among the information systems employees as they provided user support.

The second major impact was that the divisional information systems managers were asked to determine how they would create a world class information systems organization. The response to this challenge was the development of a plan with longer-term goals, status reports, a specific action plan and the means to measure results for each major project. These were then carried down to the individual level for information systems employees.

To reinforce the importance of this entire effort, the information systems executive's bonus was based on meeting company objectives (revenue and ROI), customer (user) measurements and information systems employee satisfaction.

All of this added up to some fundamental changes within the information systems organization. The message was very clear: The information systems organization, like everyone else within Xerox, must always focus on exceeding the current level of performance. Success was no longer based on a system doing what it was designed to do. Instead, it was determined by how the IS organization was contributing to the overall company objectives and through improvements to exceed performance expectations.

An Analysis of Xerox's TQM Program

In the final analysis Xerox did some things right with its TQM program and some things wrong. On the wrong side, it should have stated earlier in 1983 that customer satisfaction was the number one priority of the company. Improving profits and boosting market share were the other two objectives. Since no priorities were given, the traditional culture convinced employees that profits were still the number one objective. This led to conflict between the drive for quality and the pressure to achieve financial results. The drive to get better financial results was the basic principle of the corporation—not quality.

Other things Xerox did wrong:

✦ Early on, it failed to focus adequately on core work processes and statistics.

✦ It did not properly integrate the quality process as part of the business process.

✦ It should have been more attuned to the embedded culture of the company and the inherent difficulties in changing it.

✦ It did not initially pick the right quality officers at the start.

✦ It did not push the operating units hard enough.

Despite these shortcomings Xerox did many things right with its TQM program. For one thing it built a constituency starting at the top in a very calculated and deliberate way. Its training program played a key role in accomplishing this. The training was done in "family groups" so that managers attended with their people. In addition:

✦ It made an appropriate diagnosis of how to cure the ills of the company.

✦ Quality was the right process for the right solution at the right time.

✦ The necessary commitment was made by senior management.

✦ Information systems use was effectively aligned with its business objectives and the processes to achieve them.

✦ Executive compensation was tied to quality.

✦ Innovations and successes of the TQM program were well publicized.

✦ The pursuit of the Baldridge Award was an energizing effort within the company.

Finally, the TQM program achieved measurable results as shown in Figure 16-2.

It took Xerox nine years to really embrace quality as a way of corporate life. It took five years to train all its employees in TQM. A successful quality program takes time, commitment and never ends. It requires constant focus, commitment and self-evaluation. A summary of the key supporting elements is shown in Figure 16-3.

Figure 16-2

Reprinted by permission of Xerox Corp.

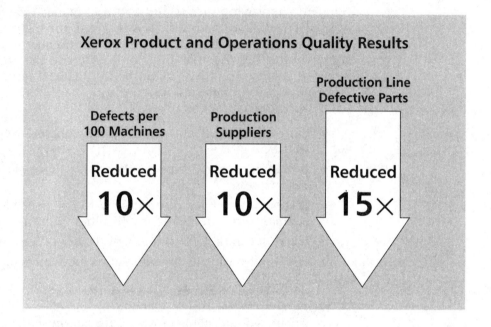

Figure 16-3

Reprinted by permission of Xerox Corp.

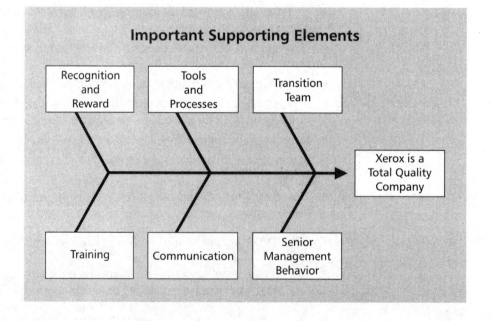

Why TQM? The Problems and the Challenges

The Japanese say that quality is no longer a competitive factor—it is a given. It is nevertheless an important topic within U.S. companies. Why have many U.S. companies pursued quality as a necessary factor in how they do everything? Maybe because it worked well at companies like Motorola, Xerox, Westinghouse, Federal Express and IBM. Xerox's Malcolm Baldridge Award publicity certainly influenced some companies. It is not uncommon to hear comments like, "We may never win the award, but the emphasis on quality makes good business sense." This may reflect recent thinking, but does not explain why the companies that were among the very first in the United States to apply TQM did what they did in the middle to late 1970s.

Was fear an explanation of what motivated companies like Xerox, Motorola and General Motors to seek solutions to business problems through quality? Was it fear of loss of market share, of loss of major customers, of being shut out of new markets, of lower earnings or even of company survival? Xerox, Motorola and General Motors were certainly not the only U.S. companies facing major threats from the Japanese. Figure 16-4 is a 1980 summary of Japanese product market share in the United States. The seriousness of this threat made many companies feel like they were fighting for their corporate lives. As noted earlier Xerox faced better quality Japanese competition whose sales prices were lower than Xerox's manufacturing costs. Unfortunately, like other historically successful companies it did not recognize the need for change until external forces dictated the necessity to do so.

✦✦✦ FUNDAMENTALS OF TOTAL QUALITY MANAGEMENT

Quality is not just building a product right, it is meeting customer expectations. Customers buy offerings—the function, the price performance, the documentation, the support and the expected effect on their business.

Quality is a management process to run the business. A common mistake is fine-tuning a bad product, the bad product being the management system. Fine-tuning will not change anything of any significance in most cases. A new management process, attitude and culture are often required. Achieving quality in even the most taken-for-granted tasks is also predicated on consistently following an orderly progression of steps.

The core problem in accomplishing all of this is how to manage a massive change in organizational behavior. A question that has been repeatedly asked at companies like General Motors, IBM and Xerox is whether anyone can actually change a large organization. The following factors are major considerations as an organization contemplates a quality emphasis program:

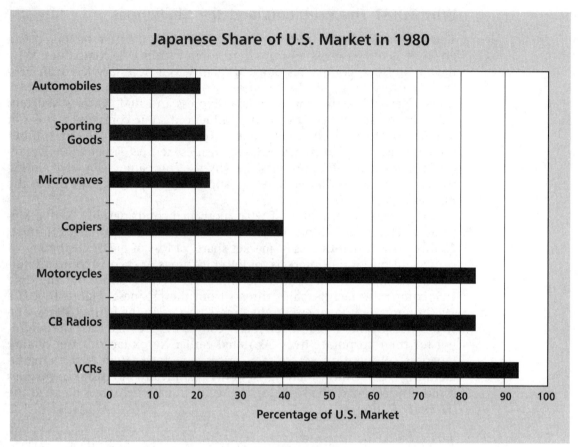

Figure 16-4

Reprinted by permission of Xerox Corp.

People are the enablers of quality. Management action, beginning at the top, and the involvement of everyone are necessary prerequisites for improvement. This lays the foundation, but employee-initiated problem solving is at the heart of any TQM initiative. Gaining employee acceptance of this effort is aided by the fact that quality gives meaning to people and their work.

Business processes are the focal point of a TQM program and are the keys to unlocking true organizational excellence. A process is a structured, measured set of activities, ordered across time and space, that is designed to produce a specified output. A process perspective focuses on how work is done, not just what is produced. It implies a horizontal view of the business that cuts across the organization and deemphasizes its functional structure. Although process innovation is important, it is imperative to step back from a process to inquire into its overall business objective.

Effecting creative and radical change to realize order-of-magnitude improvements should be done in a way that the business objective is accomplished.

Efficiency, effectiveness and competitive advantage are the direct results of a successful TQM program. It is also important to remember that improved quality does not increase total cost. The challenge is to guard against over-prioritizing short-term or narrowly defined objectives at the expense of long-term, quality-oriented goals.

A logical concern regarding a TQM program is how to tell long-time, dedicated, hardworking employees that what they felt was quality effort was not good enough. The difference between old and new quality is that the old version involved the work of individuals that, while individually good, may have been and often was integral to an inadequate process. New quality is work within a well-conceived, customer-focused business process that is in turn aligned with the goals and objectives of the business. This should be consistent with the following key elements of a successful TQM program:

- ✦ **Committed leadership:** Goals, objectives, implementation follow-up and attention to results.

- ✦ **Defined processes that can be measured.**

- ✦ **Fanatical dedication to customer satisfaction.**

- ✦ **Employee involvement:** Empowering people to make decisions through leadership and coaching. Asking people to spend time on how to do their jobs better is a valuable activity.

- ✦ **Competitive benchmarking:** Identifying and using the best as the standard.

Additional supporting elements in a successful TQM program include training, communication, and recognition and rewards that tie to profit and quality achievements.

TQM and Reengineering

Is there a fundamental difference between TQM and reengineering? Reengineering guru Michael Hammer says, "Quality programs and reengineering share a number of common themes. They both recognize the importance of processes and they both start with the needs of the customer and work back from there."[3] He then makes a major distinction by contending that a TQM program simply improves what is already in place, while a reengineering effort advocates an entirely new approach, a new beginning, a rejection of the traditional way of doing things.

---

[3] Hammer, Michael, and James Champy, *Reengineering the Corporation: A Manifesto for Business Revolution,* New York: Harper-Collins, 1993, p. 96.

What was the attitude and intention of the management at Xerox when they implemented their TQM program? Did they tell their people that they should concentrate on improving existing processes? Wayland Hicks, who headed copier development and production during the 1980s, can help answer this. He said, "Part of the mind-set we are trying to create around Xerox is that we will do business fundamentally different than we have done it before. Don't be embarrassed to try something new. Don't be embarrassed to go to someone for help if you need it. I am competing against world-class competitors and to do that I need every trick in the book."[4]

There are conceptual barriers but no official rules regarding what one can or cannot do with any approach to realizing change within an organization. The issue is not reengineering versus TQM or any other methodology; it is doing what is right for the good of the business. Contrary to the idea that reengineering and TQM compete with each other, it has been suggested that reengineering should use TQM as a logical, defined methodology. Remember that of the three letters in TQM, T is the most important. "Total" says that you maintain a balanced focus on major business factors and business results while guarding against becoming process myopic.

✦✦✦ TO MEASURE IS TO KNOW: THE ROLE OF INFORMATION SYSTEMS

Facts and data are needed for quality improvement. Pursuit of quality and operational performance goals requires that process management be based upon reliable information, data and analysis. Certain quality assessments like cost and related finances are obvious. Similar analysis must address market, customer, product and service performance, operations, competitive comparisons, suppliers, and employee-related factors. Analysis must extract broader meaning from data to support both evaluation and decision making at multiple levels within the company.

Facts and data also support a variety of company purposes such as planning, reviewing company performance, improving operations, and comparing company quality performance with competitors or with "best practice" benchmarks. The entire data collection and feedback process needs to be as robust as possible, because no one can predict the "what if this happens?" questions of the future. Careful consideration must be given to data that is indicative of current business success factors and similar factors for the future.

A major consideration relating to the use of data and analysis involves the creation and use of performance indicators. Performance indicators are measurable characteristics of products, services, processes and operations

---

[4] Jacobsen, Gary, and John Hillkirk, *Xerox: American Samurai*, New York: Macmillan, 1986, p. 31.

that the company uses to evaluate and improve performance and to track progress. The indicators should be selected to best represent the factors that lead to improved customer and operational performance. A system of indicators tied to customer and/or company performance requirements represents a clear and objective basis for aligning all activities of the company toward common goals. Through the analysis of data obtained in the tracking processes, the indicators themselves may be evaluated and changed. For example, indicators selected to measure product and service quality may be judged by how well improvement in quality correlates with improvement in customer satisfaction.

More specifically an effective measurement strategy should do the following:

✦ Evaluate how closely activities are meeting customer requirements.

✦ Suggest where adjustments might be necessary.

✦ Provide a means to organize and communicate information about the activities with the customers to generate good feedback and assure the productive use of the measurement process.

Integrating a measurement discipline into business process management should adhere to the following four guidelines:

1. The process cannot be well understood or improved in an orderly way without qualified measurements.

2. No simple measures can completely or accurately represent a complex business process.

3. Rather than wait for hoped-for improvements, the best-known current measurements should be used.

4. Learning what and how to measure is accomplished by measuring.

The Malcolm Baldridge Award includes 70 points for Information Analysis out of a total of 1,000 possible points. Does this suggest that information analysis or access to information represents 7% of the significance of a successful quality-oriented company? Absolutely not. Standing behind most if not all of the other six categories are major uses of information systems. For example, every month Xerox sends out 50,000 questionnaires to customers to evaluate their product satisfaction. The responses provide a direct input into an information system that compiles, tracks and analyzes trends in this highest value category of the Baldridge measurements (300 points).

The core of information systems support for TQM is the development and implementation of process improvements and monitoring systems. Information technology can be used to improve information flow, create measurement processes and support performance-based compensation systems. Synergy must be established between information systems and TQM goals. This suggests that representatives of the information systems organization need to be included in strategic planning to determine the appropriate focus of a TQM program. They also need to be involved in human resource decisions, including how employees will be empowered to make well-informed decisions.

The good news is that information systems employees are intellectually and culturally attuned to a TQM program. They are accustomed to a team-oriented approach and a flat organization and are trained to view possible information technology-based solutions with a broad perspective.

✦✦✦ CHALLENGES IN IMPLEMENTING A TQM PROGRAM

Organizations wishing to implement a TQM program face a number of challenges and hurdles. These include:

- ✦ Lack of leadership and direction.
- ✦ Difficulty of changing the company culture.
- ✦ Attitude problems.
- ✦ Choosing the best people.
- ✦ Understanding the business problems.
- ✦ Developing a compensation system.

The lack of strong management leadership and direction is consistently cited as the major reason that TQM programs do not realize the expected results. Unrealistic expectations, too much emphasis on process rather than results, inadequate training, poor communication and lack of patience are additional factors cited as cause for failure.

The philosophy of quality represents a culture change, which is a major challenge for any organization. People who study culture change in organizations have concluded that it takes one or two years per level to accomplish this. Six to nine levels within a company are not unusual. That translates to a minimum of six to as many as eighteen years to complete such a change.

Quality programs often must confront the attitude, "TQM doesn't apply to me. I'm not in manufacturing." To the contrary, TQM has been used successfully to close the financial books sooner at Motorola, to run more effective meetings at Xerox, to solve janitorial, cafeteria, warehousing and repair service problems.

Another challenge is picking the right people to serve on transition teams, because they are the true agents of change. These jobs demand people with the right personal credibility within the organization, receptiveness to change and interpersonal skills to sell the new way of doing things to others.

A successful TQM program requires that management understand the business problems they are trying to solve. Identifying the internal or external customer is integral to this. And finally, a performance-based compensation system is essential for achieving sustainable quality improvement.

✦✦✦ SOME WORDS FROM "MR. QUALITY," W. EDWARDS DEMING

A discussion of quality without reference to the man whose name is synonymous with the word would be incomplete. What W. Edwards Deming said makes a great deal of sense in today's business climate. In his book *Out of the Crisis* Deming held American managers responsible for causing a society-wide quality crisis. His philosophy was to put quality in human terms. He contended that when a work force is committed to doing a good job and has a solid management process in which to act, quality will flow naturally. An immediate reaction to Deming's thoughts might be, why didn't people listen to him?

Deming felt that the lack of quality in the United States was being prolonged by Seven Deadly Diseases,[5] which are:

1. A lack of constancy of purpose to plan products and services that will have a market, keep the company in business and provide jobs.
2. Emphasis on short-term profits.
3. Evaluation of performance—merit rating or annual review—based on wrong factors and individual effort.
4. Mobility of management. (Too much moving around produces managers that really do not know their business.)
5. Running a company on visual figures alone, with little or no consideration of figures that are unknown or unknowable.
6. Excessive medical costs for employee health care, which increase the final cost of goods and services.
7. Excessive costs of liability, fueled by lawyers who work on the basis of contingency fees.

To cure these diseases Deming advocates adherence to his Fourteen Points:

1. Create constancy of purpose toward the improvement of products and services with the aim to become competitive, stay in business and provide jobs.
2. Adopt the new philosophy. Management must awaken to the challenge, must learn their responsibilities and take on leadership for change.

---

[5] Both this and the Fourteen Points are based, with some minor modifications, on Deming, W. Edwards, *Out of the Crisis*, Cambridge, MA: MIT, Center for Advanced Engineering Study, 1982, pp. 97–148.

3. Cease dependence on mass inspection to achieve quality by building quality into the product in the first place.

4. End the practice of awarding business on the price tag alone. Instead minimize total cost. Move toward a single supplier for any one item based on a long-term relationship of loyalty and trust.

5. Improve constantly and forever the system of production and service, thereby improving quality and productivity, and thus decreasing costs.

6. Institute training on the job.

7. Institute leadership. The aim of supervision should be to help people and machines and gadgets to do a better job.

8. Drive out fear, so that everyone may work effectively for the company.

9. Break down barriers between departments. People in research, design, sales and production must work as a team to foresee problems of production and what may be encountered in the use of the product or service.

10. Eliminate slogans, exhortations and targets for the work force (or let workers formulate their own).

11. Eliminate numerical quotas on the factory floor. Substitute leadership.

12. Remove barriers that rob hourly workers of their right to pride of workmanship. The responsibility of supervisors must be changed from sheer numbers to quality.

13. Institute a vigorous program of education and self-improvement.

14. Everyone should work to accomplish the transformation. The transformation is everybody's job.

✦✦✦ CONCLUSION

In today's business environment a company's fortunes rest on its ability to provide superior quality products at a good value. Never forget that there is a business reason for pursuing quality. As depicted in Figure 16-5, the result of quality excellence can be delighted customers, proud and motivated employees, satisfied stockholders, successful partners and even an enhanced community.

TQM does not guarantee immediate, ultimate or sustainable business success. It is a tough, challenging, dynamic and ongoing effort. It is also a systematic and disciplined focus on business processes within an organization, which requires both management leadership and employee acceptance and empowerment. Leaders of the more successful companies

Figure 16-5

A Win-Win Proposition

profoundly believe in and promote the core values of customer-driven quality.

As was so accurately concluded in Kearns and Nadler's book on the Xerox experience, *Prophets in the Dark,* four critical success factors must be addressed. The first is **strategy**. A basic requirement for competitive success is viable competitive strategies. Qualitatively different and better strategic thinking and execution are required. The second critical factor is **quality**. Good, logical quality within an organization can make a significant difference in many respects. **Organizational design** and **organizational learning** are the final two factors. Competitive success requires successful innovation and speed. The ability to do so quickly has become critical in the global marketplace. Organizational learning ties to execution. As employees understand and accept the other three factors, they are able to achieve desired results. If at first they are not successful, a quality organization reflects upon and understands the meaning of mistakes better and faster than its competitors.

What about information systems? Information technology is and always will be the enabling resource to support the four factors cited above. It can be the catalyst for making things happen. Information technology is not the strategy; it is the enabler of the strategy. It is not quality, but the provider of data to support management by fact. It is not a flattened organization structure, but the communications link and data resource to support such an approach. Finally, information systems can be used as the foundation for new business processes and/or to help employees learn new ways of doing things. Both of these are integral to organizational learning.

A TQM program can be implemented within an organization without a major role being played by information systems. However, management by fact suggests that information systems can make a major, positive contribution to the success of a TQM effort, particularly in support of any performance measurements. The key is not unlike any information systems design and implementation. Careful consideration must be given to the data to be collected, how it will be organized and accessed by users (including managers) and whether such a system will facilitate the integration of data from multiple sources in support of decision making. Bad information systems are part of the problem and probably need to be reengineered, along with other factors that drove the need for a TQM program in the first place.

RECOMMENDED READING

Deming, W. Edwards, *Out of the Crisis*. Cambridge, MA: MIT, Center for Advanced Engineering Study, 1982.

Deming has always been known to be candid and even blunt regarding issues and those who are responsible for doing something about them. He contends that the basic sickness in American industry is failure of top management to manage. For this reason the book deals with the transformation of management style that requires a whole new structure. Deming believes that "the goal of management should be joyous workers. Too often the way that employees are treated squeezes from an individual his innate intrinsic motivation, self-esteem and dignity and builds into him fear, self-defense and extrinsic motivation." Although other publications may do a better job of explaining Deming's beliefs and approaches, one should not pass up the opportunity to see first-hand what Mr. Quality advocates.

Haavind, Robert, *The Road to the Baldridge Award: Quest for Quality*. Boston: Butterworth-Heinemann, a division of Reed Publishing, 1992.

This book provides a good summary of company experiences with TQM and the major beliefs of key quality advocates including Deming, Crosby, Juran and Reigenbaum.

Jacobson, Gary, and John Hillkirk, *Xerox: American Samurai*. New York: Macmillan, 1986.

This is an earlier account of the Xerox story written by two outsiders. They offer an objectivity and a broader perspective than many Xerox people.

Kearns, David T., and David A. Nadler, *Prophets in the Dark: How Xerox Reinvented Itself and Beat Back the Japanese*. New York: Harper Business, 1992.

Fortune magazine was right when it said that this book "is a gripping tale of life on the frontlines of the new global battlefield." It is also a classic example of the challenges faced in trying to change a company addicted to growth because of its past success in this regard.

Main, Jeremy, *Quality Wars: The Triumphs and Defeats of American Business*. A Juran Institute Report. New York: The Free Press, 1993.

This is a good summary of the experiences of a number of companies with TQM programs. Successes at Hewlett-Packard, Motorola, Ford, IBM Rochester and Xerox are certainly encouraging for those who feel that the U.S. has lost the ability to compete within the manufacturing industry.

Reid, Peter C., *Well Made in America: Lessons from Harley-Davidson on Being the Best.* New York: McGraw-Hill, 1990.

If you are not interested in copiers and Xerox, then you might find this story about Harley-Davidson more interesting. There are definite similarities in the situation faced by both companies during the early 1980s. Like Xerox, Harley-Davidson failed to respond to a Japanese threat during the 1970s. As the last motorcycle manufacturer in the U.S., Harley-Davidson was the obvious competitive target of Japanese companies like Honda and Kawasaki. In 1981 the company was offered for sale by then parent AMF, but there were no takers. The solution to this problem was a management buyout. Success was not immediate; the new independent company was on the verge of bankruptcy in 1985. Spirit, pride and a fierce determination to succeed by people from the top to the bottom within Harley-Davidson turned things around. Today it is the market leader in the U.S. in the heavyweight motorcycle market, and it has also significantly increased its international sales. Three factors were key to saving this American institution: employee empowerment, just-in-time inventory (JIT) and statistical operator control. All three of these success factors were strongly influenced by making "close-to-the-customer" a way of life for all managers and employees.

Xerox Corporation, *A World of Quality: The Timeless Passport.* Richard C. Palermo and Gregory H. Watson, eds. Milwaukee, WI: ASQC Quality Press, 1993.

This is an objective, systematic and very complete summary of the TQM program within Xerox.

EXERCISES

1. TQM and information systems.

Validate whether TQM and information systems complement each other by evaluating this premise within a specific organization.

2. A win-win proposition.

Using Figure 16-5 as a guide, explain the significance of the impact of TQM on the major stakeholders of a company.

3. Xerox as an example of an effective TQM program.

What fundamental lessons can be learned from the Xerox story in terms of business leadership, business strategy, product technology and information systems?

4. Malcolm Baldridge Award.

   a. The Baldridge Award gives very few points for information systems. What does one conclude from this lack of emphasis?

   b. Is there a correlation between companies that have won the Baldridge Award and those with high information content and related information systems support?

17

FINAL CONSIDERATIONS

I regard information technology as a precocious teenager: full of energy, irreverent, unpredictable, a source of both joy and heartache—and frequently in need of close supervision.

Kent "Oz" Nelson
Chairman and CEO
United Parcel Service

LEARNING OBJECTIVES

At some point all things, including books, need to end. By no means have all of the business-related issues that involve information systems been addressed, but it is hoped that not too many major ones have been omitted. This last chapter provides some final considerations and conclusions. An appropriate summary ends with where the book began—the business and information systems challenges that stand in the way of gaining a competitive advantage through the use of information systems. It might be necessary to go back to the first chapter and reflect on the challenges that were addressed to see if you now have a better understanding of the issues. Of equal importance, do you now have some good ideas about how to address them? Business drivers, business success factors and a systematic approach in the use of information systems are summarized because they influence whether a company can achieve and sustain competitive success.

QUESTIONS

The following final questions deserve consideration. Later in this chapter we will consider answers to these questions.

1. Do you really believe that information systems can make your organization more competitive?

2. Is this a technical or an internal marketing challenge?

3. What is the current credibility of the information systems organization?

4. What are the basic prerequisites for an organization to use information systems to compete?

5. How do you align information systems with the goals and objectives of the business?

6. What is the scope of competitively focused information systems?

7. How important is determining the value of information systems within an organization?

8. What are the organizational and personnel implications?

9. Does the use of information systems to compete ever get easy?

✦✦✦ ORGANIZATIONAL RESPONSES TO BUSINESS DRIVERS AND THE SIGNIFICANCE OF INFORMATION SYSTEMS

The possible responses to the major business drivers introduced in Chapter 1 were summarized in Chapter 15, Figure 15-1, "Integrating Information Systems with the Business Plan." Having discussed these factors throughout the book, it is now time to draw some general conclusions about them. The significance of the business drivers will be reviewed first. This is followed by a reflection on the importance of the business success factors used in Chapter 1 to begin building a better understanding of what must be present for a company to achieve and sustain success over time. This chapter concludes with a final discussion of the systematic use of information systems to gain a competitive advantage.

The responses to business drivers, shown in Figure 17-1, are a reminder of the scope of the challenges faced by a company in the current global economy. Summarizing them into the four categories of market, technology, regulation and employees/work should not suggest that there are a relatively small number of issues that must be addressed. Each of these can be both broad in scope and made up of a number of complex factors. Unfortunately there is no standard formula that might be used to arrive at a conclusion as to the right or even best combination of how to respond to each of these challenges. Picking the right combination of factors is definitely fraught with difficulty. Doing so through the use of information systems can add to the challenge.

It helps to have a particular company in mind to assess the significance of the role of information systems in support of the strategic or tactical responses. Can product marketers pursue new market opportunities in an innovative manner through the use of information systems?

Figure 17-1

Organizational Response to Business Drivers

IS Significance

	High	Medium	Low
• New Markets, Opportunities and Competitors			
• Time, Flexibility and Responsiveness as Competitive Factors			
• Product Customization			
• Process Reengineering, Redefining and TQM			
• Employee Empowerment and Cross-Functional Teams			
• Organization Downsizing, Outsourcing, Business Partnering and Alliances			

Is a computer-based approach becoming a mandatory part of a strategy that emphasizes customer responsiveness? Can a manufacturer even offer product customization without computer-based processes? Is computer data a necessary element of a TQM program or the vehicle for reengineering business processes? Does employee empowerment or cross-functional teams prompt the need to improve communications and access to information that can be facilitated through telecommunications systems? Can the same be said for interorganizational systems to support multiple forms of business partnering?

✦✦✦ BUSINESS SUCCESS AND THE ROLE OF INFORMATION SYSTEMS

The business driver evaluation focused on strategies and tactics. The business success factors summarized in Figure 17-2 have more of a people orientation. They deal with leadership, values, management style and particularly attitudes towards change and the role of employees. These factors should be evaluated based on their importance from both a business standpoint and the potential role of information systems. Once again it is better to use a specific company as the basis for this evaluation. As has been emphasized throughout this book, it is possible to evaluate the significance of the role of information systems by understanding the business environment and the specific profile of a particular company. Then and only then can you conclude the role that information systems did, could and maybe even should play.

In making information systems an important competitive resource, three general conclusions can be made. The first is that the way to gain acceptance of information systems by senior management is to focus on using it to gain a competitive advantage. Long-term viability of the business is the one-sentence job description of senior management, so competitiveness is at the top of their priority list. If there is any reason at all for them to become more interested in, and more involved with, information systems it is because of their potential use in support of competitive strategies. A second factor is realizing that the way to capitalize on this

Figure 17-2

Organizational Response

Business Success Factors	IS Role		
	Mandatory	Necessary	Marginal
• Business Leadership			
• Fitting Pieces into the Big Picture			
• Organizational Responsiveness and Resilience			
• Realizing that Solving Customer Problems Requires a Team Approach			
• A Strong Company Culture			
• Ability and Willingness to Innovate, Change and Take Risks			
• Accomplishing All of These Factors While Maintaining Necessary Balance			
• Good Communication Throughout the Entire Organization			

opportunity is through a marketing approach by those with the responsibility for the information systems resources. Finally, the way to sell anything over time is by emphasizing value as articulated by the people who are the major recipients of the benefits of information systems—the users.

✦✦✦ UNSUCCESSFUL COMPETITIVE INFORMATION SYSTEMS

The entire book has addressed how to successfully use information systems to compete. Not all organizations are successful in their attempt to use information systems to gain a competitive advantage. It could be helpful to understand why some organizations have failed in this. There are a myriad of reasons why organizations do not realize competitive success. In this analysis it is assumed that the organization attempted to use a management process similar to or even exactly like the approach advocated within this book. This would contrast to simply implementing a specific application versus an overall systems-based strategy. Within the context of a managed process approach there can still be failure. The reasons are either business- or technical-related. The business-related factors include:

- ✦ Lack of senior management sponsorship or support. See the Roles, Roles and Relationships material in Chapter 9.

- ✦ Poor employee acceptance or use. New systems represent change, and this challenge must be dealt with accordingly.

- ✦ General resistance to change within the organization. As indicated in Chapter 10 the more successful the organization, the more likely there will be resistance to changing what has made previous success possible.

- ✦ Poor alignment of information systems with the business strategy. This is probably the result of poor communication or a problem with the project team structure.

- ✦ Impatience for results. New information systems take time to develop, implement, gain acceptance by users and have a positive impact on the business. Progress often needs to be measured in months and even years.

- ✦ Vision and direction of the business is not clear. Chapter 6 stressed vision as the starting point in directing a business. An effective vision must be logical, appropriate, clear and communicated throughout the organization.

- ✦ Poor business strategy. A vision can be right and strategies misdirected. There is no automatic linkage between a good vision and an automatically successful strategy.

✦ Poor timing. Good vision, strategy and implementation but bad timing result in no value to the customer. This drives people crazy. Success is not based on formulating a direction, designing strategies or implementing tactics. The marketplace decides who wins and loses.

Information technology factors that may result in the failure of information systems to gain a competitive advantage include the following:

✦ Inadequate staffing and/or funding. This is a common occurrence and can have a very negative impact on the success of a major new system.

✦ Project size was extremely large. There is a direct correlation between project size and risk, with large projects having much higher risk than smaller projects. If a project is too big, every effort should be made to break it up into smaller subsystems.

✦ Poor project structure, particularly between the information systems organization and users. This has both business and technical implications because one drives the other. The technology must support the requirements of the business, and the project team structure is a key factor to effect an understanding regarding this.

✦ The organization lacked experience with the information technology. This concerns the experience both within the information systems organization and on the user side. Traditional guidelines caution organizations as to the number of new technologies that can be included in a new system. The greater the number of new technologies, the higher the risk.

✦ Poor systems performance. Picture this: A good job was done in defining the requirements for the new system, and it was managed well during the development and implementation phases. The day arrives to turn the system over to the users. Everything seems right with one exception—the system runs very slowly. Performance is so bad that work cannot be completed to meet necessary time windows, deadlines, etc. This can and does happen.

✦✦✦ QUESTIONS TO ASK WHEN CONTEMPLATING THE USE OF INFORMATION SYSTEMS TO GAIN A COMPETITIVE ADVANTAGE

In addressing competitive issues with people within businesses, it is far better to ask questions than to suggest that you have answers to their competitive problems. Specific questions need to be tailored to those with whom you are discussing the problem, but the following are offered as guidelines to the kinds of questions that can be asked.

Do you really believe that information systems can make your organization more competitive?

If *you* within the context of the above question refers to the executive who runs the organization day-to-day, then this is an extremely important question. Unfortunately, the only acceptable answer is Yes, not Maybe and certainly not No. "You go ahead without me" are not words that one wants to hear in response to this question, even if it includes funding approval. Do not forget that the use of information systems to compete is integral to a business strategy. This often represents a new way of doing things—a change and even a major one. This requires management leadership, sponsorship and support. Fence sitters do not make challenging, competitively focused things happen!

Is this a technical or an internal marketing challenge?

Change must always be sold within an organization. The planned use of competitively focused systems represents both a technical and a marketing challenge. There are always business and technical issues that must be addressed.

What is the current credibility of the information systems organization?

This is both a logical and necessary question to ask. If the information systems organization has a great reputation based on a strong track record, then you can pursue the use of competitive systems with a high level of confidence. If the reputation is not there to support confidence on the part of people within the organization, then this has to be addressed before going any further.

What are the basic prerequisites for an organization to use information systems to compete?

There are basically two prerequisites. The first is Roles, Roles and Relationships. The role of senior management in determining and positioning the logical and even necessary role of information systems as a competitive resource is the key prerequisite. It is also the starting point. The second prerequisite is Redefine/Define. The willingness and ability to change the business, products or services, or business processes to change value to customer is equally important.

How do you align information systems with the goals and objectives of the business?

The most succinct answer to the above question is: You work at it—*all* the time. Planning efforts to align information systems with business strategies are not an annual event but an ongoing process. This process must become an integral part of how the business is run by senior management. If the unexpected happens then the organization must respond, but it should do so within the context of a plan change and not as a spur of the moment response.

What is the scope of competitively focused information systems?

More often than not it makes sense to start with as broad a perspective as possible. Human nature suggests that if you start with a narrow approach you are very likely to stay narrowly focused. On the other hand if you start with a broad perspective you can later narrow your focus with a higher degree of assurance that the planned system clearly addresses a core problem.

How important is determining the value of information systems within an organization?

Sooner or later this will become an issue within an organization. This is true even in companies where senior management has intuitively sponsored and supported major efforts on the part of information systems. Whether this happens or not directly correlates to the total amount of information systems expenditures, the percentage of the revenue dollar of the information systems cost or the presence of a significant annual information systems expense growth rate. The key is whether senior management has hit a pain threshold regarding these expenditures. If they have they become more involved and expect better answers to the question of what the organization is getting in return for the investment in information systems.

What are the organizational and personnel implications?

In many cases the answer to this question is either Big, Many or Both of the above. Information systems can be the catalyst around which new strategies, new organizational structures, new skill profiles and new job definitions all come together at the same time. When it comes to this question, keep in mind that *competing with information systems through people* is what this is all about. Employee acceptance of a new information system can be a make or break situation.

Does the use of information systems to compete ever get easy?

No! It may get easier, but it never gets easy, and for a very basic reason: The use of information systems in support of a new and effective business strategy often prompts an organization to go after business opportunities it might not have even considered in the past. The good news is that it wins the competition for the business. The bad news is that this great new opportunity brings with it new challenges. New skills, processes, procedures, policies, etc. are required to meet these new challenges.

Responding to and successfully addressing these new challenges are what competition is all about. Once again, this may get easier, but never easy.

✦✦✦ SOME ADVICE REGARDING INFORMATION SYSTEMS IMPLEMENTATION

Because it is so important, another example of the Roles, Roles and Relationships concept is offered. Bob Wimmer, a veteran of implementing information systems in a manufacturing environment, concluded that "in thirty-two years I have learned the following four things about information systems in manufacturing companies and offer them to help you to successfully implement future systems."

Manufacturing System Guidelines

First, says Wimmer, never implement a new system without first simplifying the process. Maximize the value-added steps and minimize the non-value-added steps that have invariably crept into a manual or semi-automated manufacturing process.

Second, after working with the users to develop a solution to their problem, make sure that you stay around to help them articulate how your solution will solve their problem. They understand their part of the solution but will probably need help in explaining how information technology is going to provide the best possible solution.

Third, automate where appropriate, but only if you have a commitment from senior management.

Finally, implement through user ownership of any new system. The users may not actually own the equipment (hardware and software) on which the system is implemented, but they must have a sense of ownership of the system itself. Owners will do a much better job of successfully implementing and utilizing a new system.

While thanking Bob Wimmer for sharing the benefit of his years of experience, the heading for these guidelines is wrong: The word "Manufacturing" should be deleted. There is nothing unique about manufacturing. These four factors are generic to any system in any industry.

✦✦✦ CONCLUSION

The scope of the material and the specific aspects that have been addressed throughout this book have been both broad and content intensive. There are two reasons for this. The first deals with the importance of understanding that businesses can no longer be single dimensional in their pursuit of success. This point was addressed in Chapter 1. The second reason is that the use of information systems must parallel that which is necessary for the business to be successful. If a broad-scope, extended enterprise approach is necessary for the business, then the information systems must support it. Boeing's future success was tied to a new design system that reduced design cost and increased its ability to maintain a development schedule. The conclusion was clear that they needed to create the first computer-based design system for the entire aircraft and a new culture within the organization to accomplish it.

As difficult as it may be for those who still like to think of information technology as tools primarily for backroom administration or accounting and finance, many things suggest otherwise. The SWOT analysis model makes more sense today than it did twenty years ago when people first started suggesting its use. Threats are very real for most companies and they come more quickly and from more directions than ever before. Weaknesses can be more readily exploited by competitors, so approaches

Figure 17-3

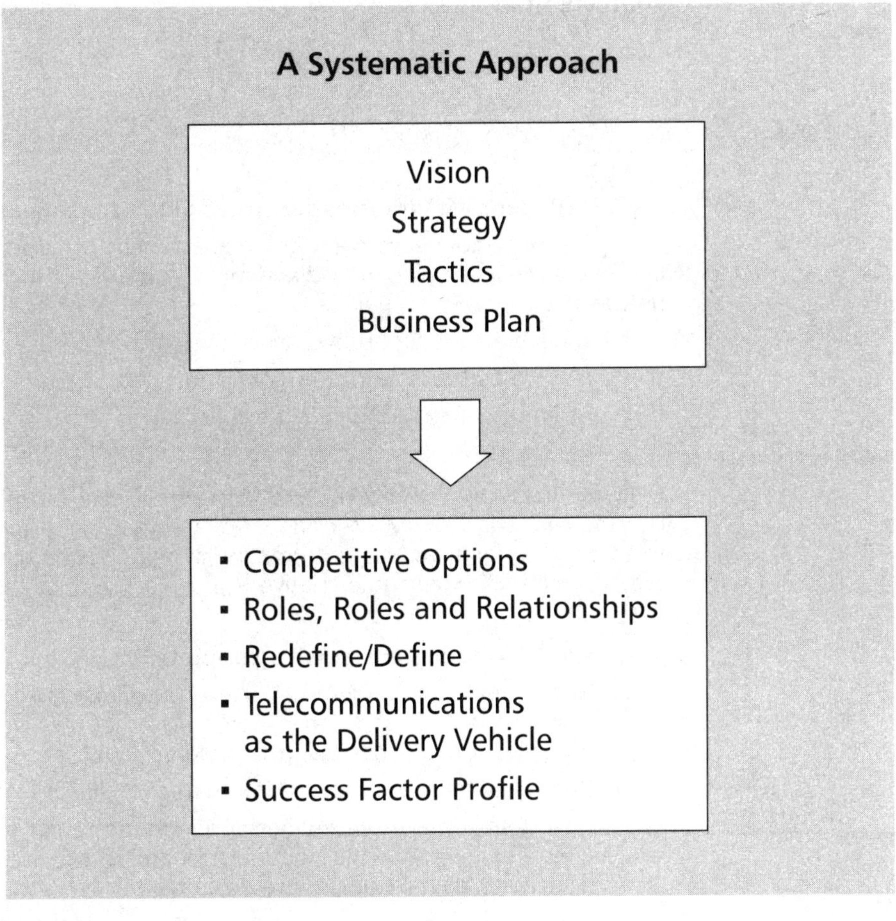

A Systematic Approach

Vision

Strategy

Tactics

Business Plan

- Competitive Options
- Roles, Roles and Relationships
- Redefine/Define
- Telecommunications as the Delivery Vehicle
- Success Factor Profile

like reengineering and total quality management become essential to the long-term viability of the business. Opportunities need to be exploited in a manner consistent with what makes fundamental sense to a particular company. This could certainly involve a global strategy backed by empowered employees and cross-functional teams with new ideas and different values. It is generally acknowledged that information technology continues to provide better price performance for both computing and telecommunications. If the technology is available to enable new ways of doing things, and the business pressures are suggesting that there is a definite need to accomplish this, then what is needed are business and IT leaders to make things happen.

Concepts and examples have been a theme throughout this book. It is often easier to remember the examples than the concepts, but it is hoped that the latter will be retained. For a comprehensive example of the concepts and format presented throughout this book see the Appendix which presents an analysis of the Boeing Company. The systematic approach that can and does work is provided once again in Figure 17-3. Done right, the use of information systems really can help a company to compete more successfully.

EXERCISES

1. The challenge of information technology management.

A number of factors have made the management of information technology a challenging task. Provide an explanation of why this is the case from three perspectives:

a. A general, overall business environment perspective.

b. A more specific business organization perspective.

c. An information technology perspective.

2. Organizational response to business drivers and business success factors.

Use the charts in Figures 17-1 and 17-2 and map them to a specific company to assess the significance of information systems to the business drivers, and the information systems role relative to business success factors.

3. Using information systems to compete.

a. How would you advise a senior executive who is key to a proposed, competitively focused application, and is not sure about approving the project but might be willing to go along with it?

b. Does it ever get easy to use information systems to compete?

c. Why does it make sense when dealing with senior management to ask questions instead of give answers regarding the use of information systems to gain a competitive advantage?

APPENDIX

AN EXAMPLE OF AN ANALYSIS PAPER

The following analysis paper was prepared by Ali Eridiaz for an MIS class in the MBA program at San Jose State University, San Jose, California, based entirely on research of public domain material.

WHY CHANGE WHEN YOU ARE FLYING HIGH?

An Analysis of The Boeing Company

by Ali Eridiaz
San Jose State University

March 1995

OBJECTIVE OF THE PAPER

SECTION I. COMMERCIAL AIRCRAFT INDUSTRY
  A. Industry Profile
  B. Typical Industry Competitive Strategy
  C. Porter Model Evaluation
  D. Globalization of the Industry
  E. Importance of Information Technology to the Industry

SECTION II. THE BOEING COMPANY
  A. Boeing Company Profile
  B. Market and Financial Performance
  C. Competitive Strategy Statement
  D. Significance of Information Systems
  E. Strengths and Weaknesses of Boeing

SECTION III. STRUCTURED ANALYSIS OF INFORMATION SYSTEMS USE
  A. Strategic Option Generator
  B. Roles, Roles and Relationships
  C. Redefine/Define
  D. Significance of Telecommunications
  E. Success Factor Profile

SECTION IV. FINAL ANALYSIS
  A. Success of Business Strategy and IT Use to Date
  B. Have the Above Factors Positioned Them for the Future?

Objective of the Paper

The objective of this paper is to analyze the strategic role of information systems within the Boeing Company. Since it represents the major portion of its business, the Commercial Airplane Group is used as the basis for this analysis. The paper is divided into four sections. The first section is an analysis of the commercial aircraft industry to provide an understanding of the competitive business environment in which Boeing competes. Section II discusses Boeing as a company and how it is positioned within the commercial airplane industry. In Section III the focus of the paper narrows from the industry to the company to the major subject of the paper—a structured analysis of Boeing's use of information systems to gain and sustain a competitive advantage. The final section concludes with an assessment of the success of the company to date with respect to their business strategy and use of information systems and whether these two factors have positioned Boeing to face the challenges of the future.

Section I: Commercial Aircraft Industry

A. Industry Profile

The worldwide market for commercial jet aircraft is primarily dependent on long-term trends in airline passenger traffic. This trend can be explained by factors such as economic growth in developed and emerging markets, political stability, profitability of the airline industry, and the globalization and consolidation of the industry. Other important factors are limitations in air transport infrastructure such as government and environmental regulations and air traffic control. Finally, product development strategy and overall competition between manufacturers also impact the market.

As shown in Figure 1, world air travel has been steadily increasing at an average annual rate of 5%, including 1994,[1] with the exception of 1991, the year of the Persian Gulf conflict. Despite the steady growth in traffic after 1991 most airlines have cut back their new aircraft orders, mainly due to their dismal financial performance. This has resulted in dramatic reductions in aircraft manufacturers' backlogs. Air France, for instance, canceled $500 million in orders from Boeing and Airbus in January 1995.[2]

Figure 1

Based on data from the Boeing 1993 Annual Report.

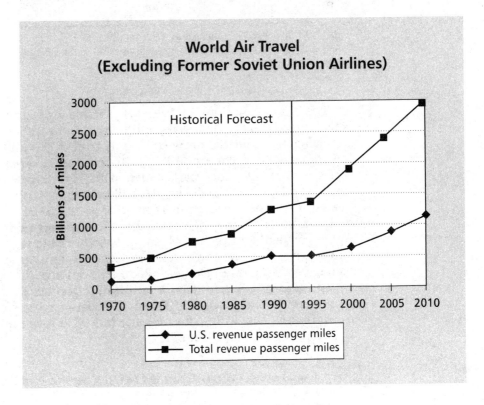

1 "Puzzle in the Skies," *The Economist,* February 11, 1995, p. 59.
2 "Steve Wolf's Soft Landing," *Business Week,* March 13, 1995, p. 91.

The commercial jet aircraft market is dominated by a limited number of manufacturers, led by Boeing, Airbus Industrie and McDonnell Douglas. Table 1 illustrates the revenues and earnings of these major players. Other minor players, such as Fokker, British Aerospace and manufacturers of short-haul, turboprop engine commuter planes are not included in the market estimates.

TABLE 1   Revenues and Market Share of Jet Aircraft Industry Leaders (Excluding Former Soviet Union)

Company	1994 Sales (in $ millions)	1994 Earnings (in $ millions)	Market Share (percentage)
Boeing	$16,851	$1,022	62
Airbus Industrie	8,000*	N/A[†]	24
McDonnell Douglas	4,760	40	14

* Estimated, full financial results not available for 1994.
[†] Airbus claims a $275 million operating profit for 1993, but this figure is being challenged by many sources.

The business outlook in 1994 deteriorated significantly, and recovery is tied directly to the financial performance of the airline industry. Worldwide aircraft shipments dropped sharply from 3,189 units to 2,402.[3] Boeing registered a decline of 14% in its revenues compared to 1993, and McDonnell Douglas lost market share with its revenues shrinking by 9%.[4] It is likely that McDonnell Douglas will halt temporarily, and perhaps permanently, the manufacturing of its wide-body MD-11 plane because of a severe shortage of orders. This may leave for the long term only Boeing and Airbus competing in the long-haul, wide-body carrier segment. The current struggle between the three vendors seems to develop at the clear disadvantage of McDonnell Douglas. Recently Scandinavian Air Service (SAS), which traditionally had been a faithful McDonnell Douglas customer—more than 70% of its current fleet is Douglas—gave preference to Boeing for thirty-five new B737-600s over the MD-95, a new model that Douglas was counting on SAS to launch.[5]

---

[3] U.S. Bureau of the Census. Report EM 545, *U.S. Exports.* Washington: GPO. This figure includes all aircraft shipments.

[4] "Corporate Scoreboard," *Business Week,* March 6, 1995, p. 101.

[5] "Boeing Win Is a Setback for McDonnell Douglas," *San Jose Mercury News,* March 15, 1995, p. 3F.

In 1994 Airbus gained on Boeing in market share, while McDonnell Douglas lost further ground. Airbus claimed it obtained "nearly 50% market share" in 1994's orders for new aircraft of more than 100 seats. Table 2 summarizes the new orders received by the three manufacturers in 1994. In terms of total backlog Boeing has 959 on-order units versus 615 for Airbus.

The commercial aircraft industry is very capital intensive and requires a long time to recoup investments characterized by long development cycles. A company also needs a large base of skilled workers, high-tech sustaining industries and sophisticated and demanding customers to thrive. Government intervention, different countries' industrial policies and international trade relationships also play a major role in shaping the industry forces.

TABLE 2   New Aircraft Orders in 1994

Company	Gross orders	Cancellations	Net orders
Boeing	120	46	74
Airbus Industrie	125	54	71
McDonnell Douglas	23	19	4

B. Typical Industry Competitive Strategy

While acknowledging the presence of McDonnell Douglas, a strong case can be made that the commercial aircraft industry is a battle between Boeing and Airbus. Their global rivalry is in many ways representative of two seemingly incompatible, even totally opposing, market philosophies. Boeing is the "free market" champion, while Airbus represents the "not so free" approach of the European Union's organized and government-subsidized competition in the so-called strategic markets.

Airbus Industrie is a multinational European consortium consisting of Aerospatiale of France, Deutsche Airbus/Deutsche Aerospace (DASA) of Germany, British Aerospace and CASA of Spain. Formed in 1970, much of its early growth and financial soundness was attributed to government subsidies. This government support has been the cause of much debate, with the United States taking the position that this is unfair competition. Airbus insists that the government subsidies are loans to aid in the development of new aircraft. Whether loans or subsidies, this funding is a luxury that Boeing and McDonnell Douglas do not have.

Michael Porter seems to imply that governments should intervene or at least play an active role in certain aspects of local, national and global businesses. But his recommendations remain vague and seem to be mainly motivated by a certain desire to reestablish an even playing field for the American companies, which he claims are being victimized by "unfair competitive practices" of some foreign countries.

In his book *Peddling Prosperity* Paul Krugman demonstrates the importance of strategic trade policy by explaining the Brander-Spencer model and by using in his explanation the Boeing versus Airbus case.[6] He explains that if Europe decides to subsidize Airbus in order to encourage it to compete against Boeing for the development of a new aircraft, where initially both companies have an equal chance of success, the subsidy can have two possible effects. If both companies decide to compete, Airbus will make a profit, all things being equal, because of the subsidy. But if Boeing does not enter a certain market segment, then Airbus will make a much higher profit than the initial subsidy. This corresponds to a transfer of wealth from the United States to Europe. Although Airbus does not seem to be extremely profitable despite the subsidies, it is difficult to argue against Krugman's logic.

Things are changing, but for the moment Europeans seem determined to support a strong aerospace industry, for good or bad reasons. It must also be considered that Airbus is acting in the interest of all consumers worldwide. Unless Airbus or a similar competitor challenges Boeing, the latter will likely become the Microsoft of commercial aviation—which it was probably about to become before the emergence of Airbus. If nothing else Airbus forced Boeing to cut its costs, become more competitive and offer commercial aircraft at more attractive prices.

If the United States, and subsequently Boeing, has developed a world-dominating aerospace industry it is because it benefited from various favorable factors. Among these are a very large territory that motivated air transport, the World War II effort of building a war machine and its post-war expansion to civil aviation and huge defense projects. If Europe decides to compete in this market, again for good or bad reasons, it can only achieve its goals by initiating a joint effort among its national aerospace champions, most of which are nationalized companies primarily coming from the defense sector.

Specific competitive strategies used by the three major players can be summarized as follows:

✦ Extensive aircraft portfolio to satisfy requirements of customer airlines across the board. Boeing is the best positioned with aircraft capacity ranging from 100 passengers (737-500) to 500 (747-400). Airbus had entered the market with small- and medium-sized carriers, but is fast catching up with the introduction of its four-engine, long-haul A340 aircraft. Only McDonnell Douglas seems to be relegated to the low-end small carriers (MD-80 and MD-90) as it is facing the decline of the MD-11 trijet.

---

[6] *Peddling Prosperity,* Krugman, Paul, New York: Norton, 1994, pp. 234–239.

✦ Pushing high-technology, electronic fly-by-wire techniques in order to reduce the number of pilots needed (from three to two) and establishing easy transfer from one type of plane to another, thus minimizing training time by developing the family concept. As an example, Airbus succeeded in obtaining approval from the FAA to have a single pool of pilots to operate its A320, A330 and A340 models.[7] Boeing received similar approval for the 757 and 767.

✦ Developing solutions to improve cost-effective exploitation of their planes. This includes the general trend toward twin-engine, widebody planes, providing fuel efficiencies and quick reconfiguration of seating layouts to optimize the ratio of seat occupancy by passenger class.

✦ Leasing and financing services to customers. As airlines face financial difficulties, financing terms become a key selling factor. All three competitors run financial services. In 1993, for instance, Boeing's customer financing activities amounted to $3,177 million, up from $2,295 million, while its sales went down to $20,568 million from an all time high of $24,133 million in 1992.[8] Airbus is also financing 5–10% of its sales.[9]

✦ Alliances, joint ventures—especially with foreign government-funded programs—and extensive lobbying and political posturing in national and international forums. "Some 45 businesses in the sixteen Asia-Pacific Economic Cooperation (APEC) economies provide Boeing with about 70 different parts and major assemblies..."[10]

C. Porter Model Evaluation

The Porter model provides a structural analysis of the industry in which a given company competes. The model does not focus just on the use of information technology; on the contrary it defines in a broad sense all the competitive forces in the market, existing alliances, potential threats and other sources of positive and negative influence.

The analysis of the commercial aircraft industry illustrated in Figure 2 shows that very few competitors compete for market share—namely Boeing, Airbus and McDonnell Douglas—and usually they have extremely close relationships with their suppliers and their customers. As already discussed, the industry is extremely concentrated.

---

7 "FAA Approves Airbus 'Mixed Fleet' Flying," *Aviation Week & Space Technology,* August 29, 1994, pp. 25–26.

8 *Boeing Annual Report,* p. 55.

9 "Puzzle in the Skies," *The Economist,* February 11, 1995, p. 59.

10 "Markets: Two-Way Trade," *Far Eastern Economic Review,* March 10, 1994, pp. 38–39.

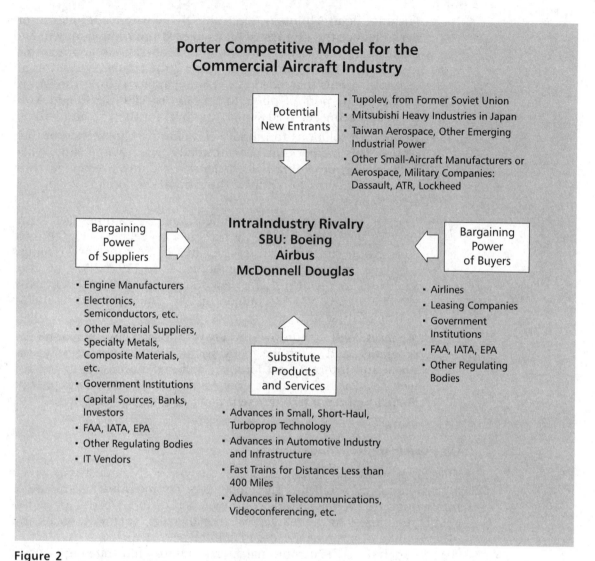

Porter Competitive Model for the Commercial Aircraft Industry

Potential New Entrants
- Tupolev, from Former Soviet Union
- Mitsubishi Heavy Industries in Japan
- Taiwan Aerospace, Other Emerging Industrial Power
- Other Small-Aircraft Manufacturers or Aerospace, Military Companies: Dassault, ATR, Lockheed

Bargaining Power of Suppliers

IntraIndustry Rivalry
SBU: Boeing
Airbus
McDonnell Douglas

Bargaining Power of Buyers

Suppliers:
- Engine Manufacturers
- Electronics, Semiconductors, etc.
- Other Material Suppliers, Specialty Metals, Composite Materials, etc.
- Government Institutions
- Capital Sources, Banks, Investors
- FAA, IATA, EPA
- Other Regulating Bodies
- IT Vendors

Buyers:
- Airlines
- Leasing Companies
- Government Institutions
- FAA, IATA, EPA
- Other Regulating Bodies

Substitute Products and Services
- Advances in Small, Short-Haul, Turboprop Technology
- Advances in Automotive Industry and Infrastructure
- Fast Trains for Distances Less than 400 Miles
- Advances in Telecommunications, Videoconferencing, etc.

Figure 2

Adapted and reprinted, with permission, from Porter, Michael E., "Forces Governing Competition in an Industry," *Harvard Business Review*, March–April 1979, p. 141.

The Bargaining Power of Suppliers

The major suppliers can be split into two groups based on their relative bargaining power. Engine manufacturers represent the single most significant group of suppliers, and it can be assumed that their bargaining power will substantially increase as they undergo concentration. General Electric, Pratt & Whitney (U.S.), Rolls-Royce (U.K.), and CFM International (jointly owned by GE and Snecma of France) are the main competitors. However, this power is somewhat balanced by the fact that often airlines enter into separate negotiations with the engine suppliers to determine the choice of the engine for their airplanes. The planes are usually designed for more than one engine type. On the other hand the required fuel efficiencies, increased reliability needs—especially for twin-engine, transatlantic wide bodies—and the need to provide more power for the new large-body aircraft require aircraft manufacturers to enter into joint development programs.

Regulating bodies such as the FAA, EPA, etc. may be considered as suppliers to the industry because they determine a number of constraints with which the industry must contend. The bargaining power of these institutions is considerable, for they can create major obstacles to the final approval of the planes.

As the industry is extremely capital intensive, all sources of investment and financing have considerable power. A recent trend is the development of financing and leasing companies who buy planes from the manufacturers, then lease them to various airlines. ILFC (International Lease Finance Corporation) is one such company that recently ordered thirty Airbus aircraft. Meanwhile Airbus Industrie itself has formed its own financing service, which has access to more than $1.5 billion revolving credit facility from forty-six different banks.[11]

On the avionics and materials side, since the military markets keep shrinking and there is heavy pressure on defense suppliers to move to commercial applications, the bargaining power of these industries as they fight for additional share of the commercial market is at the advantage of the aircraft industry.

The Bargaining Power of Buyers

The buyers, mainly airlines and leasing companies, retain considerable power. With a downturn in orders that power is increasing. As the airlines optimize their operations and cut their investments, the competition among the two major manufacturers becomes deadly.

It can also be assumed that the regulating bodies are buyers as well as suppliers. Indeed the aircraft industry has to constantly deal with these institutions to convince them to approve regulations in their favor and not make decisions that would jeopardize their competitive positioning.

New Entrants

At first look any new entrant in this market faces a steep, uphill battle. Regulations, capital requirements, extremely skilled labor needs, sophisticated support industries, necessary proven track record and the perspective of a long wait to reach profitability are but a few of the very high

---

[11] "Airbus Finance Unit Up and Running with $1.5 Billion," *Aircraft Value News*, January 9, 1995, via America Online.

barriers to entry. However, one cannot completely exclude this possibility. Just as Europe did, Japan or China may decide that this industry is strategically vital for their long-term well-being and encourage a highly subsidized entry in the market by their national champions. In the case of Japan subsidies may not even be necessary, because the sophisticated industrial infrastructure and naturally protective trade policies may very well encourage Mitsubishi Heavy Industries or another firm to engage in the battle.

The former Soviet Union represents a significant growth potential for the Big Three but also has its own national aircraft industry. While this market may be open to competition, it is also possible that the Russian Tupolev could enhance its capabilities, rationalize its operations and succeed in entering the market with a low-cost, no-frills product strategy, especially in emerging countries.

Finally, although highly unlikely, existing defense aerospace companies may be tempted by a late entry or reentry—such as Lockheed—as they see their traditional military market dwindle.

Threats of Substitute Industries

It is difficult to imagine for the foreseeable future a direct substitute for the aircraft industry, especially in the long-haul transport. Air travel is the most effective, secure, convenient and economic transportation method. However, a few threats exist, especially in the low end: Fast bullet trains between cities less than 400 miles apart offer a very attractive solution. As their speeds approach and even exceed 200 mph, these trains bring such travel below two hours from downtown to downtown, a performance difficult for any airline to match. After the start of TGV service between Paris and Lyons, Air Inter faced a 50% reduction in air travel between the two cities. If such solutions are implemented widely in the United States—a very speculative assumption—between, for example, San Francisco and Los Angeles or Washington, D.C. and New York City—a great many airlines could lose significant traffic and as a consequence reduce their fleets.

Advances in the automotive industry, such as cars capable of very high speeds, under electronic control on specially equipped freeways, could also have an impact on air travel. Finally, advances in telecommunications techniques, collaborative computing, and desktop videoconferencing based on broadband ISDN-type services may reduce business travel requirements and impact the airlines' investment in new planes and routes. This loss could be offset by forecasts of growth in the leisure travel segment.

D. Globalization of the Industry

The industry is rapidly becoming global for two reasons. There are very few players, but intense competition and very high capital requirements drive the need to maximize volume and tap all possible markets. It is unthinkable to have a national or regional strategy and expect to succeed in this industry.

Second, as many customers, including various governments across the world, consider the aircraft industry strategic, they want a share of the action. As a consequence partnerships and joint ventures are increasing. In fact, mergers and joint ventures often become necessary to remove trade barriers.

E. Importance of Information Technology to the Industry

IT's importance to the industry can be evaluated from two different perspectives:

✦ As an extremely high-technology and complex industry, integrating electronics, mechanics, chemicals, metallurgy, etc. CAD/CAM tools are used in simulation, modeling, and concurrent engineering. This IT use is not only key in reducing time to market, but also necessary to the industry's ability to cope with the complexity of the task.

✦ For operations management, such as in inventory management, IT is key to optimizing resources, reducing costs and improving efficiencies.

As can be observed from the Value Chain shown in Figure 3, information technology intervenes in almost every phase of Boeing's operations. Its role is most significant in inbound logistics, operations and service. These are the steps of the Value Chain where Boeing uses IT to gain a competitive advantage. IT's presence in the other segments is not negligible either, but its value is limited to a more traditional support role.

Section II: The Boeing Company

A. Boeing Company Profile

The Boeing Company is based in Seattle, Washington with Frank Shrontz serving as its Chairman and Chief Executive Officer and Philip M. Condit in the position of President. It currently has three business units: Commercial Airplanes, Defense and Space, and Information Services.

Commercial Airplanes (President: Ron Woodward): By far the largest, this unit designs, develops and manufactures the commercial jet aircraft. It has a very comprehensive product portfolio ranging from the 737 series, with seating capacity from about 100 to 150 passengers, to the 747, with seating capacity from 420 to 566 passengers. Other models are the twinjets Boeing 767 (long-range, 210 to 325 passengers) and the 757 (mid-range, 180 to 230 passengers). In 1995 the company introduced its newest model, the Boeing 777, with seating capacity of 305 to 440 passengers and

Porter Value Chain for Boeing

	Financial policy	Accounting	Regulatory Compliance	Legal	Government relations
Firm Infrastructure	Financial policy	Accounting	Regulatory Compliance	Legal	Government relations
Human Resource Management	Procurement training Managing relationships with suppliers	Hiring & training of engineers, test pilots, skilled workers	Training for competitiveness company-wide	People familiar with national & international economics and politics	
Technology Development	Qualification of suppliers New materials Partners	R&D, Partnerships Defense contracts		Product development Market research Regulations & Policies	
Procurement	IS inventory management JIT, production forecast	CAD/CAM systems Assembly of planes & parts tracking			Customer relationships Tracking of issues
	▪ Materials qualification ▪ Engine selection ▪ Partners & joint programs ▪ Electronics, etc.	▪ Concurrent engineering ▪ Flexible & modular manufacturing ▪ Wide choice in capacity with "family" concept ▪ Fly-by-wire technology ▪ Short development cycles ▪ Quick to market with short manufacturing cycles	▪ Worldwide presence	▪ Early involvement of customers in product definition ▪ Promotion, advertising ▪ Lobbying U.S. and foreign governments ▪ Seeking powerful partners ▪ Facilitation of financing ▪ Trade shows	▪ Repair, spare parts ▪ Maintenance service ▪ Inspection & test ▪ Upgrades ▪ Training facilities for customers
	Inbound Logistics	Operations	Outbound Logistics	Marketing and Sales	Service

Figure 3

Adapted, with permission, from Porter, *Competitive Advantage*, 1985.

the first to be 100% equipped with fly-by-wire technology. Boeing also plans to renew its 737 line, with the next-generation 737-600, -700 and -800 scheduled for delivery in 1997. Boeing's commercial aircraft sales amounted to $20,568 million in 1993.

Defense and Space (President: Jerry King): Despite the strong decline in the U.S. Department of Defense projects and Boeing's declining sales in this domain, the company had sales of $4,742 million in defense business with an operating profit of $303 million. Major contributors to the defense revenues were Space Station work packages, F-22 fighter aircraft, V-22 Osprey tiltrotor transport and RAH-66 Comanche helicopter. These programs are principally funded under cost-reimbursement type contracts.

Information Services (President: John Warner): Although this division's primary mission is to provide cost-efficient computing support for company operations, it generated revenues of $331 million mainly by competing for selected federal contracts to manage information systems. Profits for this group were a slim $2 million, down from $16 million in 1993. However, this group's main mission is to serve the other internal divisions and it is still remarkable that it is more than self-sustaining.

B. Market and Financial Performance

Highlights of Boeing's financial performance for the last five years are summarized in Tables 3 and 4. After an all-time high of revenues in 1992 Boeing faced a severe downturn, due to the dismal financial performance of most airlines and increased competition from Airbus. The trend continued in 1994. Boeing closed the fourth quarter with sales of $5,120 million, down 9% from the previous year, and the overall results in 1994 were $21,924 million, down 14% from 1993 sales. Profitability severely declined also with net earnings of $856 million: –31% compared to the previous year.[12]

Business Week lists Boeing in the Aerospace and Defense category. The average return on common equity in the industry is 13.1%, while Boeing only achieves 8.9%. However, Boeing is the least military of its group, so

TABLE 3 Summary of Boeing's Operations

Operations	1994	1993	1992	1991	1990
Sales, other operating revenue (in $ millions)					
Commercial aircraft	$16,851	$20,568	$24,133	$22,970	$21,230
Defense & space	4,742	4,407	5,429	5,846	5,862
Other industries	331	463	622	498	503
Total	21,924	25,438	30,184	29,314	27,595
Net earnings	856	1,244	1,554	1,567	1,385
Per share	2.51	3.66	4.57	4.56	4.01
Percent of sales	3.9%	4.9%	5.2%	5.3%	5.0%
R&D	1,704	1,661	1,846	1,417	827
Average employment	119,400	134,400	148,600	159,100	161,700

Based on data from the Boeing 1994 Annual Report.

---

[12] "Corporate Scoreboard," *Business Week,* March 6, 1995, p. 101.

TABLE 4 Boeing Balance Sheet Elements

Financial position at 12/31 (in $ millions)	1994	1993	1992	1991	1990
Total assets	$21,463	$20,450	$18,147	$15,924	$14,591
Working capital	3,587	2,601	1,947	2,462	1,396
Net plant & equipment	6,802	7,088	6,724	5,530	4,448
Cash & short-term investments	2,643	3,108	3,614	3,453	3,326
Total debt	2,610	2,630	1,793	1,317	315
Shareholders' equity	9,700	8,983	8,056	8,093	6,973
Contractual backlog (commercial)	60,614	70,497	82,649	92,826	91,475

Based on data from the Boeing 1994 Annual Report.

this comparison is probably not very fair. Interestingly enough McDonnell Douglas, the only other defense company with a significant commercial activity in this group, fares quite well with 15.7% return. While Boeing's defense activity is dwindling, McDonnell Douglas's remains strong and probably helps keep it afloat in the commercial aircraft business.

Boeing's employment figures show great variations and match closely its financial performance. It is expected that Boeing will further cut its employment by at least 7,000 jobs in 1995, if the industry does not show any strong recovery signs.[13]

Boeing has a strong balance sheet as of December 31, 1994, however, as seen in Table 4, there are some negative trends: debt has significantly increased during the last three years. The cash situation remains strong—although it has shrunk by nearly $1 billion in the last two years—but new aircraft orders' backlog has been steadily shrinking since 1991. Finally, its profitability still follows a negative trend, with net earnings having receded from $1,244 million in 1993 to $856 million in 1994.

C. Competitive Strategy Statement

In the 1993 annual report Frank Shrontz says: "The cornerstone of our business strategy, is **continuous improvement in the quality of products and processes**.[14] Boeing is committed to continuous improvement, and we are determined to cut waste and boost productivity with the goal of producing higher quality products in less time at the lowest possible cost."

---

[13] "Puzzle in the Skies," *The Economist*, February 11, 1995, p. 59.
[14] Also in bold characters in the original text!

It is clear that Boeing is betting on higher productivity in beating its arch rival, Airbus. The underlying assumption here is that Boeing will not be able to outspend Airbus, which can always count on government subsidies and friendly, national airlines. It must be able to match Airbus Industries lower sale prices and it must be first to the market with innovative and technologically advanced products.

D. Significance of Information Systems

Boeing's action plan as outlined by Condit and Shrontz is summarized as follows:

+ Slash costs by 25% to 30% by the year 2000.
+ Speed up manufacturing time for the 737 from 13 months to 6 months, and gain similar cycle time improvements on other models.
+ Cut inventory, moving toward a just-in-time system.
+ Train the entire work force in "competitiveness." Over 15,000 managers have completed a four-day course.
+ Bring customers and suppliers into the once-secret process of designing new airplanes.[15]

Looking again at Figure 3, the Porter Value Chain indicates where and how these efforts will enhance Boeing's competitiveness.

Boeing has nearly $8 billion of inventory that turns only twice a year, compared with nearly ten times a year or higher for world class manufacturers in other industries.[16] Since an aircraft like the 777 has about 132,500 engineered parts, plus about 3 million rivets, screws, etc., it becomes apparent that the management of such an inventory with a just-in-time system will require both world class information technology and close integration with its principal suppliers.

On the other hand the quick development and manufacturing cycles that Boeing has targeted require state-of-the-art CAD/CAM systems that enable the transition from concept to fabrication without costly and time-consuming adjustments. Ironically Boeing chose a French CAD tool, CATIA, which was developed by Dassault, a military aircraft manufacturer and designer of the famous Mirage series.

Advanced information technology tools and their application in design and development and in operations are critically important to Boeing's success in implementing its competitive strategy.

E. Strengths and Weaknesses of Boeing

Boeing's strengths and weaknesses are assessed under the light of its formulated strategy in competing with Airbus. Boeing does not believe that

---

15 "Reinventing Boeing," *Business Week*, March 1, 1993, pp. 60–67.
16 "Can Boeing Reinvent Itself?," *Fortune*, March 8, 1993, pp. 66–73.

just having the best technology will be enough to conquer the markets, but that the final battle will be fought on pricing, financing and delivering value to customers. It is therefore key for Boeing to improve its productivity and achieve the lowest possible cost structure and flexibility to beat Airbus, despite its being subsidized.

Strengths

Boeing is already on its way to achieve its goals in productivity, and it is safe to assume that it already has a lower cost structure than Airbus. It has trimmed its work force to the minimum and has plans to further cut 7,000 jobs in 1995. It has also improved its inventory management systems.

It has put in place the best CAD/CAM tools to cut development time and achieve first-time success with its new designs. It has innovated in many areas and has a very strong technological position, albeit not necessarily more advanced than Airbus.

It has a well-established, complete family of planes from the small 737 to the world's largest carrier, the 747, which allows it to serve any airline in any category. It still has a leadership position in the industry.

It has seasoned and well-focused leadership in the persons of Frank Shrontz and Phil Condit. They have identified Boeing's challenges and potential problems and have established a clear plan to keep Boeing in its leadership position.

It has understood the importance of a market-driven approach and started to invite its customers and suppliers to fully participate in new product development.

It has access to a significant, albeit declining, source of R&D funding from government defense contracts. Boeing is one of the leading U.S. exporters and as such it has the attention of the government. Although it may not count on direct government subsidies or assistance, it is well positioned to influence future U.S. trade policy decisions.

Weaknesses

While Boeing is trimming its work force and becoming lean and mean, it may also jeopardize its ability to attract and maintain skilled workers in the future. When the market conditions improve will there be a general perception that Boeing will lay off as soon as the market deteriorates? Its position and plan is to stabilize the workforce through productivity gains and process standardization.

Its balance sheet and income statement point to some weaknesses. R&D spending of $1,661 million, around 8% of sales, is rather low for this industry. Its long-term debt is also increasing, and its overall return on common equity is around 8.9%, below the average industry rate of 13.1%. This, associated with its declining defense revenues, may restrict its access to additional capital in times of crisis.

Boeing is late in adopting some of the technological innovations that its rival Airbus has implemented, such as getting family approval for different planes, thus allowing pilots to move from one model of plane to another without requiring a certification. Boeing is also behind Airbus in getting a financing and leasing operation to support its sales.

Finally, Boeing should not hope that in the foreseeable future the European Union will cut its subsidies to Airbus and let it compete without any protectionn in the world markets. On the contrary, Boeing should plan on a much longer competition period and should seek alliances that could enhance its financial position and open new markets.

Section III: Structured Analysis of Information Systems Use

This section provides an analysis of the use of information systems by Boeing to gain a competitive advantage. It focuses on business strategies that influenced the requirement for the improvements that were made possible through the use of information technology.

A. Strategic Option Generator

The Strategic Option Generator can be used as both a planning vehicle and to do an after-the-fact evaluation of the impact of information systems on major business strategies. In this case it is used as a conceptual model to identify the business opportunities pursued by the Boeing Commercial Airplane Group and to identify strategic options that they selected relative to the use of information systems. The different options selected by Boeing pertaining to targets, thrusts (strategies), modes and direction are summarized using the Strategic Option Generator in Figure 4.

Target: Boeing's key actions in changing its aircraft design process; i.e., accelerating design cycles, cooperating with suppliers and customers and reducing inventory and costs, were aimed at producing a better value for the customer. Boeing management capitalized on the threat of seeing its market erode at the benefit of Airbus. It would have been extremely difficult, if not impossible, to implement all these aggressive changes if Airbus did not represent a formidable competitive challenge to Boeing. Therefore the main target is *competitor.*

Thrust: Boeing definitely used *differentiation* as its main thrust. This differentiation is based on not only offering a better aircraft, but also providing flexibility, responsiveness and cooperation with customers. Its goal to reduce costs by 25% to 30% will help it remain competitive and profitable in a market where there is tremendous pressure on pricing and financing. Indeed, most airlines are either in financial trouble or just recently out of the red, so cost is a key factor when they make new aircraft purchasing decisions. It is also clear that there is a great deal of innovation in Boeing's thrust. The innovation is mainly in its design and manufacturing

Figure 4

Adapted from
Wiseman, *Strategy
and Computers.*

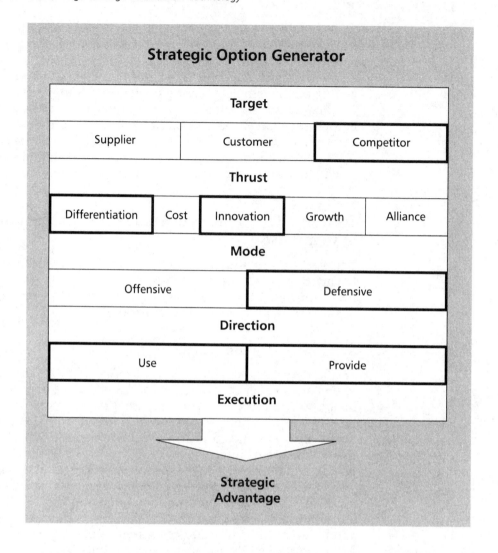

processes, but it is also reflected in the final product. The 777 encompasses many firsts, such as all electronic fly-by-wire capability—Airbus A320 is also an all fly-by-wire type of airplane—and quick cabin layout reconfiguration.

Mode: Since Boeing started its transformation as a reaction to Airbus's rise, it was in a *defensive* mode. However, the use of all-digital design and other offensive measures tend to position the company in a very aggressive stance. It is safe to assume that Boeing will use its newly acquired competitive capabilities in an aggressive mode from now on.

Direction: Boeing uses its IT tools in both *use* and *provide* modes. Obviously the *use* side is much more prevalent because the CAD/CAM system is primarily used by Boeing's internal engineering resources. However, partners, suppliers and some customers are given access to those tools, thus not only making their life easier in working with Boeing, but also in the case of the customers, providing them an additional service in letting them impact the design of the end product.

On the inventory management side, JIT methodologies require EDI between customer and suppliers and direct involvement of the suppliers in the operation of the IS tools. The *provide* aspect here relates primarily to the suppliers. Meanwhile not all inventory management improvements are based on IS; for example, Boeing opened a new distribution center in April 1994 that will control more than 450,000 parts in nearly 1 million square feet.

B. Roles, Roles and Relationships

Boeing's investment in information systems is significant. In 1992 Boeing increased its IS budget by 23% to $1.6 billion.[17] It operates a separate Computer Services Division, and its president John Warner reports directly to Frank Shrontz. Although this division also does business with external customers, about three-fourths of its work is in supporting internal company operations. Its main focus is "to help Boeing to enhance its competitive position in every sector, through the efficient use of computing technology."[18] A powerful Information Systems Division and an impressive investment in information technology show how serious Boeing is in this domain.

For Boeing to initiate this quantum change, top management vision and commitment was essential. Boeing was not necessarily in immediate danger; it was profitable, and it was the world leader in commercial aircraft. Frank Shrontz, who became chairman in 1988, was the instigator of this revolution. He was not content with Boeing's then profitable financial situation. He was able to predict that if Boeing rested on its laurels and counted on increased government protection against Airbus, it would soon find itself in trouble. Shrontz duplicated what Jack Welch did at GE. He generated a sense of urgency within the ranks of Boeing to become a world class manufacturer. He initiated a number of study missions to Japan and started a series of training from top management down to the floor level workers.

The focus was on cost cutting, inventory management, cycle time reduction and successful first-time design. Once these objectives were agreed upon, the IS tools to support them were put in place. First Philip Condit, then Alan Mullally who succeeded Condit as head of the 777 program, were instrumental in supporting the IS strategy. The program was successful because the IS strategy was driven by the business strategy, and the key players were completely aligned. The simple organization chart in Figure 5 illustrates the relationships between the key players.

---

[17] Gow, Kathleen, "Aerospace: Do it Smart and Do it Once," *Computerworld*, September 12, 1992, pp. 10–12.

[18] *Boeing Annual Report 1993*, p. 20.

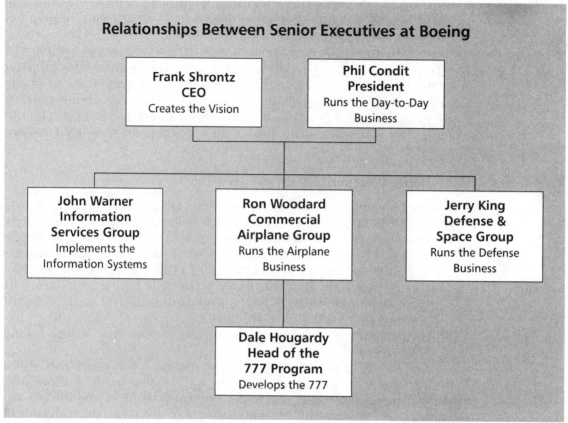

Figure 5

Even though the aerospace industry has been using computers for a long time, no one had ever been able to improve productivity significantly until Condit, as president of the airplane group, spearheaded the 100% digitally designed 777 project. Boeing had its own solids modeling software called Axxyz, but the timing on its availability for a full-scale project did not meet their needs. Management sold the internal tool to EDS and turned to CATIA (Computer-Aided Three-Dimensional Interactive Application) developed by Dassault Systems in France and licensed by IBM.

The success of this project was dependent on how much senior management was committed to support it. A handwritten agreement signed between IBM's John Akers (CEO of IBM at the time of the start of the 777 project), Frank Shrontz, and Charles Edelstenne, CEO of Dassault, stipulated that for the 777 project to work on time three things needed to happen:

1. The computer users at Boeing would have the best possible response time, computer reliability and availability.

2. Management and leadership of computer support would be the best.

3. Everything would be user friendly, and everything would work.

"That letter was pulled out a number of times during the last four years," said Larry Olson, Director of Computer Systems for the 777. "While it was not a contract, it was an agreement that carried a lot of weight."[19]

In summary, Boeing's 100% digital design program was not only supported by senior management and had very high visibility, but it had the same visibility outside the firm, at the level of the top executives of the supplier firms, in this case IBM and Dassault.

C. Redefine/Define

In the case of Boeing the option that was used to improve the competitive effort to provide value to customers was to redefine the business process. To be more specific, Boeing redefined the design and development process of an airplane. This was the first major and significant change since World War II and consisted of designing a whole aircraft—the 777 in this case—from concept to prototype using a 100% computer-based process.

CATIA, the software package used, allows the design of parts as three-dimensional, solid images and simulates how all these parts fit and work together. This approach significantly reduced design time, eliminated the lengthy trial-and-error cycle that was usually required to build full-size mockups, and enhanced the chances of first-time success. It saved Boeing both time and the cost of fixing design problems that sometimes go unnoticed until a plane is delivered to a customer.

At peak performance the design system ran on 8 mainframes that served over 2,000 workstations. The engineering workstations are located mainly in Seattle (2,033) with additional units in Wichita (484), Philadelphia (70) and Japan (220). Boeing had 7,000 people on the 777 project. About half of them were in 238 design/build teams that worked on the 132,500 unique parts for the 777.

The use of the design system was not the only innovation. The creation of design teams and the sharing of the information with suppliers, and to some extent with customers, were also new to Boeing's culture. The extensive use of cross-functional design/build teams and concurrent engineering—in other words the human factor and the reorganization of work patterns—played as significant a role as the use of advanced information technology.

In summary, these significant changes in the design process led to the following outcomes, which are graphically shown in Figure 6:

✦ Reduced design cycle, on-time completion of the project and delivery of the plane.

✦ A product that is designed to customer specifications and remains flexible for adaptation to different requirements.

---

[19] Moeller, Mike, "Boeing Goes On-Line with 777 Design," *Computer Aided Engineering*, August 1994, pp. 27–29.

Figure 6

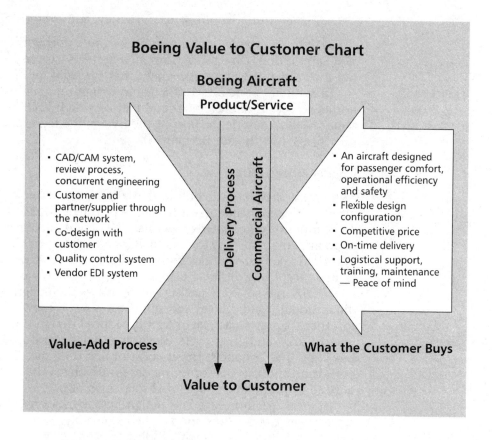

Boeing Value to Customer Chart

Boeing Aircraft

Product/Service

Delivery Process

Commercial Aircraft

- CAD/CAM system, review process, concurrent engineering
- Customer and partner/supplier through the network
- Co-design with customer
- Quality control system
- Vendor EDI system

- An aircraft designed for passenger comfort, operational efficiency and safety
- Flexible design configuration
- Competitive price
- On-time delivery
- Logistical support, training, maintenance — Peace of mind

Value-Add Process

What the Customer Buys

Value to Customer

✦ Elimination of trial and error and increases in productivity result in extremely competitive pricing.

✦ After sales support, maintenance and repair logistics are significantly improved.

D. Significance of Telecommunications

Boeing in cooperation with AT&T started to build the world's largest private telecommunications network in 1985. The system was completely operational by 1989. It consists of over 95,000 lines and handles some 1 million calls a day![20] Boeing then spent $120 million in 1988 to move its voice and data network to ISDN. It has installed four AT&T 5ESS switches in Seattle and one in Wichita.[21] It is safe to assume that Boeing considers telecommunications to be a key factor in its business success.

As the needs in telecommunications evolved towards higher bandwidth applications and more varied types of information, namely voice,

---

[20] "Boeing Pushes the Telecommunications Envelope," *AT&T Technology,* Winter 1992, pp. 2–7.

[21] "Boeing Scrapes ISDN Surface," *Computerworld,* November 14, 1988, pp. 90–91.

data and graphics, the importance of managing this telecommunications network kept growing. The CATIA design package runs on 8 mainframes and well over 2,500 IBM workstations worldwide. Although 2,033 of them are in Seattle and require on-campus local area networks (LANs), additional units in Wichita, Philadelphia and Japan require wide area network (WAN) connections. CAD/CAM applications, especially solids modeling, generate a significant amount of graphics, and interaction among engineers is key. The communications bandwidth requirements across the wide area become very important. According to Larry Olson, Director of Computer Systems for the 777, they send several terabytes of data across high-speed WAN links.[22]

Boeing's just-in-time (JIT) inventory management systems also require on-line connections with its suppliers that can only be achieved through telecommunications. Finally, Boeing's customer service also requires the same type of telecommunications links with them. These applications are less demanding in bandwidth and can be satisfied with less advanced technologies.

In both cases it is not imaginable that Boeing would be able to conduct its business, both internally and externally, without the help of a carefully planned and maintained telecommunications network. Any disruption in telecommunications services can be extremely detrimental to Boeing's business performance.

E. Success Factor Profile

This evaluation has been based on the key success factors of Boeing's 100% digital plane design process and the implementation and usage of the CAD/CAM systems. Obviously inventory management for JIT, EDI systems, etc., is also key to Boeing's competitive success, although its experience in this domain is not unique, many other companies having also successfully applied JIT principles. But in its venture in the 100% digital, paperless design Boeing stands out as a pioneer.

First of all, Boeing has very extensive IS background and experience. It has always been an early adopter and an aggressive user. For example, it started using ISDN in 1988, while the Regional Bell Operating Companies (RBOCs) started offering this technology to end-users only recently. Key factors such as pervasive computer literacy, IS architecture, IS marketing, and IS and user relations are, if not perfect, at least advanced to a degree where they are no longer critical success factors at Boeing.

This evaluation concludes that there were five major success factors for Boeing:

1. Culture.
2. Risk management.

---

[22] Moeller, "Boeing Goes On-Line," pp. 27–29.

3. Plan implementation.
4. IS integral to business.
5. Linkage to suppliers.

Culture: A culture change was absolutely critical for the success of this project. The new system required all engineers change the usual way they designed an aircraft. Concurrent engineering, cross-functional team-work, and paperless design became the norm. An open environment, supplier and customer involvement in the design process and new tools, all required a leap of faith.

Risk management: Boeing took a significant risk in deciding to develop the 777 with the new CATIA system. Although it had already used the tool to design an engine strut for the 747 and other smaller projects, committing the success of the whole program to a new tool and a new approach never tried before represented a high amount of both business and technical risk. With the involvement of senior management and a complete mobilization of all the troops, the project was a success. Boeing had to take a calculated risk in order to get ahead of Airbus at a very crucial moment.

Plan implementation: The implementation of the plan was very complex, in that it involved a new tool, and required extensive training, a great deal of dependence on outside support and cooperation with partners and suppliers. Again the timely execution of the plan was key in building Boeing's competitive advantage.

IS integral to business: The CATIA system became the very foundation of Boeing's development process. If the system stopped working, Boeing would simply be unable to continue its operations. The benefits of CATIA were so significant that Boeing decided to port existing airplane designs to CATIA as well. By doing this Boeing expects productivity gains when upgrading or changing old designs. The new generation of 737s will also be redesigned using CATIA.

Linkage to suppliers: Last but not least, since many parts of the plane are developed by external suppliers it is key to have an integrated design system with these partners. Many of Boeing's suppliers had to install workstations and the CATIA software in order to be able to work directly with Boeing.

Section IV: Final Analysis

A. Success of Business Strategy and IT Use to Date

Before expressing admiration for Boeing's success, it is important to examine Boeing's employment history and how it tracks its market performance. Undeniably, aggressive use of IS can have a negative impact on employment unless the company is in growth mode. Only in growth mode does increased productivity directly translate into increased output or additional sales. It is clear that this is not the case with Boeing. As the market contracts, albeit temporarily, and as the competition gets tougher Boeing keeps shrinking. It is interesting to note that the reduction in employment—a constant trend in the last five years—precedes the decline in sales and backlog until 1993 (see Figures 7 and 8). However, this trend falls behind the decline of sales and backlog around 1993. This may indicate that Boeing has reached an optimum ratio of sales versus headcount by 1993. In other words, significant productivity gains were made until 1993, but beyond that date employment simply followed the sales performance.

Having made these observations about employment and its direct connection to productivity, what follows is a summary of Boeing's accomplishments.

The Boeing 777 program is a big success. The first plane was rolled out in April 1994 and successfully completed flight tests. The first delivery occurred as scheduled in May 1995 to United Airlines. To date 16 customers have ordered 167 of these aircraft. Given the current downturn in demand, this is an excellent start for a new product. In fact the 777 has captured 75% of the market for airplanes of its class.

As far as CATIA is concerned, it enabled the 777 program to exceed its goal of eliminating change error and rework. According to Lyle Eveland, 777 Operations Director, since starting assembly in January 1993 there has been a range of 50% to 80% reduction in nonconformance reports compared with previous programs.[23]

Figure 7

Based on data from the 1994 Boeing Annual Report.

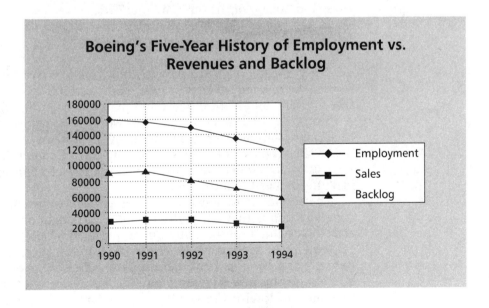

---

[23] Proctor, Paul, "Boeing Rolls Out 777 to Tentative Market," *Aviation Week & Space Technology*, April 11, 1994, p. 37.

Figure 8

Based on data from
the 1994 Boeing
Annual Report.

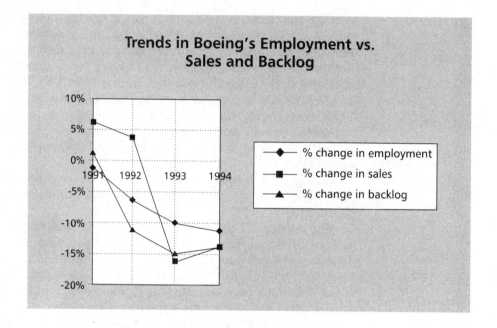

The commercial airline organization continued to make progress on the company's long-term goal to reduce costs and cycle time. The group reduced the customer introduction cycle time (measured from order implementation to delivery) from 12 months to 10 months on 737s and 757s, and 10½ months on 747s and 767s.

In September 1994 Boeing began offering next-day shipment on routine spare parts orders. Previously the company had guaranteed shipping within 10 days.

The company opened a new customer services training center south of Seattle. The training facilities include more than 200 computers with interactive software, and feature flight and maintenance training simulators.

Since late 1992 Boeing had been working to reduce computing costs in all areas—application software, delivery systems and telecommunications. The target was to reduce the unit cost of computing products and services by 36% in five years. By the end of 1994 computing costs per unit had already been reduced by 30%.

The results in inventory management are somewhat mitigated. The company claims that while the inventory balances on the 737, 747, 757 and 767 declined substantially due to production rate reductions and improvements in production inventory flow times, these declines were first partially and then in 1994 substantially offset by inventory and tooling buildup on the new 777 program. The net result is an increase of about $1 billion in total inventory from 1993. Since no detailed inventory figures per aircraft type are provided, it is difficult to judge Boeing's success in this domain, but the explanation of additional buildup due to the new 777 program is plausible. According to *Air Transport World,* in 1990 Boeing had targeted 25% cost reduction in five years by using JIT, but by mid-93 it had revised its target and now expects to reach it only in 1998.[24] On the other hand there are some significant success stories. According to Ken Bailey, Boeing's manufacturing center director at the company's new $200-million plant in Tacoma, the 480,000-square-foot facility is designed to minimize WIP (work-in-progress) and cut cycle times by 65%! The plant is equipped with 6 AGVs (automatic guided vehicles) that team with the more traditional overhead cranes to create a "pull manufacturing system." Everything is under computer control. The facility is currently used to manufacture the tail of the 777. Significant savings were achieved both in plant equipment—over $22 million—and production time.[25]

In summary, Boeing has been quite successful in making progress towards the achievement of its long-term goals. It has significantly improved its productivity, strengthened its competitiveness and successfully rolled out the 777. It succeeded in keeping its market share of 60% under difficult conditions.

B. Have the Above Factors Positioned Them for the Future?

Boeing estimates the total commercial jet transport market opportunity over the next twenty years to be approximately $1,000 billion in 1995 dollars.[26] It cautions that the realization of this market forecast depends on the airlines' ability to achieve and sustain reasonable levels of profits over the long term. Boeing is optimistic about the airlines' returning to profitability, but it could be awhile before most airlines consider aggressive growth plans again. Boeing is also content with the GATT agreement in 1993, limiting direct government subsidies to its "European competitor" to only 33%. These are long-term prospects that promise growth well into the 21st century, assuming that Boeing can weather the current storm. It is clear that Boeing has done an excellent job in maximizing its competitiveness. *Aviation Week & Space Technology* claims that "Boeing has achieved a profound conceptual shift to more efficient and effective work force teaming, digital design and advanced manufacturing techniques. These changes, plus heavy investment in testing facilities, are substantially lowering production costs and will make Boeing transports much tougher competitors in the future." [27]

In conclusion, Boeing is in much better shape today than it was at the beginning of the decade. However, the jury is still out on how it will

---

[24] Feldman, Joan M., "Just-in-Time, Not Just-in-Case," *Air Transport World,* April 1994, pp. 59–63.

[25] Forger, Gary, "Boeing Slashes Costs and Time with JIT," *Modern Materials Handling,* August 1994, pp. 47–49.

[26] *Boeing Annual Report 1994,* p. 31.

[27] Proctor, "Boeing Rolls Out 777 to Tentative Market," *Aviation Week & Space Technology,* April 11, 1994, p. 36.

meet the new challenges coming from Airbus and potential new entrants. In the second half of this decade Boeing should not focus on just preserving its 60% market share, but on aggressively pushing its leadership in every segment. After the 777 it is effectively modernizing its 737 line and also investing in R&D for small (less than 100 seats) jets. It is indeed taking the offensive on all fronts and positioning itself as a formidable force in the global commercial aircraft market.

INDEX